Antisemitism and the Russian Revolution

When the Bolsheviks came to power in 1917, they announced the overthrow of a world scarred by exploitation and domination. In the very moment of revolution, these sentiments were put to the test as antisemitic pogroms swept the former Pale of Settlement. The pogroms posed fundamental questions of the Bolshevik project, revealing the depth of antisemitism within sections of the working class, peasantry and Red Army. *Antisemitism and the Russian Revolution* offers the first book-length analysis of the Bolshevik response to antisemitism. Contrary to existing understandings, it reveals this campaign to have been led not by the Party leadership, as is often assumed, but by a loosely connected group of radicals who mobilized around a Jewish political subjectivity. By examining pogroms committed by the Red Army, Brendan McGeever also uncovers the explosive overlap between revolutionary politics and antisemitism, and the capacity for class to become racialized in a moment of crisis.

BRENDAN MCGEEVER is Lecturer in Sociology at Birkbeck, University of London. His work examines the relationship between antisemitism and racism, historically up to the present day. He is based at the Pears Institute for the study of Antisemitism at Birkbeck, University of London, where he teaches in the Department of Psychosocial Studies. He is a 2019 BBC/AHRC New Generation Thinker, with his work featuring across television and radio.

Antisemitism and the Russian Revolution

Brendan McGeever
Birkbeck, University of London

CAMBRIDGE
UNIVERSITY PRESS

University Printing House, Cambridge CB2 8BS, United Kingdom

One Liberty Plaza, 20th Floor, New York, NY 10006, USA

477 Williamstown Road, Port Melbourne, VIC 3207, Australia

314–321, 3rd Floor, Plot 3, Splendor Forum, Jasola District Centre, New Delhi – 110025, India

79 Anson Road, #06-04/06, Singapore 079906

Cambridge University Press is part of the University of Cambridge.

It furthers the University's mission by disseminating knowledge in the pursuit of education, learning, and research at the highest international levels of excellence.

www.cambridge.org
Information on this title: www.cambridge.org/9781107195998
DOI: 10.1017/9781108164498

© Brendan McGeever 2019

This publication is in copyright. Subject to statutory exception and to the provisions of relevant collective licensing agreements, no reproduction of any part may take place without the written permission of Cambridge University Press.

First published 2019

Printed in the United Kingdom by TJ International Ltd. Padstow Cornwall

A catalogue record for this publication is available from the British Library.

ISBN 978-1-107-19599-8 Hardback

Cambridge University Press has no responsibility for the persistence or accuracy of URLs for external or third-party internet websites referred to in this publication and does not guarantee that any content on such websites is, or will remain, accurate or appropriate.

Contents

List of Figures	*page*	vi
Acknowledgements		vii
A Note on Translation		x
Terms and Abbreviations		xi
	Introduction	1
1	1917: Antisemitism in the Moment of Revolution	19
2	'Red Pogroms': Spring 1918	38
3	The Soviet Response to Antisemitism, 1918	53
4	Antisemitism and Revolutionary Politics: the Red Army in Ukraine, 1919	88
5	The Soviet Response to Antisemitism in Ukraine, February–May 1919	112
6	Jewish Communists and the Soviet Response to Antisemitism, May–December 1919	140
7	Reinscribing Antisemitism? The Bolshevik Approach to the 'Jewish Question'	183
	Epilogue: In the Shadow of Pogroms	211
	Conclusions: Anti-Racist Praxis in the Russian Revolution	216
Bibliography		220
Index		240

Figures

1. Zvi Fridliand, around 1917 — page 59
2. David Davidovich (L'vovich), early 1920s — 66
3. First Conference of Jewish Communist Sections and Jewish Commissariats, Moscow, 23 October 1918 — 75
4. Poster produced by the Jewish Social Committee for the Relief of Victims of Pogroms (*Evobshchestkom*) for an exhibition on pogroms in Moscow in 1923. The caption at the top of the image, given in both Russian and Yiddish, reads: 'A breakdown of Jewish pogroms according to their organizers'. The poster was subsequently published in 1926 in Z. S. Ostrovskii, *Evreiskie pogromy 1918–1921 gg.*, 75 — 134
5. Leningradskii, S. *Kto i za chto ustraival pogromy nad evreiami* [*Who Organised the Pogroms against the Jews and for What Reason?*] (Moscow: Izdatel'stvo Krasnaia Nov', 1924) — 136
6. Jewish Red Army Unit, 1918. Banner reads: '1st Red Army Unit of the Jewish Social-Democratic Workers' Party Poalei Zion' — 149
7. Moishe Rafes, 1917 — 152
8. David Lipets and David Davidovich (L'vovich) at the Stockholm Peace Conference, June 1917 — 153
9. David Lipets, March 1927 — 155
10. Second Conference of Jewish Sections of the Communist Party, June 1919 — 165
11. Presidium of the Second Conference of Jewish Sections of the Communist Party — 166
12. Abram Kheifets, around 1917 — 172

Acknowledgements

This book is the product of a decade of conversations. From the very beginning I have relied on the wisdom and friendship of a great number of individuals, and it is a pleasure to be able to thank some of them here.

The project began its life at the University of Glasgow under the supervision of Terry Cox and Satnam Virdee. I could not have hoped for a more supportive and inspirational supervision team. Without Terry and Satnam, this book simply would not exist. I owe them my eternal thanks. I will also be forever grateful to the Centre for Russian, Central and East European Studies at the University of Glasgow for generously awarding me a PhD scholarship to undertake this research. I remain indebted to many other friends and colleagues at Glasgow, especially those in the Department of Sociology and the Department of Central and East European Studies, where I had the great privilege to be taught. In particular, I owe gratitude to my doctoral examiners, Liliana Riga and Geoffrey Swain.

The manuscript was completed at Birkbeck, University of London, which has been my academic home since 2015. I am especially grateful to my teacher and mentor, David Feldman, who has guided me through the post-PhD years and has been a constant source of inspiration, not to mention generosity. I thank my colleagues at the Department of Psychosocial Studies, where special mention must go to Lisa Baraitser, Felicity Callard, Stephen Frosh, Ben Gidley, Amber Jacobs, Gail Lewis, Yasmeen Narayan, Margarita Palacios, Sasha Roseneil, Lynne Segal, Bruna Seu and Annette van der Zaag. In particular, Miriam Zukas has been ceaseless in her guidance and support. I am hugely grateful to the Pears Institute for the study of Antisemitism, especially my colleagues Jan Davison, Tanesha Westcarr and Marc Volovici.

A number of friends and colleagues read draft chapters or engaged in fruitful discussions that helped refine and give shape to this book. In no particular order, I give thanks to: Zvi Gitelman, Jack Jacobs, Susan Milamed, Philip Spencer, Marc Caplan, Ruari Shaw Sutherland, Allan Armstrong, Aaron Winter, Gerald Surh, John Riddell, Simon Pirani,

Chris Read, Rick Saull, Eric Blanc, Alex Valdman, Peter Waldron, Sebastian Budgen, Matthias Neumann, Howard Wollman, the late Moishe Postone, Christine Achinger, Gennady Estraikh, Laura Engelstein, Aleks Reznik, Lars Fischer, Stephen Ashe, Jeff Meadowcroft, Alistair Fraser, Andy Smith, Eileen Boyle, Mark Kupovetskii, Sonya Kopelyan, Thomas Welskopp, Malte Griesse, Frank Leitenberger, George Gilbert; the organizers and participants of the 2009 Russian Archives Training Scheme (in particular, Jonathon Waterlow, Samantha Sherry, Andy Willimott, Simon Pawley and Alan Crawford), Geraldine Gould, the late Andrew McGeever, Eleanor Gordon, Elizabeth Douglas, David Douglas, Raul Cârstocea, Béla Rásky, Jeff Veidlinger, Frank Wolff, Margaret Duncan, Nathan Kurz, Rosie Cox, Anika Walke, Polly Zavadivker, David Seymour, Serhiy Hirik, Dafna Dolinko, Marc Volovici, Boris Kolonitskii, Joshua Meyers, Alexander Goldfarb, Michael Petrovsky and Tikhon Dziadko and his family.

Of special mention are Gleb Albert and Andrew Sloin, who not only read the entire manuscript but led me to countless archival sources and offered the most insightful comments anyone could hope for. My thanks also go to Dimitri Tolkatsch – without that chance encounter in the archive, the chapters on Ukraine could not have been written. While in Russia, I enjoyed the warm friendship and hospitality of Victor Remizov and his family, as well as that of Olga Loginovna and her mother, Lena Vladimirovna. I thank them for taking Caroline and me into their lives. I continue to benefit immensely from my teachers Satnam Virdee and David Feldman; their influence is on every page. Finally, Laurie Bernstein and Robert Weinberg have been friends, colleagues and so much more. I thank them for believing in this project.

The making of this work has relied on the help and knowledge of archivists and librarians in several countries. I would like to thank the staff at the State Archive of the Russian Federation; the Russian State Archive of Social-Political History; the Central State Archive of Moscow Oblast'; the Russian State Military Archive; the Russian State Archives of Literature and Art; the Central State Archives of Public Organisations of Ukraine; the Central State Archive of the Supreme Organs of Government and Administration of Ukraine; the State Archive of Zhytomyr Oblast'; the YIVO Institute for Jewish Research; and the World ORT Archive in London. I would also like to thank the librarians at the Russian State Library; the Academic Institute of Scientific Information on Social Sciences; the State Historical Library of Russia; the Houghton Library at the University of Harvard; the Bayerische Staatsbibliothek; the University of Glasgow Library; the British Library; the National Library of Scotland; and Portobello Library, Edinburgh.

Acknowledgements

The research in this book was generously supported by the Economic and Social Research Council; the Centre for Russian, Central and East European Studies at the University of Glasgow; the Bielefeld Graduate School in History and Sociology at Bielefeld University; The Pears Institute for the study of Antisemitism; The Center for Biblical and Jewish Studies at the Russian State University for the Humanities; the EU Tempus Fund; the Judaica Institute at the National University of Kyiv-Mogyla Academy; The International Forum of Young Scholars on East European Jewry; The Scottish International Education Trust; Birkbeck, University of London; The Association for Slavic, East European and Eurasian Studies; and the British Association for Slavonic and East European Studies.

I extend my gratitude to Cambridge University Press for the enthusiasm they have shown for this project, especially Lewis Bateman, Michael Watson, Liz Friend-Smith, Atifa Jiwa and Ruth Boyes. As the book progressed through to publication, I relied heavily on the guidance and expertise of Divya Arjunan, Aleksandr Kats and Judith Acevedo. I also thank the two readers consulted by the press, who were extremely generous in their critical feedback. An earlier version of Chapter 1 was published as 'Revolution and Antisemitism: The Bolsheviks in 1917', *Patterns of Prejudice*, 51 no. 3-4, (2017): 235-252. I thank the journal for allowing it to appear here.

Most important of all, I give my love and thanks to Geraldine Gould, Andrew McGeever (1950–2015) and Martin Tod for leading me to this topic, and my partner Caroline Douglas for living it with me.

A Note on Translation

I have followed the Library of Congress system for Russian transliteration, except where the more familiar form is otherwise (for example, I use Trotsky, not Trotskii). For cities and provinces, I generally use the typical or most common usage in the primary sources and secondary literature, which in most cases is Russian. However, for towns and cities in Ukraine, I have transliterated from the Ukrainian spelling (Kyiv, not Kiev; Zhytomyr, not Zhitomir). In one or two cases, the more commonly known Russian transliteration has been followed (Grigor'ev, not Hryhor'iev).

Terms and Abbreviations

Cheka	Extraordinary Commission for Combating Counterrevolution and Sabotage
Comintern	Communist International
d.	*delo*, a file within a fond (archival term)
Evkom	Jewish Commissariat of the People's Commissariat of Nationalities
Evobshchestkom	Jewish Social Committee for the Relief of Victims of Pogroms
Evsektsiia	Jewish Sections of the Russian Communist Party
f.	*fond*, document collection (archival term)
guberniia (pl. gubernii)	province, large administrative-territorial unit of the Russian empire/Soviet republics
Ispolkom	'Extecutive Committee' – a local organ of Soviet government
kulak	Soviet term for 'wealthy peasant'
l.	*list*, page (archival term)
Narkomnats	People's Commissariat for the Affairs of the Nationalities
oblast'	large region, or district, an administrative-territorial unit in the Soviet republics
op.	*opis'* or inventory (archival term)
Revkom	Revolutionary Committee
RKP(b)	Russian Communist Party (Bolshevik)
Sovnarkom	Soviet of People's Commissars
VTsIK	All-Russian Central Executive Committee (of the Russian Soviet Federative Socialist Republic)

Introduction

The Bolsheviks came to power in October 1917 and announced the overthrow of a world scarred by exploitation and oppression. Driven, first and foremost, by an unprecedented mobilization of class injuries, the revolution also offered deliverance from the injustices of gendered and racialized domination. The Bolshevik promise of a world free of racism resonated far and wide, reaching a multi-ethnic global audience, and is captured powerfully in the writings of the Jamaican American writer Claude McKay. McKay's interest in Bolshevism stemmed specifically from its opposition to antisemitism. Writing in September 1919, he proclaimed:

> Every Negro ... should make a study of Bolshevism and explain its meaning to the coloured masses. It is the greatest and most scientific idea afloat in the world today ... Bolshevism has made Russia safe for the Jew. It has liberated the Slav peasant from priest and bureaucrat who can no longer egg him on to murder Jews to bolster up their rotten institutions. It might make these United States safe for the Negro ... If the Russian idea should take hold of the white masses of the western world ... then the black toilers would automatically be free![1]

Yet the anti-racist promise ran counter to the actuality of Civil War. In the very moment of revolution, the Bolsheviks came face-to-face with mass outbreaks of antisemitic pogroms which spread across the vast regions of the former Pale of Settlement's western and south-western borderlands. Above all, the violence was carried out by forces hostile to the revolution. But the pogroms posed fundamental questions of the Bolshevik project, and revealed the nature and extent of working class and peasant attachments to antisemitism. To the dismay of Party leaders, sections of the Bolsheviks' social base participated in the violence.

---

[1] W. James, *Holding Aloft the Banner of Ethiopia: Caribbean Radicalism in America 1900-32* (London: Verso, 1999), 165–66.

Beginning in the early weeks of 1918, the pogroms continued throughout the Civil War years, reaching a devastating peak in 1919 but lasting well into the 1920s. This was the most violent assault on Jewish life in pre-Holocaust modern history: conservative estimates put the number of fatalities at roughly 50,000–60,000, but the true figure likely reached 100,000 or more.[2] At the time, some Soviet officials speculated that as many as 200,000 may have perished.[3] What is certain is that at least 2,000 pogroms took place during the revolutionary period. Amidst the carnage, hundreds of thousands of Jews fled westward, over half a million were displaced and many more were left injured and bereaved.[4] The Russian Revolution, a moment of emancipation and liberation, was for many Jews accompanied by racialized violence on an unprecedented scale.

Antisemitism and the Russian Revolution has two fundamental aims. First, it examines the complex and at times explosive overlap between antisemitism and revolutionary politics. Second, it explores Bolshevik attempts to confront antisemitism, including within the revolutionary movement itself. Such a project inevitably engages a number of debates across a range of disciplines. First and foremost, this book is in dialogue with a large literature on the pogroms,[5] a recent (and growing) interest in

---

[2] In 1922, the Commissariat of Nationalities within the Soviet government calculated that approximately 100,000 had perished. Others reached for the higher figure of 120,000. See, for example, E. Heifets, *The Slaughter of the Jews in the Ukraine in 1919* (New York: Thomas Seltzer, 1921), 180.

[3] Iu. Larin, *Evrei i antisemitizm v SSSR* (Moscow: Gosizdat, 1929).

[4] J. Veidlinger, *In the Shadow of the Shtetl: Small-Town Jewish Life in Soviet Ukraine* (Bloomington: University of Indiana Press, 2013), 37.

[5] Key works on the pogroms include: N. I. Shtif, *Pogromy na Ukraine (Period dobrovol'cheskoi armii)* (Berlin: Wostok, 1922); E. Tcherikower, *Istoriia pogromnogo dvizheniia na Ukraine 1917–1921* (Berlin: Osjudisches Historisches Archiv, 1923); I. B. Shechtman, *Pogromy dobrovol'cheskoi armii na Ukraine (K istorii antisemitizma na Ukraine v 1919–1920 gg.)* (Berlin: Osjudisches Historisches Archiv, 1932); N. Gergel, 'The Pogroms in the Ukraine in 1918–1921', *YIVO Annual of Jewish Social Science* 6 (1951): 237–51; E. Tcherikower, *Di Ukrainer Pogromen in Yor 1919* (New York: YIVO Institute for Jewish Research, 1965); P. Kenez, 'Pogroms and White Ideology in the Russian Civil War', in *Pogroms: Anti-Jewish Violence in Modern Russian History*, ed. J. D. Klier and S. Lambroza (New York: Cambridge University Press, 1992), 293–313; O. V. Budnitskii, 'Jews, Pogroms, and the White Movement: A Historiographical Critique', *Kritika: Explorations in Russian and Eurasian History* 2, no. 4 (2001): 1–23; O. V. Budnitskii, *Rossiiskie evrei mezhdu krasnymi i belymi, 1917–1920* (Moscow: ROSSPEN, 2005); L. B. Miliakova, *Kniga pogromov: Pogromy na Ukraine, v Belorussii i evropeiskoi chasti Rossii v period grazhdanskoi voiny 1918–1922 gg. Sbornik dokumentov.* (Moscow: ROSSPEN, 2008); J. Dekel-Chen et al., eds., *Anti-Jewish Violence: Rethinking the Pogrom in East European History* (Bloomington: Indiana University Press, 2011); V. P. Buldakov, *Khaos i etnos: Etnicheskie konflikty v Rossii, 1917–1918 gg. Usloviia vozniknoveniia, khronika, kommentarii, analiz* (Moskva: Novyi khronograf, 2010); L. Engelstein *Russia In Flames: War, Revolution, Civil War, 1914–1921* (Oxford: Oxford University Press, 2017), 511–40.

Introduction 3

the Soviet–Jewish encounter in the early years after 1917[6] and a now extensive literature on the 'national question' in Soviet Russia more generally.[7] Yet the story presented here stretches beyond the historiography on the Russian Revolution. The Bolshevik response to antisemitism had reverberations around the world, and found particular resonance among a layer of African American radicals engaged in the confrontation with white supremacy and anti-black racism.[8] *Antisemitism and the Russian Revolution* maintains this connection between racism and antisemitism, and in doing so, addresses recent debates within the Marxist left around race, class and anti-racist mobilization.[9] Further, in exploring how a revolutionary movement addressed the question of

---

[6] Recent key works on social, economic and cultural aspects of Jewish life in early Soviet society include: E. Bemporad, *Becoming Soviet Jews: The Bolshevik Experiment in Minsk* (Bloomington: Indiana University Press, 2013); J. Dekel-Chen, *Farming the Red Land: Jewish Agricultural Colonization and Local Soviet Power, 1924-1941* (New Haven: Yale University Press, 2005); G. Estraikh, *In Harness: Yiddish Writers' Romance with Communism* (Syracuse: Syracuse University Press, 2005); K. Moss, *Jewish Renaissance in the Russian Revolution* (Cambridge, MA: Harvard University Press, 2009); D. Shneer, *Yiddish and the Creation of Soviet Jewish Culture: 1918-1930* (Cambridge: Cambridge University Press, 2004); E. Sicher, *Jews in Russian Literature after the October Revolution: Writers and Artists between Hope and Apostasy* (Cambridge: Cambridge University Press, 2006); A. Shternshis, *Soviet and Kosher: Jewish Popular Culture in the Soviet Union, 1923-1939* (Bloomington: Indiana University Press, 2006); Andrew Sloin, *The Jewish Revolution in Belorussia: Economy, Race, and Bolshevik Power* (Bloomington: Indiana University Press, 2017); J. Veidlinger, *The Moscow State Yiddish Theater: Jewish Culture on the Soviet Stage* (Bloomington: Indiana University Press, 2006); Veidlinger, *In the Shadow of the Shtetl*; R. Weinberg, *Stalin's Forgotten Zion: Birobidzhan and the Making of a Soviet Jewish Homeland: An Illustrated History, 1928-1996* (Berkeley: University of California Press, 1998).

[7] The literature on this subject is vast. Key works include: F. Hirsch, *Empire of Nations: Ethnographic Knowledge and the Making of the Soviet Union* (Ithaca: Cornell University Press, 2005); T. D. Martin, *The Affirmative Action Empire: Nations and Nationalism in the Soviet Union, 1923–1939* (New York: Cornell University Press, 2001); R. G. Suny and T. D. Martin, eds., *A State of Nations: Empire and Nation-Making in the Age of Lenin and Stalin* (Oxford: Oxford University Press, 2001).

[8] See C. Bergin, *'Bitter with the Past but Sweet with the Dream': Communism in the African American Imaginary* (Chicago: Haymarket Books, 2016); C. Bergin, ed., *African American Anti-Colonial Thought, 1917-1937* (Edinburgh: Edinburgh University Press, 2016); James, *Holding Aloft the Banner of Ethiopia*; P. Heideman, ed., *Class Struggle and the Color Line: American Socialism and the Race Question, 1900-1930* (Chicago: Haymarket Books, 2018). On the continuing reverberations of Bolshevism in later decades among African American radicals, see M. Stevens, *Red International and Black Caribbean: Communists in New York City, Mexico and the West Indies, 1919-1939* (New York: Pluto Press, 2017). On the influence of Bolshevism on the thought of C. L. R. James, see C. L. R. James, *World Revolution, 1917-1936: The Rise and Fall of the Communist International – The C. L. R. James Archives*, ed. Christian Høgsbjerg (Durham: Duke University Press, 2017).

[9] For recent contributions to this long-standing debate, see S. Virdee, *Racism, Class and the Racialized Outsider* (London: Palgrave Macmillan, 2014); D. Roediger, *Class, Race and Marxism* (London: Verso, 2017).

anti-Jewish violence, the book sits within resurgent debates around the historical and contemporary significance of antisemitism and the left.[10]

'Red Antisemitism' in the Russian Revolution

The presence of antisemitism on the left in the Russian Revolution has long been known but, until recently, seldom examined in any depth. Foundational works by Elias Tcherikower, published in the early 1920s and mid-1960s, established that antisemitism traversed the political divide in revolutionary Russia.[11] No political formation, insisted Tcherikower, remained out of its reach, including the Bolsheviks. This was brought to a wider audience still by the journalist and playwright Isaac Babel, whose literary account of antisemitism within the Red Army led him to pose the haunting question: 'Which is the Revolution and which the counter-revolution?'[12] Yet, as the literature on the Civil War–era pogroms emerged, the focus remained largely on the culpability of anti-Bolshevik military units. And for good reason. In his classic study, Nahum Gergel calculated that the bulk of the atrocities had been carried out by the Petliura and Denikin armies (40 per cent and 17.2 per cent respectively). In contrast, the Red Army was responsible for 8.6 per cent of the Civil War pogroms, thereby making it among the least prone to anti-Jewish violence of all main military forces in the Russian Revolution.[13] Nevertheless, for decades there were no serious examinations of the nature and extent of anti-Jewish violence enacted by the Red Army. This changed with the publication of important new works by Russian historians Oleg Budnitskii and Vladimir Buldakov, which have done

---

[10] See J. Jacobs, *On Socialists and 'The Jewish Question' after Marx* (New York: New York University Press, 1992); E. Traverso, *The Jewish Question: The History of a Marxist Debate* (Leiden: Brill, 2018); J. Jacobs, ed., *Jews and Leftist Politics: Judaism, Israel, Antisemitism, and Gender* (New York: Cambridge University Press, 2017); L. Fischer, *The Socialist Response to Antisemitism in Imperial Germany* (Cambridge: Cambridge University Press, 2010); M. Kessler, *On Anti-Semitism and Socialism: Selected Essays* (Berlin: Trafo, 2005); R. Fine and P. Spencer, *Antisemitism and the Left: On the Return of the Jewish Question* (Manchester: Manchester University Press, 2017); D. Hirsh, *Contemporary Left Antisemitism* (London: Routledge, 2017); B. McGeever and S. Virdee, 'Antisemitism and Socialist Strategy in Europe, 1880–1917: An Introduction', *Patterns of Prejudice* 51, no. 3–4 (2017): 221–34.

[11] See Tcherikower, *Istoriia pogromnogo dvizheniia na Ukraine 1917-1921*; Tcherikower, *Di Ukrainer Pogromen in Yor 1919*. On Tcherikower and the gathering of his pogrom archive, see J. M. Karlip, 'Between Martyrology and Historiography: Elias Tcherikower and the Making of a Pogrom Historian', *East European Jewish Affairs* 38, no. 3 (2008): 257–80; J. M. Karlip, *The Tragedy of a Generation: The Rise and Fall of Jewish Nationalism in Eastern Europe* (Cambridge, MA: Harvard University Press, 2013), 40–45.

[12] I. Babel, *Red Cavalry* (New York: W. W. Norton & Company, 2003), 65.

[13] Gergel, 'The Pogroms in the Ukraine in 1918-1921', 248.

much to deepen our understanding of the significance of antisemitism within the Red Army during this period.[14]

Antisemitism and the Russian Revolution builds on these recent studies by offering an analysis of the articulation between antisemitism and the revolutionary process. Although marginal to the overall picture of anti-Jewish violence during the Civil War, the Red Army pogroms are placed centre stage here because of the fundamental questions they posed of the Soviet government and its commitment to internationalism and anti-racism. By moving beyond neat, categorical distinctions between 'antisemites' and 'non-antisemites', 'revolutionaries' and 'counter-revolutionaries', the book uncovers the complex ways in which antisemitism could find traction within revolutionary politics. It does so, above all, by offering the most extensive discussion yet of the role of antisemitism and pogromist violence within the Red Army.

Antisemitism was present within both the counter-revolutionary *and* revolutionary movements. It was located to a significant degree in the former, but it could be found in the latter too. Early warnings of this were apparent in the rise of antisemitism during Russia's year of revolution in 1917, when episodic reports of antisemitic agitation within the working class and socialist movement began to appear. This only came into full view, however, in the pogrom wave of the spring of 1918 – the first to follow the October Revolution. These pogroms, discussed in depth in Chapter 2, were principally carried out by loosely assembled ranks of the Red Army stationed in the borderlands of western Russia and eastern Ukraine. In the shocking case of Hlukhiv, Soviet power was constituted *through* anti-Jewish violence. These events revealed the nature and extent of antisemitism within sections of the working class and peasantry. The first test of the Bolshevik leadership's position on antisemitism, then, would be to confront pogromist violence perpetrated by its own cadres.

These dynamics reached their most violent and bloody crescendo in the pogrom wave of 1919, which extended across whole sections of the western and south-western borderlands, including into several regions of the Russian 'interior' as well. The situation was particularly acute in Ukraine, where to secure the revolution in mid-1919, the Bolsheviks were forced, however reluctantly, to rely on a social base, sections of

---

[14] Budnitskii, *Rossiiskie evrei mezhdu krasnymi i belymi*; Buldakov, *Khaos i etnos*; V. P. Buldakov, 'Freedom, Shortages, Violence: The Origins of the "Revolutionary Anti-Jewish Pogrom" in Russia, 1917-1918', in *Anti-Jewish Violence: Rethinking the Pogrom in East European History*, ed. J. Dekel-Chen et al. (Bloomington: Indiana University Press, 2011), 74–94.

which were deeply shaped by the politics of antisemitism. In its frontstage propaganda, the Soviet government framed antisemitism as the preserve of the 'counter-revolution'. Yet internal Party and government archival documents show that the actuality of revolution was considerably more complex. In the spring and summer of 1919 in Ukraine, many in the Red Army saw no contradiction between fighting for 'soviet power' (in its populist sense) and attacking what they called 'Jewish exploiters'.

Popular anti-bourgeois sentiment, on the one hand a crucial reservoir of revolutionary socialism, was at the same time a resource of antisemitic mobilization. On the ground, the categories of class struggle were sometimes deployed in ways over which the Bolsheviks often had no control. While antisemitism was primarily located on the political right, there were elements of antisemitic thinking that had a particular appeal to sections of the left. As the late Moishe Postone has perceptively noted, in moments of crisis antisemitism 'can appear to be anti-hegemonic'. Its danger for socialists and anti-capitalists lies in its unique configuration 'as a fetishized form of oppositional consciousness, [as] the expression of a movement of the little people against an intangible, global form of domination'.[15] In 1919, Bolshevism proved to be vulnerable to this very tendency as the Party's ranks swelled and its radical message was taken up in the field of mass politics.

The Bolshevik Response to Antisemitism

Antisemitism and the Russian Revolution also sets out to offer the first in-depth analysis of Party attempts to confront antisemitism. It is well known that the Bolshevik leadership opposed antisemitism and viewed the pogroms as a threat to the survival of both Jews and the revolution. However, detailed studies of the actual response of the Soviet government during the revolutionary period have been thin on the ground. Pioneering work by Oleg Budnitskii has gone some way to addressing this deficit, but there remains no book-length study in any language of the Bolshevik confrontation with antisemitism during the Russian Revolution.[16] *Antisemitism and the Russian Revolution* provides such an analysis. Studies of Bolshevik opposition to antisemitism after October 1917 generally set off from the famous Sovnarkom decree of July 1918,

---

[15] Moishe Postone, 'History and Helplessness: Mass Mobilization and Contemporary Forms of Anticapitalism', *Public Culture* 18, no. 1 (2006): 99.
[16] Budnitskii, *Rossiiskie evrei mezhdu krasnymi i belymi*, 124–34; O. V. Budnitskii, *Russian Jews between the Reds and the Whites, 1917-1920* (Philadelphia: University of Pennsylvania Press, 2012), 95–104.

signed by Lenin.[17] However, as argued in Chapter 3, this decree marked not the beginning, but the *culmination* of the first phase of the Soviet response to antisemitism. Between April and July 1918 lies a period of profound political activity in opposition to antisemitism, which until now has mostly escaped the attention of scholars.[18] As soon as the Red Army pogroms in Hlukhiv and other regions became known, a group of loosely connected non-Bolshevik Jewish socialists in the Moscow Jewish Commissariat initiated a Soviet campaign. Their crowning achievement was to successfully establish, in May 1918, the first Soviet state institution dedicated to the confrontation with antisemitism. Perhaps most important of all, these activists were the first, indeed only, group within the central institutions of the Soviet government in 1918 to raise awareness of antisemitism within the Red Army. Their campaign predates Lenin's Sovnarkom decree by three months.

However, these initiatives were to be short-lived. In mid-May 1918, the Jewish Commissariat in Moscow was dissolved at the peak of its practice, having been swept up in the wider drive towards centralization within the Soviet state. Its disbanding had immediate consequences: with neither the personnel nor institutional means available for its continuation, the Soviet campaign against antisemitism of April and May 1918 ground to a halt. When the most ferocious wave of pogroms yet broke out in Ukraine in early 1919, the Soviet government was caught unprepared. A campaign did re-emerge in the first half of 1919 in Ukraine, but it was largely reactive and sporadic.

This situation was transformed in the second half of 1919 by the incorporation into the Soviet government of a new layer of non-Bolshevik Jewish revolutionaries, in this case communist Bundists and Fareynikte activists. Having broken from their respective parties, they joined the Soviet government and constituted a renewed confrontation with antisemitism. As Chapter 6 shows, they brought with them an opposition to antisemitism born not of tactical or strategic concerns, but of an urgency and ethical imperative rooted in the experience of antisemitic violence.

---

[17] G. V. Kostyrchenko, *Tainaia politika Stalina: Vlast' i antisemitizm* (Moscow: Mezhdunarodnye otnosheniia, 2003), 56; G. Ia. Aronson, 'Evreiskaia obshchestvennost'' v Rossii v 1917-1918 g.g.', in *Kniga o russkom evreistve 1917-1967*, ed. Ia. G. Frumkin, G. Ia. Aronson, and A. A. Gol'denveizer (New York: Soiuz Russkikh Evreev, 1968), 132; S. M. Schwarz, *The Jews in the Soviet Union* (New York: Syracuse University Press, 1951), 274.

[18] The exception is Ulrich Herbeck, whose wide-ranging analysis of the 'Jewish question' in revolutionary Russia does include a discussion of the Bolshevik response to antisemitism in the spring of 1918. See U. Herbeck, *Das Feindbild vom 'jüdischen Bolschewiken'. Zur Geschichte des russischen Antisemitismus vor und während der Russischen Revolution* (Berlin: Metropol, 2009).

Just as in 1918, the flow of agency moved from the (non- or recently turned Bolshevik) Jewish left to the Party centre. Coalescing around the Central Bureau of the Evsektsiia (the Jewish Sections of the Russian Communist Party), they established in August 1919 a new state institution dedicated to the confrontation with antisemitism (the 'Committee for the Struggle against Antisemitism'). This unique initiative singled out antisemitism as a separate and dedicated sphere of Party work. Like its predecessor in 1918, the Committee's strategy was an educative one: to instil in the working class, Red Army and peasantry a cultural and political opposition to antisemitism. Yet again, however, just a matter of weeks into its work, it too was closed down by the Party centre. With its closure fell away the most promising strand of opposition to antisemitism to emerge in the Russian Revolution.

This underlines a core argument of the book: there *was* a Soviet response to antisemitism, but it was not Bolshevik in origin. Bolshevism certainly adopted a standpoint of opposition to antisemitism that stretched back to the late-imperial period. But when it came to actualizing – that is, putting into practice – such sentiments after October 1917 and through the Civil War, the process relied to a significant extent on the agency of a small grouping of non-Bolshevik Jewish radicals within the Jewish Commissariats and Evsektsii (Jewish Sections of the Communist Party).

From Standpoint to Actuality

Soviet opposition to antisemitism is widely understood to have flowed from the internationalist and assimilatory currents of Bolshevism, that is, from the Party leadership, for whom attachments to ethnicity were weak, even non-existent. Yet once disaggregated to the level of agency, we discover that the Soviet confrontation with antisemitism had rather different origins. As this study makes clear, it was profoundly overdetermined by the inclusion into the state apparatus of a group of loosely connected Jewish radicals, whose politics were as 'particular' as they were universal. Whether Marxist-Zionist or territorialist, Bundist or Bolshevik, these revolutionaries were engaged in the elaboration of a broadly defined Jewish national-cultural project. They were, in other words, part of what Ken Moss identifies as the 'Jewish renaissance' in the Russian Revolution.[19] Their route to Bolshevism was neatly captured

---

[19] Moss, *Jewish Renaissance in the Russian Revolution*. Moss locates the period of the Jewish renaissance as occurring between the interregnum of the February Revolution and the Bolshevik seizure of power (which occurred in late 1917 in Russia and late 1919 in Ukraine). Bolshevism was ultimately a damaging force for Moss; it interrupted and

From Standpoint to Actuality

by Evsektsiia leader Avrom Merezhin in 1921: 'The Jewish question was the door through which they came to us.'[20]

Such dynamics were far from unique to the Russian Revolution. As the historical sociologist Satnam Virdee has shown, the anti-racist impulse of European socialism in the late nineteenth and early twentieth centuries often had to be introduced from the outside by those 'internal others' against whom the nation was (and is) so often defined. Virdee conceptualizes this social layer as 'racialized outsiders'. Drawing on W. E. B. Du Bois,[21] he suggests that the experience of racialization and outsiderdom endowed this minority current of socialists with a 'second sight'; a 'vista' that opened up a certain perspective on society as seen from its margins. This enabled them to see 'further' than other parts of the working class and socialist movement, and to bring into view, for the benefit of the wider movement as well as for themselves, a clear-sighted critique of race and domination.[22]

Antisemitism and the Russian Revolution brings these theoretical insights to bear on its analysis of the Russian Revolution. It argues that those Jewish radicals who entered the Soviet government in 1918 and 1919 brought with them a particular approach to the question of antisemitism, accrued from their positionality within a Russian social formation defined by recurring waves of anti-Jewish violence. The story of how the world's first successful Marxist revolution dealt with antisemitism, then, is intimately bound up with the development of Jewish cultural and national projects involving diasporic Jewish socialists and Marxist Zionists, who temporarily displaced their aspirations for a Zionist homeland in order to instead contribute to the profound cultural and political revolution in Jewish social life in Soviet Russia. As Chapter 6 argues, the closer one stood politically to a Jewish socialist-national project in the Russian Revolutionary context, the more likely one was to elevate and take seriously the question of antisemitism in one's own political

---

closed down the process of Jewish cultural revival ushered in by the February Revolution. The analysis presented here, however, points in a slightly different direction: I argue that what Moss refers to as the Jewish renaissance should be extended *into* the early Soviet period. At the level of personnel, but at the level of politics, too, Jewish cultural projects of nation building flowed into Soviet Jewish political work, including, as argued here, into the Soviet confrontation with antisemitism.

[20] Z. Gitelman, *Jewish Nationality and Soviet Politics: The Jewish Sections of the CPSU, 1917-1930* (Princeton: Princeton University Press, 1972), 222–23.
[21] W. E. B. Du Bois, *Darkwater: Voices from Within the Veil* (London: Verso, 2016).
[22] Virdee, *Racism, Class and the Racialized Outsider*; S. Virdee, 'The Second Sight of Racialized Outsiders in the Imperialist Core', *Third World Quarterly* 38, no. 11 (2017): 2396–410.

practice. That is to say, proximity to a Jewish socialist-national project seems to have facilitated a more urgent form of anti-racist praxis.

But agency alone did not bring the Soviet response to antisemitism into being. What was remarkable about the Bolshevik project was that it transformed these 'outsiders' into *insiders*. In their youth, Jewish revolutionaries encountered state antisemitism, quotas in education and employment, and blocked mobility paths, all of which were integral to their political radicalization.[23] The revolution of 1917 was Russian Jewry's moment of emancipation. In opening up the state and announcing the total transformation of social relations, the Bolsheviks gave life to a revolution that had been building within Jewish social, cultural and political life over the previous century.[24] As they entered the Soviet state, these revolutionaries established Yiddish schools and journals, worker clubs and state theatres.[25] This was the Soviet-Jewish encounter: a meeting between a layer of radicalized Jewish revolutionaries and a nascent Bolshevik government that afforded unprecedented scope for ethnic minority political mobilization at the level of the state. The Evsektsiia and Jewish Commissariats were living embodiments of this Bolshevik commitment to internationalism and 'affirmative action'.[26] Previous studies have shown how the Jewish revolutionaries who staffed these institutions brought their own cultural, political and ideological agenda into the Soviet state.[27] This work suggests they also brought with them a critically important degree of anti-racist agency. In reframing our understanding of how the world's first Marxist state responded to unprecedented antisemitic violence, *Antisemitism and the Russian Revolution* aims to offer a new contribution to the complex history of the relationship between Marxism and anti-racism.

Historical Setting

By 1917, the Bolsheviks could draw on three decades of experience of socialist confrontation with pogromist violence, for the pogroms of 1917–1921 marked not the first but the third wave of anti-Jewish violence in modern Russian history. The first followed the assassination of tsar Alexander II and took place over a two-year period between 1881 and

---

[23] L. Riga, *The Bolsheviks and the Russian Empire* (Cambridge: Cambridge University Press, 2012).
[24] Sloin, *The Jewish Revolution in Belorussia*, 11.
[25] Shternshis, *Soviet and Kosher*; Veidlinger, *The Moscow State Yiddish Theater*; Shneer, *Yiddish and the Creation of Soviet Jewish Culture*.
[26] Martin, *The Affirmative Action Empire*.
[27] Shneer, *Yiddish and the Creation of Soviet Jewish Culture*, 29.

1883.[28] The second commenced with the Kishinev pogrom of 1903 and continued through to the culmination of the 1905 revolution (1903–1906). Each wave of violence was unprecedented, not just in its death toll, but in its transformative impact on Russian-Jewish life; together, they left a complicated legacy of socialist responses to antisemitism.

Russian Populists and the Pogroms of 1881–1883

Until the first outbreak of pogromist violence in 1881, Russian socialists had addressed Jewish-related matters only in passing, and the question of antisemitism remained largely peripheral to their debates in the 1870s.[29] The appearance in 1881 of mass political mobilization in the shape of antisemitic violence, however, transformed the parameters of the so-called Jewish question in Russia, especially for the 'populists', the *Narodniki*. Despite harbouring deep internal divisions, Russian populists nevertheless broadly shared a class standpoint that posited the agrarian masses as the bearers of essential values such as moral purity, integrity and truth.[30] In the populist worldview, the peasantry, especially the peasant commune, were deemed to hold the 'essence' of socialism. This agrarian-inflected class analysis proved contentious in the face of antisemitic violence.

In the immediate aftermath of the pogroms in southern Russia in the spring of 1881, some populists embraced the violence as an 'awakening' of the revolutionary potential of the peasantry, as the long-awaited appearance of 'the people' on the historical stage.[31] Although rarely seen as a desired end-goal, the pogroms were nevertheless welcomed by some populists as a necessary *means* to the formation of a more 'developed' mass social movement. The pogroms, they hoped, would help sweep

---

[28] The first significant anti-Jewish pogrom in the Russian empire actually took place in 1871, in Odessa. But it was the outbreak of violence in 1881 that constituted the first pogrom *wave* as such. On the 1871 pogrom, see J. D. Klier, 'The Pogrom Paradigm in Russian History', in *Pogroms Anti-Jewish Violence in Modern Russian History*, ed. J. Klier and S. Lambroza (Cambridge: Cambridge University Press, 1992), 20–33.

[29] J. D. Klier, *Russians, Jews, and the Pogroms of 1881-1882* (Cambridge: Cambridge University Press, 2011), 156.

[30] M. Aronson, *Troubled Waters: Origins of the 1881 Anti-Jewish Pogroms in Russia* (Chicago: University of Pittsburgh Press, 1990), 194–95.

[31] Klier, *Russians, Jews, and the Pogroms of 1881–1882*, 155; E. Haberer, 'Cosmopolitanism, Antisemitism, and Populism: A Reappraisal of the Russian and Jewish Socialist Responses to the Pogroms of 1881–1882', in *Pogroms: Anti-Jewish Violence in Modern Russian History*, ed. J. D. Klier and S. Lambroza (Cambridge: Cambridge University Press, 1992); E. Haberer, *Jews and Revolution in Nineteenth-Century Russia* (Cambridge: Cambridge University Press, 2000), 98–134.

away all 'exploiters', not just 'the Jews'. Significantly, some of those populists who privately expressed their disapproval of the pogroms were reluctant to do so publicly for fear of losing what support they had managed to acquire among the peasantry.[32] Petr Lavrov (1823–1900), who described antisemitism as the 'most tragic epidemic of our era',[33] nevertheless declined to print a pamphlet denouncing the pogroms given to him by Pavel Axelrod. Lavrov explained this 'dilemma' in a revealing letter to Axelrod himself on 14 April 1882:

> I must confess that I regard this question as a very complicated one ... an exceedingly difficult one for a party which seeks to come closer to the people. Theoretically, on paper, the question can be easily answered. But, in view of the prevailing popular passions and the need of the Russian socialists to have the people on their side wherever possible, the question is quite different.[34]

Only a small number of revolutionary populists explicitly welcomed the pogroms. But many more were willing to tolerate them as a necessary, albeit unfortunate, stage in the revolutionary process.[35]

Russian Social Democracy and the Pogroms of 1903–1906

This historical backdrop has important implications for our understanding of the Bolshevik response to antisemitism after 1917. Bolshevism emerged from the broad movement of Russian Social Democracy and from the Russian Social Democratic Labour Party (RSDRP) specifically. Formed in 1898, the RSDRP took a critical stance against the populist legacy on pogroms and antisemitism. Although it certainly harboured individual antisemites, social democracy as a whole made a decisive break with the populist acquiescence to pogromist violence.[36] The social democratic turn towards the proletariat necessitated, in part, a shift away from the antisemitic valorizations of the peasantry. Moreover, the growing belief that the pogroms had played into the hands of the tsarist regime

---

[32] Aronson, *Troubled Waters*, 203.
[33] E. Goldhagen, 'The Ethnic Consciousness of Early Russian Socialists', *Judaism* 23 (1973): 493.
[34] Ibid., 494.
[35] V. I. Pavloff, 'Revolutionary Populism in Imperial Russia and the National Question in the 1870s and 1880s', in *Socialism and Nationalism*, ed. E. Cahm and V. I. Fisera (Nottingham: Spokesman, 1978), 84; Aronson, *Troubled Waters*, 202, 210.
[36] I. V. Bobrov, 'Evreiskii vopros v ideologii i politicheskoi deiatel'nosti rossiiskikh marksistov (konets XIX v.-fevral' 1917 g.)' (PhD Dissertation, Tiumenskii gosudarstvenyi universitet, 2003), 258. Pavloff, 'Revolutionary Populism in Imperial Russia and the National Question in the 1870s and 1880s', 89; Haberer, *Jews and Revolution in Nineteenth-Century Russia*, 229; Goldhagen, 'The Ethnic Consciousness of Early Russian Socialists', 494.

had, by the 1890s, become an axiomatic position of not just social democracy but all oppositional forces (including the revived populism of the Socialist Revolutionary Party, formed in 1902).[37] In the 1880s, many populists had understood the pogroms as an 'awakening' of the masses. A generation later, the social democrats of the early twentieth century equated antisemitic violence with tsarist state reaction. This conceptualization of the pogroms as *state organized* represented an important shift in socialist approaches to antisemitism[38]. Whereas populists saw in pogroms agency from below, social democrats saw organization and manipulation from above.

Russian Social Democracy's opposition to antisemitism was underlined at the infamous Second Congress of the RSDRP in 1903. Amidst bitter divisions that led to the withdrawal of the Bund and the splitting of the party into its Menshevik and Bolshevik fractions, the Congress sat to address the question of antisemitism. The context could not have been more urgent: just weeks before, the most violent pogrom yet had taken place in Kishinev. A resolution proposed by Plekhanov at the 37th Session on 10 August 1903 called on 'comrades to use all means in their power to combat such movements and to explain to the proletariat the reactionary and class inspiration of antisemitic and all other national-chauvinist incitements'.[39] The motion was passed unanimously, though in the absence of the Bund's delegates, who had walked out five days previously.

There was nothing abstract about the question of antisemitism, and the Congress' commitments would soon be put to the test: the Kishinev pogrom of 1903 marked the beginning of a second, explosive pogrom wave in late-imperial Russia. Between 1903 and 1906, an unprecedented wave of anti-Jewish violence erupted across the Pale of Settlement.[40] It was in these formative years that social democrats confronted antisemitism at the level of *practice*. Throughout this crucial period, Bolsheviks adopted a two-pronged strategy of assisting Jewish revolutionary

---

[37] J. Frankel, *Prophecy and Politics: Socialism, Nationalism, and the Russian Jews, 1862-1917* (Cambridge: Cambridge University Press, 1981), 138.

[38] This view was shared by Jewish revolutionaries and non-revolutionaries alike. Writing in his memoirs, the Jewish liberal historian Simon Dubnov noted that before any details had emerged of the brutal Kishinev pogrom of 1903, he simply 'knew' its principle features: official collusion at the highest levels and complete passivity on the part of the police and military once the violence began. Klier, *Russians, Jews, and the Pogroms of 1881-1882*, 394.

[39] B. Pearce, *1903 Second Ordinary Congress of the RSDLP* (New York: New Park Publications, 1978), 23.

[40] For an overview of the second pogrom wave, see S. Lambroza, 'The Pogroms of 1903-1906', in *Pogroms: Anti-Jewish Violence in Modern Russian History*, ed. J. D. Klier and S. Lambroza (Cambridge: Cambridge University Press, 1992), 195–247.

organizations in physically combating pogroms and issuing scores of educational, anti-pogromist leaflets in workplaces.[41]

Opposition to antisemitism could also help to form a united front between a then bitterly divided social democratic left. Following a pogrom in Mykolaiv, a city in southern Ukraine, in October 1905, a United Committee of Social Democrats was formed, comprising Bolsheviks, Mensheviks and Bundists. The Committee soon issued leaflets to workers to form militia units to physically confront pogromists.[42] As pogroms came to be associated with the tsarist state, socialists formed strategic alliances to confront what they called the politics of 'counter-revolution'.

Antisemitism and the Limits of Social Democracy

Although social democrats made a decisive break from populist understandings of pogroms, their response to antisemitism was not without its own discontents. Just as social democrats were prolific in issuing literature that pointed to the complicity of the tsarist regime in the 1905 pogrom wave, they were often silent about the participation of workers, and their own working-class support base, in the violence. As Charters Wynn has shown, social democrats in the Donbass-Dnepr Bend region regularly opposed pogroms but sometimes chose purposefully *not* to publicly confront the antisemitism of their own working-class constituency.[43] One leaflet from October 1905 asked, 'Who is guilty? ... don't speak about the ignorance, about the barbarous instincts of the dark masses. The initiative for pogroms never comes from there.'[44] In the Pale of Settlement, Jewish revolutionaries learned through bitter

---

[41] For examples, see K. A. Sutton, 'Class and Revolution in Russia: The Soviet Movement of 1905' (PhD Dissertation, University of Birmingham, 1987); P. I. Denisenko, *Listovki bol'shevikov Ukrainy perioda pervoi russkoi revoliutsii (1905-1907 gg)* (Kiev: Gosudarstvennoe izdatel'stvo politicheskoi literatury USSR, 1955), 92–93, 207–08, 230–33, 269–70, 296–98, 514–17, 578–81; I. N. Kirillov and A. M. Tarasenko, *Listovki Ivanovo-Voznesenskoi bol'shevistkoi organizatsii 1900-1917 gg* (Ivanovo: Ivanovskoe khnizhnoe izdatel'stvo, 1957), 116–19, 143–48; I. I. P., *Listovki moskovskikh bol'shevikov v period pervoi russkoi revoloitsii* (Moskva: Gosudarstvennoe izdatel'stvo politicheskoi literatury, 1955), 487–90. See also I. Shtakser, *The Making of Jewish Revolutionaries in the Pale of Settlement: Community and Identity during the Russian Revolution and its Immediate Aftermath, 1905–1907*. (Basingstoke: Palgrave, 2014), 132–33.

[42] Denisenko, *Listovki bol'shevikov Ukrainy perioda pervoi russkoi revoliutsii (1905–1907 gg)*, 298–302.

[43] C. Wynn, *Worker, Strikes, and Pogroms: The Donbass-Dnepr Bend in Late Imperial Russia, 1870-1905* (Princeton: Princeton University Press, 1992). For a critique of this view, see G. Surh, 'Ekaterinoslav City in 1905: capa Workers, Jews, and Violence', *International Labor and Working-Class History* 64 (2003): 139–66.

[44] Wynn, *Worker, Strikes, and Pogroms*, 210.

experience about the depth of antisemitism within sections of the working class. At the same time, the response of some of their non-Jewish comrades to the violence felt like like a betrayal of the socialist promise of an internationalist future beyond ethnic discrimination.[45] These tensions surfaced in a heated exchange between Trotsky and the Bundist leader Vladimir Medem at a small socialist meeting in Karlsruhe, Germany, not long after the Kishinev pogrom of 1903. Trotsky's intervention came in response to a speech by Medem in which he had accused Russian social democrats of neglecting to confront antisemitism. Writing in his memoirs, Medem recalls Trotsky arguing:

> It [is] not necessary to fight anti-Semitism in *particular*. Anti-Semitism [is], after all, nothing more than a consequence of the universal lack of consciousness among the broad masses. Hence the need to bring them to a state of general awareness, after which anti-Semitism will fade away anyway. To make Jews a *special* subject of discussion among the broad masses [is] superfluous.[46]

This social democratic impulse to minimize or gloss over the participation of workers in antisemitic violence brought the Bund to conflict with Lenin. The dispute originated in the publication of a RSDRP leaflet issued to Jewish workers in Ekaterinoslav, which described antisemitism as a phenomenon that has 'everywhere found adherents among the bourgeois, and not among the working-class sections of the population'.[47] In January 1903, the Foreign Committee of the Bund complained bitterly that this sidestepped entirely the complicity of Russian workers in the pogroms. More specifically, the Bund complained that Russian social democrats appeared

> more interested in the enlightenment of the Jewish masses, their emancipation from prejudices ... than in the eradication of ferocious antisemitism ... there is no doubt that from a revolutionary standpoint this is a great omission.[48]

For the Foreign Committee of the Bund, antisemitism within proletarian ranks had to be confronted, and publicly so, and to deny its existence to

---

[45] I. Shtakser, *The Making of Jewish Revolutionaries in the Pale of Settlement*, 134, 139, 149.
[46] V. Medem, *The Life and Soul of a Legendary Jewish Socialist. The Memoirs of Vladimir Medem* (New York: KTAV Publishing House, 1979), 269. Trotsky comments are illustrative of a fatalism and developmentalism that characterized much (though not all) of European Marxist thinking on antisemitism. For a discussion on this point, see B. McGeever, 'Bolshevik Responses to Antisemitism during the Civil War: Spatiality, Temporality, and Agency', in *Volume 3: Russia's Home Front in War and Revolution, 1914-22. Book 4*, ed. C. Read and A. Lindenmeyr, vol. 1 (Bloomington: Slavica Publishers, 2018).
[47] V. I. Lenin, *Lenin on the Jewish Question* (New York: International Publishers, 1974), 23.
[48] Goldhagen, 'The Ethnic Consciousness of Early Russian Socialists', 495.

Jewish workers in particular was entirely unacceptable. Yet Lenin was unimpressed. In an article in *Iskra* on 15 February, he accused the Bund of having a 'truly infantile' conceptualization of antisemitism.[49] For Lenin, the Bund was ignoring 'the link that *undoubtedly* exists between antisemitism and the interests of the bourgeois, and not the working interests of the population'.[50] This was the crucial point, he argued, regardless of whether or not hundreds of workers took part in a pogrom.

At the level of practice, however, Bolsheviks and social democrats were moving beyond Lenin's narrow and reductive framing of antisemitism. Between 1903 and 1905 in the towns and cities of the Donets Basin, social democrats repeatedly called off May Day and other such demonstrations (often despite weeks of agitating and leafleting) for fear that working-class politicization would result in violence against Jews. This was principally due to the fact that the same workers striking for improved working conditions could, a mere twenty-four hours later, engage in pogromist violence. Fully aware of this, social democrats repeatedly found themselves in the position of having to curb the labour movement for fear of provoking a pogrom.[51] Similar developments were taking place elsewhere. In Kyiv, the 1903 May Day demonstration was cancelled by local social democrats, largely out of fear that the Kishinev pogrom (which had just taken place) would be replicated. When the Socialist Revolutionary Party insisted on holding the demonstration, Trotsky intervened, arguing that socialists were obligated 'to wait until after the passing of the acute moment', since mobilizing now would not 'educate the masses' but would facilitate 'a feeling of spasmodic revolutionism' that could easily turn to pogroms.[52]

What such cases reveal, above all, is that Russian social democrats were, *at the level of practice*, 'stretching' Russian Marxism, to paraphrase Frantz Fanon, beyond its own theoretical framing of antisemitism.[53]

Summary

This brief overview of the pre-revolutionary period prefigures the Bolshevik response to antisemitism after 1917 in two ways. First, during the formative years of 1903 and 1906, Bolsheviks, like all Russian social

---

[49] Lenin, *Lenin on the Jewish Question*, 23.   [50] Ibid., 23.
[51] Wynn, *Worker, Strikes, and Pogroms*, 199, 226.
[52] J. Nedava, *Trotsky and the Jews* (Philadelphia: The Jewish Publication Society of America, 1971), 52. For similar examples, see Bobrov, 'Evreiskii vopros v ideologii i politicheskoi deiatel'nosti rossiiskikh marksistov (konets XIX v.-fevral' 1917 g.)', 169; Kirillov and Tarasenko, *Listovki Ivanovo-Voznesenskoi bol'shevistkoi organizatsii 1900-1917 gg.*, 116–19, 145–46.
[53] F. Fanon, *The Wretched of the Earth* (London: Penguin Classics, 2001).

democrats, practiced the politics of the united front in their responses to antisemitism. In the borderlands of the Pale of Settlement and key cities of the Russian 'interior', Bolsheviks were deeply immersed in building strategic alliances with other revolutionaries (and indeed non-revolutionaries) at the local level to forge a progressive and collective response to the threat of anti-Jewish violence. What was particularly significant was the close cooperation with Jewish socialist organizations. Through these collaborations, the Jewish left came to play a critical role in elevating the socialist response to antisemitism in late-imperial Russia, as the dispute between Lenin and the Bund in 1903 indicated. This pattern would repeat itself in 1918 and 1919 when, after the October Revolution, non-Bolshevik Jewish socialists played the key role in actualizing, at the level of practice, the Bolshevik response to antisemitism. As Chapters 3, 6, and 7 show, these activists bridged the gap between the promise and actuality of the Soviet government's response to antisemitism after October 1917.

Second, the fact that some workers could move from striking for improved working conditions in one moment to taking part in anti-Jewish violence in the next points to the need to develop a more sophisticated understanding of the nature of the relationship between antisemitism and class formation. In the chapters that follow (specifically Chapters 1, 2, 4 and 7), *Antisemitism and the Russian Revolution* takes on this challenge and details the ways in which antisemitism could overlap with oppositional forms of political action in revolutionary Russia, sometimes with devastating consequences.

Outline of the Study

Antisemitism and the Russian Revolution unfolds chronologically: Chapter 1 examines antisemitism during Russia's year of revolution in 1917, including Bolshevik and socialist responses to it. The following two chapters are focussed tightly around the period of the spring of 1918. Chapter 2 examines the Red Army pogroms of March and April 1918, while the subsequent chapter tracks the emergence of a Soviet government response to this wave of anti-Jewish violence. The next three chapters address the year of crisis, 1919. First, the explosive articulation between antisemitism and the revolutionary process in the spring and summer of that year is examined in close detail in Chapter 4. The discussion then proceeds to an extensive analysis of the Soviet government campaign against antisemitism in the first six months of 1919 (Chapter 5), before Jewish communist responses in the latter half of the year are examined (Chapter 6). The work's final chapter offers an extended discussion of the intractability of antisemitism in the Russian revolution, and demonstrates how Bolsheviks and Jewish communists remained caught in the racializing bind of the 'Jewish question'.

A Note on Sources

Antisemitism and the Russian Revolution draws significantly on Russian-language sources. Only a small selection of Yiddish materials have been translated and incorporated into the study. This imposes limitations on the findings of the research. When non-Bolshevik Jewish socialists joined the Soviet government in 1918 and 1919, they corresponded with Soviet and Party institutions in Russian. The debate on antisemitism between Party and government institutions (including the broader campaign among the wider population) was carried out almost exclusively in Russian. In the archives of the Jewish Commissariat, for example, meeting minutes, official documents and many telegrams are in Russian, and these provide the bulk of the sources used in Chapters 3 and 6. Nevertheless, much of the internal, 'backstage' conversations within the Jewish Commissariat and Evsektsiia, including personal correspondences and private letters, were in Yiddish. It is possible that these materials offer an important (and potentially different) slant on the debates examined here. The extent to which this is the case will have to be determined by future research.

1   1917: Antisemitism in the Moment of Revolution

Introduction

The year 1917 transformed Jewish life, setting in motion a sudden and intense period of emancipation. Just days after the abdication of Tsar Nicholas II and the formation of the Provisional Government, all legal restrictions on Russian Jewry were lifted. More than 140 anti-Jewish statutes, totalling some 1,000 pages, were removed overnight. To mark this historic moment of abolition, a special meeting was convened by the Petrograd Soviet. Symbolically, the meeting happened to fall on 24 March 1917 – the eve of Passover. The Jewish delegate addressing those in attendance immediately made the connection: the February Revolution, he said, was comparable with the liberation of Jews from slavery in Egypt.[1] Formal emancipation, however, was not accompanied by the disappearance of antisemitism. In 1917, the spectre of pogroms once again returned to Russia, prefiguring the dramatic escalation of antisemitic violence that would erupt during the Civil War in 1918 and 1919.

Despite the vast literature on 1917, there has been comparatively little scholarly interest in the specific question of antisemitism during Russia's year of revolution. In fact, 1917 represents the least analyzed chapter in the history of antisemitic violence that spanned the late imperial and revolutionary years (1871–1922).[2] A century on, there exists only a handful of serious works on the subject.[3] While the scale of anti-Jewish violence between February and October in 1917 in no way matched that

---

[1] B. D. Gal'perina, O. N. Znamenskii, and V. I. Startsev, eds., *Petrogradskii Sovet Rabochikh i Soldatskikh Deputatov v 1917 godu. Dokumenty i materialy*, vol. 1 (Leningrad: Nauka Leningradskoe otdelenie, 1991), 494.
[2] Buldakov, 'Freedom, Shortages, Violence: The Origins of the 'Revolutionary Anti-Jewish Pogrom' in Russia, 1917-1918', 87.
[3] Tcherikower, *Istoriia pogromnogo dvizheniia na Ukraine 1917-1921*; V. P. Buldakov, 'Rossiiskoe evreistvo i bol'shevistskii perevorot v Petrograde, Oktriabr' 1917 - Ianvar' 1918 goda', in *Arkhiv evreiskoi istorii, tom 4*, ed. O. V. Budnitskii (Moscow: ROSSPEN, 2007), 92–124; Buldakov, *Khaos i etnos*; M. Beizer, 'Antisemitism in Petrograd/Leningrad, 1917–1930', *East European Jewish Affairs* 29, no. 1–2 (1999): 5–28; Budnitskii, *Rossiiskie evrei mezhdu krasnymi i belymi*, 52–93.

of, say, the 1903–6 or 1918–22 pogrom waves, Russian society in 1917 bore witness to a sharp increase in antisemitism. Newspaper reports indicate that at least 235 attacks against Jews were carried out in 1917. Although totalling just 4.5 per cent of the population, Jews were victims of around a third of all recorded acts of physical violence against national minorities in that year.[4] Just as in 1905, violent antisemitism in 1917 was closely connected to the ebb and flow of revolution. Although levels of antisemitism were comparatively low during the February Revolution, they would escalate later in the year at precisely those moments of revolutionary upheaval: the July Days, the Kornilov Affair in August and the October Revolution.

The Bolshevik response to such antisemitism in 1917 was part of a broader, cross-party strategic alliance stretching back to 1905, comprising revolutionaries, reformist socialists and liberals.[5] Within this milieu, antisemitism was understood from 'the standpoint of the bourgeois revolution': that is, the belief that the founding of a bourgeois, capitalist democratic republic would create the conditions for the eradication of antisemitism and indeed all forms of national oppression.[6] Since the turn of the century, most Russian socialists (Jewish and non-Jewish alike) had identified antisemitism with tsarism. Following the February 1917 Revolution, antisemitism now came to be seen as the most reactionary form of restorationist counter-revolution. This view was shared not just by socialists but by many non-socialists in Jewish political life. For example, an editorial in the liberal Jewish newspaper *Evreiskaia Nedelia* (The Jewish Week) in September 1917 asked:

Who needs this [pogromist] agitation? A priori, it is those elements who seek a return to the old regime. If, before [February 1917], pogromist agitation supported the old regime by turning the masses away from revolutionary propaganda, then now it is carried by those elements who want to return the old regime to power.[7]

---

[4] Buldakov, *Khaos i etnos*, 1019.
[5] On socialist responses to antisemitism in Russia prior to 1917, see G. D. Surh, 'Russian Jewish Socialists and Antisemitism: The Case of Grigorii Aronson', *Patterns of Prejudice* 51, no. 3–4 (2017): 253–68; Bobrov, 'Evreiskii vopros v ideologii i politicheskoi deiatel'nosti rossiiskikh marksistov (konets XIX v.-fevral' 1917 g.)'; B. McGeever, 'The Bolshevik Confrontation with Antisemitism in the Russian Revolution, 1917-1919' (Unpublished PhD thesis. University of Glasgow, 2015), 25–30.
[6] McGeever, 'Bolshevik Responses to Antisemitism During the Civil War: Spatiality, Temporality, and Agency'. For a broader discussion of this theme, see E. Traverso, *The Marxists and the Jewish Question. The History of a Debate 1843-1943* (New York: Humanity Books, 1994).
[7] 'Pogromist Danger and the Means of Self-Defence' (*Pogromnaia opastnost' i mery samozashchity*), *Evreiskaia Nedelia*, no. 36–7, 12 September 1917, 1.

This perspective had a significant mobilizing capacity, particularly within the socialist movement. Despite their deep-rooted differences, almost all socialists had an entrenched interest in defending the gains of the February Revolution.[8] This was captured by the concept of the *demokratiia*, a key term in Russian revolutionary discourse. Essentially, *demokratiia* was invoked to distinguish 'people's power' from the 'bourgeoisie' and the 'ruling classes'. As such, socialist, Marxist and indeed all radical and progressive political parties claimed to act in the spirit of the '*demokratiia*' and the 'people' (*narod*).[9] Institutionally, the *demokratiia* came increasingly to be rooted in the soviets and the three main parties which controlled them (the Bolsheviks, the Mensheviks and the Socialist Revolutionaries [SRs]).[10] From the perspective of the *demokratiia*, then, antisemitism represented a return to the 'old regime' of tsarism, and hence was viewed principally as a form of restorationist counter-revolution. Committed to the standpoint of the bourgeois revolution, socialists of the *demokratiia* set aside their party differences and confronted antisemitism and pogromist violence.

The Soviets

The institutional hub of the socialist response to antisemitism in 1917 was the soviets of workers' and soldiers' deputies. Conceived during the 1905 Revolution, the Petrograd soviet was re-established in the Russian capital following the February Revolution of 1917. By March 1917, there were more than 600 soviets in various regions and, by the summer, they had been established across the whole of Russia, a process bringing about the unique phenomenon of *dual power*: the balance of forces between the ostensibly ruling Provisional Government and the increasingly powerful soviets.[11] The soviets initially constituted a formally self-limiting form of government, agreeing as a matter of principle

---

[8] L. Trotsky, *The Permanent Revolution and Results and Prospects* (London: New Park Publications Ltd., 1971), 163.
[9] On the *demokratiia*, see the classic essay: R. G. Suny, 'Toward a Social History of the October Revolution', *The American Historical Review* 88, no. 1 (1983): 31–52. See also B. I. Kolonitskii, "Democracy' in the Political Consciousness of the February Revolution', *Slavic Review* 57, no. 1 (1998): 95–106; B. I. Kolonitskii, "Democracy' as Identification. Towards the Study of Political Consciousness During the February Revolution', in *Social Identities in Revolutionary Russia*, ed. K. P. Madhavan (Basingstoke: Palgrave, 2001).
[10] E. Mawdsley, *The Russian Civil War* (Edinburgh: Birlinn, 2008), 16–19.
[11] N. N. Smirnov, 'The Soviets', in *Critical Companion to the Russian Revolution, 1914-1921*, ed. E. Acton, V. Iu. Cherniaev and W. G. Rosenberg (Bloomington: Indiana University Press, 1997), 429–30.

to the formula of *postol'ku-poskol'ku*, a phrase denoting the soviets' agreement to recognize the Provisional Government *to the extent* that it in turn recognize the soviets.[12] However, by the summer of 1917, the ministers of the Provisional Government, their deputies and the leaders of urban dumas and zemstvos began to report not to 'the state' proper (i.e. the Provisional Government) but to the soviets themselves. Similarly, from July onwards, the soviets began to hold more sway than the organs of military command. State power was concretely transferring to the soviets.[13] Politically, the Mensheviks and the SRs were in control of the soviets between February and June. Yet as the Mensheviks and the SRs stuck harder and faster to their moderate programmes, the Bolsheviks gained support. From the moment of the Kornilov Affair in August, the soviets swung dramatically to the side of the Bolsheviks.[14]

The soviets were non-party institutions that engaged in cross-class, broad political campaigns. Despite bitter inter-party fighting in 1917, cross-party alliances were the defining characteristic of the soviet model, as was shown in August when the threat of counter-revolution in the shape of the Kornilov Affair was swiftly put down by an alliance of all formations left of the Kadets.[15] It was from these cross-party, strategic alliances that the soviet confrontation with antisemitism emerged in Russia's year of revolution.

The Soviets Respond to Antisemitism

The soviets responded to antisemitism almost immediately following the February Revolution. Just five days after its formation, on 3 March, the Petrograd soviet established a commission, headed by the Bundist Moishe Rafes, whose task was to stop 'black hundreds' from trying to 'sew national hatred among the population'. Three days later, on 6 March, the commission sent representatives to the north-west of

---

[12] Ibid., 430. [13] Ibid., 431.
[14] N. N Sukhanov, *The Russian Revolution, 1917: A Personal Record*, ed. Joel Carmichael (Princeton: Princeton University Press, 1984), 522–23; A. Rabinowitch, *The Bolsheviks Come to Power. The Revolution of 1917 in Petrograd* (New York: W. W. Norton, 1978); Suny, 'Toward a Social History of the October Revolution'; D. J. Raleigh, 'Political Power in the Russian Revolution: A Case Study of Saratov', in *Revolution in Russia: Reassessments of 1917*, ed. E. R. Frankel, J. Frankel and B. Knei-Paz (Cambridge: Cambridge University Press, 1992), 34–53.
[15] D. Koenker, 'The Evolution of Party Consciousness in 1917: The Case of the Moscow Workers', *Soviet Studies* 30, no. 1 (1978): 61. The Kornilov Affair was an attempted military coup led by General Kornilov against the Provisional Government; the Kadets were members of the liberal democratic Konstitutsionno-Demokraticheskaia Partiia (Constitutional Democratic Party).

Petrograd to respond to an increase in 'antisemitic agitation'. Later that week, reports came in of 'pogrom literature' being distributed in the capital.[16] Similarly, just days after it was established, the Moscow soviet began to monitor instances of antisemitism.[17] By April, the Petrograd soviet was also receiving warnings about impending pogroms,[18] and although actual outbreaks of antisemitic violence remained few and far between, the Poalei Zion party nevertheless felt moved to demand that the Petrograd soviet come out with a specific set of measures to confront antisemitism[19]. This initiative was likely put forward by Zvi Fridliand, a member of the Central Committee of the Poalei Zion party. These early initiatives within the soviets around the question of antisemitism underlined the agency of Jewish socialists in the Bund (Rafes) and the Poalei Zion party (Fridliand). Later, after the October Revolution, both Rafes and Fridliand would play a vital role in developing the first Soviet government's response to antisemitism (see Chapter 3), but already in early 1917 their presence could be felt.

In June 1917, antisemitism increased markedly on the streets of the Russian capital and beyond, in the former Pale of Settlement. In mid-June, the Petrograd soviet sent a special commission to the Ukrainian city of Elisavetgrad and its neighbouring towns in an attempt to ensure a local soviet response in the event of an outbreak of anti-Jewish violence.[20] By the third week of June, crowds of workers were reportedly gathering in Petrograd to welcome pogromist speeches purporting to reveal the 'real' names of the Jewish members of the Petrograd soviet.[21] Bolshevik leaders sometimes came face-to-face with such antisemitism. When walking through the streets of the capital in early July, the Bolshevik Vladimir

---

[16] Gal'perina, Znamenskii, and Startsev, *Petrogradskii Sovet Rabochikh i Soldatskikh Deputatov v 1917 godu. Dokumenty i materialy.*, 1:84, 132, 176, 190, 342. The Commission continued to take measures to combat antisemitism throughout 1917. On 22 May, for example, it instructed the Ministry of Military Affairs to take action against reported antisemitism within the Russian Army. See B. D. Gal'perina and V. I. Startsev, eds., *Petrogradskii Sovet Rabochikh i Soldatskikh Deputatov v 1917 godu. Dokumenty i materialy*, vol. 3 (Moscow: ROSSPEN, 2002), 132.

[17] See the documents in Tsentral'nyi gosudarstvennyi arkhiv Moskovskoi oblasti (hereafter TsGAMO), f.66 o.25 d.45 l.1–45. The folder containing these files is titled 'Black Hundred material (pogromist agitation against Jews, attacked on the Moscow Soviet 31/3/1917-1/11/1917)'.

[18] Letter titled 'To the Soviet of Workers Deputies' by a church representative in St. Petersburg warning of impending pogroms. Dated 4 April 1917. Gosudarstvennyi arkhiv Rosiiskoi Federatsii, Moscow (hereafter GARF), f.504 o.1 d.528 l.1.

[19] Beizer, 'Antisemitism in Petrograd/Leningrad, 1917–1930', 6–7.

[20] H. Rogger, 'Conclusions and Overview', in *Pogroms: Anti-Jewish Violence in Modern Russian History*, ed. J. D. Klier (New York: Cambridge University Press, 1992), 350.

[21] Buldakov, *Khaos i etnos*, 317.

Bonch-Bruevich – Lenin's future secretary – encountered various groups of people openly calling for anti-Jewish pogroms.[22] Around the same time, the Jewish historian Simon Dubnov noted in his diary that he too had heard people calling for pogroms, at the Aleksandr Market in Petrograd.[23] More and more reports came in of similar gatherings. At some of them, class resentment and antisemitic representations of Jewishness overlapped: in late July, speakers at a street-corner rally in the city centre called on the crowd to 'smash the Jews and the bourgeoisie!'[24] As the socialist newspaper *Izvestiia* put it, 'Lately, on the streets of Petrograd and other cities, pogrom-like persecution of the Jews goes on almost before our very eyes.'[25] Whereas, in the immediate context after the February Revolution, such speeches had failed to have any real traction on the streets of Petrograd, they now were drawing large audiences.[26] Despite the socialist insistence that antisemitism was the preserve of the counter-revolutionary right, it increasingly asserted itself across the political divide. It was in this context that the First All-Russian Congress of Soviets of Workers' and Soldiers' Deputies gathered in Petrograd.

This First Congress of Soviets was composed of 1,090 delegates from all socialist parties and represented more than 336 local soviets, scores of military units and more than 20 million Russian citizens.[27] By any assessment, this was a historic gathering of the revolutionary movement. Throughout the month of June, the Congress met daily to discuss a range of political issues, including the convocation of a constituent assembly, the ongoing war, the land question and many others matters. On 22 June, as reports of 'pogromist agitation' continued to flood in, the Congress turned to the question of antisemitism.

The discussion had been initiated by the Bund's delegate Mark Liber, who insisted that the Congress directly address the persistence of antisemitic sentiment in Russia.[28] His request met with resounding success.

---

[22] These recollections were included in a speech delivered by Bonch-Bruevich on 28 October 1917. The speech was reprinted in V. Bonch-Bruevich, *Krovavyi navet na khristian* (Moscow: Gosudarstvennaia tipografiia, 1919), 11. A copy of this title is held in Bonch-Bruevich's personal files in the manuscripts department of the Rossiiskaia gosudarstvennaia biblioteka, Moscow (Russian State Library), Fond rukopisei, f. 369 o. 49 d. 28.
[23] S. Dubnov, *Kniga zhizni. Materialy dlia istorii moego vremeni: Vospominaniia i razmyshleniia* (Moscow: Mosty kul'tury, 2004), 417.
[24] Rabinowitch, *The Bolsheviks Come to Power*, 43.
[25] Beizer, 'Antisemitism in Petrograd/Leningrad, 1917–1930', 8.
[26] Beizer, 7; Budnitskii, *Rossiiskie evrei mezhdu krasnymi i belymi*, 83–84.
[27] V. L'vov-Rogachevskii, *Goniteli evreiskogo naroda v Rossii. Istoricheskii ocherk* (Moscow: Moskovskii Sovet Rabochikh Deputatov. Otdel izdatel'stva i knizhnogo sklada, 1917), 1.
[28] J. Meyers, 'To Dance at Two Weddings: Jews, Nationalism, and the Left in Revolutionary Russia' (Unpublished PhD thesis. Stanford University, 2018), 150–51.

On the morning of 22 June, the Congress's special Commission on the National Question met to draft a resolution 'On the Struggle against Antisemitism'.[29] This task was allocated to the Bolshevik Evgenii Preobrazhenskii,[30] who just two days previously had openly condemned the Provisional Government for delaying its decision to take measures to protect 'oppressed national minorities'.[31] Preobrazhenskii's resolution on antisemitism was passed unanimously by the Commission on the National Question, and was then immediately put to the Congress delegates later that same day. It was, without question, the most authoritative statement on antisemitism by the socialist movement yet. Prior to reading out his resolution before the assembled delegates, Preobrazhenskii began with an impassioned speech:

> Congress cannot let this issue pass without making a special appeal to the whole *demokratiia* [socialist movement], it cannot let this pass without proposing a series of measures to fulfil its duty to the Jewish people and show to the masses that this anti-Jewish demagogy is carried out in order to restore tsarism and destroy the freedoms won by the revolution.[32]

Preobrazhenskii identified antisemitism as an attempt to enact a counter-revolution against February and restore tsarism, a perspective firmly in keeping with 'the standpoint of the bourgeois revolution' discussed earlier. It is also worth noting that, despite the deepening split between the soviet leadership and the increasingly radicalized and bolshevized cadres, Preobrazhenskii continued to appeal to the 'whole *demokratiia*', without party distinction. In other words, for the Bolshevik Preobrazhenskii, the campaign against antisemitism was an issue that could forge alliances across the socialist left, and, indeed, it was something that *required* such unity.

The resolution itself had two important things to say about antisemitism. First, Preobrazhenskii instructed 'all local soviets ... to carry out relentless propaganda and educational work among the masses in order to combat anti-Jewish persecution'.[33] This underscored the profoundly

---

[29] L'vov-Rogachevskii, *Goniteli evreiskogo naroda v Rossii. Istoricheskii ocherk*, 3.

[30] Preobrazhenskii would again return to the question of antisemitism two years later, in 1919, when he included a special subchapter dedicated specifically to antisemitism in *ABC of Communism*; see N. Bukharin and E. Preobrazhenskii, *The ABC of Communism* (Wiltshire: The Merlin Press, 2006), 199–200.

[31] M. F. Vladimirskii et al., eds., *Pervyi Vserossiiskii S'ezd Sovetov Rabochikh i Soldatskikh Deputatov, tom 2* (Moscow: Gosizdat, 1931), 182. See also R. P. Browder and A. F. Kerensky, eds., *The Russian Provisional Government 1917. Documents (in 3 Volumes)*. (Stanford: Stanford University Press, 1961), 318–19.

[32] Vladimirskii et al., *Pervyi Vserossiiskii S'ezd Sovetov Rabochikh i Soldatskikh Deputatov, tom 2*, 241.

[33] Ibid., 239–41.

educative role of the soviets. Second, the resolution warned of the 'great danger' posed by the 'tendency for antisemitism to disguise itself under radical slogans' (*radikal'nye lozungi*). This admission was relatively new territory for the Russian socialist movement, which until then had tended to frame antisemitism as the preserve of the counter-revolutionary right. Here, however, Preobrazhenskii acknowledged that antisemitism could find expression in left discourse. Such antisemitism, he continued, represented 'an enormous threat to the Jewish people and the whole revolutionary movement, since it threatens to drown the liberation of the people in the blood of our brothers, and cover in disgrace the entire revolutionary movement'. When Preobrazhenskii finished reading aloud the resolution, a Jewish delegate rose to state his wholehearted agreement with it, before adding that, although it would not bring back his fellow Jews murdered in the pogroms of 1905, it would nevertheless help heal some of the wounds that continued to cause so much pain in the Jewish community. The resolution was passed unanimously by the Congress.[34]

What were the consequences of this historic meeting? Writing in September 1917, the veteran Menshevik, Vasili L'vov-Rogachevskii, lamented that the soviets had not taken antisemitism seriously following the Congress, pointing out that the promised educational campaigns had not materialized and that the soviets had generally failed to publish literature on antisemitism.[35] Whilst the soviets may well have failed to respond to the growth of antisemitism in late June and July, newspaper sources from August and September indicate that a campaign was indeed eventually set in motion by various regional soviets. For example, in response to growing reports of antisemitic agitation, the Moscow soviet undertook a series of measures, including organizing lectures and talks in Moscow factories on antisemitism.[36] On 20 August, the Moscow soviet also convened a meeting to debate the sharp increase in antisemitic propaganda, and a special commission was formed to campaign locally against antisemitism. The following day, on 21 August, the commission organized another meeting, this time one that included not only the deputies from the local Moscow district soviets but trade unionists and representatives of the regional Duma as well.[37] In the former Pale of Settlement, local soviets were instrumental in preventing antisemitic pogroms. For example, in Chernihiv (Ukraine) in mid-August, Black

---

[34] Ibid., 241.
[35] L'vov-Rogachevskii, *Goniteli evreiskogo naroda v Rossii. Istoricheskii ocherk*, 102.
[36] *Evreiskaia Zhizn'* (Jewish Life), no. 38–9, 29 September 1917, 20.
[37] *Rassvet* (Dawn), no. 8, 30 August 1917, 24.

Hundred accusations that Jews were stocking up grain led to a series of violent anti-Jewish disturbances. Crucially, it took a delegation from the Kyiv soviet to organize a group of local troops to put down the unrest.[38] Other small-scale interventions occurred in places further afield: in late August, the local soviet in Slutsk – a city south of Minsk – issued a special resolution against antisemitism in light of pogromist agitation by a group of monks at a local monastery.[39]

Soviet attempts to combat antisemitism continued throughout September. Early in the month, the Moscow soviet again issued a special proclamation against pogroms, calling on meetings to be set up for workers to discuss antisemitism[40]. On 17 September, L'vov-Rogachevskii delivered a lecture to the Moscow branch of the Menshevik party on the topic 'The Jews in Russia and Their Role in the Revolutionary Movement'. Other lectures on similar themes continued to be delivered in workplaces and soviets throughout September.[41] On 13 September, yet another commission was established to confront pogroms, this time by the Kyiv soviet, and its work included arranging meetings for 'various democratic organizations' on the topic of antisemitism.[42] This again points to the centrality of cross-party and cross-class alliances in the campaigns against antisemitism. Despite the growing bolshevization of the soviets, the confrontation with antisemitism was something that continued to require the participation of all socialist parties.

Moderate socialists in the Provisional Government, we should note, attempted to initiate their own response to antisemitism. On 14 September, at a meeting of the government, the Menshevik A. M. Nikitin explicitly raised the issue of pogroms. Government representatives responded by passing a resolution that promised to take 'the most drastic measures against all pogromists'.[43] At another meeting, on 29 September, government ministers were given 'all powers at their disposal' to put down pogroms.[44] In the government's own words, stopping pogroms was to be achieved by strengthening 'military and civil authorities' and 'local organs of government'.[45] Despite these and other related initiatives, however, the Provisional Government's power had virtually disintegrated: with its ideological and repressive state apparatuses almost

---

[38] Buldakov, *Khaos i etnos*, 389–99. [39] *Rassvet*, no. 8, 30 August 1917, 33.
[40] Buldakov, *Khaos i etnos*, 429. [41] *Evreiskaia Zhizn'*, 38–9, 29 September 1917, 20.
[42] Buldakov, *Khaos i etnos*, 432. [43] Buldakov, 423.
[44] Tcherikower, *Istoriia pogromnogo dvizheniia na Ukraine 1917-1921*, 207; Buldakov, *Khaos i etnos*, 423.
[45] Browder and Kerensky, *The Russian Provisional Government, 1917*, 1644.

completely paralyzed by mid- to late 1917,[46] it was in no position to respond adequately to outbreaks of antisemitism.[47] An editorial in the pro-government newspaper *Russkie Vedomosti* on 1 October captured the situation in stark terms: 'the wave of pogroms grows and expands ... mountains of telegrams arrive daily ... [yet] the Provisional Government is snowed under ... the local administration is powerless to do anything ... *the means of coercion are completely exhausted*'.[48]

Not so with the soviets. As the political crisis deepened in October, scores of provincial soviets established their own repressive state apparatuses for combatting antisemitism. For example, on 7 October in Vitebsk, a city 350 miles west of Moscow, the local soviet formed a military unit to protect the city from pogromists.[49] The following week, the Orel soviet passed a resolution to take up arms against all forms of antisemitic violence.[50] By the middle of the month, the campaign had even spread to the Russian Far East, where a meeting of the All-Siberian soviet issued a resolution protesting against pogroms, declaring that the local revolutionary army was prepared to take 'all measures necessary' to prevent them.[51] This remarkable display of solidarity shows how deeply ingrained the fight against antisemitism was within sections of the organized socialist movement. Even in places in the Far East where there were comparatively few Jews and even fewer pogroms,[52] local soviets identified with the Jews on the Western Front who were suffering at the hands of pogromists and antisemites.

That the soviets had become, by mid-late 1917, the principle source of socialist opposition to antisemitism seems beyond doubt. In mid-September, even the highly critical liberal Jewish newspaper *Evreiskaia Nedelia* admitted in an editorial: 'We must give them their dues, the soviets ... have carried out an energetic struggle [against pogroms] ... and in many places it has only been thanks to their strength that peace

---

[46] The concepts 'repressive' and 'ideological' state apparatuses are used here in the Althusserian sense to identify and distinguish between two spheres of state activity: the 'repressive state apparatuses' that predominantly function through coercion (the army, police and courts); and the 'ideological state apparatuses' that function through ideology and persuasion. See L. Althusser, *On the Reproduction of Capitalism: Ideology and Ideological State Apparatuses* (London: Verso, 2014).
[47] Buldakov, *Khaos i etnos*, 318; Buldakov, 'Freedom, Shortages, Violence', 74.
[48] Browder and Kerensky, *The Russian Provisional Government, 1917*, 1646. Emphasis added.
[49] Buldakov, *Khaos i etnos*, 446.   [50] Ibid., 454.
[51] 'Protest against Jewish Pogroms', *Izvestiia VTsIK*, 21 October 1917, 2.
[52] Although see L. Kalmina, 'The Possibility of the Impossible: Pogroms in Eastern Siberia', in *Anti-Jewish Violence: Rethinking the Pogrom in East European History*, ed. J. Dekel-Chen et al. (Bloomington: Indiana University Press, 2011), 131–44.

has been restored'.[53] However, the socialist response to antisemitism was unevenly developed at the local level. In mid-October in Tambov (a city 300 miles south of Moscow), the local soviet met to discuss measures to stop the recent outbreak of pogromist violence. During the discussion, members of the soviet reportedly shouted, 'Why stop the pogrom? Let's join in (*idem podsobliat'*)!'[54] Nevertheless, the overall picture that emerges from even the critical Jewish press in 1917 is one that points to the soviets playing a leading role in combatting antisemitic violence.

Such opposition to antisemitism from below was replicated from above, by the All-Russian Executive Committee (Vserossiiskii Tsentral'nyi Ispolnitel'nyi Komitet, VTsIK) – the head organization of the soviets – when it wrote to all soviet deputies on 7 October demanding that a commission consisting of all soviet parties and trade unions be formed in every city to fight antisemitism. The commissions were also instructed to issue leaflets and brochures denouncing anti-Jewish violence.[55] Three days later, on 10 October, the VTsIK met again to outline further measures against antisemitism, with the Bundist Abramovich leading the discussions.[56] Most symbolic of all, however, was the resolution passed against antisemitism by the Second All-Russian Congress of Soviets on 26 October: 'The honour ... of the revolution demands that no such pogroms take place ... the whole of revolutionary Russia and the world is watching you'.[57] The timing could not have been more dramatic: the resolution was issued at the very moment that Red Guards seized the Winter Palace. The wording of this resolution appeared to reveal a concern on behalf of the Congress that a revolutionary insurrection might enlarge the scope for pogroms. This fear that revolution – and, in particular, a *Bolshevik* revolution – would exacerbate the threat of the pogroms was something that was felt across the socialist left.

Antisemitism within the Revolutionary Movement

For the Bolshevik leadership, revolutionary politics was simply incompatible with antisemitism: the two were antithetical. As a front-page

[53] 'Pogromist Danger and the Means of Self-Defence', *Evreiskaia Nedelia*, no. 36–37, 12 September 1917, 1.
[54] 'The Soviet of the Russian Republic' (editorial), *Evreiskaia Nedelia*, no. 41, 15 October 1917, 1.
[55] Telegram sent to all soviets from the Moscow Soviet from the Central Executive Committee of the Soviet of Workers' and Soldiers' Deputies, instructing them to form commissions to combat pogroms. Dated October 7 1917. TsGAMO, f.66 o.3 d.865 l.1-2.
[56] Buldakov, *Khaos i etnos*, 446.
[57] Iu. A. Akhapkin, M. P. Iroshnikov and A. V. Gogolevskii, *Dekrety sovetskoi vlasti o Petrograde: 25 oktiabria (7 noiabria) 1917 g - 29 dekabria 1918 g* (Leningrad: Lenizdat, 1986), 14.

headline in the party's main newspaper *Pravda* would later put it in 1919, 'To be against the Jews is to be for the Tsar!'[58] Yet, when it came to the party rank and file, the overlap between revolutionary politics and counter-revolutionary antisemitism in 1917 appears to have been real. Revolution and antisemitism existed not only in conflict but in articulation as well.

Although the Bolsheviks played an unquestionably crucial role in the broad socialist response to antisemitism in 1917, newspaper reports from the summer and autumn of that year show that they were frequently accused by other socialists of perpetuating antisemitism and even harbouring antisemites within the party's social base. To be sure, we ought to treat with caution those accusations from the Bolsheviks' socialist adversaries that the party membership had an antisemitism problem, for there was much political capital to be gained by associating the Bolsheviks with 'counter-revolutionaries'. Nevertheless, the frequency with which such reports appeared is striking and raises the question of whether there was a real – if overstated – issue of antisemitism among the rank and file.[59]

For example, in June, Georgii Plekhanov's anti-Bolshevik newspaper *Edinstvo* reported that, when Menshevik agitators spoke at the Moscow barracks in the Vyborg region of Petrograd during the regional Duma elections, soldiers, apparently egged on by Bolsheviks, shouted, 'Down with them! They're all Yids!'[60] According to the Bundist Mark Liber, when hundreds of thousands of workers protested in Petrograd on 18 June, Bolsheviks reportedly tore down Bundist banners and shouted antisemitic slogans. When Liber raised this at a session of the Petrograd soviet on 20 June, he went so far as to accuse the Bolsheviks of being pro-pogromist.[61] The Menshevik newspaper *Vpered* also reported in June that, at an open meeting in the Mar'ina Roshcha district of Moscow, Bolsheviks shouted down Mensheviks, accusing them of being 'Yids'

---

[58] I. Bardin, 'To Be Against the Jews Is to Be for the Tsar', *Pravda*, 14 May 1919, 1.
[59] Beizer, 'Antisemitism in Petrograd/Leningrad, 1917–1930', 8.
[60] *Evreiskaia Nedelia*, no. 25, 25 June 1917, 25. Plekhanov, we should note, was vehemently anti-Bolshevik by mid-1917, so this source ought to be treated with some caution. Also, in 1917 radicalized soldiers regularly took liberty to speak at political meetings 'as Bolsheviks', even when they had no party credentials. This sometimes led Bolshevik leaders to demand party credentials to be shown before rank-and-file members could speak at rallies. See V. Sol'skii, *Vatslav Sol'skii 1917 god v zapadnoi obslati i na zapadnom fronte* (Minsk: Tesei, 2004), 141. I thank Gleb Albert for bringing this source to my attention.
[61] Gal'perina and Startsev, *Petrogradskii Sovet Rabochikh i Soldatskikh Deputatov v 1917 godu. Dokumenty i materialy*, 2002, 3:348, 352. See also Beizer, 'Antisemitism in Petrograd/Leningrad, 1917–1930', 8.

who 'exploit the proletariat'.[62] Reports of Bolshevik antisemitism aimed at Mensheviks in Moscow continued throughout the July Days[63] and were replicated in other cities too. In Odessa, for example, reports reached the Zionist press that Bolshevik agitation among soldiers had an explicitly antisemitic character. In response, the local Odessa soviet closed down Jewish shops in an attempt to prevent a pogrom.[64] Such reports became even more frequent during the critical weeks in October and November. Ilia Ehrenburg, who would go on to be one of the most prolific and well-known Jewish writers in the Soviet Union, wrote the following letter to his friend M. A. Voloshin a few days after the October insurrection. It stands as perhaps the most vivid description of the articulation between antisemitism and the revolutionary process in 1917:

> Yesterday I was standing in line, waiting to vote for the Constituent Assembly. People were saying 'Whoever's against the Yids, vote for number 5! [the Bolsheviks]', 'Whoever's for world-wide revolution, vote for number 5!' The patriarch rode by, sprinkling holy water; everyone removed their hats. A group of soldiers passing by started to belt out the *Internationale* in his direction. Where am I? Or is this truly hell?[65]

In this startling account, the apparently obvious distinction between revolutionary Bolshevism and counter-revolutionary antisemitism is blurred. Around the same time, in the Okhta region of Petrograd, the writer Solomon Lur'e similarly observed Bolsheviks assuring voters queueing up to vote in the Constituent Assembly elections that the head of the Provisional Government, Alexander Kerensky, was in fact a Jew and that, for this reason, they should choose to support the Bolsheviks.[66] Kerensky, of course, was not Jewish, but such antisemitism did not operate according to logic, and often what gave it such fantastic appeal was precisely its rejection of social reality.[67] Indeed, the Provisional Government was frequently labelled by antisemites as 'Jewish', despite the fact that there were no Jews in the government. One arresting illustration of the extraordinary degree to which antisemitism could take flight from reality is captured when Kerensky, leaving the Winter Palace by car on the night of the Bolshevik insurrection, noticed that someone had painted in huge letters across the palace wall: 'Down with the Jew

---

[62] *Evreiskaia Nedelia*, no. 25, 25 June 1917, 26.   [63] Buldakov, *Khaos i etnos*, 340.
[64] Buldakov, 341, 344.   [65] Budnitskii, *Rossiiskie evrei mezhdu krasnymi i belymi*, 88.
[66] B. Ia. Koprzhiva-Lur'e, *Istoriia odnoi zhizni* (Paris: Athenuem, 1987), 79.
[67] Antisemitism, as Adorno once noted, is often not concerned with the 'real', 'empirical' Jew, but rather has as its object 'bogies rather than real opponents, that is to say, it builds up an imagery of the Jew, or of the Communist, and tears it to pieces, without caring much how this imagery is related to reality'; T. Adorno, *The Stars Down to Earth* (London: Routledge, 2002), 222.

Kerensky, Long Live Trotsky!'[68] These examples prefigured Isaac Babel's haunting question in *Red Cavalry*: 'Which is the Revolution and which the counter-revolution?'[69] Despite Bolshevik insistence that antisemitism was a purely 'counter-revolutionary' phenomenon,[70] it clearly eluded such neat categorization and could be found across the political divide.

What constituted the social basis of this apparent antisemitism on the revolutionary left? In a Jewish newspaper issued shortly after the October Revolution, it was claimed that antisemitic 'Black Hundreds' were 'filling up the ranks of the Bolsheviks' across the whole country'.[71] While such claims should certainly be treated with a strong degree of caution, the notion that the Bolshevik insurrection could appeal to far-right antisemites was not entirely without substance: in some far-right circles the October Revolution was *welcomed* in the hours immediately following the seizure of power. For example, an astonishing editorial in the antisemitic paper *Groza* (Thunderstorm) on 29 October declared:

The Bolsheviks have seized power. The Jew Kerensky, lackey to the British and the world's bankers, having brazenly assumed the title of commander-in-chief of the armed forces and having appointed himself Prime Minister of the Orthodox Russian Tsardom, will be swept out of the Winter Palace, where he had desecrated the remains of the Peace-Maker Alexander III with his presence. On October 25th, the Bolsheviks united all the regiments who refused to submit to a government composed of Jew bankers, treasonous generals, traitorous land-owners, and thieving merchants.[72]

It is abundantly clear that the Bolshevik leadership sought to arrest this articulation between the antisemitism of the far right and the radicalism of the Bolshevik project (the *Groza* newspaper, for example, was immediately closed down after the revolution). Nevertheless, the editorial underscored a troubling issue that had developed throughout the year:

---

[68] M. Ferro, *The Bolshevik Revolution: A Social History of the Russian Revolution* (London: Routledge & Kegan Paul, 1985), 238.
[69] Babel, *Red Cavalry*, 65.
[70] When an editorial published in the Kronstadt soviet newspaper *Izvestiia* claimed that 'antisemitism and counter-revolution are one and the same thing' (Budnitskii, *Rossiiskie evrei mezhdu krasnymi i belymi*, 87.), it expressed a long-standing and oft-repeated tenet of the socialist understanding of antisemitism.
[71] *Evreiskaia Nedelia*, no. 43–4, 29 October 1917, 4.
[72] Budnitskii, *Rossiiskie evrei mezhdu krasnymi i belymi*, 87. The apparently 'pro-Bolshevik' antisemitism of the newspaper *Groza* was discussed at a session of the Petrograd soviet on 16 October. See B. D. Gal'perina and V. I. Startsev, eds., *Petrogradskii Sovet Rabochikh i Soldatskikh Deputatov v 1917 godu. Dokumenty i materialy*, vol. 4 (Moscow: ROSSPEN, 2003), 524, 530.

antisemitism, though principally a phenomenon of the political right, could combine with the politics of the left as well.

In mid-late 1917, Lenin's pre-revolutionary conception of a small conspiratorial party was discarded as the doors were opened wide to tens of thousands of new members, many of whom were becoming politicized for the first time.[73] With many more non-members subscribing to the party's radical anti-bourgeois critique, the Bolsheviks had truly become a mass party. It is not difficult to imagine that the Bolshevik project unwittingly attracted racist and antisemitic elements of society, including among the working class. In such circumstances, statements by the party leadership on antisemitism were clearly not always going to be representative of the thoughts and feelings of the party rank and file as a whole. Events in 1918 and 1919 would reveal just how acute this problem was when, in some regions of the former Pale of Settlement, the Red Army suddenly found swathes of pogromists in their midst marching behind the slogan 'Smash the Yids, long live Soviet Power!'

Revolution and Antisemitism?

Concern about the overlap between antisemitism and Bolshevism in late 1917 was most commonly expressed by moderate socialist intellectuals. What underscored their anxiety was a fear that Lenin's insistence on insurrection would produce a series of unintended consequences, including anti-Jewish violence. Attempts to overthrow the Provisional Government and (prematurely) construct a socialist society would necessarily lead to 'pogroms',[74] so they argued. For the Jewish Menshevik L'vov-Rogachevskii, the 'tragedy' of the Russian revolution lay in the apparent fact that the 'the dark masses (*temnota*) are unable to distinguish the provocateur from the revolutionary, or the Jewish

---

[73] Rabinowitch, *The Bolsheviks Come to Power*, xxi.
[74] The Russian word *pogrom* went through something of a transformation in 1917 and began to take on a much broader signification. Throughout October and November, for example, the front pages of soviet and Bolshevik newspapers carried headlines warning of pogromist violence, and it is clear that the term was deployed to mean disorder in general, not just antisemitic violence per se. See, for example, *Izvestiia VTsIK*, no. 187, 3 October 1917, 1–2; no. 193, 10 October 1917, 4; no. 201, 19 October 1917, 2; no. 204, 22 October 1917, 1; *Izvestiia Moskovskogo Soveta Rabochikh Deputatov*, no. 201, 1 November 1917, 2; no. 202, 2 November 1917, 2; and *Soldatskaia Pravda*, no. 98, 7 December 1917, 1. We should note, therefore, that when socialists and leftists warned of 'pogroms' (as they frequently did), they often had this more generalized conception in mind, and when referring specifically to antisemitic pogroms, they would often insert the adjective *evreiskie* (Jewish) to denote '[anti-]Jewish pogroms' (*evreiskie pogromy*).

pogrom from a social revolution'.[75] Maxim Gor'kii epitomized this strand of thinking in his *Novaia Zhizn'* writings throughout 1917.[76] On 18 October, for example, he warned that an insurrection would see an 'unorganized mob pour out into the streets, not knowing what it wants and [it] ... will begin to "make the history of the Russian revolution". If the Bolsheviks took power, he predicted that 'this time events will assume an even bloodier pogrom character'.[77] Two days earlier, at a session of the Petrograd soviet on October 18, the Menshevik Internationalist Isaak Astrov gave a detailed description of how 'pogrom agitation' was finding traction within sections of the working class. Pogromists, he said, were awaiting a Bolshevik insurrection with anticipation.[78] On 24 October, on the eve of revolution, the Menshevik Fedor Dan pleaded with the radicalized Petrograd soviet to step back from revolution, warning that 'counter-revolutionists are waiting with the Bolsheviki to begin riots and massacres'.[79] In Vitebsk, the Socialist Revolutionary newspaper *Vlast' Naroda* reported that Black Hundreds would try to start an anti-Jewish pogrom in the event of any Bolshevik attempt to take power.[80] As late as 28 October, the Mensheviks' Petrograd Electoral Committee issued yet another desperate appeal to workers in the capital, warning that all forms of protest would *necessarily* lead to pogroms: the Bolsheviks have seduced 'the ignorant workers and soldiers', and the cry of 'All power to the Soviets!' will all too easily turn into Beat the Jews, beat the shopkeepers.[81] That same day, the Bolshevik Vladimir Bonch-Bruevich also issued an appeal against antisemitism. Though he laid the blame squarely with the Black Hundreds, and not the Bolsheviks or their working-class supporters, the timing of his intervention reflected a widely held anxiety about the relationship between revolution and antisemitism.[82] These fears were replicated in

---

[75] L'vov-Rogachevskii, *Goniteli evreiskogo naroda v Rossii. Istoricheskii ocherk*, 108.
[76] *Novaia Zhizn'* was a newspaper established by Maxim Gor'kii after the February Revolution. Politically orientating itself towards the Menshevik Internationalists (a number of whom sat on the editorial board), it was sharply critical of revolutionary Bolshevism in late 1917. Gor'kii himself wrote a series of articles denouncing the Bolshevik attempt to seize power. See M. Gorky, *Untimely Thoughts. Essays on Revolution, Culture and the Bolsheviks, 1917–1918*, 1st Edition (London: Garnstone Press, 1968).
[77] Browder and Kerensky, *The Russian Provisional Government, 1917*, 1766.
[78] Gal'perina and Startsev, *Petrogradskii Sovet Rabochikh i Soldatskikh Deputatov v 1917 godu, dokumenty i materialy*, 2003, 4:524. The Menshevik Internationalists were a faction of the Russian Social Democratic Labour Party that took an anti-war position in 1914.
[79] J. Reed, *Ten Days That Shook the World* (Harmondsworth and New York: Penguin, 1977), 84.
[80] Buldakov, *Khaos i etnos*, 488.   [81] Reed, *Ten Days That Shook the World*, 289.
[82] Bonch-Bruevich, *Krovavyi navet na khristian*.

the Jewish liberal press. For example, a lead article in *Evreiskaia Nedelia* on 15 October claimed:

> Comrade Lenin and his fellow Bolsheviks call in their speeches and articles on the proletariat to 'turn their words into action' (*pereiti ot slov k delu*), but ... wherever Slavic crowds gather, the turning of 'words into action' means, in reality, 'striking out at the Yids'.[83]

The following week, the same publication warned on its front page that 'social revolution in the minds of the Petrograd masses has become synonymous with 'Jewish pogrom''[84].

Contrary to these alarmist predictions, in the hours and days immediately following the Bolshevik seizure of power, there were no mass pogroms in the Russian interior. In the immediate sense, then, the revolution did not translate into antisemitic violence, as had been predicted. These warnings reveal just how deeply ingrained the fear of the 'dark masses' was among sections of the socialist left who claimed to speak in their name. Notable, too, was the presence of Jews among those who voiced their concerns. Indeed, most of those aforementioned non-Bolshevik socialists who expressed their fear about rising antisemitism in 1917 were Jewish (e.g. the leading Mensheviks L'vov-Rogachevskii and Feder Dan). Bundists exhibited particular sensitivity in this area, and for understandable reasons. Many of the party's leading activists went into 1917 with first-hand experience of confronting antisemitic violence during the bloodshed of the 1905 revolution. For Grigorii Aronson, the great danger of 1917 lay in the possibility that the rage of the masses would be turned against Jews, thus 'drowning the Revolution in Jewish blood' as had happened twelve years previously.[85] Similarly, Bundist leader David Lipets warned that the revolution could be double-edged, since in Russia, 'freedom and Jewish pogroms [have] a strange connection, a wild insanity'.[86]

Such fears were widely shared among the intelligentsia (both socialist and liberal, Jewish and non-Jewish), which approached the notion of a proletarian uprising with horror due to the violence they believed it would unleash. In contrast, and as captured in Nikolai Sukhanov's classic memoirs, what defined the Bolsheviks during this period was

---

[83] *Evreiskaia Nedelia*, no. 41, 15 October 1917, 1.
[84] *Evreiskaia Nedelia*, no. 42, 22 October 1917, 1. The Zionist liberal press was as hostile to Bolshevism as it was sensitive to the question of antisemitism, so it is not suprising that such reports appeared with regularity throughout late 1917.
[85] Meyers, 'To Dance at Two Weddings', 89.
[86] J. Meyers, 'A Portrait of Transition: From the Bund to Bolshevism in the Russian Revolution', *Jewish Social Studies* 24, no. 2 (2019): 113.

precisely their confidence in the Petrograd masses so greatly feared by the intelligentsia.[87] In many of the industrial regions of western Russia, that confidence was well placed. However, just six months later, in the spring of 1918 in the former Pale of Settlement, the warnings from the previous year began to ring true: a new wave of pogroms swept the Ukrainian northeast – the first since the October Revolution – and they were carried out by Red Guards and local 'Bolsheviks'. In Hlukhiv, Bolshevik power was actually consolidated through anti-Jewish violence.[88] At the party's congress in mid-May 1918, the Bund leadership pointed out in no uncertain terms that the pogroms were 'principally a consequence of the presence of dark elements (*temnykh elementov*) who have attached themselves to the Bolshevik movement'.[89] These pogroms occurred not in Petrograd but in the quite different context of Ukraine. Nevertheless, they showed that the exhortations of the anti-Bolshevik socialist left in late 1917 were not entirely without substance.

Beyond 1917

The events of 1917 prefigured in embryonic form the parameters of the so-called Jewish question in the Civil War of 1918 and 1919. From June and July 1917 onwards, it became increasingly apparent that antisemitism was a problem within sections of the now enlarged Bolshevik support base. The challenge facing the Bolshevik leadership, then, was not only to combat the antisemitism of the radical right but to disentangle the overlap between Bolshevik radicalism and antisemitism within the movement itself. These problems would heighten dramatically in 1918 and 1919 when the Civil War extended into parts of the former Pale of Settlement, where the bulk of the Jewish population resided. Here, when the Red Army fought for 'Soviet power', the lines of demarcation between 'antisemite' and 'internationalist' and 'revolutionary' and 'counter-revolutionary' often collapsed along an axis of antisemitic violence. These events did not come from nowhere: the articulation between antisemitism and revolutionary Bolshevism had been prefigured in 1917.

---

[87] Sukhanov, *The Russian Revolution, 1917*. I would like to thank Christopher Read, who helped to develop this point in a private correspondence.

[88] Tcherikower, *Istoriia pogromnogo dvizheniia na Ukraine 1917-1921*, 287–97; Miliakova, *Kniga pogromov*, 6–8; McGeever, 'The Bolshevik Confrontation with Antisemitism in the Russian Revolution, 1917-1919', 103–04. See Chapter 3 for a full discussion.

[89] See K. M. Anderson, V. V. Shelokhaev, and Iu. N. Amiantov, *Bund: Dokumenty i materialy, 1894-1921* (Moscow: ROSSPEN, 2010), 1124–25. An edited version of this conference resolution – with the passage quoted above removed – was published in the Bund's newspaper *Evreiskii Rabochii*, no. 3, 30 May 1917, 6.

What 1917 also showed, however, is that the Bolsheviks responded to such antisemitism, and they did so by helping to build a broad socialist cross-party alliance comprising all progressive social forces. The political expression of this cross-party alliance was the soviets of workers' and soldiers' deputies. Despite the increasingly acute political differences and inter-party tensions that engulfed the soviets in the latter part of 1917, the Bolsheviks, like all socialists, continued to stress the importance of building a broad alliance to combat antisemitism. In sum, 1917 produced a historic bloc of subalternity that offered a real challenge not just to class exploitation but to forms of oppression such as antisemitism.

However, if February 1917 produced such alliances, October pulled them apart. Disagreeing profoundly on the Bolshevik acquisition of power, social democrats were pushed into opposing camps on the question of whether to support the new Soviet government. The trajectory of the main Jewish socialist party, the Bund, illustrates well the dilemmas thrown up by the actuality of revolution in October. On the evening of 25 October 1917, at an emergency meeting to discuss the Bolshevik insurrection, the Central Committee of the Bund called on 'all revolutionary democratic forces to fulfil the main task of the *demokratiia* and form a coalition to fight against the coalition of counter-revolution'.[90] The writing, however, was already on the wall: the 'democratic forces' of the soviets no longer stood on the same platform. The strategy of the united front to defend the gains of the February Revolution had now been superseded by the actuality of the October revolution. Later, in 1918, the Bund would split into left (pro-Soviet) and right (anti-Soviet) factions. The *fact* of Soviet power had pushed the party into 'revolutionary' and 'reformist' camps, and eventually this would bring about a formal split and the establishment of the Communist Bund. In the radically changed conjuncture of post-October 1917, new alliances and new collective forms of anti-racist agency had to be forged to confront the ferocious pogroms of 1918 and 1919.

[90] Ibid., 1104.

2 'Red Pogroms': Spring 1918

Introduction

The Bolsheviks had come to power in October 1917 on a wave of revolutionary optimism that a new society could be constituted free of the oppression and exploitation of the capitalist world. However, in the weeks and months that followed, these hopes were kept in check by a dramatic increase in antisemitism. In early 1918, open antisemitic agitation increasingly began to assert itself in the industrial heartlands of Moscow and Petrograd.[1] By the spring, the first pogrom wave to follow the October Revolution broke out in various regions of the former Pale of Settlement. What shocked the Bolshevik leadership most of all was the participation of Red Guards in this violence. Whereas in mid- to late 1919 the majority of pogroms were carried out by anti-Bolshevik military forces, in the spring of 1918 antisemitic violence flowed principally from Red Guards in the former Pale. Consequently, the first Soviet response to antisemitism was directed at those who were ostensibly committed to the Bolshevik project. The pogroms of the spring of 1918 revealed the extent to which antisemitism could articulate with the revolutionary process: in some regions of the former Pale, Bolshevik power was actually constituted *through* anti-Jewish violence. Although marginal in the overall picture of anti-Jewish violence during the Civil War, the Red pogroms of the spring of 1918 will be placed centre stage by virtue of the fundamental questions they posed of the Soviet government and its anti-racist strategy.

From October to March: Revolution and Retreat

The Red pogroms took place against the backdrop of the Bolshevik defeat in 'The Eleven Days War'[2] and the German advance into Finland,

---

[1] Buldakov, 'Freedom, Shortages, Violence'.
[2] 'The Eleven Days War' was the name given by Lenin to the German advance into Soviet Russia between 18 February and 3 March. The Treaty of Brest-Litovsk, which saw the Bolsheviks surrender the vast regions of the western borderlands, was signed on 28 February.

Estonia, Ukraine and the surrounding borderlands. In the first weeks after the October Revolution, Lenin and Trotsky had expressed complete confidence in the 'triumphal march of Soviet power' as it spread across the vast regions of the former empire. The Bolsheviks, however, were soon in retreat. On 24–25 February, the Estonian cities of Tartu and Tallinn were occupied by German troops. Even more worrying was the fall of Narva on 4 March, whose proximity to Petrograd (a mere 100 miles) convinced many that the Soviet capital was doomed.[3] Reflecting on the situation at the Seventh Party Congress just three days later on 7 March (after the signing of the Brest-Litovsk peace treaty with Germany), Lenin summed up the essence of the threat which the Bolsheviks had faced: '[W]e believed that we would lose Petrograd in a few days when the advancing German troops were only a few days' march away'.[4] Symptomatic of Petrograd's increasing vulnerability was the decision on 12 March to relocate the capital (and the Soviet government) to landlocked Moscow. The fear that Petrograd would be captured by German troops continued well into May, with Lenin in particular remaining convinced that the city would be taken.[5]

In the western and south-western borderlands, the situation was even more desperate. In late February, German troops took hold of Minsk, Mogilev and Zhytomyr as they advanced along the Dnepr River. In early March they took Kyiv, deposing the Ukrainian Soviet Republic, and in April even Kharkiv – the Bolsheviks' working-class stronghold in Ukraine – fell. Summarizing the situation at the aforementioned Seventh Party Congress, Lenin noted that Soviet power was passing through an 'extraordinarily difficult and painful situation': whereas in October, November and December 1917 the Bolsheviks had swept aside the threat of internal counter-revolution, they now came face to face with an external and much more menacing threat in the shape of imperialism.[6] The ground the Bolsheviks ceded in the Treaty of Brest-Litovsk had already been lost militarily in the war with Germany, and they kept on losing: the Central Powers marched on for another 500 miles such that by early May they occupied the whole of Ukraine and territories beyond.[7] As Rosa

---

[3] Mawdsley, *The Russian Civil War*, 47; A. Rabinowitch, *The Bolsheviks in Power: The First Year of Soviet Rule in Petrograd* (Bloomington: Indiana University Press, 2007), 241–42.

[4] Gosizpolit, *Sed'moi ekstrennyi s'ezd RKP(b) mart 1918 goda. Stenograficheskii otchet* (Moscow: Gosudarstvennoe izdatel'stvo politicheskoi literatury, 1962), 20. See also L. Trotsky, *On Lenin: Notes towards a Biography* (London: Harrap, 1971), 100 for a recollection on Lenin's fear that the Bolsheviks would lose power in late February – early March.

[5] Rabinowitch, *The Bolsheviks in Power*, 241.   [6] Mawdsley, *The Russian Civil War*, 60.

[7] Ibid., 48.

Luxemburg perceptively noted in late 1918, the signing of the Brest-Litovsk Treaty resulted not in peace but in continued war, a war characterized by 'systematic German advance and tacit Bolshevik retreat'.[8]

In the early weeks after October 1917, when hopes of world revolution remained high, the Bolshevik leadership adopted a dual strategy of relying on the European proletariat to overthrow their own bourgeois regimes on the one hand, and on the revolutionary vigour of volunteer detachments to protect Soviet Russia from the threat of counter-revolution on the other. Defeat at the hands of the Central Powers, however, revealed just how weak these local detachments were.[9] The 'Soviet military' during this period was predicated on Lenin's notion of a popular militia, the 'Red Guards' – a volunteer army drawn from the ranks of workers and poor peasants. In early 1918, these units operated with weak leadership and virtually no overarching command structure, resulting in the Soviet government having little control over its own military campaign.[10] During the Soviet retreat from the borderlands north-east of Ukraine in the spring of 1918, the uneven and contradictory nature of class consciousness among these Red Guards was exposed. It was precisely in these regions that the first wave of antisemitic violence since the October Revolution broke out. These pogroms were by and large carried out not by the newly arriving 'counter-revolutionaries' and 'imperialists', but by the same Red Guards upon whom the Bolsheviks were relying to extend the revolution to Ukraine. The first Soviet state confrontation with antisemitism was principally a confrontation with the antisemitism of its own cadres.

The Pogroms of the Spring of 1918

As chronicled in the pioneering work of the historian and activist Elias Tcherkower, the pogrom wave of the spring of 1918 occurred in the borderlands of the north-east, in Voronezh, Gomel, Kursk and, above all, the towns and cities of the Chernihiv region, a large multi-ethnic administrative area on the Ukrainian left bank.[11] The violence was

---

[8] R. Luxemburg, *Selected Political Writings* (London: Jonathon Cape, 1972), 236.
[9] R. R. Reese, *Red Commanders: A Social History of the Soviet Army Officer Corps, 1918-1991* (Lawrence: University Press of Kansas, 2005), 18.
[10] R. I. Kowalski, *The Bolshevik Party in Conflict: The Left Communist Opposition of 1918* (Pittsburgh: University of Pittsburgh Press, 1991), 137–38; E. H. Carr, *The Bolshevik Revolution, 1917-1923. Volume 3* (London: Penguin Books, 1973), 72–75.
[11] Tcherikower, *Istoriia pogromnogo dvizheniia na Ukraine 1917-1921*, 143; Budnitskii, *Rossiiskie evrei mezhdu krasnymi i belymi*, 119. Much of what follows in this chapter draws on the research of the diaspora Yiddishist, Elias Tcherikower. Born in Poltava

unique in that it brought into play an entirely new social agent in the history of Russian pogroms: militarized Bolshevik and Red Guard cadres. Between March and May in the towns and cities of the Chernihiv region, volunteer Red Guards and sailors attacked Jews in the same moment as they marched under the Red flag. In these regions, the 'class struggle' was overdetermined by antisemitism such that 'the Jew' became a principal signifier of anti-bourgeois sentiment.

Such sentiment was by no means confined to the north-east of Ukraine. In Ekaterinoslav (today Dnipro), a major city in the south with a long history of pogromist violence,[12] the 'defence of the revolution' and the 'fight against the bourgeoisie' became inseparable from antisemitic violence among some sections of the population. In late March, local Bolsheviks joined Red Guards, members of the local Revolutionary Committee (*Revkom*, the local soviet government) and a group of anarchists in attacking all Jewish self-defence units in the city. As they laid siege to a building where a self-defence unit organized by the United Jewish Socialist Workers Party was based, Red Guards were heard shouting 'Yids!' and 'counter-revolutionaries!'.[13] The next day, Bolsheviks, Red Guards and members of the local *Revkom* further disarmed self-defence units set up by the Bund, Poalei Zion and the Union of Jewish Soldiers on the pretext that the units were 'protecting the bourgeoisie'.[14] Ironically, just as Red Guards were attacking the United

---

in 1881, Tcherikower grew up speaking Russian and Yiddish in a household that combined moderate religious observance with a commitment to Zionism. By the time of the 1905 Revolution, Tcherikower was moving in Menshevik circles and had become something of a moderate Marxist. Increasingly, however, he moved away from revolutionary activism and towards diasporic Yiddish nationalism. During the years of repression from 1907 onwards, he turned more and more to cultural work. Though he was close, at times, to Poalei Zion, Tcherikower remained aloof from Zionism, instead retaining his firm commitment to diaspora nationalism. A decade later, when the pogrom wave of 1918–21 swept the former Pale of Settlement, Tcherikower became its chief chronicler as head of the 'Editorial Board for Gathering and Researching Materials Regarding the Pogroms in Ukraine', an initiative funded by a range of Russian Jewish organizations. Though several public intellectuals and activists sat on the editorial board, Tcherkower carried the weight of the day-to-day work. In the summer of 1919, he collected scores of documents, photographs, eyewitness accounts and newspaper reports, copying each document twice to preserve the material in case of the loss of the original. See Karlip, *The Tragedy of a Generation*, 40–45, 165–66; Karlip, 'Between Martyrology and Historiography', 265. It is important to note that Tcherikower was hostile to Bolshevism, and this surely influenced his work. Nevertheless, the materials he collected represent the most authoritative set of resources on the pogrom wave of the spring of 1918, and as such they form the basis for the discussion that follows.

[12] Wynn, *Worker, Strikes, and Pogroms*; Surh, 'Ekaterinoslav City in 1905'.
[13] Tcherikower, *Istoriia pogromnogo dvizheniia na Ukraine 1917-1921*, 152, 302.
[14] Ibid., 302.

Jewish Socialist Workers Party and Poalei Zion in Ekaterinoslav, 900 miles to the north, in Moscow, leading activists from these same parties were coordinating the Soviet government's response to the pogroms taking place in Ukraine (see Chapter 3). Such was the uneven and contradictory nature of the revolutionary process in the spring of 1918.

One of the most brutal incidents took place at the end of March in Novhorod-Siverskyi, a mid-sized city in the Chernihiv province with a population of around 10,000, of whom 3,000 were Jewish. When a 600-strong rear-guard unit of Red Guards on the retreat from the town of Sosnitsa stopped in Novhorod-Siverskyi, they established a city soviet. Having done so, they then carried out searches for local Jews, demanding that they hand over their weapons and money. On 30 March, a newly arrived unit of Red Guards subjected all Jews to a 'contribution' of 750,000 rubbles. The following day, local Bolsheviks tried to start a pogrom, only to be met by fierce resistance from Jewish self-defence units. Despite overcoming the Jewish self-defence squads, the Bolsheviks chose to flee the city and continue on their direction to Briansk, having heard rumours that German troops were approaching.[15] On 6 April, however, a local Jewish community organization ('The Committee for Providing Help to Victims of Pogroms') issued a memorandum warning that a large group of Bolsheviks was returning to the city, having been agitating among the peasants to 'slaughter the Yids' (*rezh'te' zhidov!*) on their arrival. When the Bolsheviks entered the city that same evening, a large pogrom broke out in which at least eighty-eight Jews were killed and eleven injured.[16] Ukrainian newspapers also reported that the Bolsheviks again attacked Jewish self-defence units during the violence.[17] According to one report, Jews were murdered irrespective of their class background: 'if you were a Jew, they simply killed you'. After three hours of violence, the Bolsheviks again fled the city as German troops arrived. On their retreat, however, they continued attacking Jews in neighbouring villages.[18]

Such violence continued into May. In the city of Smolensk, on 15 May, two groups of Red Army soldiers took to the streets demanding that 'Jewish commissars' be removed immediately from their posts. In Chernihiv, as the Red Army retreated from Konotop in the direction of Briansk, a unit under the command of Afanasii Remnev killed twenty Jews and injured another nineteen at the Zernovo railway station. In

---

[15] *Evreiskaia Nedelia*, no. 15–16, 15 June 1918, 23; Tcherikower, *Istoriia pogromnogo dvizheniia na Ukraine 1917-1921*, 298–99; Miliakova, *Kniga pogromov*, 11.
[16] Tcherikower, *Istoriia pogromnogo dvizheniia na Ukraine 1917-1921*, 299–301.
[17] Buldakov, *Khaos i etnos*, 717.
[18] Tcherikower, *Istoriia pogromnogo dvizheniia na Ukraine 1917-1921*, 147–49, 299.

nearby Surazh, a small city of 4,000 inhabitants, over half of whom were Jewish, Red Army soldiers attacked Jewish self-defence groups.[19] After having been forced out of the city by the German advance, the Bolsheviks again retook Surazh with the help of twenty train carriages of soldiers from the 'First Cavalry in the name of V. I. Lenin'. On its arrival, however, 'Lenin's cavalry' put a call out to destroy Jewish houses as a 'punishment for the counter-revolution'.[20] The Surazh pogrom was stopped by the arrival of another Red Army unit, this time a cavalry unit under the leadership of the Bolshevik Lobanov, which had been sent from a neighbouring town. However, having put down the pogrom, Lobanov then gathered his troops and organized a large rally in the city centre, where in a speech he declared that 'in various towns the Jews welcome the Germans with open arms [*evrei ... vstrechali nemtsev khlebom sol'iu*]', and if this happens [here], severe punishments will follow.[21] The notion that Russia was in the grips of a German–Jewish conspiracy found expression across the political divide during this period.[22] That such sentiment was articulated by the Bolshevik Lobanov shows that even within those Red Army units that could be relied upon to resist the slaughtering of the Jews, antisemitism could *still* find expression.

In areas such as Odessa, Ekaterinburg, Kharkiv, Holovanivsk and Podolia, Jewish self-defence units proved to be the only reliable form of opposition to antisemitism.[23] In some cases, they were successful in stopping Red pogroms: in Gomel, for example, Jewish self-defence units killed a number of Red Guards who had attempted to start a pogrom during their retreat from the city in the wake of the German advance.[24]

In the regions of the former Pale where pogromist violence was less pronounced, some Soviet institutions still struggled to operate without the structuring impact of antisemitism. According to the Bund's weekly paper *Evreiskii Rabochii* (The Jewish Worker), when a deputy in the Vitebsk soviet called the Bolshevik leader Boris Abromovich Breslav a 'pathetic Yid' in early May, a debate took place within the soviet about whether to exclude the deputy for antisemitism.[25] In the vote, six members abstained and others argued that to exclude people

---

[19] Buldakov, 'Freedom, Shortages, Violence', 85.   [20] Buldakov, *Khaos i etnos*, 765.
[21] Tcherikower, *Istoriia pogromnogo dvizheniia na Ukraine 1917-1921*, 145, 286.
[22] See, for example, Buldakov, 'Freedom, Shortages, Violence', 77.
[23] For more information on self-defence squads in these regions, see Buldakov, *Khaos i etnos*, 716.
[24] Tcherikower, *Istoriia pogromnogo dvizheniia na Ukraine 1917-1921*, 144, 284; Buldakov, *Khaos i etnos*, 765–66; Buldakov, 'Freedom, Shortages, Violence', 85–86.
[25] The situation in Vitebsk was, like the country as a whole, profoundly uneven: just a few weeks later, in June, a peasant congress in the same region called for a broad fight against all forms of antisemitism; Buldakov, *Khaos i etnos*, 733.

from the soviet for antisemitism would be to 'persecute the whole of Russia'.[26] According to the Bundist Kossovskii, shouts of 'chase the Jews out of the soviets' were also heard in the Vitebsk soviet during this period.[27]

It is often assumed that the Red Army was the only saviour of the Jews in the Civil War. In the spring of 1918, however, when Bolsheviks arrived in various towns and cities of the former Pale, a mass exodus of Jews would often take place out of fear that Soviet power would be secured through yet more pogromist violence.[28] Whereas in 1919, Jews and Bolsheviks would often flee Ukrainian cities together when the Whites arrived, between March and May 1918, Jews often found themselves running *from* Bolshevik power. Throughout the revolution and Civil War, Bolshevik propaganda framed antisemitism as the preserve of the 'counter-revolution'. However, in the Ukrainian north-east and elsewhere in mid-1918, such lines of demarcation often did not exist, and for many Jews in these regions, distinctions between revolution and counter-revolution collapsed along the axis of antisemitic violence. The episodes described above evoke the tragic dilemma facing Jews during the Russo–Polish War of 1920, so powerfully captured in Isaac Babel's *Red Cavalry*:

> The Pole shoots because he is counter-revolution. And you shoot because you are the Revolution. But Revolution is happiness. And happiness does not like orphans in its house. A good man does good deeds. The Revolution is the good deed done by good men. But good men do not kill. Hence the Revolution is done by bad men. But the Poles are also bad men. Who is to say which is Revolution and which is counter-revolution?[29]

The nature and extent of antisemitism within Red Guards in 1918 very much depended on the composition of local units. For instance, just as Red pogroms raged in the north-east throughout early to mid-March, the local soviet in central Ukrainian city of Fastiv mobilized a unit of Red Guards to successfully put a stop to pogroms. During the same period, Red Guards also played a crucial role in stopping pogroms in the south, in the city of Kremenchuk.[30]

A key question thus emerges: What was the composition of the Red detachments responsible for such pogroms? Were they predominantly

---

[26] *Evreiskii Rabochii* 1, 7; Buldakov, *Khaos i etnos*, 746.
[27] John Spargo, *The Jew and American Ideals* (New York and London : Harper & Brothers, 1921), 89–90.
[28] Tcherikower, *Istoriia pogromnogo dvizheniia na Ukraine 1917-1921*, 150.
[29] Babel, *Red Cavalry*, 64–65.
[30] Buldakov, *Khaos i etnos*, 682; Buldakov, 'Freedom, Shortages, Violence', 84.

working class, peasant based, Russian or Ukrainian? Were they local or from other towns and cities? Unfortunately, and as others have noted, it is frustratingly difficult to arrive at an accurate picture of the social makeup of these formations.[31] According to Tcherikower, the pogroms of the spring of 1918 were carried out by 'demoralized' Red soldiers who nonetheless were fully committed to the principles of the Soviet army, and who even considered themselves to be proper Bolsheviks.[32] Regardless of the extent of their commitment, they were certainly not 'old Bolsheviks', since most had probably only aligned themselves with the party after October 1917. The Red Guards were largely formed by the commanders Anotonov-Ovseenko (Bolshevik) and Muraviev (Left SR) in Moscow; that is to say, the bulk of the arms and personnel were from Russia[33] and were largely 'proletarian' (though for how long and to what extent they had been proletarianized is difficult to determine).[34]

Pogromist violence in this period was highly dependent on the support and participation of local Ukrainian peasant populations, whose political loyalty could (and did) change on a regular basis.[35] Moreover, many Red Guard detachments in 1918 were trained and led by former tsarist officers who had been enlisted by the Bolsheviks.[36] Given the depth of antisemitism in the Russian army in the Pale of Settlement during the Great War we should not be surprised to find its expression in the early, formative stages of the Red Army.[37]

An important factor which perhaps goes some way towards explaining the nature and degree of antisemitism in the Red Army during this period is the fact that these units rarely submitted themselves to centralized Bolshevik authority. Characteristic of the situation was the description offered by Antonov-Ovseenko to Lenin about the 8th Army in Voronezh: 'the 8th Army', he said, 'is in complete disorder ... in this situation the commander in chief throws directly into Voronezh the still untrained,

---

[31] H. Abramson, *A Prayer for the Government. Ukrainians and Jews in Revolutionary Times, 1917-1920* (Boston: Harvard University Press, 1999), 111.
[32] Tcherikower, *Istoriia pogromnogo dvizheniia na Ukraine 1917-1921*, 150.
[33] Y. Bilinsky, 'The Communist Takeover of the Ukraine', in *The Ukraine, 1917–1921: A Study in Revolution*, ed. T. Hunczak (Cambridge, MA: Harvard University Press, 1977), 110.
[34] G. Swain, 'Russia's Garibaldi: The Revolutionary Life of Mikhail Artemevich Muraviev', *Revolutionary Russia* 11, no. 2 (1998): 60; J. Borys, *The Sovietization of Ukraine, 1917-1923: The Communist Doctrine and Practice of National Self-Determination* (Edmonton: Canadian Institute of Ukrainian Studies, 1980).
[35] Tcherikower, *Istoriia pogromnogo dvizheniia na Ukraine 1917-1921*, 144.
[36] Reese, *Red Commanders*, 12.
[37] On antisemitism in the Russian army during World War I, see E. Lohr, 'The Russian Army and the Jews: Mass Deportation, Hostages, and Violence during World War I', *Russian Review* 60, no. 3 (1 July 2001): 404–19.

unblooded and politically uneducated ... falling into semi-panic these units quickly fall apart'.³⁸ In general, most Red units were poorly trained, undisciplined and highly prone to rebellion.³⁹ These bitter experiences in the spring of 1918 consolidated the view among Bolshevik leaders that the fate of the revolution depended on the formation of a disciplined, centrally organized, standing Red Army.

The Hlukhiv Massacre

The most violent manifestation of 'Red antisemitism' in 1918 was undoubtedly the pogrom in early March in Hlukhiv, a city in the east of the Chernihiv region of Ukraine, close to the Russian border. Hlukhiv was one of the largest and most ethnically diverse cities in north-east Ukraine: according to the 1897 census, the city had just over 15,000 inhabitants: 8,600 Ukrainians, 2,200 Russians and around 4,000 Jews. In January 1918, at the tail end of the 'triumphal march of Soviet power', Hlukhiv was taken by a Red Guard unit under the command of V. O. Tsyganok. In early March, the Reds found themselves pushed out of the city by the 300-strong Ukrainian Baturinskii regiment which sought to 'cleanse the city of Bolshevism'.⁴⁰ However, having regrouped on the outskirts of the city, the Bolsheviks soon joined forces with the Roslavl'skie Red Partisans, recently arrived from Kursk, and plans were put in place to recapture the city. After securing the support of local peasants, pro-Bolshevik forces mounted a successful assault on Hlukhiv, first taking the railway station, the post office and then other key points of the city.⁴¹ With power now established militarily, the Bolsheviks did not set out to intensify the class struggle or secure working-class hegemony as one might have expected; instead, the principal Bolshevik slogan after recapturing Hlukhiv was *'eliminate the bourgeoisie and the Yids!'* Eyewitness statements reveal the full extent of the horror unleashed.⁴²

Firstly, with the Reds now firmly in control of the city, the Ukrainian Baturinskii regiment changed sides and aligned themselves with the Bolsheviks, proclaiming to the latter that they only fought against Soviet

---

³⁸ A. E. Adams, *Bolsheviks in the Ukraine: Second Campaign, 1918-1919* (New Haven: Yale University Press, 1963), 51.
³⁹ Ibid., vi–vii.
⁴⁰ Tcherikower, *Istoriia pogromnogo dvizheniia na Ukraine 1917-1921*, 286–87.
⁴¹ I. Rogatyns'kyi, 'Hlukhivs'ka tragediia. Iz zapysok Ilii Rogatyns'kogo', *Zhyttia i Znannia* 8, no. 32 (1930): 31; Tcherikower, *Istoriia pogromnogo dvizheniia na Ukraine 1917-1921*, 287.
⁴² Tcherikower, *Istoriia pogromnogo dvizheniia na Ukraine 1917–1921*, 146, 287–97; Miliakova, *Kniga pogromov*, 6–8; Rogatyns'kyi, 'Hlukhivs'ka tragediia'.

power in the first place because the 'Yids' had paid them to do so.[43] The Baturinskii troops thus seemed to be appealing to Bolshevik antisemitism in a bid to save themselves from punitive measures. After the regiment was incorporated, the now enlarged Red Guard unit proceeded to go from door to door, asking: 'Where do all the Yids live?' According to a contemporary eyewitness, many among the local Christian population pointed out the Jewish neighbourhoods to the Red Guards.[44] In his memoir, written in 1930, Rogatyns'kyi recalls that once they arrived, the Red Guards simply lined up entire Jewish families and shot them on the spot.[45]

The pogrom started at 5 PM on 7 March, and over the course of the next two and a half days at least 100 of the town's Jewish inhabitants were murdered, perhaps many more.[46] According to newspaper reports and eyewitness accounts, the town's entire Jewish intelligentsia were slaughtered, as was each and every Jewish schoolboy. Eight Jews were apparently thrown from a moving train, 70-year-old Rabbi Berel was shot and as many as 140 Jews were reportedly buried in a single mass grave.[47] In one account, the Bundist Vladimir Kossovskii claimed that 'the street which housed the [local] soviet was literally sodden with Jewish blood'.[48] As they ransacked Jewish homes and killed Jews, Red soldiers shouted, 'We are going to slaughter all the bourgeoisie and Yids!' When one Jew asked why they were being killed, soldiers reportedly answered, 'We've been given orders [from above] to kill all the Jews'.[49] The complicity of the local Bolshevik regime in the violence is confirmed by other contemporary sources. For example, in a newspaper report in the Petrograd Yiddish daily *Unzer Togblat*, the unnamed author details the role of the local soviet in the violence. After two days of incessant killing, the soviet eventually issued the following order: 'Red Guards! Enough blood!' Yet this was by no means the end of the Hlukhiv massacre, for the very same Bolshevik commissars who called for the

---

[43] Tcherikower, *Istoriia pogromnogo dvizheniia na Ukraine 1917–1921*, 287.

[44] This is based on a report by an unnamed inhabitant of the town, written in mid-March and published in the Petrograd Yiddish weekly *Unzer Togblat* on 19 April. The account is republished in Tcherikower, *Istoriia pogromnogo dvizheniia na Ukraine 1917–1921*, 286–91.

[45] Rogatyns'kyi, 'Hlukhivs'ka tragediia', 31.

[46] The journal of the Poalei Zion party *Bor'ba* (The Struggle) reported in its 1 May edition that 270 Jews were murdered; *Bor'ba*, 1 May, 29. The Kharkiv-based Menshevik newspaper *Sotsial Demokrat*, however, put the figure at 425, while some reports even speculated that as many as 5,000 Jews had been killed. See Tcherikower, *Istoriia pogromnogo dvizheniia na Ukraine 1917-1921*, 145; Buldakov, *Khaos i etnos*, 679.

[47] See 'EVENTS IN 5679: June 1, 1918, to May 31, 1919', 1919, 287.

[48] Spargo, *The Jew and American Ideals*, 88.

[49] Tcherikower, *Istoriia pogromnogo dvizheniia na Ukraine 1917-1921*, 288.

shootings to stop then immediately initiated large-scale lootings of Jewish property and homes.[50] The local synagogue was destroyed and the Torah torn to pieces. Once the killing had stopped, the head of the local soviet then demanded (on the eve of Passover) that the remaining Jews hand over 10,000 rubbles; failure to do so, he warned, would see the violence resume. Meanwhile, Red Guard pogromists who had fallen in the struggle for power in Hlukhiv were given official burials in the town centre under a red banner bearing the words 'Long Live the International!'[51] As is clear, in the case of Hlukhiv, Soviet power was secured by and through antisemitism.

On the back of the events in Hlukhiv and elsewhere, Petrograd Jewish Community organizations declared 23 May 1918 to be a Jewish National Day of Mourning across the whole of Russia. The pogrom was reported widely in the Jewish press. That day's edition of *Unzer Togblat* appeared in a black border, with articles titled 'Protest by Mourning' and 'The Day of Sorrow'.[52] But how did Bolshevik newspapers handle the explosive fact that Red Guards had participated in this violence?

'The Glorious Roslavl'skii Regiment': Bolshevik Newspapers and the Hlukhiv Massacre

Writing in his diary on 7 April (exactly one month after the start of the pogrom), the Jewish historian Simon Dubnov complained that the Bolshevik leadership in Petrograd had 'kept silent' about the Hlukhiv pogrom 'because it was the work of the Red Army'.[53] Dubnov, based in Petrograd at the time, perhaps had in mind a startling telegram published in the Red Army's newspaper *Zvezda* on 10 March, and again in the main Bolshevik organ, *Pravda*, on 18 March:

On March 8 the city of Hlukhiv was taken by the glorious Roslavl'skii regiment ... the Reds took the city, showing no remorse. The Roslavl'skie troops ... have established Soviet power along with the armed local peasants, workers and soldiers.[54]

---

[50] Ibid., 290; Spargo, *The Jew and American Ideals*, 88.
[51] Tcherikower, *Istoriia pogromnogo dvizheniia na Ukraine 1917-1921*, 291.
[52] Spargo, *The Jew and American Ideals*, 90.   [53] Dubnov, *Kniga zhizni*, 436.
[54] *Pravda*, 18 March; *Zvezda*, 10 March. The telegram was also republished in full in S. M. Korolivskii, N. K. Kolensnik and I. K. Rybalka, *Grazhdanskaia voina na Ukraine 1918-1920. Tom pervyi, Kniga pervaia*. (Kiev: Izdatel'stvo naukova duma, 1967), 33. The original copy of the telegram is held in GARF f.1235 o.93 d.114. l.1. It was sent to the Party leadership on 9 March and is identical to the various published versions. I thank Mikhail Pogorelov for tracking down the original and making copies. I also thank Gleb

The account here is evidently at odds with events in Hlukhiv, where 'establishing Soviet power' meant, in practice, wiping out whole sections of the Jewish population. The telegram even celebrates the 'heroic' nature of this Bolshevik 'victory'. Were the editors of *Pravda* aware of what was happening in Hlukhiv when this telegram was published? The historian Elias Tcherikower assumed that the Bolshevik leadership was in full knowledge of the events, and as far as he was concerned, the Party was indifferent to the tragic reality of 'Bolshevizing' the city through the spilling of Jewish blood.[55]

However, the first letters of protest notifying the Soviet government about the pogrom did not arrive until 4 April,[56] that is, a full month after the pogrom had taken place and nearly three weeks after the *Pravda* telegram had been published. Indeed, the first eyewitness reports about Hlukhiv did not appear in the Jewish press until mid-April,[57] again indicating that it took some weeks before the full extent of the violence became known. Given that the Soviet government tended to rely upon the Jewish press for information about pogroms in the former Pale of Settlement,[58] it seems likely that they were unaware of the nature of the Bolshevik 'victory' in Hlukhiv before the publication of the *Pravda* telegram.

Nevertheless, once news of the pogrom began to spread, Soviet newspapers made no reference whatsoever to *who* had actually been responsible for the violence.[59] This unwillingness on the part of the Bolsheviks to publicly discuss Red Army involvement in pogroms would recur throughout the Civil War period. There was evidently some truth, then, to Dubnov's complaint that the Bolshevik press shied away from openly discussing the problem of 'Red antisemitism'.

Agency in the Hlukhiv Pogrom: The Problem of Sources

It is difficult to build a picture of the individual and collective forms of agency responsible for the Hlukhiv massacre. Perhaps unsurprisingly,

---

Albert for bringing to my attention the *Pravda* publication of this telegram and for the fruitful discussion that followed.

[55] Tcherikower, *Istoriia pogromnogo dvizheniia na Ukraine 1917-1921*, 147.
[56] GARF f.130 o.2 d.212 l.1 and f.1318 o.1 d.561 l.437.
[57] Tcherikower, *Istoriia pogromnogo dvizheniia na Ukraine 1917-1921*, 287.
[58] For example, the Information Department of the Central Evkom closely monitored the Jewish press and put together a biweekly report detailing all published information relating to Jewish life. Each report contained special sections on 'antisemitism and pogroms'. See, for example, GARF f.1318 o.1 d.841 l.24-27; f.1318 o.1 d.412 l.1-53; f.1318 o.1 d.560 l.234-238.
[59] Tcherikower, *Istoriia pogromnogo dvizheniia na Ukraine 1917-1921*, 150.

memoirs from leading Bolsheviks in the Civil War and official post-war Soviet histories of the Hlukhiv region pass over the events of March 1918 without mention of the pogrom.[60] Some Soviet publications in the 1920s at least mentioned that a pogrom had taken place in Hlukhiv, but said nothing whatsoever of the role of the Red Guards in it.[61] The Jewish Communist Samuil Agurskii acknowledged in his 1926 monograph, *The Jewish Worker in the Communist Movement, 1917-1921* that 'antisemitism even penetrated some Soviet institutions' in early to mid-1918, but he did not say anything about the scale and specificity of the slaughter that took place during this period.[62] The problem is further compounded by the fact that both Bolshevik and anti-Bolshevik newspaper reports from 1918 say so little about the individuals and groups responsible for the Hlukhiv pogrom. The following schematic overview is all that can be drawn from the available sources: when the Bolsheviks first took Hlukhiv in January 1918, the regional party organization was made up of forty 'Communists'. By late February – that is, a week before it recaptured the city and carried out the pogrom – the Roslavl'skii red partisans were apparently 3,000 strong.[63] The Roslavl'skii unit had been formed in Smolensk, a western Russian city some 400 kilometres north of Hlukhiv. Soon after its formation it joined the larger southern unit which oversaw the Red Army's attempt to maintain control in the Chernihiv region during the war with Germany. In late February, the Roslavl'skii unit was sent from Smolensk to Hlukhiv in order to 'help the struggle against German bourgeois-nationalist counter-revolution'.[64] Again, it is unclear who these soldiers actually were. The fact that the unit was formed in Smolensk indicates that it may have been composed mainly of Russians, and indeed this is corroborated in one memoir.[65] Other accounts, however, suggest a strong level of support for the pogrom on the part of the local armed Ukrainian peasantry, who aligned

---

[60] See, for example, V. A. Antonov-Ovseenko, *Zapiski o grazhdanskoii voine. Tom 1* (Moscow: Vysshii voennyi redaktsionnyi sovet, 1924); I. Ia. Makukhin, ed., *Istoriia gorodov i sel Ukrainskoi SSR. Tom 19 sumskaia oblast'*, vol. 19 (Kiev: Institut istorii Akademii Nauk USSR, Ukrainskoi sovetskoi entsiklopedii Akademii Nauk USSR, 1974), 232.
[61] E. S. Ostrovskii, *Evreiskie pogromy 1918-1921* (Moscow: Emes, 1926), 36.
[62] S. Agurskii, *Evreiskii rabochii v kommunisticheskom dvizhenii (1917-1921)* (Minsk: Gosudarstvennoe izdatel'stvo Belorussii, 1926), 152.
[63] Makukhin, *Istoriia gorodov i sel Ukrainskoi SSR*, 19:231–32.
[64] Korolivskii, Kolensnik and Rybalka, *Grazhdanskaia voina na Ukraine 1918-1920. Tom pervyi, Kniga pervaia*, 757.
[65] Rogatyns'kyi, 'Hlukhivs'ka tragediia'.

themselves with the Bolsheviks in the days preceding the entry of the Roslavl'skii unit into Hlukhiv.[66]

What of the commissars who led the Hlukhiv soviet, which, if we recall, officially sanctioned the pogrom? Only two names have emerged from the existing literature: 'Vlasov' (also noted in newspapers of the time as 'Ulasov'), described in one account as a 'kulak'; and Pil'chenko, who apparently held a criminal record for fraud.[67] Vlasov, it seems, was part of the original group of Bolsheviks who had captured the city in January, though it remains unclear if Pil'chenko was among them. The chief commissar and commander of the Southern Front unit (to which the Roslavl'skii regiment belonged) were 'Lopatin' and 'Sobakin', respectively, but again, little else is known about them.[68]

Just over a week after the Hlukhiv massacre, the Supreme Commander of the Red Army in Ukraine, Antonov-Ovseenko, ordered the immediate recomposition of all Red Army units in Hlukhiv and the surrounding regions. On the evening of 19 March he instructed all 'autonomous Red units' to be dissolved and reconstituted under the single command of the Bolshevik General Rudolf Sivers.[69] To underline the point, he ordered Sivers to summarily execute any Red troops who offered resistance to these measures.[70] It seems likely that Antonov-Ovseenko took this measure in light of the Hlukhiv pogrom. As the events of 1919 would show, the drive for centralization in Ukraine was born not only of a desire for one party rule but also because centralization was often the only means of overcoming local Bolshevik and Red Army antisemitism.

Conclusion

Although occupying only a marginal position in the overall picture of anti-Jewish violence during the Civil War, the Red pogroms of the spring of 1918 have been placed centre stage here by virtue of the fundamental questions they posed of the Soviet government and its broader anti-racist strategy. Whereas the pogroms of late 1919 were largely carried out by anti-Bolshevik military forces, in the spring of 1918, pogromist violence

---

[66] Tcherikower, *Istoriia pogromnogo dvizheniia na Ukraine 1917-1921*, 187; Buldakov, *Khaos i etnos*, 679.
[67] Tcherikower, *Istoriia pogromnogo dvizheniia na Ukraine 1917-1921*, 286.
[68] Korolivskii, Kolensnik and Rybalka, *Grazhdanskaia voina na Ukraine 1918-1920. Tom pervyi, Kniga pervaia*, 33.
[69] Sivers, born in Petrograd in 1892, led the Soviet Fifth Army during the fight against Germany in March and April 1918.
[70] T. F Kariaeva and N. N. Azovtsev, eds., *Direktivy komandovaniia frontov Krasnoi Armii, 1917-1922. Sbornik dokumentov*, vol. 1 (Moscow: Voennoe izdatel'stvo Ministerstvo Oborony SSSR, 1971), 108.

emerged principally from the ranks of Red Guards and the Red Army. The first test the Bolsheviks faced on the question of antisemitism after coming to power in October 1917, then, was to confront antisemitism within their own social base. In the most extreme case in Hlukhiv, Bolshevik power was constituted *through* anti-Jewish violence. Elsewhere, there was a widespread presence of antisemitism within local Bolshevik and Soviet institutions. How did the Bolshevik leadership address this? What sorts of measures did it take in response to the articulation of antisemitism and the revolutionary process? And which forms of individual and collective agency were responsible for bringing these campaigns into being? It is to these questions that we now turn.

3 The Soviet Response to Antisemitism, 1918

Introduction

The leadership of the broader Russian socialist movement made its position on antisemitism clear in the very moment of revolution itself. On 26 October 1917, as power passed into the hands of the Bolsheviks, the Second All Russian Congress of Soviets passed a resolution against pogroms.[1] However, in the first nine months of Soviet power, the Bolshevik leadership did not broach the question of antisemitism even once. By late July 1918, no response had been made to the devastating Red pogroms in Chernihiv during the spring of that year. Eventually, on 26 July 1918, the Soviet government issued a decree on anti-Jewish violence. Traditionally, historians begin their discussions of the Bolshevik response to antisemitism after 1917 by citing this important document.[2] However, the decree marked not the beginning but the *culmination* of the first phase of the Soviet response to antisemitism. Between April and July 1918, a small group of Jewish socialists were engaged in an intensive phase of anti-racist praxis within the lower echelons of the Soviet state apparatus. Until now, this chapter in the history of the Russian Revolution has been almost entirely overlooked.[3]

---

[1] Akhapkin, Iroshnikov and Gogolevskii, *Dekrety sovetskoi vlasti o Petrograde*, 14.
[2] Kostyrchenko, *Tainaia politika Stalina*, 56; Aronson, 'Evreiskaia obshchestvennost'' v Rossii v 1917-1918 gg.', 132; Schwarz, *The Jews in the Soviet Union*, 274.
[3] To date, the emergence of a Soviet response to antisemitism in the spring of 1918 has not been addressed in either the English- or Russian-language literature. Oleg Budnitskii offers a brief paragraph-length discussion but says nothing of the individual and collective types of agency that brought this campaign into being or the specific political context in which it arose. See Budnitskii, *Rossiiskie evrei mezhdu krasnymi i belymi*, 124–25. The exception to this rule is the excellent study by Ulrich Herbeck, *Das Feindbild vom 'jüdischen Bolschewiken'*. I would like to thank Ulrich for a hugely productive conversation in 2012, where he generously shared his work and listened to my ideas, providing important feedback.

The Moscow Jewish Commissariat

The first Soviet response to antisemitism did *not* emerge from the Party leadership. Recently published documents from the Petrograd Committee of the RKP(b) and the Petrograd-based Soviet government – the Council of Peoples' Commissars headed by Lenin – indicate that antisemitism was not put on the agenda at *any* of the meetings held by these key institutions between October 1917 and the spring of 1918.[4] Instead, the first Soviet campaign against antisemitism emerged from a very specific institution: the Moscow Jewish Commissariat (hereafter Moscow Evkom).

The Moscow Evkom was part of a wider structure of thirteen loosely connected regional Jewish commissariats throughout Soviet Russia, all ostensibly under the control of the central Commissariat for Jewish National Affairs (hereafter Central Evkom).[5] The establishment of Central Evkom was part of the Soviet government's broader strategy of affording ethnic minority groups within the Russian interior a degree of institutional and cultural representation. This led to the formation of various national commissariats, which were essentially governmental institutions responsible for establishing educational and cultural materials in minority languages.

The Central Evkom was formed in Petrograd on 20 January 1918 and was headed by the 'old Bolshevik' Semon Dimanshtein – a member of the party since 1904.[6] The reason for the Commissariat's formation was

---

[4] Iu. N. Amiantov et al., eds., *Protokoly zasedanii Soveta Narodnykh Komissarov RSFSR. Noiabr' 1917 - mart 1918 gg.* (Moscow: ROSSPEN, 2006); T. A. Abrosimova, ed., *Peterburgskii komitet RKP(b) v 1918 godu: Protokoly i materialy zasedanii* (Saint Petersburg: Peterburgskii gosudarstvennyi universitet. Filologicheskii fakul'tet, 2013).

[5] Agurskii, *Evreiskii rabochii v kommunisticheskom dvizhenii (1917-1921)*, 64–67; Gitelman, *Jewish Nationality and Soviet Politics*.

[6] Semon Dimanshtein (1886–1938) was born into a family of craftsworkers in Sebezh, in the Vitebsk province. His early life was shaped by an Orthodox, religious upbringing. During his childhood the local rabbi lived in the Dimanshtein household; by the time Semon was twelve, he was studying in the yeshiva. Indeed, Dimanshtein would go on to study at both the Slobodka and Lubavitch yeshivas, and by the age of eighteen had received two rabbinical ordinations, one from the renowed rabbi Khaim Ozer Grodzenskii of Vilna. In 1903, however, Dimanshtein broke from his rabbical career and entered a *gymnasium*, where he came into contact with illegal socialist circles. Soon after, he joined the Russian Social Democratic Labour Party, and subsequently the Bolsheviks, helping the party to translate materials into Yiddish and Hebrew. He was arrested in 1906 and 1908 for participating in underground groups in Riga and Minsk. In 1909, he was sentenced to five years' exile in Sibera, some of which he served, before fleeing abroad, first to Germany and then to France. In Paris, still a committed Bolshevik, Dimanshtein worked in a factory and founded a Jewish workers' club in Montmartre. Events in Russia pulled him back, however: in May 1917, he returned to Riga, where he joined the Bolshevik committee and edited the newspaper *Okopnaia Pravda* (Trench Truth). Later that summer, the Bolshevik Central Committee requested

to promote, or rather translate, the principles of the October Revolution for the Yiddish-speaking Jewish working class, among whom the Bolsheviks held virtually no influence whatsoever.[7] This task was carried out by the Commissariat's Sub-department for Culture and Enlightenment. The Central Evkom's second aim was to fight against 'socialist-nationalist elements such as the Bund, and other petty bourgeois parties', which for a long time had held a significant degree of influence within the working-class districts of the former Pale.[8] However, such was the paucity of Bolshevik cadres with any organic relationship to the Yiddish-speaking Jewish masses, the Central and regional Evkoms had to rely on precisely these 'petty bourgeois elements' in order to function, and as such, membership of the Evkoms was extended to non-Bolshevik Jewish socialists, in particular the Left SRs and the left faction of the Poalei Zion party.[9] It was out of this Jewish socialist milieu that

his services in Petrograd. Following the outbreak of the October Revolution, Dimanshtein was appointed head of the Jewish Commissariat in the People's Commissariat for Nationalities. In this role, he led the Party's Jewish work, editing the first Soviet Yiddish newspaper *Di varhayt* and its successor *Der emes*, and chairing, from 1919 to 1920, the Central Bureau of the Evsektsiia (the Jewish Section of the Russian Communist Party). Throughout the 1920s, Dimanstein held various senior posts in the Party and Soviet government. His main sphere of work remained in the Jewish arena. Like so many in the Evsektsiia and Evkom milieu, his stock fell as the nightmare of Stalinism took hold: he was arrested on 18 February 1938 and executed on 25 August for 'counter-revolutionary' activities; Gitelman, *Jewish Nationality and Soviet Politics*, 130–32; Z. Gitelman, *A Century of Ambivalence: The Jews of Russia and the Soviet Union, 1881 to the Present* (Bloomington: Indiana University Press, 2001), 65; A. Zel'tser, 'Dimanshtein, Semen Markovich', in *The YIVO Encyclopedia of Jews in Eastern Europe*, ed. G. D. Hundert, Vol. 1 (New Haven: Yale University Press, 2008).

[7] On the founding of the Jewish Commissariat, see RGASPI f.272 o.1 d.71 l.5. On the lack of Bolshevik influence among the Yiddish-speaking Jewish working class, see Gitelman, *Jewish Nationality and Soviet Politics*, 105; Agurskii, *Evreiskii rabochii v kommunisticheskom dvizhenii (1917-1921)*, 42.

[8] Agurskii, *Evreiskii rabochii v kommunisticheskom dvizhenii (1917–1921)*, 42. We should note, though, that Agurskii made this comment in 1926, at the height of the anti-Bundist campaigns in Belorussia, and it is quite possible that he overstated the Evkom's hostility to the Bund during the period of 1918. I thank Andrew Sloin for this point. For a broader discussion of the anti-Bund campaigns in Belorussia in the mid- to late 1920s, see his superb study: Sloin, *The Jewish Revolution in Belorussia*.

[9] Gitelman, *Jewish Nationality and Soviet Politics*. On the splitting of Poalei Zion in Moscow into right and left factions, see Budnitskii, *Rossiiskie evrei mezhdu krasnymi i belymi*, 118. For a provincial take on the same process in Vitebsk, see A. Zel'tser, *Evrei sovetskoi provintsii: Vitebsk i mestechki 1917-1941* (Moscow: ROSSPEN, 2006), 43–44. The Bund refused to collaborate with the Bolsheviks in the spring of 1918. At its Moscow conference in May 1918 a resolution was passed instructing all Bund members to continue to refuse any form of cooperation with the 'bureaucratic' Jewish Commissariats, whose inclusion of Jewish socialist and non-Party members acted as a cover for their 'non-democratic character'; Anderson, Shelokhaev and Amiantov, *Bund*, 1124. Bundists often mocked the fact that the Bolsheviks were working so closely with Poalei Zion, a party which sought to build a Zionist homeland in Palestine. *Evreiskii Rabochii* 4, 14.

the Soviet response to the Red pogroms of early 1918 emerged, and its institutional expression was the regional Moscow Evkom.

The Moscow Evkom was established at a gathering of non-Bolshevik Jewish socialists in Moscow in early March 1918.[10] At this meeting, key positions in the newly formed commissariat were allocated to a small group of Yiddish-speaking Jewish revolutionaries active within Poalei Zion, the United Jewish Socialist Workers Party and the Left SRs. Although it was predicated on an openly pro-Soviet politics, the Moscow Evkom, like many other Jewish commissariats during this period, did not contain a single Bolshevik.[11] Three 'commissions' were established within the Moscow Evkom's internal structure: the Commission for Cultural Enlightenment; the Commission for Social Relief; and the Commission for the Fight against Pogroms. Of these, it was the latter which was by far the most active: an internal report on the activities of the Moscow Evkom written in early June 1918 noted that the campaign against antisemitism and pogroms had taken up virtually all of the Evkom's work to date, to the extent that work in the other two commissions had barely even started.[12]

Despite the profound political disagreements between Poalei Zion and the United Jewish Socialist Workers Party on the so called Jewish question,[13] key activists from both parties coalesced around the apparatuses of the Moscow Evkom. Unlike well-known Jewish Bolsheviks such as Trotsky, Sverdlov and Zinoviev, these Jewish radicals were far less traversed along the path of assimilation, and most of them had active and very real connections to Yiddish-speaking cultural worlds. Moreover, their differences notwithstanding, leading members of both the Poalei Zion and the United Jewish Socialist Workers Party were committed to the idea of a Jewish national project, however broadly defined. They held similar assessments of the crisis facing the Jewish population, and in this sense they shared more in common than was apparent at the time.[14] These political formations were part of a much

---

[10] TsGAMO f.4619 o.2 d.148 l.21

[11] Indeed, most provincial Jewish commissariats were staffed by non-Bolsheviks, i.e. Left SRs, Poalei Zionists, Left Bundists and non-affiliated workers. In Perm, for example, the Evkom consisted of two Poalei Zionists, one Left SR and not a single Bolshevik; Gitelman, *Jewish Nationality and Soviet Politics*, 138.

[12] GARF f.1318 o.1 d.561 l.104-104ob; TsGAMO f.4619 o.2 d.148 l.21ob

[13] Broadly speaking, the Poalei Zion advocated a Zionist solution to the 'Jewish question', whereas the politics of the United Jewish Socialist Workers' Party were rooted in an 'extraterritorial' approach that promoted the autonomy of the Jews in Russia. For a classic account of these divisions, see Frankel, *Prophecy and Politics*.

[14] Barry Trachtenberg, *The Revolutionary Roots of Modern Yiddish, 1903-1917* (New York: Syracuse University Press, 2008), 14, 39.

wider process identified by Ken Moss as the 'Jewish renaissance' in the Russian Revolution.[15] As we shall see, their embeddedness in a Jewish socialist politics had significant implications for their political response to antisemitism.

The Composition of the Moscow Evkom

Although it drove the Soviet state response to antisemitism in the spring of 1918, the Moscow Evkom was a remarkably small institution that boasted no more than ten staff at any one time. An internal report dated 23 May 1918 shows that the 'Department for the Struggle against Antisemitism' (now changed from its original title of the 'Commission for the Struggle against Pogroms') consisted of a mere six individuals.[16] Throughout its existence, the Department repeatedly wrote to the Moscow Sovnarkom stating the 'urgent need' for more financial support to collate information on antisemitism and develop a political response.[17] Officially the work of the Department was overseen by Poalei Zion activist Naum Markovich Asarkan, but in actuality he was not centrally involved in the development of a Soviet response to antisemitism. When a report of the Moscow Evkom's activities between April and June was submitted to the Moscow Sovnarkom, Asarkan was noted as being 'absent' from his duties.[18] As such, it fell to staff from other departments of the commissariat to carry out the campaign against antisemitism.

The two figures who played the key role were the Evkom's Secretary, Zvi Fridliand (Grigorii Samoilovich) and Il'ia Dobkovskii. Fridliand, born in Minsk in 1896, joined the Poalei Zion party in 1913. In 1917 he became a member of the party's Central Committee. Over the course of 1917, divisions emerged within the Poalei Zion party, with a small, broadly pro-Bolshevik current emerging at the party's Moscow conference in April 1917.[19] By the time of its August

---

[15] Moss, *Jewish Renaissance in the Russian Revolution*.
[16] These were: Poalei Zion activist Naum Markovich Asarkan (who headed the department), one typist, one clerk and three unnamed assistants; GARF f.1318 o.1 d.561 l.258ob. The three unnamed assistants were only recruited on 22 April after the Moscow Evkom leadership had appealed to the Moscow Sovnarkom for additional staff to collate information on the nature and extent of antisemitism.
[17] TsGAMO f.4619 o.3 d.19 l.15; GARF f.1318 o.1 d.561 l.258ob.
[18] GARF f.1318 o.1 d.561 l.104-104ob; TsGAMO f.4619 o.2 d.148 l.21-21o6. Asarkan appears to have left the Soviet government in 1918 and continued his work in Moscow with Poalei Zion. See, for example, the documents held in RGASPI f.272 o.1 d.13.
[19] See *Listok Petrogradskogo Komiteta Evreiskoi Sotsial-Demokraticheskoi Rabochei Partii (Poalei Tsiona)*, 17 April 1917.

conference, the party had split into three factions: a rightist group which was close to the Mensheviks and supported the Provisional Government; a 'centrist' grouping that campaigned for an end to the war; and a left-wing camp which openly supported the Bolsheviks. Fridliand, by this point a member of the party's Central Committee, led the left faction. Though he was still a member of Poalei Zion, the revolution pulled him ever further towards Bolshevism. During the October Revolution he was active among the Red Guards, arming workers to seize the Winter Palace. After the Bolsheviks came to power, Fridliand moved to Moscow where, along with other Poalei Zion activists such as Rabinovich, he helped establish the Moscow Jewish Commissariat.[20]

[20] Aronson, 'Evreiskaia obshchestvennost'' v Rossii v 1917-1918 g.g.', 133; B. Gurevitz, *National Communism in the Soviet Union, 1918-1928* (Pittsburgh: University of Pittsburgh Press, 1980), 47–48; O. V. Budnitskii, "Evreiskie batal'ony' v Krasnoi Armii', in *Mirovoi krizis 1914-1920 godov i sud'ba vostohnoevropeiskogo evreistva*, ed. O. V. Budnitskii et al. (Moscow: ROSSPEN, 2005), 190; Ts. Fridliand, *Kommunisticheskii Internatsional i Kommunisticheskii Poalei-Tsionizm* (Minsk: Gosudarstvennoe izdatel'stvo Belorussii, 1921), 92–95. Fridliand sat on the Central Committee of the Poalei Zion between 1917 and 1919. At the decisive Second Congress of Soviets in November 1917, he argued that Poalei Zion delegates should not walk out with Mensheviks, but should remain and work with the Bolsheviks. See *Evreiskaia Rabochaia Khronika* no. 14 (20), 11 April 1917, 19. In early 1919, he moved from Moscow to Minsk, where, as a Poalei Zion representative, he sat on the Executive Committee of the short-lived Lithuanian-Belarussian Soviet Socialist Republic. When the Poalei Zion party endured a second split in August 1919, Fridliand led a left faction and formed the Jewish Communist Party (Poalei Zion). By 1921, however, he initiated the dissolution of the party and joined the Bolsheviks (see Chapter 6 for more). Shortly after this, he moved back to Moscow to become an academic, taking up a specialist interest in the French Revolution. Later, he became professor at the Moscow State University, where in 1934 he became Dean of the Faculty of History. Yet just two years later, he was arrested during Stalin's purges and murdered on 7 March 1937; A. N. Artizov, 'Sud'by istorikov shkoly M. N. Pokrovskogo (seredina 1930-kh godov)', *Voprosi Istorii* 7 (1994): 34–38; A. G. Slutskii, 'Doktor Istoricheskikh Nauk, Professor Grigorii Samoilovich Fridliand (k semidesiatiletiiu so dnia rozhdeniia)', in *Istoriia i istoriki. Istoriografiia vseobshchei istorii. Sbornik statei.*, ed. M. A. Alpatov (Moscow: Izdatel'stvo 'Nauka', 1966); Serhiy Hirik, 'Neviadomaia pratsa Ryhora (Tsvi) Frydlianda ab levym Paalei-Tsyianiz'me u Belarusi', *Zapisy BINIM* 39 (2017): 491–99. Although Fridliand's 'Jewish work' largely came to an end when he joined the Bolsheviks in 1921, he did, on occasion, return to matters Jewish: in 1925, he reviewed a Yiddish monograph by the former Bundist Ester Frumkina; Ts. Fridliand, 'Ester: Lenin i ego trudy', *Pechat' i Revoliutsiia*, 4 (1925): 176–77. The following year he authored the entry on '*antisemitizm*' in the first edition of the Great Soviet Encyclopaedia; Ts. Fridliand, 'Antisemitizm', in *Bol'shaia Sovetskaia Entsiklopediia*, vol. 4, 65 vols (Moscow: Gosudarstvennoe slovarno-entsiklopedicheskoeizdatel'stvo 'Sovetskaia Entsiklopediia', 1926). Fridliand's most substantive statement on Jewish politics after joining the Party was his monograph *Kommunisticheskii Internatsional i Kommunisticheskii Poalei-Tsionizm*. This book, published in 1921, was unknown to scholars until a copy was recently uncovered by the historian Serhiy Hirik. For a discussion, see Hirik, 'Neviadomaia pratsa Ryhora (Tsvi) Frydlianda ab levym Paalei-Tsyianiz'me u Belarusi', See also Fridliand *Kommunisticheskii Internatsional i Kommunisticheskii Poalei-Tsionizm*. I thank Serhiy for generously sharing this material.

Figure 1 Zvi Fridliand, around 1917.
Image courtesy of Tikhon Dziadko and family

The other key activist was Il'ia Dobkovskii. Born in 1882 in Belorussia, in the Diatlovskii region of Grodno, Dobkovskii received a religious Jewish education. By the turn of the century he joined the Union of Socialist Revolutionary Maximalists, a radical offshoot of the Socialist Revolutionary Party which distinguished itself by incorporating assassinations and robbery into its political programme. Following the October Revolution of 1917, Dobkovskii joined the ranks of the Left Socialist Revolutionaries, who were now in coalition government with the Bolsheviks. At the start of 1918, Dobkovskii approached Stalin to publish a pro-Soviet newspaper in Yiddish. When, shortly after, the Central Evkom was established in Petrograd, Dobkovskii was appointed vice-Commissar under Dimanshtein.[21] Dobkovskii was also active in the Bureau of the Moscow Evkom,[22] and it was in this latter role that he

---

[21] GARF f.1318 o.1 d.22 l.12; Agurskii, *Evreiskii rabochii v kommunisticheskom dvizhenii (1917-1921)*, 40; Gitelman, *Jewish Nationality and Soviet Politics*, 132; Miliakova, *Kniga pogromov*, 913; David Engel, *The Assassination of Symon Petliura and the Trial of Sholem Schwarzbard 1926-1927: A Selection of Documents* (Göttingen: Vandenhoeck and Ruprecht, 2016), 43.

[22] TsGAMO, f.4619 o.2 d.148 l.21-21ob; GARF f.1318 o.1 d.561 l.104-104ob.

helped to initiate the first Soviet state response to antisemitism in April 1918.[23]

The Structural Weaknesses of the Moscow Evkom

The Moscow Evkom ostensibly reported to the Central Evkom; in actual fact, however, it was more organically part of the Moscow regional (*oblastnoi*) Council of Peoples' Commissars (hereafter Moscow Sovnarkom).[24] This was a separate entity from the Central Sovnarkom headed by Lenin in Petrograd, and compared to the latter, it was politically heterodox: not only was the Moscow Sovnarkom led by Left Communists, but over a third of its membership were Left SRs.[25] This meant that the Moscow Evkom was under threat from almost its very inception. After the transfer of the Soviet government from Petrograd to Moscow in mid-March 1918, Moscow now found itself home to two Jewish Commissariats: the regional Moscow Evkom but also the Central Evkom, newly relocated from Petrograd under the leadership of Dimanshtein.

---

[23] Dobvkovskii's position in the Moscow Evkom was cut short, however: on 22 April he was arrested by the Cheka for alleged involvement in the tsarist secret police. Despite being cleared by a revolutionary tribunal in June 1918, Dobkovskii did not return to work in the Evkom. After emigrating to Paris in the early 1920s, Dobkovskii testified in the 1926 trial of Schwartzbard, the assassin of Symon Petliura, leader of the Ukrainian Directorate and widely held accountable for many of the 1919 pogroms; Gitelman, *Jewish Nationality and Soviet Politics*, 133. For more on Dobkovskii's role in the Schwartzbard trial, see Engel, *The Assassination of Symon Petliura and the Trial of Sholem Schwarzbard 1926-1927*, 43–51. On Dobkovskii's expulsion from the Evkom in April 1918, see GARF f.1318 o.1 d.561 l.312, 313; f.1318 o.1 d.1 l.10-11; and *Izvestiia VTsIK* 29 June 1918.

[24] GARF f.1318 o.1 d.561 l.104-104ob.

[25] The key positions in the Moscow Sovnarkom were taken up by M. N. Pokrovskii (Left Communist), Chairman; A. A. Bitsenko (Left SR), Vice Chairman; G. N. Maksimov, Vice Chairman; V. M. Smirnov (Bolshevik, later a leader of the Left Opposition in 1923), Commissar for Finance; V. P. Nogin (moderate Bolshevik who in late 1917 argued against the closure of the Constituent Assembly and the formation of a Bolshevik-only government), Commissar for Labour; V. F. Zitta, Commissar for Agriculture; P. K. Shtenberg (Bolshevik), Commissar for Enlightenment; A. I. Rykov (Bolshevik who, like Nogin, was against the closure of the Constituent Assembly), Commissar for Food; A. Lomov (Left Communist), Commissar for National Economic Affairs; V. E. Trutovskii (Left SR), Commissar for Regional Economic Affairs; Braun, Commissar for Transport; V. N. Iakovleva (Left Communist), Commissar for Communications; N. Ia. Zhilin, Commissar for Control and Accounts; S. Ia. Budzyn'skii, Commissar for Care; Golubkov, Commissar for Health; N. I. Muralov (Bolshevik, later member of the Left Opposition and supporter of Trotsky in the United Opposition), Commissar for Military Affairs; and finally V. M. Friche (Bolshevik) Commissar for Foreign Affairs. The Moscow Evkom was established under Friche's Commissariat for Foreign Affairs. See S. Khromov, ed., *Grazhdanskaia voina i voennaia interventsiia v SSSR. Entsiklopediia* (Moscow: Sovetskaia Entsiklopediia, 1983), 358.

The Campaign Emerges: April 1918

Given Dimanshetin's Bolshevik credentials – he was the *only* 'old Bolshevik' within the entire Evkom structure – and the fact that the Moscow Evkom did not contain a single Communist, it was somewhat inevitable that the regional commissariat would lose out to its central counterpart.[26] However, the future of the Moscow Evkom was more specifically bound up with the wider power struggle between the Left Communist–controlled local government in Moscow and the central Sovnarkom headed by Lenin, now based in the Kremlin following the relocation of the capital. This conflict had been simmering for some time, and was underlined as early as January 1918 when the regional Moscow Sovnarkom declared its intention to recognize Lenin's central authorities only in so far as they recognized its own right to coordinate affairs on a federative basis.[27]

Given its location, the Moscow Evkom was bound to become entangled in the wider conflict with the central agencies of Soviet power.[28] Stalin was particularly disposed to criticizing the regional Moscow Sovnarkom (and by extension its sub-commissariats such as the Moscow Evkom). For instance, although the formation of the Moscow Evkom was noted at an 7 April session of the Commissariat for National Affairs (hereafter Narkomnats),[29] just eleven days later, on 14 April, Stalin (who headed Narkomnats) proposed that 'all regional Commissariats for national affairs should be closed down immediately'.[30] This came just as the Moscow Evkom had set to work on initiating a state response to antisemitism. The writing was on the wall from the very beginning: whatever headway the Moscow Evkom could make in initiating a Soviet government response to antisemitism would have to be secured fast.

The Emergence of a Soviet Response to Antisemitism: April 1918

The first known discussion about antisemitism within the central institutions of the Soviet government took place on 7 April at the fourth

---

[26] Agurskii, *Evreiskii rabochii v kommunisticheskom dvizhenii (1917-1921)*, 57.
[27] T. J. Colton, *Moscow: Governing the Socialist Metropolis* (Cambridge, MA: Harvard University Press, 1995), 102.
[28] For Lenin's criticisms of the Left Communists in the Moscow Sovnarkom, see his article in late February 1918, *Strannoe i chudovishchnoe* (Strange and Monstrous); V. I. Lenin, *Polnoe sobranie sochinenii*, vol. 35 (Moscow: Izdatel'stvo politicheskoi literatury, 1974), 399–407.
[29] GARF f.130 o.1 d.1. l.3-3ob; see also V. P. Kozlov, *Arkhiv noveishei istorii Rossii. Seriia 'Katalogi' tom VII: Protokoly rukovodiashchikh organov narodnogo komissariata po delam natsional'nostei RSFSR 1918-1934 gg. Katalog dokumentov* (Moscow: ROSSPEN, 2001), 17.
[30] GARF f.1318 o.1 d.1 l.7-9ob. See also Kozlov, 18.

session of the Collegium of Narkomnats, headed by Stalin.[31] The only existing documentation of this discussion is a single sentence in the meeting's minutes, merely stating, 'the session acknowledges the information given by Dimanshtein about Jewish pogroms'.[32] We know more, however, about the background to this meeting. A few days earlier, Dimanshtein received fresh reports – most likely from Zvi Fridliand (Secretary of the Moscow Evkom) – about the pogroms carried out by the Red Army in Chernihiv. Fridliand apparently handed Dimanshtein the reports so that Stalin, Commissar for National Affairs, would take the issue to the executive of the Soviet government (the Sovnarkom). Fridliand's hope was that the Sovnarkom would 'come out *with its own protest* against the pogroms currently being carried out in Russia'.[33] It appears, however, that the issue was never passed on to the Sovnarkom: any record of this would most certainly have been noted by either the Evkom or the Sovnarkom in their exhaustive internal reports, yet there is no such record in the archives of either institution. Nor was the question of antisemitism brought before the Collegium of Narkomnats again. This general inactivity on the part of the central institutions prompted key members of the Moscow Evkom to take matters in their own hands by appealing directly to the most senior figures in the Soviet government.

The first such appeal came four days later, on 11 April, when the Moscow Evkom delegated David Davidovich (L'vovich) of the United Jewish Socialist Workers Party to put the question of the Red pogroms on the agenda at the fifth meeting of the All-Russian Central Executive Committee (hereafter VTsIK) – ostensibly the highest legislative body within the nascent Soviet state.[34] Davidovich opened his remarks by

---

[31] For more on Narkomnats, see J. Smith, 'Stalin as Commissar for Nationality Affairs, 1918-1922', in *Stalin: A New History*, ed. S. Davies and J. Harris (Cambridge: Cambridge University Press, 2005), 45.

[32] GARF f.130 o.1 d.1 l.4-6. See also Kozlov, *Arkhiv noveishei istorii Rossii*, 18.

[33] GARF f.1235 o.19 d.5 l.42.

[34] *Izvestiia Sovetov Rabochikh Soldatskikh i Krest'ianskikh Deputatov gor. Moskvy i Moskovskoi Oblasti*, 6 April 1918. David Davidovich (L'vovich) was born in southern Russia in 1882 into an assimilated Jewish family. He graduated in law and economics from Saint Petersburg University, and also studied engineering in Munich. After becoming interested in the Jewish labour movement in his teenage years, he joined Poalei Zion. In 1905, however, he joined the Zionist Socialist Workers Party, which in 1917 merged with the Jewish Socialist Workers Party to become the United Jewish Socialist Workers Party. From 1908 he lived in the United States, in connection with Jacob Schiff's 'Galveston Plan'. After returning to Russia in January 1918, he stood as the United Jewish Socialist Workers Party's only candidate in the Constituent Assembly on the slate of the Socialist Revolutionaries (SRs). Indeed, he was one of the very last speakers at the Constituent Assembly before it was dispersed by the Bolsheviks. A few weeks later, in March 1918, he worked closely with the Moscow Evkom, and it was in this capacity that he made the first recorded appeal to the Soviet government to initiate a

The Campaign Emerges: April 1918

reminding the chairman of the VTsIK, the Bolshevik Iakov Sverdlov, that the Moscow Evkom had already submitted a request to the Narkomnats, requesting that the Soviet government issue a statement against the pogroms. He then asked that the VTsIK take a special interest in the matter, but not before qualifying his comments:

> I am aware that there are much more important issues in Russia just now, such as Entente troops landing in Vladivostok and Murmansk ... and that the other issues on the agenda of today's meeting are also much more important.[35]

Davidovich broached the question of antisemitism, then, in a tentative and almost apologetic tone. To ensure the message was pressed home, he added: 'I also understand that the people are suffering from issues far more important than the one I come to you about today.' When reading these remarks, we should bear in mind that the confrontation with antisemitism was absolutely central to Davidovich's political practice, as it was for his comrades in the Moscow Evkom. It formed a crucial part of their revolutionary subjectivity and their collaboration with the nascent Soviet regime. Within a Moscow Evkom milieu, opposition to antisemitism did not have to be rationalised or justified; yet when presenting his case to Sverdlov, Davidovich framed the question of pogroms as one of only secondary concern. 'Nonetheless', Davidovich told Sverdlov, eventually getting to the point,

> You have probably read ... about the pogrom in Hlukhiv in which the Jewish population was butchered ... about the pogroms in Turkestan and in Galicia ... I consider these events to be enough for the VTsIK to come out and state its own opinion and to issue a protest of its own.[36]

Sverdlov responded by promising to instruct the Presidium of the VTsIK to establish a special commission (to include Evkom representatives),

---

response to the outbreak of pogroms in the former Pale of Settlement. However, following the expulsion of the Left SR's (and, by extension, the left Zionists) from the Soviet government in mid-1918 (see below for a discussion), Davidovich fled to Kyiv where he came into contact with the work of the Society for Handicraft and Agricultural Labour among the Jews of Russia (ORT); World ORT Archive (hereafter: WORTA), d07a008, 26. See also Miliakova, *Kniga pogromov*, 911; G. Estraikh, 'From Foreign Delegation to World ORT Union', in *Educating for Life: New Chapters in the History of the ORT*, ed. R. Bracha, A. Drori-Avraham and G. Yantian (London: World ORT, 2010), 77–86; G. Estraikh, 'From Berlin to Paris and Beyond: The 1930s and 1940s', in *Educating for Life: New Chapters in the History of the ORT*, ed. R. Bracha, A. Drori-Avraham and G. Yantian (London: World ORT, 2010), 123–24; L. Shapiro, *The History of the ORT: A Jewish Movement for Social Change* (New York: Schocken Books, 1980), 148; ORT, *The Hope and the Illusion. The Search for a Russian Jewish Homeland: A Remarkable Period in the History of the ORT, 1921 to 1938* (London: World ORT, 2006), 135–37.

[35] GARF f.1235 o.19 d.5 l.42-43.   [36] GARF f.1235 o.19 d.5 l.42-43.

whose task it would be to develop a public statement, outlining in no uncertain terms that Soviet power would 'take all measures necessary to ensure that no such pogroms occur anywhere in Russia or in other countries'.[37] However, no such commission was ever formed, the VTsIK did *not* issue an appeal for pogroms to be put down, and as such the central organs of the Soviet state had still to form any kind of response to the antisemitic violence being perpetrated in Ukraine and elsewhere. This inactivity did not go unnoticed by Jewish political parties: on 25 April the Temporary Jewish National Soviet – a body representing all the major socialist and non-socialist Jewish parties – issued a complaint that the ruling authorities in the regions of the former empire, including the Soviet government, had 'failed to take any serious measures to prevent pogroms', and that the Jews have been left to 'defend themselves, their honour, life and property'.[38] Similar statements from Jewish community organizations soon followed. In early June, a meeting of the Petrograd Jewish Communal Council (*Evreiskii Obshchinnyi Sovet*) pointed out that those responsible for the pogroms were the 'very same armed groups upon which the Soviet government depends [for its existence]'.[39] It is difficult to trace what impact, if any, such protests had on the Soviet leadership, though the Central Evkom certainly paid close attention to them.[40]

The exchange between Davidovich and Sverdlov gives an illustration of the centrality of Jewish politics to the Soviet response to the Red pogroms of 1918. It is not insignificant that the question of antisemitism had been brought to the VTsIK by Davidovich, a long-standing member of the Jewish socialist movement. Born in 1882 in southern Russia, he had joined the Poalei Zion party by his teenage years. Like so many other Jewish radicals of his generation, 1905 was the pivotal year, a moment defined by both revolution and antisemitism.[41] Davidovich's role in 1905 was to lead a Jewish self-defence unit in Odessa against pogromist violence.[42] Soon after, he became a 'Territorialist', joining the Zionist

---

[37] GARF f.1235 o.19 d.5 l.43–44.
[38] *Razsvet* no. 16–17, 28; G. Ia. Aronson, 'Evreiskii vopros v epokhu Stalina', in *Kniga o russkom evreistve 1917-1967*, ed. Ia. G. Frumkin, G. Ia. Aronson and A. A. Gol'denveizer (New York: Soiuz Russkikh Evreev, 1968), 15.
[39] *Evreiskaia Nedelia* no. 16–17, 15 June 1918; Miliakova, *Kniga pogromov*, 765. GARF f.1318 o.1 d.560 l.234-238.
[40] Such protests were monitored in the central Evkom's biweekly internal report on the Jewish press. See, for example, GARF f.1318 o.1 d.552 l.3; GARF f.1318 o.1 d.560 l.234.
[41] Trachtenberg, *The Revolutionary Roots of Modern Yiddish, 1903-1917*.
[42] As fellow territorialist and ORT leader Aaron Syngalowski put it at Davidovich's funeral in 1950, 'We met over 40 years ago. It was the Jewish Revolution, the insurrection

Socialist Workers' Party, which in 1917 was amalgamated into the United Jewish Socialist Workers' Party. In other words, Davidovich engaged with the Russian Revolution both as a socialist and as a Jew. Combatting antisemitism and antisemitic violence was integral to his socialist activism, not just in 1905, but in 1918 as well, including thereafter.[43]

In contrast, Sverdlov's political biography was largely free of any Jewish dimension. Born in 1885, just three years after Davidovich, he too threw himself into the 1905 revolution, as a committed Bolshevik. He did so in the Urals, far from the ravages of pogromist violence, where he led a local Soviet of Workers' Deputies. Sverdlov's estrangement from the Jewish world was not only geographic: he did not participate in the Jewish socialist movement in his youth, and nor did he encounter antisemitism during the formative period of 1903–1907. 'I never felt a nationalist yoke or was persecuted as a Jew', he once noted. 'In fact, during the first days of the Kishinev pogrom I felt nothing which separated me from the attitude of the non-Jewish population'.[44] Whereas Jewishness was a claimed identity for Davidovich, Sverdlov identified as Russian and married a non-Jewish woman.

In other words, when the Soviet government sat for the first time to discuss the question of antisemitism, it took the form of an exchange between the Jewish socialist Davidovich and the assimilated Bolshevik

against the physical and moral distress of our people, the rebellion against its utter passivity which had brought us together. Our bond was a great dream, the dream of a normal life in a Jewish land.' WORTA d17a001, 257.

[43] WORTA d07f144, 4. While in Kyiv in April 1919, Davidovich was appointed to the Foreign Delegation of the ORT alongside Leon Bramson. He immediately left for Minsk, a perilous journey which took him through pogrom-torn Ukraine and Belorussia. In his memoirs, Davidovich recounts his fear of being attacked by 'Petliura gangs' at any moment. Though he would eventually leave for Paris in March 1920, Davidovich's relationship with Soviet Russia was far from over: the World ORT continued to place the bulk of its campaign work on providing financial aid for Soviet Jews. In August 1921, Davidovich met with I. Rashkes of the Evsektsiia in Berlin to discuss relief aid to Jews suffering from pogroms. In 1926, Davidovich returned to Moscow to attend the first congress of the Society for Agricultural Settlement of Jewish Toilers (OZET), an organization established by the Soviet government to promote (both domestically and internationally) the agricultural settlement of Jews on Soviet territory. After moving to New York in 1939, Davidovich presided over the ORT's Emergency Committee. Following World War II, he returned to Paris, where he would remain until his death in 1950. WORTA d07a008, 26. See Miliakova, *Kniga pogromov*, 911; Estraikh, 'From Foreign Delegation to World ORT Union', 77–86; Estraikh, 'From Berlin to Paris and Beyond: The 1930s and 1940s', 123–24; Shapiro, *The History of the ORT*, 148; ORT, *The Hope and the Illusion*, 135–37. For a general history of the ORT, see J. Radar, *By the Skill of Their Hands: The Story of the ORT* (Geneva: World ORT, 1965).

[44] Riga, *The Bolsheviks and the Russian Empire*, 82.

Figure 2 David Davidovich (L'vovich), early 1920s.
World ORT Archive

Sverdlov: while the former elevated the issue, the latter, while certainly opposed to antisemitism, did not give it the same urgency. It was the non-Bolshevik Jewish socialist who pressed antisemitism onto the agenda of the Bolsehvik leadership. This dynamic would resurface time and again in the course of the Russian Revolution.

With the government still to make any public statement on pogroms, the leaders of the Moscow Evkom accelerated their efforts to initiate a Soviet campaign against antisemitism. On 19 April, the Secretary of the Moscow Evkom, Zvi Fridliand, wrote a pointed letter to the highest authority in Soviet Russia, Lenin's central Sovnarkom, to demand that the Soviet government respond to the sharp rise in antisemitism. Whereas the previous week Davidovich had raised the issue with Sverdlov almost apologetically, Fridliand, in his letter, went straight to the heart of the matter:

The Moscow Evkom has received information about pogroms in Hlukhiv (in which the entire Jewish intelligentsia was wiped out), in various parts of Vitebsk, and also about pogromist agitation in Petrograd and Moscow ... The government of the workers and peasants must do everything possible to prevent attempts at pogroms in Soviet territories [*vnutri strany*] and fight against the growth of antisemitism. The ommissariat for Jewish Affairs in the city of Moscow and the Moscow Region [Moscow Evkom] invites the government of workers and peasants to take, in front of the whole world ... the appropriate measures to ensure that all pogroms are put down. The defence of the honour and life of the peaceful Jewish proletariat is the cause of the international proletariat, *it is the task of the Russian socialist government.*[45]

On the same day (19 April), Moscow Evkom activist Il'ia Dobkovskii wrote a separate letter, this time directly to Lenin himself. Again, the severity of the situation was underlined:

The [central] Sovnarkom must once and for all put an end to this provocation [antisemitism] and *come out in its own authoritative voice with a resolute protest against pogroms* and those traitors to the revolution who want to build their own politics through it. The Jewish Commissariat, expressing the will of the Jewish workers, has a key interest in ensuring that all working people clearly understand who is responsible for pogroms and hence we ask you, respected comrade, to ensure that the fight against pogroms is put on the agenda at the next meeting of the [central] Sovnarkom.[46]

That same week, Fridliand authored another Moscow Evkom circular, this time addressed to the whole of Soviet Jewry, requesting that all information about pogroms be sent to the Jewish Commissariat. Interestingly, Fridliand added that all quieries regarding the Soviet response to antisemitism should also be directed to the Evkom.[47]

There are three crucial points to bring out from these interventions. First, it is abundantly clear that the impetus for a political praxis in opposition to antisemitism was emerging *not* from the central apparatuses of the Soviet state, but from the Moscow Evkom. *It* was pressuring the centre. Second, as the tone of Fridliand and Dobkovskii's letters clearly illustrates, the Moscow Evkom felt that the Soviet government was failing to confront antisemitism, so much so that, in Fridliand's case, he felt it necessary to 'remind' the Sovnarkom that it was *its duty* to do so. Third, it is instructive to look carefully at the ways in which Davidovich, Dobkovskii and Fridliand broached the complex issue of agency and responsibility for the 1918 pogroms. They did so delicately, making no mention of the uncomfortable fact that the pogroms within Soviet territories had largely been carried out by the Red Army. Fridliand,

---

[45] GARF f.130 o.2 d.212 1.1 (emphasis added). The document is also available in GARF f.1318 o.1 d.561 1.437; f.1318 o.1 d.22 1.125-125ob. Fridliand's letter was also published in the journal of the Jewish Commmissariat, *Evreiskaia Tribuna*, no. 1–2, 13April 1918, 12–13. See also Miliakova, *Kniga pogromov*, 754–55.
[46] GARF f.130 o.2 d.212 1.3; ibid., f.1318 o.1 d.555 1.485 (emphasis added). See also Miliakova, 755–56.
[47] See also *Evreiskaia Tribuna* no. 1–2, 13 April 1918, 12.

Dobkovskii and Davidovich certainly knew these pogroms were the work of the Red Army and local 'Bolshevik' forces.[48] When debating the issue among other Moscow Evkom activists just four days later on 21 April, for example, Dobkovskii and Fridliand framed the issue quite differently, and specifically identified the complicity of the Red Army in the spring pogrom wave.

Other efforts were made by the leading activists of the Evkom during this time. In the third week of April, Fridliand was involved in drafting a statement on antisemitism for the Central Committee of the Poalei Zion party, which was published in its main Russian-language newspaper, *Bor'ba*. In a tone similar to his aforementioned letter to Lenin, the statement demanded, once again, that the Soviet government come out definitively against the pogroms, and that meetings and protests be organized immediately.[49] Later that week, Fridliand was also involved in organizing a Poalei Zion meeting in Moscow in protest against the pogroms, during which he issued another public statement on the issue.[50] Around the same time, Moscow Evkom representative Dobkovskii met with Georgii Chicherin, the Commissar for Foreign Affairs, to discuss the spread of pogroms to Galicia and Bessarabia. During the meeting, Dobkovskii demanded that specific measures be taken by the Soviet government to protest against the violence.[51]

How, then, did Lenin and the Soviet government respond to these repeated appeals by the activists of the Moscow Evkom? On 23 April, Lenin's secretary, V. D. Bonch-Bruevich, responded to Fridliand and Dobkovskii's 19 April letters by inviting Dimanshtein's Central Evkom to enter into discussions with the Soviet government to develop a 'concrete list of measures for fighting pogroms and provocation'.[52] However, these discussions would not take place for another three months,[53] meaning that between April and July, with the Bolshevik leadership yet to take any action, the Moscow Evkom was left to develop a Soviet confrontation with antisemitism on its own. Even less successful was Dobkovskii's aforementioned appeal to Chicherin, which apparently went unanswered.[54]

---

[48] As noted above, the Moscow Evkom had been raising awareness about the pogrom in Hlukhiv since at least 11 April, and probably 7 April, by which time the Jewish press had published various articles about the role of the Bolsheviks in the Hlukhiv massacre and other outbreaks of anti-Jewish violence.
[49] *Bor'ba*, 1 May 1918, 35–36.   [50] *Bor'ba*, 1 May 1918, 37–38.
[51] *Evreiskaia Tribuna*, no. 1–2, 13 April 1918, 13.   [52] GARF f.130 o.2 d.212 l.2.
[53] RGASPI f.19 o.1 d.164 l.92-93; see also GARF f.1235 o.93 d.77 l.199.
[54] *Evreiskaia Tribuna*, no. 1–2, 13.

The Consolidation of a Soviet Response to Antisemitism: Mid- to Late April 1918

A series of requests to the VTsIK, Sovnarkom, Chicherin, Narkomnats and even to Lenin himself had all ended in bureaucratic delay or unfulfilled promises to draft appeals and set up commissions. The activists in the Moscow Evkom found a much more receptive and immediately proactive audience in the shape of the Moscow Sovnarkom. On 17 April, at the request of the Moscow Evkom, a meeting was held at the offices of the Moscow Sovnarkom to discuss the recent pogroms in Chernihiv and the sharp growth of antisemitism in the Moscow region. The first Soviet state response to antisemitism had thus been initiated in the Soviet capital, in the regional Moscow government. Unlike the previous attempts outlined above, this meeting produced a set of resolutions in which all soviets in the vast Moscow region (oblast') were instructed to hold special meetings explaining to workers the threat posed by antisemitism. Perhaps most remarkably, the meeting also instructed Feliks Dzerzhinskii and the Cheka – the single most authoritative body in the repressive state apparatus – to take measures against pogroms. That the members of the Moscow Evkom and the Moscow Sovnarkom, both peripheral institutions, felt able to give orders to the Cheka indicates the extent to which they saw themselves as *the* centre of the Soviet state response to antisemitism. The meeting further instructed Soviet newspapers to 'publish *all* proven facts about pogroms'. This was likely a veiled criticism of the failure of the Bolshevik press to make, by that point, any mention of the complicity of the Red Army and local Bolshevik forces in pogromist violence. More concretely, the meeting instructed the Moscow Evkom, together with the Moscow Commissariat for Military Affairs (also part of the wider Moscow Sovnarkom), to form a special commission for fighting pogroms.[55]

Four days later, on 21 April, such a commission was duly established, with Dobkovskii and S. M. Tsvibak[56] from the Central Evkom and A. Ia.

---

[55] Copies of the resolutions of the 17 April meeting are held in GARF f.1235 o.93 d.378 l.5; GARF f.1318 o.1 d.561 l.369; TsGAMO f.4619 o.2 d.148 l.1; f.66 o.3 d.865 l.8; f.4619 o.1 d.3 l.58. The resolutions were also sent to the Moscow Cheka and the Commissariat for Military Affairs: TsGAMO f.4619 o.2 d.140 l.25; f.4619 o.2 d.178 l.3. They were also published in *Izvestiia TsIK* on 28 April 1918; the Poalei Zion newspaper *Bor'ba* on 1 May 1918, 29–30; and in the Jewish newspaper *Razsvet* on 28 April 1919, 26. Several years later, the resolutions were again published in Agurskii, *Evreiskii rabochii v kommunisticheskom dvizhenii (1917-1921)*, 153.
[56] Not much is known about Tsvibak. In addition to being Secretary of the Central Evkom in 1918, he was also close to the *Soiuz Evreev-Voinov*, the Union of Jewish Soldiers.

Arosev[57] and Rabinovich[58] from the Military Commissariat appointed as its core members of staff. The newly formed commission issued a set of recommendations which were to prove deeply controversial, and which led to a heated debate on Bolshevik strategy on antisemitism within the wider Moscow Sovnarkom structure. The controversy pivoted around the Commission's insistence that special military units for the specific purpose of fighting antisemitism and pogroms be formed 'with immediate effect'. The units were to move from city to city, combating all forms of antisemitism across the entire region of the vast Moscow oblast'. Most controversially, the Commission stated that units, where necessary, could be composed in part, or even *entirely*, of activists from 'non-Soviet' socialist parties, 'so long as they are absolutely committed to the fight against pogroms'. In other words, this was an open call for Mensheviks, SRs, the Bund and other Jewish socialist parties who rejected the October Revolution to assist the Soviet state in confronting antisemitism. Accompanying this was the demand that commanders of each unit include representatives from the Moscow Evkom. The activists of the Jewish Commissariat were attempting to ensure that they would not only establish these institutions but lead them as well.

Most important of all, at the meeting of 21 April, Dobkovskii broached the issue of responsibility for the pogroms. In contrast to the delicate approach taken in his letter to Lenin on 19 April, Dobkovskii now stated that the 'soil is entirely fertile for antisemitic propaganda within the Red army, where the cultural level is low due to a complete absence of any political or educative work being carried out there'.[59] For the first time the specific problem of *antisemitism within the Red Army* had been stated explicitly within a Soviet state institution. Crucially, the Moscow Evkom

---

Apparently, he worked as a 'commissar' in the Union in order to bring it under Soviet control. See Miliakova, *Kniga pogromov*, 914–15. There is further evidence to suggest he was a Bolshevik by early 1918. According to one source, a certain 'S. M. Tsvibak' was a member of the Executive Bureau of the Bolshevik high school students' union, which worked under the Cheka for a brief period after the October Revolution. See A. V. Krasnikova, 'Studencheskaia organizatsiia pri Peterburgskokm Komitete RSDRP(b) i ee vklad v sovetskoe gosudarstvennoe stroitel'stvo v pervye posleoktiabr'skie mesiatsy 1917 g.', in *Problemy gosudarstvennogo stroitel'stva v pervye gody sovetskoi vlasti*, ed. Iu. S. Tokarev (Leningrad: Trudy LOIN, 1973), 76. I thank Gleb Albert for bringing this source to my attention.

[57] Alexandr Iakovlevich Arosev, born 1890, joined the Bolsheviks in 1907 and was a leading participant in the October Revolution in Moscow.

[58] It is unclear who 'Rabinovich' actually was. Most likely, it was 'D. Rabinovich' who worked in the Moscow Evkom during this period; GARF f.1318 o.1 d.561 l.298.

[59] TsGAMO f.4619 o.2 d.148 l.3-3ob; f.4619 o.2 d.25 l.129-129ob; f.4619 o.2 d.178 l.20; f.4619 o.2 d.177 l.2-3.

finally had a captive audience and a political platform from which to develop a Soviet response to antisemitism.

In an attempt to concretize these proposals, they were presented by the commission six days later to a session of the Moscow Sovnarkom on 27 April.[60] Unfortunately, detailed minutes of this meeting have not been preserved. However, what is clear is that the core proposal to form special military defence squads was flatly rejected. Instead, the 27 April meeting produced a new set of recommendations for confronting antisemitism, which were published widely in the Moscow-based Soviet press. In place of military units, the Moscow Sovnarkom proposed an alternative strategy based entirely on the politics of education and persuasion.

It proposed, for example, that 'systematic cultural-enlightenment work' be carried out in the Red Army, that the Moscow Evkom 'immediately' publish leaflets on antisemitism, and that the Soviet press carry regular articles on this issue.[61] These were not empty promises: throughout the remainder of April and May, a number of articles about antisemitism were indeed published in the Moscow edition of *Izvestiia*.[62] Most important of all, Rabinovich of the Moscow Evkom was instructed at the 27 April meeting to form a new 'commission', whose task it would be to coordinate educational work on antisemitism within the Red Army specifically. In a seeming rebuttal to Dobkovskii and Tsvibak's proposals of 21 April, Rabinovich's commission was to include *only* activists from pro-Soviet parties.[63]

The disagreements around military units notwithstanding, what is most striking about the resolutions passed at both the 21 April and 27 April meetings is that they specifically identified the Red Army as the principal, indeed the *only* section of Soviet society within which an antiracist politics was to be carried out. This was the Moscow Evkom's single most important achievement during this intensive period of campaigning around antisemitism: they had succeeded in pushing the question of Red Army antisemitism centre stage in the regional Moscow government. The resolutions passed at the 27 April meeting can be seen to have had some impact: the Moscow soviet immediately

---

[60] TsGAMO f.4619 o.2 d.148 l.2; f.4619 o.1 d.3 l.27; f.4619 o.1 d.3 l.19; f.66 o.2 d.69 l.54-55. An edited version of the resolution was also published in *Izvestiia Sovetov Rabochikh Soldatskikh i Krestianskikh Deputatov Goroda Moskvy i Moskovskoi Oblasti* (86, 1).

[61] TsGAMO f.4619 o.1 d.3 l.19; f.4169 o.2 d.178 l 8; f.4619 o.2 d.177 l.20; RGASPI f.272 o.1 d.71 l.8.

[62] The Moscow Evkom wrote to the *Izvestiia* editorial board in late April reminding it of its duty to publish such articles; TsGAMO f.4619 o.2 d.148 l.4.

[63] See RGASPI f.272 o.1 d.71 l.8; TsGAMO f.4619 o.1 d.3 l.19; f.4619 o.2 d.177 l.20; f.4169 o.2 d.178 l.7, 8.

telegrammed the core recommendations, including the instruction *not* to set up special military units, to all thirteen provinces (*gubernii*) within the vast Moscow region (*oblast'*).[64] The following month, on 15 May, the Tambov soviet replied, confirming that they had received the resolution and that posters had been put up around the city warning workers and soldiers that 'all attempts at starting pogroms will be put down and any person found guilty will be shot on the spot'.[65] The extent to which such threats were enforced by the local repressive state apparatuses, however, is not clear.

On 2 May, the Moscow Evkom invited the Central Evkom to the first meeting of the newly formed commission (now given the full title of The Commission for The Struggle against Antisemitism and Pogroms).[66] This was a key moment: the Central and Moscow Evkoms having entered into discussions around antisemitism, the Commission ostensibly had more reach and influence. The following day, on 3 May, the formation of the Commission was announced on the front page of the Moscow *Izvestiia*.[67] Over the course of the next four weeks, regular updates appeared in the same newspaper detailing the development of the Commission's work. For example, on 9 and 14 May, it was noted that the Commission had successfully initiated 'a widespread agitational campaign against antisemitism within the Red Army'.[68] These reports contained appeals to 'all proletarian organisations and individual educators [*lektory*] and orators' interested in participating in the commission's work to contact the Moscow Evkom. It is unknown how many responded, but by all accounts, the scope of the Commission's campaign grew extensively over the next two weeks: by 30 May, the Commission had successfully established a 'Board of Educators' within the Moscow Soviet's Department for Cultural Enlightenment, whose main task it was to move between factories and Red Army units, agitating on the topic of antisemitism. In addition, the board also scheduled courses on antisemitism for Party members undertaking training in agitation and propaganda. Further, by the end of May, it had initiated a series of educational lectures in agricultural, trade union and cooperative courses in Moscow, and plans were put in place to extend these to the surrounding provinces. Lecture themes included: 'Nation and Class', 'The Historical Roots of National Oppression and Antisemitism', 'The Jewish Working Class and

---

[64] TsGAMO f.4619 o.2 d.178 l.2.
[65] TsGAMO f.4619 o.2 d.26 l.130. It is not clear how local soviets responded in the thirteen other provinces.
[66] GARF f.1318 o.1 d.561 l.314.   [67] *Izvestiia*, 3 May 1918, 1.
[68] *Izvestiia*, 9 May 1918, 4; 14 May 1918, 6.

the Revolutionary Movement', 'The Role of Jews in Social Life' and 'Jews and the Economy'.[69]

The brutal events in Hlukhiv and elsewhere in the spring of 1918 had revealed that Bolshevism was not immune from antisemitism. During the same period, it also became clear that if a Soviet response to antisemitism were to emerge, it would have to be *actualized*. Such a response did indeed emerge, but the critical role was played not by the Bolshevik leadership, but by the non-Bolshevik activists of the Moscow Evkom. By the end of May 1918, they had had successfully established the first Soviet state institution dedicated to the confrontation with antisemitism.

The Dismantling of the Soviet Response to Antisemitism: May–June 1918

However, just as the campaign against antisemitism got off the ground, plans were put in place to dissolve the Moscow Evkom and indeed the entire Moscow Sovnarkom state apparatus. Since mid-April, Stalin had sought to do away with all regional commissariats for national affairs.[70] Moreover, since February, Lenin himself had also been attacking the Left Communist–dominated regional institutions of government in Moscow.[71] Following an intense political conflict between the two Moscow-based Sovnarkom governments in the wake of the signing of the Brest-Litovsk treaty,[72] Lenin's Central Sovnarkom eventually won out and the Moscow regional Sovnarkom was disbanded. The centralization process proceeded in stages: on 13 May, the Moscow Evkom was closed down by the Central Evkom (headed by Dimanshtein).[73] Two weeks later, on 28 May, the Moscow Sovnarkom itself was dismantled,[74] and by 21 June even the Moscow Sovnarkom's newspaper, the Moscow *Izvestiia*, was relaunched as a more explicitly pro-Bolshevik organ.

---

[69] *Izvestiia*, 25 May 1918, 3; 30 May 1918, 2; *Evreiskaia Tribuna – Organ Otdela Kul'tury i Prosvishcheniia Kommissariata po evreiskim nacional'nym delam*, no. 3–4, 3 June 1918, 12.

[70] GARF f.1318 o.1 d.1 l.7-9ob. See also Kozlov, *Arkhiv noveisheii istorii Rossii*, 18.

[71] Lenin, *Polnoe sobranie sochinenii, tom 35*, 399–407; Kowalski, *The Bolshevik Party in Conflict*, 121–37; R. V. Daniels, *The Conscience of the Revolution. Communist Opposition in Soviet Russia* (London: Harvard University Press, 1960), 70–91; L. Schapiro, *The Origin of the Communist Autocracy. Political Opposition in the Soviet State. First Phase: 1917-1922. Second Edition* (London: Macmillan, 1977), 130–46.

[72] For the Left Communists, the treaty was a betrayal of the revolution. So strong was the discontent that on 24 February the Left Communist–dominated Moscow Regional Bureau of the Russian Communist Party declared that it had 'no confidence' in Lenin's Central Committee and that it would refuse to obey any of the decisions that flowed from the treaty; Daniels, *The Conscience of the Revolution*, 76.

[73] GARF f.1318 o.1 d.547 l.1; TsGAMO f.4619 o.2 d.148 l.2.

[74] TsGAMO f.4619 o.2 d.28 l.18.

The institutions that had established and led the Soviet response to antisemitism were dissolved at the peak of their political practice, having been swept up in the wider drive towards centralization within the Soviet state. In a mere five weeks, a handful of Moscow Evkom activists had pressed the issue of antisemitism onto the agenda within each of the main Soviet state apparatuses (the VTsIK, Sovnarkom and Moscow Sovnarkom). What is more, they initiated and then led the first-ever propaganda campaign against antisemitism in the Soviet press. Above all, though, the Moscow Evkom activists were the only group in the central institutions of the Soviet government to take measures against the growth of *Red Army* antisemitism specifically.

The disbanding of the Moscow Evkom had immediate consequences: first, the planned campaign in the press was curtailed with immediate effect and no further articles appeared in the Moscow *Izvestiia* throughout the rest of the summer. The plan to have *Pravda*, the main Party newspaper, run a series of articles also failed to materialize. Indeed, with the Moscow Evkom now dissolved, *Pravda* failed to publish a single agitational piece on the topic of antisemitism throughout the whole of 1918. Above all, though, the demise of the Moscow Evkom led to the abrupt cancellation of the educational workshops and courses on antisemitism organized by the aforementioned 'Board of Educators'. The Soviet response to antisemitism had been brought to an end at the level of both structure and of agency.

We are confronted, therefore, with a deep irony: whereas in the former Pale, the centralization of the Soviet military and the creation of a centrally controlled regular standing 'Red Army' was crucial in preventing the Red pogroms, in Moscow those same centralizing tendencies led to the dismantling of the first Soviet campaign against antisemitism.

The Central Evkom and the Attempt to Reconstitute a Soviet Response to Antisemitism, May–July 1918

With the Moscow Evkom now disbanded, the Central Evkom headed by Dimanshtein took over Soviet Jewish work in Moscow. The Central Evkom was a small institution with a large remit. On the eve of its first conference in October 1918 it boasted forty-nine members of staff, yet the work of the commissariat extended across the whole of Soviet Russia and those parts of the former Pale under Soviet control.[75] After

---

[75] GARF f.1318 o.1 d.548 l.4-4ob.

Figure 3 First Conference of Jewish Communist Sections and Jewish Commissariats, Moscow, 23 October 1918. Zvi Fridliand is seventh from the left, third row.
From the Archives of the YIVO Institute for Jewish Research, New York

the closure of the Moscow Evkom in May 1918, the Central Evkom moved to establish a new Soviet campaign against antisemitism. In the first instance, Dimanshtein wrote to the Cheka to ask that a special department be formed within the Cheka itself to deal with antisemitism. Dimanshtein even suggested a name for such an institution: The Department for the Struggle against National Antagonism. We should note its universalist framing: Dimanshtein pitched this in general terms, not as a 'Jewish department'.[76] However, the request went unfulfilled, and no such institution was ever set up in the Cheka. Instead, the Evkom was left to establish its own apparatus, which it immediately began to do.

This process was helped by the fact that two of the members of staff from the dissolved Moscow Evkom were transferred to work in the Central Evkom. One of these was the aforementioned Zvi Fridliand, the key architect of the first Soviet campaign against antisemitism in

[76] GARF f.1318 o.1 d.563 l.465.

the spring of 1918. On 1 June he established a new Department for the Struggle against Antisemitism within the Central Evkom[77] (no such department had previously existed in this institution, this work having previously been carried out by the now defunct Moscow Evkom). According to Dimanshtein, it was Fridliand's initiative: '[H]e collected materials and developed concrete measures to direct a wide campaign to combat antisemitism across the whole of Russia – in the scale required for our times'.[78]

However, the project would be short-lived. On 6 July, the Left SR uprising in Moscow brought about an end to the period of coalition government and the expulsion of many 'non-Bolsheviks' from the state apparatus. Fridliand, along with other Poalei Zion activists, was subsequently removed from the Jewish Commissariat, and the recently established Department for the Struggle against Antisemitism collapsed.[79] Once again, the centralization process had interrupted the Soviet response to antisemitism. With no dedicated campaign in place and some of its key activists removed from government, the Central Evkom struggled to carry out any meaningful work in this area. Nevertheless, attempts were made to retain a Soviet campaign against antisemitism.

Following on the back of the activities of the Moscow Evkom, the beginnings of a campaign began to emerge in Petrograd. At the behest of the Central Evkom, a public meeting on antisemitism was held on 21 April at the 'Modern' Circus, with several members of the Jewish Commissariat giving speeches. The main attraction, however, was Zinoviev, who opened the proceedings.[80] In his speech, Zinoviev described antisemitism as a form of 'national hatred', 'implanted into the consciousness of workers' by the bourgeoisie. Zinoviev made no mention of antisemitism in the Red Army, but in a closing comment clearly addressed to Russian workers, he demanded that urgent measures be taken 'to kill off this deadly plague at its root' (*chtoby v zarodyshe ubit' etu gubitel'nuiu iazvu*).[81] This was, in fact, one of three speeches delivered by Zinoviev on the subject of antisemitism that week in Petrograd.[82] Concurrently, the Petrograd Soviet – headed by Zinoviev – issued a call

---

[77] GARF f.1318 o.1 d.555 l.33; f.1318 o.1 d.555 l.104; f.1318 o.1 d.561 l.104-104ob; f.1318 o.1 d.561 l.298; f.1318 o.1 d.561 l.276; f.1318 o.1 d.561 l.283. See also TsGAMO f.4619 o.2 d.148 l.21-21ob.
[78] S. Agurskii, *Di Yidishe komisariatn un di yidishe komunistishe sektsies* (Minsk: Gosudarstvennoe izdatel'stvo Belorussii, 1928), 14–15.
[79] Gitelman, *Jewish Nationality and Soviet Politics*, 139.
[80] A report in the Evkom's press noted that the meeting on 21 April had been arranged 'on the initiative of the Jewish proletariat'. In all likelihood, this meant the Evkom had played the key role. See *Evreiskaia Tribuna*, no. 3–4, 3 June 1918, 14.
[81] *Evreiskaia Tribuna*, no. 3–4, 3 June 1918, 14–15.   [82] Ibid., 12.

for contrubutors to write a series of ten pamphlets on pogroms, at least four of which saw the light of day.[83] Despite this brief flurry of activity, however, the campaign in Petrograd was not sustained and soon fell away.

On 22 July 1918, shortly after Fridliand was removed from his position, the head of the Central Evkom, Dimanshtein, sent a telegram to Trotsky, then Commissar for Military Affairs, to inform him that 'open pogromist agitation' was being carried out throughout the regions of the former Pale. What is more, Dimanshtein added that antisemites had taken up positions in local Soviet government apparatuses and that entire sections of the Red Army had 'succumbed to this pogromist agitation'. Soviet institutions on the ground, argued Dimanshtein, had quite simply failed to develop any response to antisemitism and were in fact even complicit in the problem. Dimanshtein's closing lines were revealing: '[T]he [Central] Evkom', he wrote, 'takes great interest in the fight against antisemitism ... and to this end it has decided to delegate its own representatives S. M. Tsvibak and Iu. A. Shimeliovich ... to make sure that the struggle against this phenomenon *begins*.'[84]

There are three important points to draw out from this short telegram. First, it is striking that Dimanshtein sent Shimeliovich and Tsvibak to these regions to *begin* a Soviet response to antisemitism: clearly, no such campaign had been initiated either by the central or local state apparatuses. Indeed, those local institutions were apparently themselves interpolated by antisemitism. Second, the telegram once again showed that the Evkom played an absolutely central role in putting the specific question of *Red Army antisemitism* on the political agenda. Third, the initiative for this political confrontation originated from the same network of Jewish socialists who had led the first campaign earlier in 1918.

---

[83] The titles of the ten proposed pamphlets were: 'What Is Nationalism?'; 'Are Jews the Enemy?'; 'The Tsar and Jewish Pogroms'; 'Who Are the Pogromists?'; 'Who Needs National Strife?'; 'The Arminian Question'; 'The Polish Question'; 'Down with Pogromists'; 'The Counter-revolution and the Pogroms'; 'How to Fight against Jewish Pogroms' and 'Nationalism and Internationalism'. The Petrograd Soviet committed itself to publishing the pamphlets at the 'cheapest price and in the widest circulation in the countryside among soldiers and workers no less'. See *Evreiskaia Tribuna*, no. 3–4, 3 June 1918, 12. In 1918, the following four pamphlets were published by the Petrograd Soviet on the subject of antisemitism and pogroms: M. Stogov, *Komu nuzhny pogromy?* (Petrograd: Izdatel'stvo Petrogradskogo Soveta, 1918); N. Gorlov, *Temnyie sily, voina i pogromy* (Petrograd: Izdatel'stvo Petrogradskogo Soveta, 1918); *Evrei, klassovaia bor'ba i pogromi* (Petrograd: Izdatel'stvo Petrogradskogo Soveta, 1918); *Vragi li evrei rabochim i krest'ianam?* (Petrograd: Izdatel'stvo Petrogradskogo Soveta, 1918).

[84] GARF f.1318 o.1 d.554 l.239; f.1318 o.1 d.412 l.1 (emphases added). This communication was reported in the Soviet Yiddish-language newspaper *Emes* on 13 August. See GARF f.1318 o.1 d.412 l.9.

78   The Soviet Response to Antisemitism, 1918

Tsvibak, if we recall, had been a member of the special commission established by the Moscow Evkom on 21 April, the commission responsible for the controversial proposal to form military units to fight antisemitism. As Dimanshtein's telegram to Trotsky illustrates, this network of activists continued into July 1918, and its reach extended far beyond the interior of Moscow and into the provinces of the former Pale, where antisemitic violence was most sharply experienced. But quite what impact two Moscow-based Jewish Evkom activists could exert in confronting antisemitism within the provincial apparatuses of the Soviet state in the former Pale remains unclear. If anything, the telegram revealed just how precarious the Soviet response to antisemitism was and how much it was reliant on a thin layer of activists whose work was continually disrupted by the trend towards centralization.

Lenin Responds: July 1918

It was on the back of Dimanshtein's 22 July telegram to Trotsky that the Soviet government finally moved to address the question of antisemitism. If we recall, a number of requests had been put to the Soviet government by the Moscow Evkom in mid-April, demanding that Bolshevik leaders issue an authoritative statement on the spring 1918 pogroms. Three months on, no such statement had been issued. On 25 July, however, three days after Dimanshtein's telegram to Trotsky outlining the threat of anti-Jewish sentiment within the Red Army, Lenin's Sovnarkom met to discuss the question of antisemitism for the first time. The meeting had immediate results: the following day, a Sovnarkom decree on antisemitism was issued to all regions of Soviet Russia,[85] and on 27 July it was published in the Soviet press.[86] This was a significant moment: a Soviet government's response to antisemitism had been set in motion.

It was Dimanshtein who had played the key role, not just in initiating the meeting, but in drafting the decree itself.[87] Crucially, it was endorsed by Lenin, who personally added its concluding sentence in red pen: 'The

---

[85] GARF f.1235 o.93 d.77 l.199-199ob.
[86] *Pravda*, 27 July 1919; *Izvestiia VTsIK*, 27 July 1918. The decree is available in English in Lenin, *Lenin on the Jewish Question*, 141–42. See also V. I. Lenin, *Polnoe sobranie sochinenii*, vol. 5 (Moscow: Izdatel'stvo politicheskoi literatury, 1967), 567–68; Lenin, *Polnoe sobranie sochinenii*, vol. 35, 666.
[87] Later in 1918, Dimanshtein wrote that the 'Jewish Commissariat' had drafted the decree; Agurskii, *Di yidishe komisariatn un di yidishe komunistishe sektsies*, 14–15. Writing in 1924 just after Lenin's death, Dimanshtein indicated that he had in fact written the decree himself, and that Lenin had proofread it; V. I. Lenin, *O evreiskom voprose v Rossii* (Moscow: Kooperativnoe izdatel'stvo 'Proletarii', 1924), 15. In the late 1920s, however, two competing interpretations emerged: in 1929, Lunacharskii claimed that the original

Sovnarkom instructs all Soviet institutions to take uncompromising measures to tear the antisemitic movement out by the roots. Pogromists and pogrom-agitators are to be placed outside the law.'[88] Shortly after, Dimanshtein proudly announced the significance of Lenin's addition: '[This] is a very severe decree ... that makes anti-Jewish pogroms punishable by death.'[89]

The extent to which this pledge was actualized, however, appears to have been limited, since in mid-1918 the repressive state apparatuses were in complete disarray, and consequently the promise to place pogromists 'outside the law' was unlikely to have been enforced in those localities where antisemitism was most pronounced.[90] More pertinently, the decree was issued in late July 1918, by which time the Bolsheviks had already lost those regions of the former Pale of Settlement where the Red pogroms had taken place. The impact of the decree on the ground was therefore negligible. Further, while Dimanshtein's telegram to Trotsky on 22 July had explicitly identified the problem of antisemitism within the Red Army and Soviet institutions, the decree passed over the issue in silence: instead, antisemitism was simply identified as 'counter-revolution'.

Nevertheless, the decree was important, since it marked the first intervention by the Bolshevik leadership on the question of antisemitism since the October Revolution of 1917. Moreover, it met one of the key demands tabled by Moscow Evkom activists back in April, namely that the Soviet government come out decisively against pogromist violence. In the existing literature this decree is usually cited as the first Soviet government response to antisemitism.[91] However, as the discussion here has revealed, the decree came on the back of three months of consistent political action against antisemitism on the part of the Moscow Evkom and Dimanshtein's central Jewish Commissariat. The decree, then, marked not the beginning but in fact the *culmination* of the first phase of the Soviet response to antisemitism.

---

draft was written by Sverdlov. See A. Lunacharskii, *Ob antisemitizme* (Moscow: Gosudarstvennoe izdatel'stvo, 1929), 38. Lenin's secretary, Bonch-Bruevich, claimed in 1927 and again in 1929 that the decree had in fact been written by Lenin himself. See *Ogonek*, no. 24, 1927 and *Krasnaia Niva*, no. 23, 1929. It is quite possible, however, that Bonch-Bruevich was overstating the role of Lenin long after his death.

[88] GARF f.1235 o.93 d.77 l.199-199ob; RGASPI f.19 o.1 d.164 l.92-93. See also Lunacharskii, *Ob antisemitizme*, 38.
[89] Agurskii, *Di yidishe komisariatn un Di yidishe komunistishe sektsies*, 14–15.
[90] Aronson, 'Evreiskaia obshchestvennost'' v Rossii v 1917-1918 g.g.', 132–33.
[91] Kostyrchenko, *Tainaia politika Stalina*, 56; Aronson, 'Evreiskaia obshchestvennost'' v Rossii v 1917–1918 g.g.', 132; Schwarz, *The Jews in the Soviet Union*, 274.

The Bund and the Pogrom Wave of the Spring of 1918

In May 1918, as the Soviet state was struggling to initiate its response to the devastating Red pogroms in Chernihiv, the largest Jewish Marxist party, the Bund, stepped into the fray. The Bund had famously denounced the October 1917 insurrection as outright 'insanity' and pure 'adventurism', and its opposition to Soviet power was well known.[92] At its All-Russian Conference in Moscow in mid-May 1918, the party leadership laid the blame squarely on the Bolsheviks: 'the pogroms in Hlukhiv, Gomel', Novhorod-Siverskyi, declared a resolution passed by the conference, 'are principally a consequence of the presence of dark elements who have attached themselves to the Bolshevik movement [*temnykh elementov, pristavshikh k bol'shevistkomu dvizheniiu*]'. Not stopping there, the resolution further blamed the Bolsheviks for 'creating particularly favourable conditions for the appearance of Jewish pogroms'. 'The growth of pogromist sentiment', it continued,

is feeding from the sharp dissatisfaction of the wide masses, hastened by economic ruination, hunger, speculation, unemployment and the unbearable political regime ... Bolshevik power deepens the economic breakdown of the country, deepens the civil war, and its politics and terror creates an atmosphere of anarchy and impunity.

In the face of seeming inaction from the Soviet state, the Bund initiated its own response by entering into discussions with the Mensheviks in an attempt to develop a joint response to antisemitism.[93] On 23 May, at a public meeting organized by the Petrograd Committee of the Bund, the Bundist V. Kantorovich made an appeal to 'all social democratic parties' to form a series of 'democratic institutions' capable of confronting antisemitism. The meeting ended with a resolution passed by an 'overwhelming majority' that restated the charge against Bolshevism for creating 'particularly favourable conditions' for pogroms.[94] Shortly after, the Bund's weekly newspaper *Evreiskii Rabochi* (The Jewish Worker) announced the formation of The Cross-Party Socialist Committee for the Struggle against Antisemitism (*Mezhpartiinaia Sotsialisticheskaia Organizatsiia dlia Bor'by s Antisemitizmom*). Consisting of representatives from the Russian Social Democratic Labour Party (the Mensheviks), the Bund, Poalei Zion, United Jewish Socialist Workers Party and the SRs,

---

[92] Anderson, Shelokhaev and Amiantov, *Bund*, 1103. On the Bund in 1917, see Meyers, 'To Dance at Two Weddings'.
[93] *Evreiskii Rabochi*, no. 2, 7. See also Anderson, Shelokhaev and Amiantov, *Bund*, 1124–25.
[94] *Evreiskii Rabochii*, no. 2, 8.

the committee set out to hold demonstrations, publish leaflets and brochures and establish educational courses on the theme of antisemitism.[95] This was, in effect, an attempt to reconstitute cross-party alliances that had been so crucial in 1917 (see chapter 1). And coming in the wake of the closure of the Moscow Evkom, it was an attempt to breathe new life into the socialist confrontation with antisemitism. It seems, however, that the initiative failed to materialize. Aside from a founding statement that appealed to 'all democratic organizations' to help assist in the work of the committee, it seems nothing came of the venture. The Bundist weekly *Evreiskii Rabochii* did not mention it again during the rest of the summer, and in the archives of the Jewish Commissariat there is not one single reference to the Committee. With the rapid drive towards political centralization in Petrograd and Moscow, it became increasingly clear that any comprehensive response to antisemitism would have to come through the apparatuses of the Soviet state.

The Central Evkom's Attempt to Reconstitute a Soviet Campaign against Antisemitism: October–December 1918

Yet for a number of months the Soviet government was not up to the task. Once Zvi Fridliand had been removed from the Central Evkom following the Left SR uprising in July 1918, his position as head of the Department for the Struggle Against Antisemitism remained vacant from August through to October. During this period, the Soviet response to antisemitism ground to a halt. The situation changed, however, in mid-October when the Yiddish writer Zalman Vendrovskii (also known as Wendroff and Vendrof)[96] joined the Central Evkom as a journalist. Vendrovskii had been invited to take up this post by Daniel Charney who, along with his older brother and renowned Yiddish literary critic,

---

[95] *Evreiskii Rabochii*, 8, 15–16.
[96] GARF f.1318 o.1 d.546 l.5-5ob; f.1318 o.1 d.563 l.207; Rossiiskii Gosudarstvennyi Arkhiv Literatury i Iskusstva (hereafter RGALI), f.631 o.6 d.251 l.27. See also: http://narodknigi.ru/journals/101/vozvrashchenie_zalmana_vendrova/. Vendrovskii (1887–1971) was born in Slutsk, Belorussia. After spells in Britain and America, he moved to Warsaw in 1908, where he became one of the best-selling Yiddish writers. In 1918, he settled in Moscow, where he took up a position in the Central Evkom. Vendrovskii struggled to carve out a publishing profile throughout the 1920s and 1930s. In 1950, he was arrested along with many of his Yiddishist colleagues, and served six of his ten-year prison sentence before being freed in 1956. He died in 1971. G. Estraikh, 'Zalmen Vendrof', in *The YIVO Encyclopedia of Jews in Eastern Europe*, ed. D. H. Gershon (New York: YIVO Institute for Jewish Research, 2008); G. Estraikh, 'Zalman Wendroff. The *Forverts* Man in Moscow', in *Leket: yidishe shtudyes haynt*, ed. M. Aptroot et al. (Dusseldorf: Dusseldorf University Press, 2012), 509–28.

Shmuel Niger, also worked for the Central Evkom at this time. Charney, Niger and Vendrovskii were anything but Bolsheviks,[97] and had all been fiercely critical of the October Revolution. However, by mid- to late 1918, a stratum of the Jewish cultural intelligentsia, particularly the Yiddishists, began to re-evaluate their position and see in the October Revolution an opportunity to extend and deepen the Jewish cultural revolution which had been in process since February 1917.

That they gravitated to Moscow, to the Jewish Commissariat, is no coincidence. After the October Revolution, Moscow had become the hub of Soviet Yiddish radical culture. From early 1918 onwards, a number of non-communist Yiddish intellectuals moved towards the Soviet state, and this collaboration took place, above all, through the Jewish commissariats.[98] As Daniel Charney noted in his memoirs, 'There was not a single Yiddish writer in Russia in those days [1918–1922] who did not pass through Moscow.'[99] Indeed, the central Jewish Commissariat led by Dimanshtein was initially located in the same building as a group of Zionist publishing houses. Evkom activists ate together with their Zionist neighbours in the shared kosher canteen.[100]

The institution that brought the Jewish and Bolshevik revolutions together was the Jewish Commissariat – the Central Evkom. As noted earlier, the Evkom desperately lacked skilled Yiddish-speaking journalists and editors.[101] Individuals such as Charney, Niger and Vendrovskii were employed not as revolutionaries, but as cultural 'specialists', and they arrived at a crucial time: the staff of the Evkom had just been reduced due to the expulsion of Poalei Zion party members.[102] Concurrent to this was the emergence of 'Jewish Sections' (*Evsektsii*) of the Russian Communist Party. Unlike the Evkom, which was located within the Soviet

---

[97] Niger and Charney were active in Simon Dubnov's non-socialist Folks Party, which advocated Jewish National Autonomy within Russia; Moss, *Jewish Renaissance in the Russian Revolution*, 218. Vendrovskii was not aligned with any political party but had been involved in anarchist and Zionist circles in Britain in the early 1900s; Estraikh, 'Zalman Wendroff', 509.

[98] Estraikh, *In Harness*, 37–45.   [99] Ibid., 41.

[100] Gitelman, *Jewish Nationality and Soviet Politics*, 136; G. Estraikh, 'Evreiskaia literaturnaia zhizn' v posrevoliutsionnoi Moskve: Moskovskii kruzhok evreiskikh pisatelei i khudozhnikov', in *Arkhiv evreiskoi istorii*, tom 2, ed. O. V. Budnitskii (Moscow: ROSSPEN, 2005), 190. According to Charney, 'the household harmony between the floors was extraordinarily good; while the Zionists upstairs eagerly studied every word of the Balfour Declaration, the Jewish Communists downstairs pored over Bukharin's *ABC of Communism*'; Gitelman, *Jewish Nationality and Soviet Politics*, 136.

[101] Charney, Niger and Vendrovskii edited *Emes*, the Evkom's daily newspaper, and *Kultur un bildung*, the first Soviet-Yiddish cultural journal; Estraikh, 'Zalman Wendroff', 510; Aronson, 'Evreiskaia obshchestvennost' v Rossii v 1917-1918 g.g.', 133.

[102] Estraikh, 'Zalman Wendroff', 510; Moss, *Jewish Renaissance in the Russian Revolution*, 217–20.

government, the Evsektsii were part of the Party structure. In practice, the distinction between the Evkom and Evsektsiia was marginal: Dimanshtein was in charge of both, and staff members moved between the two organisations.[103]

The gravitation of Yiddish cultural intellectuals towards Moscow and Bolshevism had important implications for the campaign against antisemitism. On 20 October Dimanshtein called the first Conference of Jewish Sections and Jewish Commissariats. Of the sixty-four delegates, thirty-three were non-Bolsheviks. A resolution was passed noting the 'sad and unfortunate fact that antisemitic elements can be found in Soviet institutions'.[104] The statement was published in the Yiddish Soviet press, but not, it seems, to Russian-speaking audiences. The conference also announced the formation of a newly reconstituted 'Department for the Struggle against Antisemitism and Pogroms', to be headed by the newly recruited Zalman Vendrovskii.[105] He set to work immediately: on 18 October, Vendrovskii wrote to all editors of the Soviet press requesting information on all cases of antisemitism, particularly those involving Soviet government officials.[106] On 14 October, Vendrovskii, together with Dimanshtein, made renewed efforts to establish a dedicated institution within the Cheka for combatting antisemitism. In their appeal, Vendrovskii and Dimanshtein complained that several Soviet governmental institutions, including the Cheka itself, had not done enough to confront antisemitism. Even more serious, the appeal pointed out, was that 'open antisemites' were occupying positions of authority within the Soviet government. To address the situation, Vendrovskii and Dimanshtein proposed that a 'Department for the Struggle against National Antagonism' be established within the Cheka. However, just as in May, the calls went unanswered.[107] All was not entirely lost: in November, Vendrovskii did manage to secure an agreement with the publishing house of the VTsIK to issue literature on antisemitism to the Red Army.[108]

Generally speaking, Vendrovskii's Department for the Struggle against Antisemitism and Pogroms did *not* pressure the central Party and governmental institutions to intensify the campaign against antisemitism, as its Moscow Evkom precursor had done in April 1918. Instead, under Vendrovskii's stewardship, the department was essentially reduced to an

---

[103] Gitelman, *Jewish Nationality and Soviet Politics*, 141.
[104] Agurskii, *Di yidishe komisariatn un di yidishe komunistishe sektsies*, 35–36.
[105] GARF f.1318 o.1 d.563 l.207. See also Agurskii, *Di yidishe komisariatn un di yidishe komunistishe sektsies*, 36.
[106] GARF f.1318 o.1 d.563 l.48.   [107] GARF f.1318 o.1 d.563 l.465.
[108] *Zhizn' Natsional'nostei*, 8 December 1919, 7.

information-gathering institution: Vendrovskii's main role seems to have been to maintain a weekly internal report detailing Soviet and international press clippings on pogroms and antisemitism both in Soviet Russia and the surrounding western borderlands.[109] Vendrovskii was a writer and a journalist, not a political activist, and the work of the department in late 1918 reflected this. Vendrovskii continued to work in the department until the end of the year,[110] but in early 1919 he left his position to become a journalist in the Commissariat for Transport.[111] As such, the Department for the Struggle against Antisemitism and Pogroms yet again fell by the wayside. This situation was compounded at the close of 1918 when the head of the Jewish Commissariat Dimanshtein left Moscow for Vilna to serve as commissar in the short-lived Lithuanian-Belorussian Soviet Republic.[112] The key individuals who had led the first Soviet response to antisemitism – Fridliand, Dimanshtein, Dobkovskii and Vendrovskii – had all now left the Jewish Commissariat. Once again, there was no Soviet state institution dedicated to confronting antisemitism, and as before, the political campaign ground to a halt. Indeed, this would remain the case until a new grouping of non-Bolshevik Jewish socialists entered the Soviet government in mid-1919. It was only then that a renewed and deepened Soviet confrontation with antisemitism re-emerged.

Conclusion

What we have come to know as the 'Bolshevik' response to antisemitism was the work of a group of *non-Bolshevik* Jewish radicals who coalesced around the regional apparatuses of the local Moscow Soviet government. Repeatedly, and often against great odds, they campaigned for and brought into being the first Soviet state response to antisemitism. And it was a response that depended, to a significant degree, upon the agency of a group of individuals who were deeply embedded within a *Jewish* socialist politics. Zvi Fridliand spoke in synagogues in Yiddish before Jewish workers[113]; his replacement, Zalman Vendrovskii, was immersed

---

[109] GARF f.1318 o.1 d.412 l.1-49. Vendrovskii was well placed to carry out this monitoring role: between 1917 and 1919, he also acted as the Moscow Correspondent for the New York Yiddish socialist paper *Forwerts*; Estraikh, 'Zalman Wendroff', 511–12.
[110] GARF f.1318 o.1 d.548 l.16.
[111] This is stated in an autobiographical note written by Vendrovskii in 1938: RGALI f.631 o.6 d.251 l.27.
[112] Estraikh, *In Harness*, 39.
[113] For a report of Zvi Fridliand speaking at a synagogue in September 1917, see *Evreiskaia Rabochaia Khronika*, no. 15 (21), 25 November 1917, 26.

Conclusion

in Yiddish literary circles and the international Jewish socialist movement. He was by all accounts a Yiddishist, not a Bolshevik. David Davidovich (L'vovich) was similarly embedded in Jewish socialism: his background was in Poalei Zion and then, later, the United Jewish Socialist Worker's Party. Never a Bolshevik, he was nevertheless the first to raise the question of antisemitism before the Soviet government in April 1918.

It is also instructive that nowhere in the founding documents of the Evkom was it stated that its activists would even take part in, let alone lead, the Soviet response to antisemitism.[114] That Moscow Evkom activists *did* choose to take the lead in this area is significant and reveals much about the nature of their approach to the question of antisemitism. To prefigure an argument that will be developed later, I suggest that their activism did not stem from tactical or instrumental considerations, but from an ethical spontaneity.[115] What is more, when Moscow Evkom activists did assume the role of developing a Soviet response to antisemitism, they did so by continually appealing *to* the central authorities to develop a more rigorous campaign. In 1918, the central authorities generally failed to respond adequately, and in the face of such inactivity, the activists of the Moscow Evkom developed their own campaign.

A crucial question thus emerges: Why did the central organs of Soviet power fail to elaborate an effective response to antisemitism before late July? An answer may lie in the profound nature of the crisis facing the Bolshevik leadership during this period. Throughout April and May 1918, Party leaders continued to believe that Petrograd was bound at any moment to be taken by German troops.[116] Even more pressing was the rebellion of the Czech Legion, which provoked a crisis so grave that Trotsky declared in July that the fate of the entire revolution was now under threat.[117] We here touch on a crucial issue that distinguished the Moscow Evkom activists from the Bolshevik leadership: for Jewish socialists such as Dobkovskii, Fridliand and Davidovich, the slaughtering of Jews was not epiphenomenal, nor was it a mere facet of the revolutionary process. It was *the* fundamental question in the spring of 1918, and it shaped their own engagement with the revolution during this period. For the Bolshevik leadership, however, the central issue was not the plight of the Jews of Chernihiv, but the survival of the Soviet state which, as noted

---

[114] RGASPI f.272 o.1 d.71 l.5; GARF f.1318 o.1 d.22 l.12; Agurskii, *Evreiskii rabochii v kommunisticheskom dvizhenii (1917-1921)*, 40.
[115] See Chapter 6.   [116] Rabinowitch, *The Bolsheviks in Power*, 241–42.
[117] Mawdsley, *The Russian Civil War*, 62–68; Rabinowitch, *The Bolsheviks in Power*, 242–43.

above, was by no means certain. In this context, pogroms were simply part of a much wider political crisis, and indeed they were not even the main source of that crisis. In other words, Moscow Evkom activists and Bolshevik leaders, despite whatever shared political ground existed between them, clearly attached different levels of importance to the question of pogromist violence.

The Soviet campaign against antisemitism in 1918 can therefore only be understood by situating it within the Jewish political world out of which it emerged. Whether Zionist or territorialist, these Jewish radicals were engaged in the elaboration of a Jewish national-cultural project broadly defined. They were of a generation born at a decisive turning point of modern Jewish history: the pogroms of 1881–1882.[118] They encountered a world transformed by the processes of rapid modernization and proletarianization. Unlike their predecessors, they studied not in the *yeshiva*, but in universities abroad, where they encountered not just sociology, philosophy and law, but revolutionary politics as well.[119] By the time they were young adults in 1905, they found themselves in the throes of revolution and antisemitic violence. Frankel captures it vividly:

They were extremely young in 1905, utterly committed both to the cause of revolution and to that of armed Jewish self-defence against pogroms ... By 1906, the revolution had absorbed their every waking moment, every ounce of strength and every hope. However, to them the revolution meant a struggle not only for social equality and political freedom, but also for national, for Jewish, liberation.[120]

There was an elective affinity between combatting antisemitism in 1918 and what Ken Moss calls the 'Jewish renaissance in the Russian revolution'.[121] That is to say, the story of how the world's first successful Marxist revolution dealt with antisemitism is, on close inspection,

---

[118] J. Frankel, 'The Crisis of 1881-1882 as a Turning Point in Modern Jewish History', in *The Legacy of Jewish Migration, 1881 and Its Impact*, ed. David Berger (New York: Brooklyn College Press, 1983), 9–22.

[119] Trachtenberg, *The Revolutionary Roots of Modern Yiddish, 1903-1917*, 40.

[120] Frankel, *Prophecy and Politics*, 329. For a brilliant analysis of youth and revolutionary experience in the Pale of Settlement, see I. Shtakser, *The Making of Jewish Revolutionaries in the Pale of Settlement: Community and Identity during the Russian Revolution and its Immediate Aftermath, 1905–1907* (Basingstoke: Palgrave), 2014.

[121] Moss, *Jewish Renaissance in the Russian Revolution*. For Moss, the Bolshevik Revolution 'violently altered' and ultimately closed down the avenues of cultural revival ushered in by the February Revolution. In other words, Moss locates the period of the Jewish renaissance between February 1917 and the Bolshevik seizure of power (which occurred in October of that year in Russia, and in late 1919 in Ukraine). See Moss, 10. The analysis here, however, suggests a slightly different reading: the activists of the Evkom, I suggest, should be placed *within* the framing of what Moss calls the 'Jewish renaissance'.

Conclusion

intimately bound up with a much wider Jewish cultural and national project involving diasporic Jewish socialists and Marxist Zionists, who temporarily set aside their aspirations for a Zionist homeland to contribute to the profound cultural and political revolution in Jewish social life in Soviet Russia. These non-Bolshevik Jewish intellectuals, as David Shneer has pointed out, brought their own cultural, political and ideological agenda with them into the Soviet state.[122] What the discussion here has shown is that they provided a vital resource of anti-racist agency that breathed life into the Soviet confrontation with antisemitism.

However, by late 1918, most of these individuals had been expelled from the Evkom or had moved on to other areas of work within the Soviet government. When the most ferocious wave of pogroms hitherto broke out in Ukraine in early 1919, the Soviet government was caught unprepared: its institutional campaign against antisemitism had either been dismantled by the growing drive towards centralization or had fallen by the wayside owing to a shortage of staff. As we shall see later, it was not until the summer of 1919, when of a new stratum of non-Bolshevik Jews (in this case, communist Bundists and Fareynikte activists) were incorporated into the Soviet government, that a renewed campaign against antisemitism fully emerged again. Just as in 1918, this group of non-Bolshevik outsiders played the crucial role in bringing to fruition a concrete Soviet response to the ongoing problem of antisemitism, and Red Army antisemitism in particular. They did so against the backdrop of the most extensive wave of pogromist violence in Ukraine yet, a period which also witnessed a ferocious growth in antisemitism within the Red Army. Once again, the Bolshevik response to antisemitism would be a response to the antisemitism of its own social base.

---

[122] Shneer, *Yiddish and the Creation of Soviet Jewish Culture*, 29.

4 Antisemitism and Revolutionary Politics: the Red Army in Ukraine, 1919

Introduction

The arc of antisemitic violence in the Russian Revolution peaked in Ukraine in 1919. Following the Bolshevik retreat in April 1918, a new Hetman government backed by the Central Powers was formed, with Pavlo Skoropadsky as head of state. The Hetman regime, however, was ousted in December 1918 by the Ukrainian uprising led by Simon Petliura and Volodymyr Vynnychenko, who formed the Directory government within a newly constituted Ukrainian People's Republic.[1] The Directory's existence would also be short lived: no sooner had it been established, the Bolsheviks commenced what became known as their 'second campaign' to retake control of Ukraine, which they did with relative ease.[2] On 3 January 1919, the Red Army secured Kharkiv, and by 4 February, just as in 1918, the Party was once again in control of Kyiv.[3] During the ensuing war between the Ukrainian Army and the Soviet Red Army in January and February 1919, a number of pogroms were carried out by Petliura's forces, most notably in Zhytomyr and Berdychiv in January, and, worst of all, Proskuriv (present-day Khmel'nytskyi) in February.[4] In the latter case, more than 1,650 Jews were murdered in just four hours by the Ukrainian Army following an unsuccessful attempt by the Bolsheviks to capture the town.[5]

---

[1] S. Yekelchyk, *Ukraine: Birth of a Modern Nation* (Oxford: Oxford University Press, 2007), 79.
[2] Adams, *Bolsheviks in the Ukraine*.
[3] Borys, *The Sovietization of Ukraine, 1917-1923*, 153.
[4] Gergel, 'The Pogroms in the Ukraine in 1918-1921', 241.
[5] Harvard University Library (hereafter HUL), f.3050 o.1 d.162 l.8. For further information on the Proskuriv pogrom, see Miliakova, *Kniga pogromov*, 47–70; Heifets, *The Slaughter of the Jews in the Ukraine in 1919*, 39–40. Reports in Menshevik newspaper *Nash Golos* (Our Voice) suggested that around 3,000 Jews were killed in Proskuriv on February 15. See V. G. Korolenko, *Dnevnik. Pis'ma 1917-1921* (Moscow: Sovetskii pisatel', 1997), 144. For an overview of the debate about Petliura's complicity in the pogroms of 1919, see C. Gilley, 'Beyond Petliura: The Ukrainian National Movement and the 1919 Pogroms', *East European Jewish Affairs* 47, no. 1 (2017): 45–61.

Introduction   89

Over the course of 1919, the Proskuriv pogrom became something of a touchstone for Bolshevik conceptualizations of antisemitism, since it seemed to confirm the Party leadership's assumption that the pogroms were necessarily 'anti-Soviet' as well as 'anti-Jewish'. However, as this chapter demonstrates, the reality of the political field in Ukraine in 1919 was far more complex than the Bolshevik theorization of antisemitism implied. Indeed, anti-Jewish violence found expression *across* the political divide, and no political formation remained unaffected by its structuring impact, including Bolshevism. The Bolshevik revolution in Ukraine had a very particular articulation with antisemitism. The initial source of the Bolsheviks' victory in Ukraine in early 1919 – the mobilization of peasants around a populist anti-bourgeois politics – would, by the spring and summer of the same year, come to be a key source of antisemitic violence in the region. The articulation of antisemitism and the revolutionary process, already prefigured in the spring of 1918, now presented itself even more sharply in 1919, and with consequences considerably more devastating.

It is important to once again underline, however, that Bolshevism was far from the main source of antisemitism in Ukraine in 1919. In fact, the Red Army was the least prone to pogroms of all the military forces in Ukraine. In his classic study, Gergel calculated that the Reds were responsible for 8.6 per cent of the Civil War pogroms, with the bulk of the atrocities being carried out by the Petliura and Denikin Armies (40 per cent and 17.2 per cent, respectively).[6] Yet, important though they are, these statistics offer only a snapshot of antisemitic violence, and they do not tell us anything about the nature and extent of antisemitic *sentiment* within the Red Army.

We need, in other words, a more granular analysis to uncover the presence or absence of antisemitism in the Bolshevik movement in Ukraine in 1919. This chapter offers such an analysis by bringing together internal Bolshevik security reports (*svodki*[7]), memoirs, newspapers and internal Party and governmental communications. In doing

---

[6] Gergel, 'The Pogroms in the Ukraine in 1918-1921', 248.
[7] Since the opening of the former Soviet archives, there has been fruitful debate about the limitations of internal Party, government and Cheka/NKVD reports (*svodki*), which ostensibly provide insight into the 'moods' of the Soviet population. These discussions have largely focussed on the use of such sources for the Stalin era. In contrast, the discussion in this chapter relies extensively on *svodki* from the earlier, Civil War period. Nevertheless, their limitations need to be noted. As critics have pointed out, these reports reveal less about popular opinions than about Soviet government perceptions of them. To mitigate this tension, Lesley Rimmel suggests garnering as broad a range of *svodki* as possible, including examples from both 'peripheral' and central regions. To an extent, the discussion here achieves this by examining *svodki* in each and every province of Ukraine

so, it shows that while the Red Army may only have been responsible for less than one-tenth of all Civil War pogroms, antisemitism was a considerable problem in the majority of Red Army units in Ukraine in 1919. Just as in the previous year, the Bolshevik confrontation with antisemitism in 1919 was principally a confrontation with the antisemitism of its own cadres.

The Ukrainian Social Formation in 1919

To understand how antisemitism found traction within the Bolsheviks' social base in Ukraine in 1919, it will be useful to offer a sketch of the Ukrainian social formation during the revolutionary period.[8] Ukraine in 1919 was a society markedly polarized by class and ethnicity. In urban regions, the working class was overwhelmingly drawn from Ukraine's minority ethnic populations, above all Russians and Jews.[9] Moreoever, those sections of the working class that were ethnically Ukrainian tended to be politically and culturally orientated to Russia.[10] In contrast, the vast rural regions were predominantly Ukrainian.[11] The first Soviet census of 1926 captured it well: while Ukrainians constituted 80 per cent of the total population of Ukraine, they represented a mere 4 per cent of the

---

for the year 1919. These reports were carried out every two to three days throughout the year by Bolsheviks on the ground, and they cover both rural and urban regions of the country. Nevertheless, to make inferences about the extent of antisemitism based purely on, say, Red Army *svodki* is problematic, not least because these sources tend to chart sudden sharp increases in antisemitism, and not the longer-term patterning of such sentiments. To balance this, the chapter also draws on newspaper sources and memoirs to broaden the analysis. On the usage of *svodki* in Soviet history, see T. D. Martin, 'Obzory OGPU i sovetskie istoriki,' in *'Sovershenno sekretno': Lubianka – Stalinu o polozhenii v strane (1922-1934 gg.), Tom 1, chast' 1* (Moscow: Institut rossiiskoi istorii rossiiskoi Akademii Nauk, 2001); L. A. Rimmel, 'Svodki and Popular Opinion in Stalinist Leningrad,' *Cahiers du Monde Russe: Russie, Empire Russe, Union Soviétique, États Indépendants* 40, no. 1 (1999): 217–34; P. Holquist, 'Letter,' *Slavic Review* 55, no. 3 (1996): 719; T. McDonald, *Face to the Village: The Riazan Countryside Under Soviet Rule, 1921-1930* (Toronto: University of Toronto Press, 2011); S. Davies, *Popular Opinion in Stalin's Russia: Terror, Propaganda and Dissent, 1934-1941* (Cambridge: Cambridge University Press, 1997); T. Johnston, *Being Soviet: Identity, Rumour, and Everyday Life Under Stalin 1939-1953* (Oxford: Oxford University Press, 2011), xliv–xlvi.

[8] The term 'social base' is used here to refer not only to Party members in the narrow sense but to the broader social forces on which the Bolsheviks depended to secure power in Ukraine. Significantly, this includes Red Army soldiers, many of whom were not Party members. In a context of all-out Civil War in 1919, Bolshevik power in Ukraine, wherever it existed, was largely a militarized form of statecraft.

[9] Borys, *The Sovietization of Ukraine, 1917-1923*, 70–71.

[10] E. H. Carr, *The Bolshevik Revolution, 1917–1923. Volume 1.* (London: Penguin Books, 1950); Riga, *The Bolsheviks and the Russian Empire*.

[11] L. Trotsky, *Trotsky's History of the Russian Revolution, Volume 3* (London: Sphere Books, 1967), 46.

industrial working class. Meanwhile, they totalled 91 per cent of the peasantry, and according to some historians, that figure may have been as high as 97 per cent in 1917.[12] Those who where Ukrainian by ethnicity thus frequently found themselves to be minorities in the major cities, and in no case did they ever constitute the majority of the urban population.[13] These dynamics had significant implications for class relations. Nationality, ethnicity and class frequently manifested as interlocking experiences, and consequently, relations between urban traders and peasants were intersectional in character: they were simultaneously processes of class *and* identity formation. In Ukrainian peasant popular culture, the 'cityman' represented a ruthless profiteer, an oppressor of the poor Ukrainian toiler. The crisis of the revolutionary period frequently provided the foil for these representations to come to the fore, particularly when the breakdown of exchange channels left peasants without vital manufactured goods such as boots, cloth, nails and ploughs.[14] In Ukraine, the national question was keenly felt at the point of production, and in particular in the realm of distribution and exchange.[15]

'Down with the Communists, Long Live Soviet Power!'

The political consequences of this were profound. Writing in early June 1919, the Bolshevik Nikolai Podvoiskii admitted that the Party's only real semblance of governmental power was in the capital cities of Kharkiv, Ekaterinoslav, Poltava and Chernihiv[16] – industrial regions located in the east and north-east of the country in areas heavily populated by so-called non-Ukrainians. These contradictions found expression in popular representations of Bolshevik power, which, in the eyes of many Ukrainians, was 'foreign' and 'urban'.[17] In the Ukrainian popular imaginary,

---

[12] Abramson, *A Prayer for the Government*, 16.
[13] Borys, *The Sovietization of Ukraine, 1917-1923*, 64–67.
[14] Adams, *Bolsheviks in the Ukraine*, 10.
[15] C. Ford, 'The Crossroads of the European Revolution: Ukrainian Social-Democrats and Communists (Independentists), the Ukrainian Revolution and Soviet Hungary 1917–1920', *Critique* 38, no. 4 (2010): 573. As the Bolshevik Nikolai Podvoiskii admitted in early August 1919, 'the distinction between the city and the countryside in Ukraine strongly exacerbated national oppression'; YIVO Institute for Jewish Research (hereafter YIVO), RG80 Folder 48, 3852.
[16] RGASPI f.71 o.35 d.691 l.2. Or, as the Bundist Moishe Rafes put it, the only 'genuinely revolutionary proletarian elements in Ukraine were to be found in the mass of the proletariat of national minorities – Russians and Jews'; Borys, *The Sovietization of Ukraine, 1917–1923*, 385.
[17] In its propaganda the Party tried to overcome the popular perception that the Bolsheviks were not 'Ukrainian'; see Tsentral'nyi Derzhavnyi Arkhiv Hromadians'kykh Ob'iednan' Ukrainy (hereafter TsDAHO) f.57 o.2 d.342 l.139.

'the Communist' was a construct defined by the intersections of class, ethnicity and place: Communists were urban, non-Ukrainians who stood aloof from peasant life; they were 'Russian oppressors' and, above all, 'speculating Jews'.[18]

These representations were taken up within revolutionary politics, particularly among sections of the radicalized Ukrainian peasantry, which in 1919 began to mobilize around the slogans 'We are for Bolshevik power but without Communists!' and 'Down with the Communists, long live Soviet power!' This emergent form of revolutionary subjectivity was closely connected to the politics antisemitism. Internal Bolshevik security reports show that across Ukraine in mid-1919, sections of the peasantry, along with other social classes too, were deeply attached to the Jew/Communist conflation.[19] The fight for the popular conception of 'Soviet power' often became associated with a fight against 'Jewish communism'.[20] In Poltava in late April, for example, peasants shouted 'down with the Yids, down with this Moscow Communist government, long live Soviet power!'[21] The spring and summer of 1919 would reveal just how entrenched these sentiments had become, including within sections of the Bolsheviks' social base.

The Composition of Red Army Antisemitism in Ukraine, 1919

To grasp the phenomenon of antisemitism in the Red Army in 1919 we must first outline the composition of the forces which fought, ostensibly, to consolidate the Bolshevik revolution in Ukraine. The Bolshevik victory in Ukraine in early 1919 was due substantially to the collapse of the Ukrainian Army, which decreased from 100,000 troops in December 1918 to a mere 21,000 by the third week of January 1919.[22] The contrast in the fortunes of the Red Army could not have been more marked:

[18] See, for example, RGASPI f.17 o.6 d.369 l.112-113, 248.
[19] TsDAHO f.1 o.20. d.35 l.11-12; Tsentral'nyi Derzhavnyi Arkhiv Vyshchykh Orhaniv Vlady ta Upravlinnia Ukrainy (hereafter TsDAVO), f.5 o.1 d.17 l.72.
[20] For the most comprehensive account to date on the overlap between left Ukrainian nationalism and antisemitism in 1919, see the work of Christopher Gilley, in particular: C. Gilley, 'The Ukrainian Anti-Bolshevik Risings of Spring and Summer 1919: Intellectual History in a Space of Violence', *Revolutionary Russia* 27, no. 2 (2014): 120; C. Gilley, 'Otamanshchyna? The Self-Formation of Ukrainian and Russian Warlords at the Beginning of the Twentieth and Twenty-First Centuries', *Ab Imperio* 2015, no. 3 (2015): 83–84; C. Gilley, 'Fighters for Ukrainian Independence? Imposture and Identity among Ukrainian Warlords, 1917–22', *Historical Research* 90, no. 247 (2017): 183–84.
[21] TsDAVO f.5 o.1 d.17 l.64.
[22] Ford, 'The Crossroads of the European Revolution', 587.

according to calculations by Red Army Commander Vladimir Antonov-Ovseenko, the Reds started out in late 1918 with some 7,000–8,000 troops, and by mid-February that number has risen sharply to over 46,000. This included at least 5,000 soldiers who had transferred directly from the Ukrainian Army to the side of the Soviet Army. Even more substantial were the numbers of peasant militias (at least 14,000), who now aligned themselves to ad hoc Red partisan units.[23] Although nominally Soviet, the Bolshevik leadership could scarcely be confident of their allegiance, let alone attempt to control them. The centralization of the Red Army, so vigorously called for by Lenin and Stalin in 1919, was simply impossible in Ukraine.[24]

In such circumstances, the Ukrainian Bolsheviks unsurprisingly leaned heavily on more reliable forces such as the International Division, a multi-ethnic regiment composed of Jewish self-defence units and Chinese, Hungarian, Austrian and German workers.[25] These regiments often played a crucial role in putting down pogroms carried out by partisan Soviet units. However, from February onwards, Red Army Commander Antonov-Ovseenko repeatedly lost his most reliable troops as the Party centre in Moscow ordered Red units stationed on the Ukrainian front to be sent to fight on the southern and eastern fronts, where Admiral Kolchak was making westward gains on the Bolsheviks. The Ukrainian Bolsheviks were therefore forced to accelerate the formation of new partisan units and Red Guard detachments.[26] Such was the scramble for troops, Antonov-Ovseenko was in no position to check and screen those who volunteered for the Reds. If partisans simply declared that they would fight for the Reds, that they would defeat the 'bourgeois enemy', they were admitted.[27] Writing in June 1919, Podvoiskii claimed that an astonishing 90 per cent of Soviet troops stationed in Ukraine were in fact composed of partisan and insurgent units.[28] In contrast to the first Bolshevik government of 1917–1918, which relied predominantly on Russian Red Guards, the second Bolshevik attempt to come to power

---

[23] V. A. Antonov-Ovseenko, *Zapiski o grazhdanskoii voine. Tom 3.* (Moscow: Gosudarstvennoe voennoe izdatel'stvo, 1932), 166–67. See also RGASPI f.71 o.35 d.507 l.79-82.

[24] Heifets, *The Slaughter of the Jews in the Ukraine in 1919*, 89–90; Adams, *Bolsheviks in the Ukraine*, 133. See also RGASPI f.17 o.109 d.43. l.16-19ob. On Lenin and Stalin's call to centralize the Red Army, see S. M. Korolivskii, N. K. Kolensnik and I. K. Rybalka, *Grazhdanskaia voina na Ukraine 1918-1920. Tom vtoroi* (Kiev: Izdatel'stvo 'Naukova Duma', 1967), 1.

[25] See Adams, *Bolsheviks in the Ukraine*, 147–48; I. Deutscher, *The Prophet Armed: Trotsky, 1879-1921* (London: Oxford University Press, 1970), 428.

[26] Adams, *Bolsheviks in the Ukraine*, 147–48; Deutscher, *The Prophet Armed*, 428, 439.

[27] Adams, *Bolsheviks in the Ukraine*, 148.   [28] RGASPI f.71 o.35 d.691 l.3.

in Ukraine in 1919 drew almost exclusively on a Ukrainian peasant social base.[29] 'Bolshevism' in Ukraine, noted Podvoiskii in August 1919, had taken the form of agrarian *partizanstvo*, not the dictatorship of the proletariat.[30] As the ranks of the Reds swelled, the Bolsheviks were now approaching the mass army required to consolidate power in Ukraine. Its political and ideological foundations, however, were deeply contentious.

The consequences of this soon became apparent. As early as February 1919, internal Bolshevik reports began to note the profound degree of antisemitism in various units and divisions of the Red Army.[31] By early April, reports indicated that *entire* Red Army divisions in Ukraine (such as the 2nd Division) were composed of troops formerly attached to the army of the Ukrainian Directory. Needless to say, such divisions were plagued by antisemitism.[32] On 5 April, Podvoiskii gave a start assessment of the situation facing the Bolsheviks: '[W]e have to our own detriment absorbed not only counter-revolutionaries, not only white guard scum, but even more so the masses of poor peasants [*bedniakov*] ... who, having been mobilised previously by the counter-revolution, have fled that camp and now joined ours.'[33] In sum, antisemitism had its basis in the overwhelmingly partisan composition of the Red Army in Ukraine: the worldview of the Bolsheviks' social base contrasted sharply with that of the Party leadership.[34]

Throughout March and April, the fragility of Soviet power was cruelly exposed as various partisan Red Army units rose up against the Bolsheviks. Ostensibly under the control of Red Army commander Antonov-Ovseenko, these rebel units were, in actuality, loyal to their charismatic, independently minded leaders – *otamany*, self-styled 'warlords', who frequently changed sides in the Civil War.[35] According to the head of the Ukrainian Soviet government, Khristian Rakovskii, between 1 April and 1 May, at least ninety-three uprisings occurred within the ranks of the Soviet Ukrainian Army.[36] As they attacked buildings where the soviets convened and shot Cheka agents, these rebels called for a

---

[29] Borys, *The Sovietization of Ukraine, 1917-1923*, 194, 201.
[30] YIVO RG80 folder 48, 3851.   [31] TsDAVO f.5 o.1 d.17 l.23-23ob.
[32] TsDAHO f.1 o.20 d.35 l.5-6. For more on the composition of the 2nd Division see Korolivskii, Kolensnik, and Rybalka, *Grazhdanskaia voina na Ukraine 1918-1920. Tom pervyi, Kniga pervaia*, 22.
[33] RGASPI f.71 o.35 d.507 l.80.   [34] RGASPI f.272 o.1 d.81 l.65.
[35] The name given to commanders of these partisan units – *otamany* – was a reference to Zaporozhian Cossack leaders from the Early Modern period, who were seen by Ukrainian nationalists as the true bearers of the Ukrainian national idea. See Gilley, 'Otamanshchyna?'
[36] Adams, *Bolsheviks in the Ukraine*, 233.

'Soviet power' in its populist sense, that is, local self-government without communes, without grain requisitioning, without 'Communists' and, above all, without 'Jews'. The uprisings revealed the extraordinary confluence between left populism, Ukrainian nationalism and antisemitism. Most threatening of all was the Grigor'evshchina of May 1919, the rebellion of Red Army units under the control of Nikifor Grigor'ev. These uprisings deserve close examination, for they reveal the depth of antisemitism within the Bolsheviks' social base during this period.

The Grigor'evshchina of May 1919

A former officer in the tsarist army during World War I, Nikifor Grigor'ev initially sided with the German-backed Skoropads'kyi regime, before then forming an alliance with the Ukrainian nationalist Petliura in 1918, where he commanded a number of partisan units in the south of Ukraine. In February 1919, however, Grigor'ev joined forces with the Bolsheviks, a defection which crucially opened up the front to the Red Army. At a time when the most reliable Soviet armies were being taken out of Ukraine and sent to the eastern and southern fronts, Grigor'ev provided the vital military resources needed to secure the key cities and regions in the Ukrainian south. His newly constituted Soviet unit – the 1st Transdneprian Red Army Division[37] – was huge, comprised of some 13,000–16,000 soldiers, many of whom described themselves as 'Bolshevik'.[38] Their 'Bolshevism', however, differed markedly from the politics of Lenin and Trotsky: in Grigor'ev's army, socialism meant a defence of peasant values and a support for direct self-government at the local level – in other words, the popular peasant conception of 'Soviet power', with all its attendant forms of contradictory consciousness.[39]

On 6 April, the same day that the short-lived Bavarian Soviet Republic was established in Munich, Grigor'ev proved his worth by taking Odessa

---

[37] This would soon be expanded to the 6th Soviet Ukrainian Rifle Division, again under the command of Grigor'ev.

[38] In his memoirs, Antonov-Ovseenko put the figure at 13,000, whereas Zatonskii suggests it was nearer 16,000. On 12 May 1919, in a telegram to the Ukrainian Sovnarkom, Antonov-Ovseenko estimated the number at 15,000. See Antonov-Ovseenko, *Zapiski o grazhdanskoii voine. Tom 4*, 131; V. P. Zatonskii, Vodovorot (iz proshlogo), *Etapy bol'shogo puti. Vospominaniia o grazhdanskoi voine*, ed. V. D. Polikarpov, (Moscow: Voennoe izdatel'stvo Ministerstvo Oborony, 1963), 157. T. F Kariaeva and N. N. Azovtsev, eds., *Direktivy komandovaniia frontov Krasnoi Armii, 1917-1922. Sbornik dokumentov*, vol. 2 (Moscow: Voennoe izdatel'stvo Ministerstvo Oborony SSSR, 1971), 202.

[39] Heifets, *The Slaughter of the Jews in the Ukraine in 1919*, 89–90; Adams, *Bolsheviks in the Ukraine*, 165. For information on the composition of Grigor'ev's units, see TsDAHO f.57 o.2 d.342 l.98.

from the occupying French and Greek armies. The head of the Ukrainian Soviet government Rakovskii could scarcely conceal his delight: 'Of all the glorious victories with which the Red Army has covered itself ... the taking of Odessa has the most worldwide significance ... Long live the Red Army of the Ukraine! Long live Red Odessa!'[40] Yet the 'Red Army' that captured Odessa was far from a Communist Army, and 'Red Odessa' was far from 'Bolshevik'. In actuality, the Bolshevik leadership in Ukraine were gambling the future of the revolution on a partisan and highly contentious social base.[41]

By the following week, Bolshevik intelligence reports began noting that soldiers in Grigor'ev's 6th Soviet Army were openly shouting slogans such as 'long live soviet power, down with Communists, all Communists are Yids'.[42] Although these reports were all sent to the Bolshevik Central Committee, the Party leadership continued to depend on Grigor'ev in the hope, as Commander of the Ukrainian Soviet Army Antonov-Ovseenko put it, 'that his military strength might be put to use'.[43] As late as 2 May 1919, Antonov-Ovseenko dispatched a confidential memorandum to the Soviet government, advising it to maintain close cooperation with Grigor'ev, even praising him as 'a local man' who has 'always stood up against the oppressors of the peasantry'. While acknowledging Grigor'ev's unpredictability, Antonov-Ovseenko asserted, 'it should be quite possible to keep him under control'.[44]

The gamble backfired. No sooner had the memorandum been sent, a ferocious wave of antisemitic violence broke out from the ranks of Grigor'ev's army. Buoyed by his recent victories, Grigor'ev now turned against the Soviet government, initiating the most deadly of all the Civil War pogroms. In just eighteen days his units, formerly attached to the Red Army and now in open revolt, carried out at least fifty-two pogroms

---

[40] Antonov-Ovseenko, *Zapiski o grazhdanskoii voine. Tom 3*, 249–50.
[41] Adams, *Bolsheviks in the Ukraine*, 201. For a Menshevik take on Bolshevik rule in Odessa following the capturing of the city by Grigor'ev's troops, see V. Brovkin, *Dear Comrades: Menshevik Reports on the Bolshevik Revolution and the Civil War* (Stanford: Hoover Press, 1991), 167–70.
[42] Bolshevik reports from mid-April detailing the extent of antisemitism within Grigor'ev's units are discussed in Antonov-Ovseenko, *Zapiski o grazhdanskoii voine. Tom 4*, 75–80. See also TsDAVO f.5. o.1 d.17 l.55. Some reports sounded the alarm bell as early as late March. A briefing by a political inspector for the Commissariat of Military Affairs on 29 March, for example, noted that there was no political work being carried out among Grigor'ev's troops, and that antisemitism was rampant; S. M. Korolivskii, N. K. Kolensnik and I. K. Rybalka, *Grazhdanskaia voina na Ukraine 1918-1920. Tom pervyi, Kniga vtoraia* (Kiev: Izdatel'stvo 'Naukova Duma', 1967), 278, 332.
[43] Antonov-Ovseenko, *Zapiski o grazhdanskoii voine. Tom 4*, 79.
[44] V. P. Butt et al., eds., *The Russian Civil War: Documents from the Soviet Archives* (New York: Palgrave Macmillan, 1996), 84–85.

in which more than 3,400 Jews were murdered.[45] Although representing only a fraction of the total number of Jews killed in 1919, these massacres were distinguished by having the highest fatality rate of all the Civil War pogroms.[46]

Despite a flurry of Party and Soviet government decrees ordering Grigor'ev's troops to be shot on the spot,[47] the apparatuses of Soviet power in Ukraine were in no position to enforce these orders, such was their lack of centralization and inability to rely on local forces. The seriousness of the situation was underlined when one of the most dependable Soviet regiments, the 1st Regiment of Red Cossacks, was pulled out of Kyiv and sent to fight Grigor'ev at Kremenchuk. En route, it attacked Cheka units and started a pogrom in Lubny under the slogan 'death to the Yids and Communists'.[48]

The Confluence of Antisemitism and Revolutionary Politics in Ukraine

What the Grigor'evshchina revealed was the startling extent to which Bolshevik revolutionary discourse could overlap with antisemitic conceptions of Jewishness, and with such devastating consequences. To give an illustration, on 29 March, on the eve of his advance into Odessa, Grigor'ev issued a telegram to all Volunteer Army soldiers to 'throw your generals into the sea, raise the Red Flag, put down your weapons and in place of 'God Save the Tsar', come with us peacefully and sing 'Arise, Arise, Working People' [the opening lines of the chorus to the Russian version of *The Worker's Marseillaise*]'.[49] Just six weeks later, however, in a

---

[45] Grigor'ev's troops carried out pogroms in Zlatopol (2–5 May), Znamenka (3 May), Lebedyn (5 May), Gorodishche (11–12 May), Zolotonosha (12 May), Rotmistrivka (13–14 May), Matusovo (13–14 May); Belozerie (14–15 May), Smila (14–15 May), Elisavetgrad (15–17 May), Novomyrhorod (17 May), Cherkasy (16–21 May), Raihorod (20 May), Oleksandriia (22 May), Chyhyryn (25 May), Oleksandrivka (15–18 May), Stepanivka (18 May) and Semonivka (18–19 May). See HUL f.3050 o.1 d.162 l.4 See also Heifets, *The Slaughter of the Jews in the Ukraine in 1919*, 70 and S. I. Gusev-Orenburgskii, *Kniga o evreiskikh pogromakh na Ukraine v 1919 g. Sostavlena po ofitsial'nym dokumentam, dokladam s mest i oprosam postradavshikh* (St. Peterburg-Berlin: Izdatel'stvo Z. I. Grzhebina, 1921), 10; S. I. Gusev-Orenburgskii, *Bagrovaia kniga. Pogromy 1919-1920 gg. na Ukraine* (New York: Ladoga, 1983), 7. Other reports estimate the total number of Jews murdered in the Grigor'evshchina at 6,000. See RGASPI f.272 o.1 d.81 l.92.
[46] Gergel, 'The Pogroms in the Ukraine in 1918-1921', 250.
[47] RGASPI f.71 o.35 d.500 l.38; TsDAHO f.57 o.2 d.305 l.39, 45-46; TsDAHO f.57 o.2 d.342 l.85-86; Korolivskii, Kolesnik and Rybalka, *Grazhdanskaia voina na Ukraine 1918-1920. Tom pervyi, Kniga pervaia*, 33, 48.
[48] TsDAVO f.5 o.1 d.19 l.5.   [49] Adams, *Bolsheviks in the Ukraine*, 190.

dramatic declaration of war against the Soviet state, Grigor'ev issued his defining statement, known as the *Universal*:

> 'Ukrainian people! ... The political speculators have deceived you and, with clever methods, have taken advantage of your trustfulness. In place of land and freedom they have subjected you to the commune, to the Cheka, and to the commissars, those gluttonous Muscovites from the land where they crucified Christ ... Holy Toiler! Man of God! Look at your calloused hands and look around! Injustice! You are the Tsar of the land ... but who governs you? All those who desire the blood of the people ... Down with the political speculators! ... Long live the power of the soviets of the people of Ukraine!'[50]

As part of a wider attack on a range of 'exploiters' of the peasants, Grigor'ev was expressing a non-referential antisemitism. 'The Jews' were not named explicitly, but the key signifiers of an antisemitic discourse were all in place: the Ukrainians had been 'deceived' by a people more 'clever' than them; the spectre of the 'bloodsucker' was invoked; the 'honest' workers with 'calloused hands' are ruled by 'Christ killers' and speculators. Here we see the signification of a well-worn antisemitic conception of 'labour': in contrast to the 'non-productive' Jew stands the 'real' toiler, the oppressed, the authentic bearer of 'concrete', 'productive' labour: the Ukrainian peasant, who, unlike 'the Jew', has an 'organic' relation to the land and the nation.[51] Later, in the same declaration, Grigor'ev demanded the formation of new soviets based effectively on the notorious *numerus clausus* quota system[52]: 80 per cent of places in the soviets were to be reserved for ethnic Ukrainians, and Jews were to be allocated no more than 5 per cent. This is but one illustration of the explosive capacity for revolutionary discourse and populist anti-bourgeois sentiment in 1919 Ukraine to be expressed through antisemitism.

Later, towards the end of his uprising in late May 1919, Grigor'ev's antisemitism came into full view as he openly attacked what he called the 'Yid' Soviet government. Yet his antisemitism remained wedded to a left populist discourse. In a series of leaflets addressed to Red Army soldiers, workers and peasants, Grigor'ev proclaimed in one breath 'Long live world socialist revolution, long live the International' while in another he

---

[50] Antonov-Ovseenko, *Zapiski o grazhdanskoii voine. Tom 4*, 203–04.
[51] M. Postone, 'Anti-Semitism and National Socialism: Notes on the German Reaction to 'Holocaust'', *New German Critique*, no. 19 (1 January 1980): 97–115.
[52] The *numerous clausus* was a quota system introduced in tsarist Russia between 1882 and 1887, which set entry levels for Jews in education and various other professions at 5–10%; B. Nathans, *Beyond the Pale: The Jewish Encounter with Late Imperial Russia* (Berkeley: University of California Press, 2002), 262–67.

called on his troops to attack Bolshevik commissars, 99 per cent of whom, he claimed, were 'Yids'.[53]

Grigor'ev's rebellion illustrates that the lines of demarcation between revolutionary and counter-revolutionary, so clear in Bolshevik propaganda,[54] were, in actuality, fluid and porous. Radicalized peasants and workers moved between these categories. Grigor'ev was, in part, drawing upon the same experiential triggers that the Bolsheviks themselves had mobilized earlier in the year: class injustices, the desire for local control, left-populist resentment. What is more, Grigor'ev was recruiting from the very social base that the Bolsheviks had mobilized to come to power in the first place. In other words, antisemitism provided a nexus that enabled people to move between the seemingly antithetical categories of revolution and counter-revolution. The following two case studies in Elisavetgrad and Uman' provide a vivid illustration of this.

Elisavetgrad, May 1919

In 15–18 May, one of the most ferocious pogroms of the spring and summer of 1919 took place in Elisavetgrad, a city in central Ukraine in the north of the Kherson region. Surrounded by a large peasant population, the city was home to the Elvorti agricultural equipment factory, which in 1917 employed more than 7,000 workers[55]. In March 1919, the local Soviet state apparatuses were controlled largely by the Left SRs who, according to Bolshevik internal reports, frequently accused the Soviet government of being 'a government of Yids'. However, such sentiments were hardly restricted to the Left SRs: the same reports note that the head of the local *ispolkom* (executive committee), a Bolshevik named Ul'ianov,[56] campaigned for Jews to be removed from local government and replaced by Orthodox Christians.[57] The dynamic in

---

[53] TsDAHO f.5 o.1 d.265 l.1341, 1346-1347. In one document, Grigor'ev denounces the 'people's provocateurs Rakovskii, Rafes and Bronshtein Trotsky', whose rule has led 'eighty percent of the labouring peasants of the land of Ukraine to fall in to the hands of a few little Yids (*zhidki*) and political speculators'; TsDAHO f.5 o.1 d.265 l.1349. I thank Dimitri Tolkatsch for bringing these documents to my attention. Grigor'ev's leaflets around this time are also discussed in Gilley, 'The Ukrainian Anti-Bolshevik Risings of Spring and Summer 1919', 121.

[54] For an appeal by the Odessa Bolsheviks against the Grigor'ev pogroms, see R. Wade, ed., *Documents of Soviet History. Volume 1. The Triumph of Bolshevism, 1917-1921* (New York: Academic International Press, 1991), 384–85.

[55] www.chervonazirka.com/index.php?part=static&cname=about (accessed 24 June 2019).

[56] 'Ul'ianov' was apparently expelled from the Russian Communist Party in early 1919 but made his way back into Party work by moving to Elisavetgrad. TsDAHO f.1 o.20 d.91 l.25.

[57] TsDAHO f.1 o.20 d.35 l.1.

the soviet did not fare much better: throughout February and March, there were speeches repeatedly demanding that the Jews be expelled from the soviet or pogroms would ensue.[58] In one particular session of the soviet, seventeen of its representatives debated for four and a half hours whether or not to 'beat the Jews', before finally resolving to vote in the negative.[59] Evidently, there were serious problems concerning antisemitism in Elisavetgrad *before* the arrival of Grigor'ev's troops.

In mid-April, 3,000 of Grigor'ev's partisans arrived in Elisavetgrad,[60] and by 10 May they had succeeded in dissolving the local Soviet government. Grigor'ev's aforementioned *Universal* to the 'Ukrainian people', which depicted the Bolsheviks as 'Christ killers', was now plastered around the town. In a desperate attempt to hang on to power, a Soviet division of sailors from Odessa was sent to Elisavetgrad. Although they succeeded initially, when Grigor'ev's troops returned on 15 May, many defected. Later that day, the very same Red sailors participated in a vicious pogrom in which at least 1,526 Jews were murdered.[61]

On the morning of the pogrom, a committee of trade unionists, metalworkers and members of the local Peasant Congress tried to put a stop to the massacre by forming armed detachments. The working class, however, was significantly divided on the issue. On 20 May, the local social democratic newspaper *Nasha Zhizn'* (Our Life) reported that the pogrom had in fact been carried out not only by Grigor'ev units and Red sailors, but by workers as well.[62] Internal Bolshevik reports also indicate that those Communists who refused to change sides and continued to fight against Grigor'ev (the bulk of whom were Jewish) were rounded up and shot by workers from the local Elvorti factory, the same factory from which the Bolsheviks had drawn their support throughout the preceding months.[63] To make matters worse, local members of the Party who

---

[58] OKK, *Gody bor'by. Sbornik materialov po istorii revoliutsionnogo dvizheniia na Zinov'evshchine* (Zinov'evsk: Okruzhnaia oktiabr'skaia komissiia, 1927), 78.

[59] Gitelman, *Jewish Nationality and Soviet Politics*, 165.

[60] Antonov-Ovseenko, *Zapiski o grazhdanskoii voine. Tom 4*, 78. Grigor'ev's unit was composed almost exclusively of peasants from the Kherson region. See HUL f.3050 o.1 d.130 l.1.

[61] HUL f.3035 o.1 d.130 l.1; TsDAHO f.1 o.20 d.91 l.25. See also Heifets, *The Slaughter of the Jews in the Ukraine in 1919*, 244–45; E. B. Bosh, *God bor'by: Bor'ba za vlast' na Ukraine s aprelia 1917 g. do nemnetskoi okkupatsii* (Moscow: Gosudarstvennoe izdatel'stvo, 1925), 89. The figure of 1,526 is from a report by the Russian Red Cross: HUL f.3050 o.1 d.162 l.8. Other reports, however, put the figure at 3,000; RGASPI f.71 o.35 d.486 l.412-413.

[62] HUL f.3050 o.1 d.130 l.33. One report even claimed that up to 75% of the pogromists were workers; HUL f.3050 o.1 d.130 l.12ob.

[63] TsDAHO f.1 o.20 d.91 l.25.

stayed following the arrival of Grigor'ev's units *also* took part in the pogrom.[64]

As is clear, antisemitism was a problem that crossed the military and political divide in Elizavetgrad. As one local Communist admitted in a frank and revealing telegram written in late June, 'the entire work of Elisavetgrad Soviet institutions ... including the Communists, is fundamentally compromised'.[65]

Uman', May–July 1919

Even more shocking were the events that unfolded in the struggle for power in Uman', a mid-sized town in central Ukraine in what was then the Kyiv province (now Cherkasy oblast'). Its population in 1919 was around 60,000–65,000, the majority of whom were Jewish (approximately 35,000), with Russians and Ukrainians together making up 22,000.[66] Soviet power was established in Uman' on the evening of 11 March, when partisan units of the 8th Ukrainian Soviet Regiment pushed out the Directory army. Almost immediately, the same Soviet units engaged in an extensive pogrom that was only brought to an end by the arrival of a second Soviet detachment.[67] Following a brief occupation of the city by Ukrainian Cossack insurgents, who were no friends of the Jews,[68] the pogrom-prone 8th Soviet Regiment again took the city on 22 March. Antisemitism was not confined to the Red Army, but was present in the local organs of Soviet power as well. Within the Executive Committee, Left SRs succeeded in expelling Jews from office. They did so by making the now familiar charge that true 'soviet power' had been taken out of the hands of the 'toilers' and sabotaged by 'strangers' and 'foreigners' – in other words, Jews. Around the same time, an antisemitic campaign was also initiated by the local Ukrainian and Russian population in Uman', who accused 'Bolshevik Yids' of closing down Orthodox churches.[69]

This was the background to the arrival of Grigor'ev's troops on 12 May. The political field in Uman' was one in which ostensibly pro-Bolshevik Red soldiers carried out pogroms; pro-soviet Left SRs successfully campaigned for the expulsion of Jews from the Executive

---

[64] TsDAHO f.1 o.20 d.91 l.25.   [65] TsDAHO f.1 o.20 d.91 l.25ob.
[66] Heifets, *The Slaughter of the Jews in the Ukraine in 1919*, 316.
[67] I have been unable to determine which Soviet regiment this was.
[68] According to a report of the Russian Red Cross, the Cossacks had murdered 300 Jews in the town of Teplik. On arrival, they threatened to do the same in Uman', but were apparently persuaded not to on the payment of contributions in kind in the shape of shoes, money and other garments. Miliakova, *Kniga pogromov*, 129.
[69] Miliakova, *Kniga pogromov*, 118–19; Gusev-Orenburgskii, *Bagrovaia kniga*, 83–85.

Committee; and sections of the local population waged a populist campaign against the 'Yid Soviet power'. Antisemitism traversed the political divide in Uman' in 1919.

When Grigor'ev's insurgents arrived and deposed the local Soviet government, they initiated a ferociously violent pogrom in which at least 300 Jews were murdered.[70] In some cases, well-known Soviet officials joined Grigor'ev's troops in carrying out the assault.[71] The pogrom was finally brought to an end on the morning of 22 May by the arrival of the 7th Soviet Regiment.[72] However, just three days later the 7th Regiment was pulled out of Uman' by the central authorities to put down uprisings in the surrounding provinces, and in its place returned the dreaded 8th Soviet Ukrainian Regiment, the same unit responsible for the pogrom in March.[73] With its return came a new wave of pogromist violence every bit as brutal as first. Reports by the Russian Red Cross in Ukraine[74] give details of armed Red soldiers stopping civilians on the street, asking, 'Are you a Yid?' Those who did not answer convincingly were mercilessly beaten.[75] Jews who risked appearing in public to go to synagogue had to run a gauntlet of soldiers from the 8th Soviet Army, who would stand outside shouting, 'Who is your god?'[76]

The situation in Uman' is illustrative not only of the extent of antisemitism within sections of the Red Army but also of the inability of the Soviet government to deal with antisemitic violence, even when there was a desire

---

[70] P. F. Kurinnyi, *Uman' ta umanchany ochyma P. F. Kurinnoho (z osobystykh shchodennikiv za 1918-1929 hh.)*, (Uman: uman'skyi kraieznavchyi muzei, 2014), 208. I thank Dimitri Tolkatsch and Igor Opatskiy for bringing this source to my attention. Reports compiled by the Russian Red Cross in Ukraine detail entire families being massacred and tortured, with hands, feet, ears, noses and women's breasts cut off. See Miliakova, *Kniga pogromov*, 122.

[71] Miliakova, *Kniga pogromov*, 124.

[72] According to the Ukrainian Left SR newspaper *Bor'ba*, Soviet troops did not arrive in Uman' until 23 May; RGASPI f.71 o.35 d.486 1.217-219. However, a memoir from a local Uman' lawyer suggests the Red Army arrived at 9 o'clock on the morning of 22 May. See Kurinnyi, *Uman' ta umanchany ochyma P. F. Kurinnoho (z osobystykh shchodennikiv za 1918-1929 hh.)*, 205.

[73] This was an enlarged 8th Regiment now totalling some 2,100 troops; RGASPI f.71 o.35 d.498 l.167ob. Just two weeks earlier the regiment had carried out a pogrom in Gaisin, a town in central Ukraine Committee of the Jewish Delegations. *The Pogroms in the Ukraine under the Ukrainian Governments (1917–1920). Historical Survey with Documents and Photographs.* (London: John Bale, Sons and Danielsson, ltd. 1927), 228, 232.

[74] The Russian Red Cross was legalized by the Ukrainian Soviet government in 1919 and was allowed to exist until 1921. See Miliakova, *Kniga pogromov*, 849. In mid-late 1919, it carried out extensive investigations into pogroms and collected testimonies by survivors and witnesses. See, for example, the files in TsDAHO f.1 o.20 d.126.

[75] Miliakova, 126. See also Kurinnyi, *Uman' ta umanchany ochyma P. F. Kurinnoho (z osobystykh shchodennikiv za 1918-1929 hh.)*, 209.

[76] J. Veidlinger, *Pogrom: The Origins of the European Genocide of the Jews* (New York: Metropolitan Books, 2020), 282.

to do so at the local level. As the pogrom raged from 22 May onwards, local Communist Party cells tried to fight the 8th Soviet Regiment, and several orders making pogroms punishable by death were issued. While local Bolsheviks did succeed in ensuring that ten Red Army pogromists were shot by firing squads, they were unable to halt the violence. Despite repeated appeals by Bolsheviks to the central authorities in Kyiv that the 8th Regiment be immediately dissolved, relieved of its duties and replaced by another, *non-antisemitic* unit, seemingly there were no such forces at the state's disposal. Consequently, the 8th Regiment remained in Uman' throughout the whole month of June.[77] Perhaps most controversially, according to reports by the Russian Red Cross, the 8th Regiment was *intentionally* kept in Uman' by the Bolshevik leadership because it had proven itself more than capable of maintaining 'Soviet power' by fending off various rebel movements throughout late May and June.[78] In six weeks of violence, the 8th Regiment killed approximately 150 Jews.[79] To be clear, then, in the spring and early summer of 1919, the Bolsheviks were kept in power in Uman' by and through militarized antisemitism in the shape of the 8th Soviet Regiment.

Finally, on 3 July, the 8th Regiment was replaced by the First Ukrainian Soviet Cavalry under the command of Fedor Gribenko.[80] However, it proved to be just as antisemitic as its predecessor: upon arrival, Soviet cavalrymen robbed and attacked Jewish neighbourhoods while declaring that they were there to fight 'the Yids and the Communists'. It was only with the arrival of the multi-ethnic International 4th Soviet Regiment on 5 July that two months of anti-Jewish violence at the hands of the Soviet military was finally brought to an end. The International 4th Regiment was composed of Jewish self-defence groups as well as Chinese, Hungarian, German and Russian workers. Often, it proved the most reliable Soviet unit in Ukraine and the one most capable of confronting Red Army antisemitism.[81] More pogroms would follow in Uman' in late July, but these would be carried out by anti-Bolshevik

---

[77] Miliakova, *Kniga pogromov*, 127.
[78] Rossiiskii Gosudarstvennyi Voennyi Arkhiv (hereafter RGVA), f.103 o.1 d.49 l.355-356. I wish to thank Dimitri Tolkatsch for bringing this source to my attention. See also Miliakova, *Kniga pogromov*, 127; Heifets, *The Slaughter of the Jews in the Ukraine in 1919*, 87–88.
[79] Veidlinger, *Pogrom*, 282.
[80] For more on Gribenko, see Miliakova, *Kniga pogromov*, 850; Zatonskii, 'Vodovorot (iz proshlogo)', 160.
[81] When the International 4th Division arrived in Uman', the pogrom-prone First Soviet Cavalry was sent to Poltava. See Miliakova, *Kniga pogromov*, 118–30. Other sources give the date of the arrival of the 4th Division as 8 July. See Kurinnyi, *Uman' ta umanchany ochyma P. F. Kurinnoho (z osobystykh shchodennikiv za 1918-1929 hh.)*, 223.

peasant insurgents. This time, the new Soviet government, backed by the International 4th Regiment, took an unconditional opposition to the violence.[82]

The Grigor'evshchina in the Spring and Summer of 1919

These were not isolated incidents. In Cherkasy, a city 190 kilometres north-east of Uman' on the Dnepr River, a substantial section of local Bolsheviks openly interpreted the struggle against the bourgeoisie as one against 'Jewish speculators'.[83] When Grigor'ev's troops arrived there on 10 May, a call was immediately issued for self-defence units to be formed within the trade unions. However, local 'Christian' workers refused, leaving 100–200 Jews to defend themselves (all were reportedly killed).[84] The pogrom by Grigor'ev's troops in Cherkasy commenced on 16 May and lasted for five days. In the ensuing violence some 617 Jews were murdered.[85] Reports stated that 'Christian' workers in the soviet of trade unions either took part in the violence or were indifferent to it.[86] When local Bolshevik leaders tried to mobilize their Red Army division to put down the violence, copies of Grigor'ev's *Universal* were found circulating among the soldiers waiting to depart. By the time they were ordered to fight, sections of the Red Army refused and declared their intention to side with Grigor'ev instead. When asked why they had defected, they stated their agreement with the *Universal*.[87] Although a Red Army regiment *did* eventually put up a fight against Grigor'ev's troops, testimonies by local Red soldiers reveal how those who defected to Grigor'ev did so on the grounds that Christian 'brothers' should unite to fight the 'Communist Yids'.[88] By 21 May, the Bolsheviks had regained control of Cherkasy. Many of the soldiers who had rebelled now rejoined the Soviet army and patrolled the streets with the same rifles they had used to terrorize Jews just days before.[89]

---

[82] University of Glasgow, Russian Revolutionary Literature Collection, Reel 47, Document 1162.
[83] Heifets, *The Slaughter of the Jews in the Ukraine in 1919*, 251.
[84] HUL f.3050 o.1 d.162 l.17ob. For more on Jewish self-defence units in Cherkasy, see RGASPI f.272 o.1 d.81 l.90-91.
[85] Miliakova, *Kniga pogromov*, 351.
[86] Heifets, *The Slaughter of the Jews in the Ukraine in 1919*, 257.
[87] Gilley, 'The Ukrainian Anti-Bolshevik Risings of Spring and Summer 1919', 114.
[88] Miliakova, *Kniga pogromov*, 140–41; Heifets, *The Slaughter of the Jews in the Ukraine in 1919*, 268–69. For more on the aftermath of the Cherkasy pogrom, see Johnson, 'Sholem Schwarzbard', 111–13.
[89] Veidlinger, *Pogrom: The Origins of the European Genocide of the Jews* (New York: Metropolitan Books, 2020), 270–72.

Similar developments occurred in the town of Zolotonosha, in the Poltava province, where the Bogunskii regiment of the Red Army was stationed.[90] The regiment was utterly pervaded with antisemitism; it had perpetrated pogroms back in February.[91] In mid-April, prior to their arrival in Zolotonosha, Bogunskii soldiers apparently tore the red stars off their uniform, shouting, 'This is a Yid star!' This antisemitism was further underlined with the arrival of Grigor'ev's troops on 12 May, which saw the Bogunskii regiment defect en masse and help carry out a pogrom under the slogan 'down with Jewish power!' When asked by a local Bolshevik why they had deserted the Red Army, Bogunskii soldiers answered: 'Because they [Grigor'ev's troops] stand for Soviet Power, but they also beat the Yids and Communists'.[92]

The stakes for the Bolshevik leadership could not have been higher. Ukraine was geographically and politically the only channel through which the Bolsheviks could extend aid to the newly constituted Soviet Hungary.[93] Moreover, when White Army general Denikin launched a major offensive from the Kuban into the Ukrainian left bank in May, the Grigor'evshchina had left the Red Army stretched and vulnerable. Although the Grigor'evshchina would be put down in just under three weeks, the uprising had consequences all out of proportion with its actual military threat: by keeping Red Army divisions engaged in the south, the Grigor'evshchina seriously undermined the fight against Denikin, who was able to march forward into Ukraine with great ease. Indeed, he brought about the catastrophe of which Lenin had long warned by seizing the Donbas and depriving Russia of its coal, iron and steel production. On 25 June, Denikin captured the Bolshevik stronghold Kharkiv, and by the end of the July Ekaterinoslav and Poltava had also fallen. On 9 August, Trotsky tried desperately to instil discipline by ordering those Soviet armies still in Ukraine to be 'cleaned up' and have their pogromists removed,[94] but it was all in vain. By 19 August, Denikin's army was in control of those regions west of the Dnepr River (known as the Ukrainian left bank), most of southern Ukraine, and even parts of the

---

[90] On the composition of the Bogunskii regiment, see Miliakova, *Kniga pogromov*, 856.
[91] GARF f.1318 o.1 d.426 l.5-5ob.
[92] TsDAHO f.1 o.20 d.35 l.116, 121-123; f.5 o.1 d.17 l.55; TsDAVO f.5 o.1 d.17 l.61; HUL f.3050 o.1 d.162 l.4ob; RGASPI f.272 o.1 d.81 l.65. See also Gusev-Orenburgskii, *Bagrovaia kniga*, 9; Gilley, 'The Ukrainian Anti-Bolshevik Risings of Spring and Summer 1919', 114.
[93] Mawdsley, *The Russian Civil War*, 173.
[94] See Trotsky's 'Instructions to the responsible political workers of the 14th Army', where he calls on all units to be 'cleaned up' and warns that 'kulak elements are carrying out agitation … turning Red Army soldiers to pogroms and banditism'; RGASPI f.17 o.109 d.45 l.36.

Ukrainian right bank (east of the Dnepr River). And he did not stop there: in October his troops had marched into Russia as far as Orel', a mere 200 kilometres from Moscow. Once more, the fate of the entire revolution hung in the balance.[95]

Beyond Grigor'ev: Antisemitism in the Red Army and Party in 1919

The Grigor'evshchina was an expression of a much deeper problem of antisemitism in the apparatuses of Bolshevik power at the local level in Ukraine in 1919. Intelligence reports sent to the Party Central Committee in April and May reveal that antisemitism was strongly developed within the Red Army across the *whole* of Ukraine, uncluding in many regiments and brigades that did *not* carry out pogroms.[96] Although the wave of pogromist violence subsided after May,[97] reports from both June and July illustrate that antisemitism continued to be a profound problem within the Red Army and local Bolshevik and Soviet institutions.[98] The situation was so grave in some regions that Bolshevik agitators simply could not go near the Red Army for fear that they would be shot on the spot as 'Yid speculators'.[99] Typical of such reports was an inspection carried out into the Ukrainian Soviet 1st Army in early June. It concluded that 'political work among the troops is entirely impossible' owing to antisemitism, which is so 'strongly developed ... pogroms have become a regular occurrence (*obychnoe iavlenie*)'.[100] Bolsheviks who wished to distribute propaganda against antisemitism faced equally challenging circumstances in many rural regions. In Lityn (Podolia province) and Fastiv (Kyiv province), the local Party had virtually no contact with the peasant population, which on more than one occasion rose up against the regime under the slogan 'we are the Bolsheviks, beat

---

[95] Adams, *Bolsheviks in the Ukraine*, 349–83; Borys, *The Sovietization of Ukraine, 1917-1923*, 360.
[96] Security reports for the months of April and May show that antisemitism found traction in Red Army units all across Ukraine, from the regions of the north such as the Volyn oblast', Konotop and Berdychiv; to Bila Tserkva, Poltava, Vasylkiv, Oleksandriia, Koziatyn and Kryvyi Rih in central Ukraine; and from Konstantingrad (present day Krasnohrad) and Donestk in the east to Ochakiv and Kherson in the south and Koziatyn in the west. See the reports held in TsDAHO f.1 o.20 d.35 l.40-42, 126-128, 156-158; f.1 o.20 d.41 l 2-12, 25; f.57 o.2 d.283 l.19-21; and RGASPI f.17 o.6 d.369 l.109-111; f.71 o.35 d.507 l.363-394.
[97] HUL f.3050 o.1 d.162 l.4ob-6.
[98] RGASPI f.71 o.35 d.507 l.363-394; f.71 o.35 d.489 l.251-292; TsDAVO f.5 o.1 d.20 l.6-30.
[99] TsDAHO f.1 o.20 d.35 l.95, 146-148; f.5 o.1 d.17 l.23-23ob.
[100] TsDAHO f.1 o.20 d.35 l.95.

up the Yids!'[101] The disjuncture between the Party leadership and rural communities was often profound: one report, from the Pustovoity village in the Vinnytsia province, revealed that local peasants did not even know what Soviet power was, and nor did they know which party was in government in Moscow. They were, however, convinced that the Bolsheviks were all 'Yids'.[102]

Similar difficulties appeared within the Party itself. In Fastiv, for example, a Party report noted that of the twenty-two Communists in the local Party organization in mid-June, only two were actual card-carrying members, with the rest being antisemitic 'Petliura agitators'. Membership, so the report indicated, was being coordinated through interpersonal friendship groups, and the antisemites in the party could not be arrested, such was their dominance.[103] Again, it is important to note that these were not isolated cases.[104] In some regions, antisemitism had become so pervasive that local party/soviet organizations had split into opposing camps. In Lypovets (Kyiv province), the soviet was composed of sixty Communist Bundists, twenty Mensheviks and twenty Bolsheviks. The principal divide, however, was *not* a party one: according to a local Party report written in mid-May, the soviet was split along ethnic lines, with Jewish and Russian groups effectively operating as separate, opposing camps.[105] In Ovruch (Zhytomyr region), the local Communist organization was similarly divided between a non-Jewish group which 'openly tried to start pogroms' and a Jewish group composed of 'honest workers'. The report concluded by demanding that the Central Committee immediately replace the antisemitic individuals with 'real Communists'.[106]

The central authorities were simply in no position to effect such changes. Illustrative of this is the fact that on 30 May, just days after the Grigor'evshchina, a meeting of the Cheka and Soviet government leadership declared that responsibility for dealing with local outbreaks of 'counter-revolution' rested at the local level, in Soviet institutions

---

[101] TsDAHO f.1 o.20 d.35 l.78-81, 162.   [102] RGASPI f.71 o.35 d.489 l.118.
[103] TsDAHO f.1 o.20 d.35 l.142-143
[104] See, for example, the following reports sent to the Party Central Committee in June 1919: TsDAHO f.1 o.20 d.35 l.118-119, 127-128, 139-141; TsDAHO f.1 o.20 d.41 l.19; and RGASPI f.71 o.35 d.507 l.374. As an article about pogroms and counter-revolutionary sentiment in the Kharkiv Bolshevik daily *Kommunar* put it, '[T]he great hindrance and deficiency of our [Party] work derives from the complete absence of conscious party workers in the provinces'; *Komunar*, no. 57 (71), 29 May 1919, 1.
[105] TsDAHO f.1 o.20 d.35 l.86-87.
[106] TsDAHO f.1 o.20 d.35 l.78-81. Similar cases were reported in Fastiv: TsDAHO f.1 o.20 d.35 l.142-143.

such as the executive committees.¹⁰⁷ However, these were *precisely* the bodies that were prone to antisemitism during the spring and summer of 1919. The central authorities often tried to send 'honest Communists' to the provinces, to ensure some stability. However, in some cases, things did not work out as planned: in Pavlohrad (a town in the Ekaterinoslav region), the 'Communist' sent by the Party centre, named 'Panov', turned out to be an antisemite.¹⁰⁸ This, again, was not an isolated case.¹⁰⁹ Such were the levels of separation between the centre and the periphery that the Bolshevik leadership were simply unable to check the composition of Party institutions at the local level, and as such, these institutions were often staffed with antisemites over whom the leadership had little control.¹¹⁰ All of this led the Central Bureau of the Jewish Sections of the Communist Party (the Evsektsiia) to conclude that non-Bolshevik Jewish socialists were '*often the only source of local resistance*' to Red Army pogroms and anti-Soviet uprisings in mid-1919.¹¹¹

Perhaps the sharpest insight into the everyday nature of 'Red antisemitism' in 1919 is given in the following testimony by Il'ia Shmulevich, a local Jewish citizen from Rosava, a town of 5,000 inhabitants (210 Jewish families) in the Kanivskyi district of the Kyiv Province. Rosava bore witness to a Red Army pogrom from 27 February until 3 March 1919.¹¹² The account that follows is from 2 March, and begins with Shmulevich having been arrested by the local Bolshevik regime and sentenced to death by a Revolutionary Tribunal along with six other Jews for no reason other than their being Jewish. It is worth quoting at length:

They loaded their revolvers. Sensing the inevitability of death ... I spluttered, 'I'm a poor worker, I'm a Bolshevik' ... the passion of my words and my sobbing, stuttering voice seemed to soften up the menacing Commander. He agreed to grant us the 'temporary' right to life ... and added poisonously, 'I may be your

---

¹⁰⁷ TsDAVO f.2 o.1 d.25 l.72.   ¹⁰⁸ TsDAHO f.1 o.20 d.35 l.24.
¹⁰⁹ Reports by the Information Bureau of the Ukrainian Commissariat for Military Affairs reveal that in Vasylkiv (Kyiv region), the 'communists' sent from the centre to put a stop to peasant uprisings were themselves interpolated by antisemitism. RGVA f.25860 o.1 d.148 l.81ob. I thank Dimitri Tolkatsch for bringing this source to my attention.
¹¹⁰ TsDAHO f.1 o.20 d.35 l.40-42, 118-119; f.57 o.2 d.342 l.30-33. A report by Poalei Zion in June 1919 (sent to Lenin) complained that several Red Army units responsible for carrying out pogroms had yet to be disbanded. Similarly, it warned that 'openly counter-revolutionary bandits' continued to occupy key positions in local organs of the Soviet government. RGASPI f.272 o.1 d.141 l.18-19.
¹¹¹ RGASPI f.445 o.1 d.1 l.78 (emphasis in the original).
¹¹² For more on the Rosava pogrom, see Heifets, *The Slaughter of the Jews in the Ukraine in 1919*, 85; Budnitskii, *Rossiiskie evrei mezhdu krasnymi i belymi*, 451. See also *Zhizn' Natsional'nostei*, no. 9 (17), 16 March 1919, 3.

brother, but I don't trust you Jews, there are too many of you among us' ... We were met by an officer whom the soldiers called the Assistant Commissar ... 'I'll shoot them here and now' he said. However, to our relief, the revolver malfunctioned ... After some time a large cavalry appeared with several automatic rifles. The Political Commissar (*politkom*) ordered the cavalry to stop – 'prepare your rifles, it's time to shoot these counter-revolutionaries'. Several soldiers got off their horses. They loaded their rifles. Standing in line in the face of death, one of our group, Konstantinovskii, lost his mind and began to laugh hysterically. Another of the condemned, Podol'skii, for some reason kept his hands deep within his pockets ... the Political Commissar ordered him to take them out, but Podol'skii remained motionless and looked into the distance. He refused to take them out. Thrown into a rage by this 'refusal to follow orders', the Commissar took out his sabre and struck Podol'skii several times to the head. The blows were so hard his skull split open ... and his brains spilled out. My death now seemed inevitable ... I began frantically stating my commitment to the Bolsheviks, to the working class and to its liberation ... To my great fortune ... the Political Commissar ordered me to step aside. Gun shots rang out. My fellow comrades had all fallen ... I was taken to the telegraph station ... where I was interrogated by the Political Commissar of the Fifth Regiment ... he pushed me up against the wall and put a revolver to my head ... 'Are you a Jew?' he asked. 'I am not a Jew, I am a soldier of the army, of labour and of the revolution.' This declaration finally brought the Commissar over to my side. After a short meeting with his entourage, he said, 'very well, off you go'. Before leaving though I asked to be issued with some kind of pass in case I was to run into trouble again. Initially he refused, stating that he had no such papers, but then later I was given a note with 'In solidarity with Soviet power' written in pencil. At the first checkpoint I was detained ... When I showed my pass one of the soldiers asked, 'What is your nationality?' I answered with a phrase now filled with happiness: 'I am a soldier of the army, of labour and of the revolution.' The soldier replied, 'I too am an internationalist, however I want to know if you are a Jew or not.' I answered, 'for an internationalist it makes no sense to ask what nationality one belongs to.' The soldier, waving his hand as if to get rid of a bad smell, allowed me to go.[113]

Such problems were not confined to 1919, and in fact persisted into the latter stages of the Civil War. During the Soviet–Polish war in the summer of 1920, for example, some of the most brutal Red Army pogroms were carried out by one of the Soviet government's most trusted and decorated army units, the First Red Cavalry, led by Semen Budennyi.[114] Elsewhere,

---

[113] Gusev-Orenburgskii, *Bagrovaia kniga*, 79–83.
[114] RGASPI f.17 o.109 d.73 l.60-60ob; GARF f.R-1339 o.1 d.424 l.119-119ob. See also Babel, *Red Cavalry*; O. V. Budnitskii, 'The Reds and the Jews, or the Comrades in the Arms of the Military Reporter Liutov', in *The Enigma of Isaac Babel. Biography, History, Context*, ed. G. Freidin (Stanford: Stanford University Press, 2009); O. Figes, 'The Red Army and Mass Mobilization during the Russian Civil War 1918-1920', *Past & Present*, 129 (1990): 195–96; S. Brown, 'Communists and the Red Cavalry: The Political

outbreaks of antisemitic violence continued throughout 1920 and 1921 in various divisions of the Red Army.[115]

Conclusion

Bolshevik power was secured in Ukraine in early 1919 through what became known as *partizanstvo*, the partisan basis of the Red Army. This is neatly captured in the memoirs of Zatonskii, a key figure in the Soviet government in Ukraine in 1919:

> We submitted ourselves to elements of the peasantry who, although very much sympathetic to Bolshevism, were nonetheless very suspicious, to say the least, of Communism. The peasant partisan enthusiastically interpreted our battle slogans during the period of the overthrow of the old regime, and saw us as willing allies in his fight against the landlords. But having won that fight, the partisan wanted one further thing: he wanted rid of everything foreign [*chuzhdoe*] and imposed [*nanosnoe*] (urban) so that he might finally be the master of his own land ... [Previously] the Bolsheviks had said 'arm yourself, beat the landlord and seize his land!' The Communists now say 'give the state your bread, subject yourselves to discipline ... give us your weapons' ... it is no surprise that ... they turned against us with almost the same ferocity with which they had risen up against the *Hetman* and Petliura.[116]

Antisemitism provided a conduit for these partisan Red Army soldiers to make the journey from 'revolution' to 'counter-revolution'. It should again be restated, however, that the Red Army was by no means the only force complicit in antisemitic violence. Many of the towns and cities discussed in this chapter suffered successive waves of pogroms as various armies and insurgent units passed through. In Skvyra (Kyiv province), there were no less than seven pogroms during the Civil War years, 'only' two of which were carried out by Red Army regiments (anti-Bolshevik forces were responsible for the other five).[117] And just as there were Ukrainian peasants who saved Jews from certain death during pogroms, equally there were Bolsheviks and other socialists at the local level who rejected the pogromist worldview of their so-called 'comrades'. But

---

Education of the Konarmiia in the Russian Civil War, 1918–1920', *Slavonic and East European Review* 73, no. 1 (1995): 86–89; V. L. Genis, 'Pervaia Konnaia armiia: Za kulisami slavy', *Voprosy istorii*, no. 12 (1994): 64–77. On the Soviet–Polish War more generally, see T. C. Fiddick, *Russia's Retreat from Poland. From Permanent Revolution to Peaceful Coexistence* (Basingstoke: Palgrave Macmillan, 1990).

[115] For example, a Red Army pogrom was carried out by the 6th Regiment in Bohuslav in 1921. See YIVO RG80 folder 38, 3474. On antisemitism within the 12th Division of the Red Army in the summer of 1920, see YIVO RG80 folder 39, 3519.

[116] Zatonskii, 'Vodovorot (iz proshlogo)', 155. I thank Dimitri Tolkatsch for bringing this source to my attention.

[117] Miliakova, *Kniga pogromov*, 339.

Conclusion

looking at the social formation holistically, it is clear that antisemitism was a *dominant* form of consciousness within this conjuncture. To borrow from the cultural theorist Raymond Williams: its dominance met contestation from other 'emergent' and 'residual' worldviews,[118] and as we shall soon see, the Bolshevik leadership *did* try to provide such an alternative. However, the difficulties in doing so were profound owing to the fact that antisemitism and 'Bolshevism' were often co-extensive projects in the popular imaginary. The Grigor'evshchina seemed to represent what many within the Bolsheviks' social base in Ukraine desired: a populist leftist government that represented 'true Bolshevism' or true 'Soviet power'; a power of 'the people' (*narod*), of the 'labouring people' (*trudiashchiisia*). These were standard categories of revolutionary Bolshevism, and as far as leading Bolsheviks were concerned, they were precisely the kinds of concepts that were best equipped to cut through antisemitic discourse and show the way towards a truly class consciousness. However, in the Ukrainian revolutionary conjuncture, class and ethnic categories could not be so easily separated. Indeed, the terms 'Ukrainian' and 'Jew' simultaneously bore both class *and* ethnic overdeterminations. The 'Ukrainian' was a 'true' and 'honest' 'toiler' who put their hands to 'productive' labour. 'The Jew', in addition to being a 'Communist', was also 'non-labourer', a 'speculator'. In other words, the categories Bolshevik leaders deployed in their class analysis – 'bourgeois', 'toiler', 'the people', 'exploiter' and 'exploited' – were, on the ground, understood in profoundly complex and racialized dimensions.[119] Equally porous was the notion of 'Soviet power', whose meaning was fought over among revolutionaries. By May and June 1919, the Party appeared to have lost that fight, as a racialized conception of the revolution gained a 'material force' deep within the ranks of the Bolsheviks' own support base.[120]

---

[118] R. Williams, *Marxism and Literature* (Oxford University Press, 1977).

[119] The place of 'speculation' within popular conceptions of Jewishness has been addressed in Andrew Sloin's pioneering work on Bolshevik power in Belorussia. For Sloin, the Soviet state's designation of 'speculation' as a criminal (not to mention 'counter-revolutionary') act coincided and often overlapped with the widespread antisemitic identification of 'speculation' as a defining feature of Jewishness. There was a 'tendency inherent in the Soviet project', writes Sloin, 'to conflate Jewish economic practices with the workings of 'merchant capital' and problematically impute to Jewish actors a certain agency over basic economic functions'. See Andrew Sloin, 'Speculators, Swindlers and Other Jews: Regulating Trade in Revolutionary White Russia', *East European Jewish Affairs* 40, no. 2 (2010): 112. These stereotypes had a long history. In late imperial politics and culture, Jews were often depicted as 'commercial' in contrast to a Russian peasantry defined by its 'productivity' and organic relation to the soil. See L. Engelstein *The Keys to Happiness. Sex and the Search for Modernity in Fin-de-Siècle Russia.* (London: Cornell University Press, 1992), 299.

[120] On ideas gaining 'material force', see K. Marx, *Early Writings* (London: Penguin Books Limited, 1992).

5 The Soviet Response to Antisemitism in Ukraine, February–May 1919

The Re-Emergence of a Soviet Confrontation with Antisemitism, February 1919

When the Red pogroms and the Grigor'evshchina broke out in Ukraine in 1919, the Soviet government in Moscow was caught unprepared. The campaigns against antisemitism initiated in the spring of 1918 had been dismantled by the growing drive towards centralization. How, then, did the Party leadership respond to the explosion of antisemitic violence in early to mid-1919?

In 1918, the Soviet campaign against antisemitism emanated specifically from non-Bolshevik Jewish radicals within the Moscow Jewish Commissariat. In early 1919, however, the beginnings of a new campaign were initiated not in Moscow, but in Ukraine itself, by the newly constituted Ukrainian Soviet government. Nine months after the Bolsheviks' defeat at the hands of the German Army, Soviet forces retook Kharkiv on 3 January 1919, and by the beginning of February, Kyiv was once again under Bolshevik control. These key military breakthroughs paved the way on 28 January 1919 for the formation of a Ukrainian Sovnarkom, headed by the Bolshevik Khristian Rakovskii. It was *this* institution that initiated the beginnings of a campaign against antisemitism in early 1919.

The reestablishment of a Ukrainian Soviet government took place alongside a ferocious eruption of antisemitic violence. If we recall, in the early weeks of 1919, a number of pogroms were carried out by Petliura's Ukrainian Army, including in Zhytomyr and Berdychiv in January, and most horrific of all in Proskuriv in mid-February, in which more than 1,650 Jews were murdered.[1] However, the Ukrainian Soviet government's intervention came not in response to *these* pogroms, but to the growth of antisemitism within the ranks of the *Red Army*.

On 4 February 1919, a mere six days after its formation, the Ukrainian Sovnarkom heard a report by the Commissar for Internal Affairs, Vasilii

---

[1] Miliakova, *Kniga pogromov*, 47–70.

Averin, detailing evidence of 'pogromist agitation' within the 13th Regiment of the Soviet Army. According to Averin's report, this had resulted in an attack on Jews by Red soldiers in broad daylight in the city of Pavlohrad (Ekaterinoslav region).² It was *this* report, not the more extensive attacks on Jews then being carried out by Petliura's army, that propelled the Ukrainian Bolshevik Party into a confrontation with antisemitism. The following day, on 5 February, a meeting of the Ukrainian Sovnarkom was called to formulate a Soviet governmental response to the growth of antisemitism in the Red Army.³ The measures taken were extensive, particularly when set against the relative inactivity of Lenin's Moscow-based Sovnarkom during the spring of the previous year.

First, commitments were made to develop an educational programme through the Soviet press. A. Gorokhov was instructed to ensure that 'a whole number of [newspaper] articles and brochures on the question of antisemitism are published'. Further, V. Mezhlauk was given the specific task of ensuring that the Bolshevik newspaper *Kommunist* carried regular features on antisemitism.⁴ However, these commitments were only partially fulfilled: in the month of February, only one⁵ pamphlet on antisemitism was published and only two⁶ articles on antisemitism appeared in *Kommunist*. A consistent press campaign against antisemitism in the Ukrainian Soviet press only really commenced in mid-May, that is, *after* the wave of Red Army antisemitism had already broken out.

The most significant decisions taken at the 5 February meeting concerned the punitive measures to be adopted by the Ukrainian Soviet government on the question of antisemitism. At the meeting, Chairman of the Sovnarkom Rakovskii was instructed to draft an 'order' (*prikaz*)

---

² TsDAVO f.2 o.1. d.16 l.32.
³ In attendance at the meeting was virtually the entire Central Committee of the Ukrainian Communist Party: Kh. Rakovskii (Chairman of the Ukrainian Sovnarkom), A. M. Zharko, F. A. Zemit, M. L. Rukhimovich, B. O. Magidov, I. I. Shvarts, A. G. Shlikhter, V. I. Mezhlauk, E. I. Kviring, A. I. Khmel'nitskii, V. P. Zatonskii, S. N. Vlasenko, N. A. Skripnik, K. E. Voroshilov Chernyi, G. G. Iagoda, P. P. Tytyshkin, A. F. Gorokhov and V. G. Iudovskii. TsDAVO f.2 o.1 d.16 l.14.
⁴ TsDAVO f.2 o.1 d.16 l.17.
⁵ I. Shelit, *Doloi pogromov* (Kiev: Izdatel'stvo narodnogo kommisariata po voennym delam Ukrainy, 1919). See RGASPI f.71 o.35 d.691 l.123-124 for more information.
⁶ See Budnitskii, *Russian Jews*, 366. One of these articles was simply an edited version of the report from Pavlohrad presented at the meeting of the Ukrainian Sovnarkom on 4 February, and the other was a reproduction of the appeal written by Rakovskii in light of the meeting on 5 February (discussed later here). It seems, therefore, that the Party leadership was unsuccessful in generating a regular flow of new articles on antisemitism for *Kommunist*. At the same time, however, we should note that at least two articles against antisemitism were published in the Kharkiv-based *Izvestiia Vseukrainskogo Tsentral'nogo Ispolnitel'nogo Komiteta*: one on 14 February and another two weeks later, on 28 February. RGASPI f.71 o.35 d.490 l.111-112.

threatening all those participating in 'antisemitic propaganda' with arrest.[7] The following week, Rakovskii's document was sent to all Soviet state institutions in Ukraine, published in the Kyiv-based Bolshevik newspaper *Kommunist* on 12 February, and then subsequently distributed separately as a poster.[8] Its opening sentence was a frank and public admission that 'pogromist agitation' was being carried out 'not only among workers and peasants, but in the ranks of the Red Army also'. The document further warned that those found to have taken part in antisemitic acts would be subject to 'the most brutal and severe measures', irrespective of their position in the Soviet army. Rakovskii's intended audience was made explicit: 'Comrades, workers and peasants! Do you really not understand that this [antisemitism] can only bring harm to our work?'[9]

This was a significant moment. For the first time, a Bolshevik leader had publicly acknowledged that antisemitism was a problem within *the Red Army specifically*. The publication of Rakovskii's 'order' signalled that the Bolshevik leadership in Ukraine was more readily inclined to address the issue than the Russian Party had been in the spring of 1918.

Perhaps even more significant was the ratification of the Decree against National Hatred, passed on 10 February, and drafted in light of the Ukrainian Soviet government's discussion on antisemitism just five days previously.[10] If Rakovskii's 'order' had been somewhat vague in its threat to issue the most 'brutal and severe' punishments to those found guilty of antisemitism, the Decree was far more specific: all those found guilty of 'national hatred' were to be arrested immediately and sentenced to 'a minimum of five years imprisonment'. Those found to be 'directly agitating for pogromist violence' were to be executed.[11] For the first time since the October Revolution of 1917, a specific set of punishments for antisemitism had been detailed and outlined by the Party leadership.[12]

---

[7] TsDAVO f.2 o.1. d.16 l.16-17.

[8] RGASPI f.71 o.35 d.507 l.434; *Zhizn' Natsional'nostei*, 23 March 1919, 3. A copy of the poster is preserved in the archives of the Institut Iudaiki (the Judaica Institute) in Kyiv (hereafter IJ), f.19 o.1 d.4 l.50.

[9] IJ, f.19 o.1 d.4 l.50.   [10] TsDAVO f.2 o.1. d.16 l.16.

[11] TsDAVO f.2 o.1. d.16 l.69.

[12] The severity of the measures was broadly in line with the discourse pertaining to the fight against the 'counter-revolution' that had been emanating from Moscow since early 1918. For example, on 21 February 1918, the Sovnarkom in Petrograd issued a decree ordering 'all counter-revolutionaries to be shot on the spot'; Lenin, *Polnoe sobranie sochinenii*, Vol. 35, 359–60. This particular decree was drafted in response to the threat of the German invasion which sparked the Eleven-Day War, and thus the usage of the term 'counter-revolutionary' in this context did not specifically refer to 'antisemites'.

Revolutionary Justice: The Judicial Confrontation with Antisemitism at the Local Level

In the context of 1919, however, the Party leadership was in no position to ensure that these commitments were enforced on the ground. At the 5 February meeting, the Ukrainian Soviet government resolved that the campaign against antisemitism be carried out by local soviets.[13] Yet as noted earlier, Bolsheviks were unable to carry out political work within the Red Army on the question of anti-Jewish violence, such were the levels of antisemitism. In some cases, local soviets became battlegrounds where antisemites and internationalists fought for control over the revolutionary process. In Elisavetgrad, the latter lost out to the former.[14] Soviet power at the local level sometimes acted as a *barrier* to the implementation of directives from above.

Similar problems befell the judicial component of the campaign against antisemitism. Responsibility for delivering 'revolutionary justice' rested with the Revolutionary Tribunals, a series of judicial institutions established by the Bolsheviks in late November 1917 in Russia and early December 1918 in Ukraine.[15] Their principal aim was to deal with the 'counter-revolution' broadly defined, that is, any form of activity deemed by the Party to undermine the goals and aims of the revolution.[16] Tribunals were overseen by provincial or city soviets, and often Bolsheviks struggled to find politically reliable personnel to staff these institutions.[17] The degree, then, to which the punishments outlined in the Ukrainian Sovnarkom's Decree against National Hatred would be heeded was highly dependent on the political and ideological composition of the

---

[13] At the meeting it was stated: '[W]e must organize a political power capable of taking the most decisive measures against antisemitism. Such a power is to be found in the shape of the local soviets.' TsDAVO f.2 o.1 d.16 l.16-17.

[14] OKK, *Gody bor'by*, 78; Gitelman, *Jewish Nationality and Soviet Politics*, 165.

[15] Between December 1918 and June 1919, all Military Revolutionary Tribunals in Ukraine were carried out under the auspices of the Ukrainian Commissariat for Military Affairs headed by Podvoiskii. At the local level, regular Revolutionary Tribunals were organized by provincial and city soviets. After June 1919, all Revolutionary Tribunals came under the jurisdiction of the Russian Soviet government; E. I. Melamed and M. S. Kupovetskii, eds., *Dokumenty po istorii i kul'ture evreev v arkhivakh Kieva* (Kiev: DUKh i LITERA, 2006), 254.

[16] For more on the Revolutionary Tribunals, see M. Rendle, 'Revolutionary Tribunals and the Origins of Terror in Early Soviet Russia', *Historical Research* 84, no. 226 (2011): 693–721; M. Rendle, 'Defining the 'Political' Crime: Revolutionary Tribunals in Early Soviet Russia', *Europe-Asia Studies* 65, no. 9 (2013): 1771–88; A. Retish, 'Power, Control, and Criminal Activity', 2011.

[17] S. Kucherov, *The Organs of Soviet Administration of Justice: Their History and Operation* (Leiden: Brill, 1970), 45; Rendle, 'Revolutionary Tribunals and the Origins of Terror in Early Soviet Russia', 705–08.

soviets at the local level. In some regions of Ukraine, these institutions were often staffed by antisemites (and at times even outright pogromists), and in such cases it was highly unlikely that the directives set out in the Decree would be fulfilled.

Further research in regional archives is needed to form a complete picture of the range of sentences handed out for antisemitism by the Revolutionary Tribunals at the local level across Russia and Ukraine. We can, however, glean some insight by looking at the small sample of cases held in the central archives in Kyiv and Zhytomyr. From these files, it is clear that the sentences given to those convicted of antisemitism were significantly more lenient than the punishments prescribed in the Decree. In Zhytomyr, a series of Revolutionary Tribunals were organized between May and July 1919 to administer punishments to those accused of participating in the two pogroms which took place in the city in January and March earlier that same year. From the reports, we know that those found guilty of looting Jewish property during the pogroms were imprisoned rather than executed, and their prison sentences were considerably shorter than the suggested five years: in some cases, the sentences were between four and six weeks[18]; in others, between four and six months.[19] In no case was the death penalty invoked. The Zhytomyr Revolutionary Tribunals took place under the auspices of the Ukrainian Soviet government's Commissariat for Justice.[20] Running alongside these were the trials conducted by the 'Justice Department' of the local Zhytomyr Cheka. The punishments administered in these trials seem to have been much closer to those prescribed in the Decree against National Hatred. For example, when one Red Army soldier was found to have taken part in the looting of Jewish property in the March pogrom, he was shot by the Cheka firing squad.[21] Even within the same region, sentences for identical crimes varied significantly depending on which repressive state apparatus was assigned the case.

---

[18] Derzhavnyi Arkhiv Zhytomyrs'koi Oblasty (hereafter DAZhO) f.R-1820 o.5 d.174 l.57-58; f.R-1820 o.5 d.128 l.1-1ob,18,25; f.R-1820 o.5 d.176 l.1-3.

[19] DAZhO f.R-1820 o.5 d.136 l.1-4ob,44-47,75-77; f.R-1820 o.5 d.151 l.1-2,30

[20] E. I. Melamed, ed., *Dokumenty po istorii i kul'ture evreev v regional'nykh arkhivakh Ukrainy. Putevoditel'. Volynskaia, Zhitomirskaia, Rovenskaia, Cherkasskaia Oblasti* (Kiev: Rossiiskii Gosudarstvennyi Gumanitarnyi Universitet, Tsentr Bibleistiki i Iudaiki, 2009), 166–67.

[21] The Red Army soldier in question was Valentin Gagan who looted the flat belonging to Meer Gol'man during the pogrom on 10 January 1919, stealing a wallet and two watches in the process. He was shot by the Cheka on 25 May after a trial in which Gol'man was present as a witness. DAZhO f.R-1820 o.5 d.124 l.1-2, 46-47, 56. According to Rendle, tribunals increasingly began to be conducted by the Cheka rather than the Revolutionary Tribunals, and their sentences were invariably harsher. See Rendle, 'Revolutionary Tribunals and the Origins of Terror in Early Soviet Russia', 694, 711.

Elsewhere, punishments for antisemitism fell significantly short of the measures set out in the Decree. In Okhtyrka in Kharkiv, Bolsheviks found guilty of antisemitism were temporarily expelled from the Party only to be re-admitted providing they behaved 'impeccably' (*bezuprechno*) during their period of expulsion. In some cases, those expelled for antisemitism managed to retain their party membership. For example, in Ovruch in early June, internal Party reports indicate that a mere two weeks after his expulsion for participating in a pogrom, the Bolshevik 'Iurchenko' was still working in the local Party structure and continued writing articles for the Soviet press.[22] This was not an isolated case: elsewhere in Ovruch, a number of known pogromists continued to work in the local apparatuses of the Soviet government in the summer of 1919, partly because of the inadequacies of Revolutionary Tribunals, but also because Jews, fearful of any reprisals, sometimes refused to name those who had carried out pogroms.[23]

In other regions, however, the Decree appeared to find more support at the local level. In Vitebsk, fifteen individuals were given the death penalty at a Revolutionary Tribunal into the pogrom in the 'Novka' factory in 1919.[24] In Golynka, Smolensk, a Commissar of the local Cheka was shot for leading a pogrom.[25] In Nemyriv, a city in the Vinnytsia region of western Ukraine, the local Military Revolutionary Committee issued an appeal on 9 April warning that all 'antisemitic agitators' would be sent to a Revolutionary Tribunal and shot.[26] Whether this threat was actually followed, however, remains unknown.

The process of bringing those found guilty of antisemitism to justice was also interrupted by the ongoing Civil War. In the town of Ivanovo (Kyiv province), local Bolsheviks and Jewish community organizations established a series of tribunals to punish those found to have participated in a pogrom carried out on 25 June by insurgents under the command of the Otaman Struk.[27] In late July, the trials had to be abandoned, however, as the Bolsheviks lost control of the town. Later that year, in September, a

---

[22] TsDAHO f.1 o.20 d.30 l.46-47, 96, 118. On the leniency of the sentences issued by the Revolutionary Tribunals in Russia in 1917 and 1918, see Rendle, 708–09.
[23] Miliakova, *Kniga pogromov*, 42–43.
[24] I. Slavin, *Evreiskii pogrom na zavode 'Novki'* (Vitebsk: Izdanie vitebskogo gubvoenrevkoma, 1920), 9.
[25] Buldakov, *Khaos i etnos*, 1032.   [26] TsDAHO f.57 o.2 d.273 l.26.
[27] TsDAVO f.4572 o.1 d.12 l.1-18. Il'ia Timofeevich Struk (1896–1969) was a leader of an anti-Bolshevik insurgence movement in Ukraine during the Civil War; Miliakova, *Kniga pogromov*, 847. His attempts to mobilize the peasantry were invariably accompanied by claims that the 'Yid Trotsky-Bronstein' was closing down Orthodox Churches. One of his slogans was 'Death to Nakhamkes [a reference to the Jewish Bolshevik Iu. Steklov] and Bronstein ... Down with the Judas Red Star!' Nedava, *Trotsky and the Jews*, 165.

Revolutionary Tribunal was convened in Moscow to resume the case after the Bolsheviks had lost power in Ukraine. However, the Moscow Tribunal concluded that no punishment could be issued owing to a lack of evidence (all witnesses were either still in Ukraine or had emigrated). As this case illustrates, even when there was the desire at the local level to bring antisemites to justice, the military situation sometimes prevented the Party from honouring its commitment to the Decree. In regions such as Slovechne in Volyn, it took until 1921 before those guilty of participating in the pogroms of the spring of 1919 were tried and shot by firing squad.[28]

There is evidence to suggest that punishments were more severe when antisemitism was used to incite workers and peasants against Bolshevik rule. In Myrhorod, a city in the Poltava region, the former officer of a Soviet battalion Sergei Dubchak led an uprising against the Soviet regime in early April 1919 under the slogan 'Death to the Yids and Communists, long live Soviet Power!' When the Bolsheviks regained control of the city on 4 April, Dubchak, along with seven other leaders of the uprising, was sentenced to death by the Revolutionary Tribunal. Among the charges brought against them was their explicit use of antisemitism to agitate *against the regime*.[29] This latter case is instructive, since it suggests that antisemitism was punishable by death not because the accused had participated in antisemitic political action in and of itself, but rather, because such action represented a crime against the Soviet state. Indeed, a statute issued by the Moscow-based Commissariat for Justice on 21 February 1919 made it clear that those to be brought before the Revolutionary Tribunals were to include individuals accused of 'organizing, participating in or calling for counter-revolutionary actions *against the Workers-Peasants' Government* (that is, uprisings, pogroms, mass disorders etc)'.[30] Pogromist violence, then, was a crime first and foremost because it represented a threat to the *Soviet state*, not to Jews as such.

Abramson has stated that this Bolshevik response to antisemitism in early to mid-1919 was 'very effective'.[31] To substantiate this claim,

---

[28] GARF f.R-1339 o.1 d.418 l.28.

[29] TsDAVO f.5 o.1 d.17 l.43. See also TsDAHO f.1 o.20 d.35 l.20. In 2009, a large monument to Dubchak was erected in the place where he was executed by the order of the Revolutionary Tribunal. The plaque accompanying the monument commemorates the 'victims of Bolshevik-Chekist terror ... Glory to Heroes of Ukraine!' No mention is made of the fact that this 'hero' of the Ukrainian nation was a leader of a pogrom and that he was, in part, shot for this reason.

[30] GARF f.1250 o.21 d.24 l.13.

[31] Abramson, *A Prayer for the Government*, 150. For a critique of Abramson's general thesis, see L. Fischer, 'The Pogromshchina and the Directory: A New Historiographical Synthesis?', *Revolutionary Russia* 16, no. 2 (2003): 47–93.

he cites the aforementioned 'order' written by Rakovskii following the meeting on 5 February, which threatened those found guilty of antisemitism with 'the most brutal and severe measures'.[32] However, as the material presented here demonstrates, the 'order' was met with an uneven reception on the ground. This flowed from the nature of 'Bolshevik power' itself: whatever semblance of hegemony the Bolsheviks had managed to achieve by early 1919 in Ukraine existed largely at the level of the repressive apparatuses of the Soviet state. The Bolshevik response to antisemitism, like so many other Party campaigns of that period, was predicated on the politics of coercion, not consent. This is neatly captured in a stark letter by the Bolshevik Iurii Steklov to the Party Central Committee in June 1919: 'In the purely peasant and semi-proletarian provinces soviet power in general and the Communist Party in particular has no social base ... Terror reigns. We hold on only through terror.'[33] In this respect, the Soviet confrontation with antisemitism reflected the broader weaknesses of the Bolshevik project in Ukraine.

The Soviet State Response to Antisemitism: February–July 1919

The beginnings of a new campaign against antisemitism in early 1919 emanated principally from the Bolsheviks in Ukraine. However, two important interventions were also made by leading Party members in Moscow. In late March, five weeks after the meeting of the Ukrainian Sovnarkom, Lenin recorded a short gramophone speech titled, 'On the Pogromist Persecution of the Jews' (*O pogromnoi travle evreev*).[34] The speech was played on loudspeaker in workplaces and agitational-political trains, and apparently also at meetings and demonstrations.[35] Its impact, however, appears to have been limited, since it only appeared in print form after Lenin's death in 1924.[36]

---

[32] IJ, f.19 o.1 d.4 l.50.
[33] S. A. Smith, *The Russian Revolution: A Very Short Introduction* (Oxford: Oxford University Press, 2002), 91.
[34] Lenin, *Polnoe sobranie sochinenii*, Vol. 35, 242; Lenin, *Lenin on the Jewish Question*, 135–36.
[35] Agurskii, *Evreiskii rabochii v kommunisticheskom dvizhenii (1917-1921)*, 155; Larin, *Evrei i antisemitizm v SSSR*, 7.
[36] The pogrom speech was omitted from the first edition of Lenin's Works (published in 1925), though was later included in the Second Edition. See Schwarz, *The Jews in the Soviet Union*, 289. Although the speech continued to appear in subsequent editions of Lenin's works, it was consistently omitted in post-war published collections of Lenin's seven other gramophone recordings.

During the same week Lenin recorded the speech, Bukharin and Preobrazhenskii presented their *ABC of Communism* to the Eighth Party Congress. The *ABC* was a highly influential document that was republished countless times by the Party during the Civil War, including a 1921 Yiddish edition issued by the Jewish Commissariat.[37] In the chapter titled 'Communism and the Problem of Nationality', Preobrazhenskii authored a special section dedicated to antisemitism.[38] This was not Preobrazhenskii's first public statement on antisemitism – in the summer of 1917, he also proposed a resolution on pogroms at the First All-Russian Congress of Soviets (see Chapter 1).

Yet unlike Rakovskii's interventions cited earlier, neither Preobrazhenskii's 1919 text nor Lenin's speech made any reference to working class or Red Army agency in the pogroms. Lenin, for example, defined antisemitism purely as the work of 'capitalists, who strive to sow and foment hatred between workers of different faiths, different nations and different races'.[39] Similarly, for Preobrazhenskii, antisemitism was the preserve of the 'Russian bourgeoisie' who 'raised the hunt against the Jews' in order to 'divert the anger of the exploited workers'.[40] As is clear from the preceding discussion, these somewhat reductive conceptualizations failed to account for the many-sided nature of antisemitism, and, in particular, the way it traversed the political divide, finding expression within the left as well as the right.[41]

Their limitations notwithstanding, these interventions did represent an attempt on the part of the most senior members of the Party leadership to intervene on the issue. Unfortunately, these were to be isolated interventions: from January to May 1919, there would be no further statements by the Moscow Party leadership on antisemitism. Instead, the Bolshevik response to antisemitism in the first half of 1919 flowed singularly from Ukraine, and from the Ukrainian Party leadership.

However, in Ukraine, the campaign appeared to stall almost as soon as it had begun. Following the meeting of the Ukrainian Sovnarkom on 5 February, the next intervention by the Bolshevik leadership in Ukraine would not come for a full two months. During this period pogroms continued, and in March in particular, Red Army pogroms broke out

---

[37] GARF f.1318 o.24 d.13b l.13; f.1318 o.24 d.15 l.30. On the *ABC*, see L. T. Lih, 'The Mystery of the ABC', *Slavic Review* 56, no. 1 (1997): 50–72.
[38] Bukharin and Preobrazhenskii, *The ABC of Communism*, 199–200.
[39] Lenin, *Polnoe sobranie sochinenii*, Vol. 35:242; Lenin, *Lenin on the Jewish Question*, 135–36.
[40] Bukharin and Preobrazhenskii, *The ABC of Communism*, 199.
[41] For a detailed discussion of Lenin's speech, see McGeever, 'Bolshevik Responses to Antisemitism during the Civil War'.

in Rosava and Uman'.[42] Bolshevik leaders continued to receive reports about these and other such outbreaks,[43] and thus their silence during these critical two months underlines the limited degree to which a consistent political practice in opposition to antisemitism had been established. In other words, the campaign in Ukraine during the first half of 1919 was sporadic and reactive. Whenever the Ukrainian Bolsheviks did intervene, they did so in response to antisemitic incidents that had already taken place; and not all incidents were met with a response.

On 7 April, two months after the Ukrainian Sovnarkom interventions, the Party Central Committee in Ukraine entered the fray, passing a resolution which exhibited a strikingly open admission of the nature of the problem facing the Bolsheviks:

> The kulak counter-revolution is peddling an evil, demagogic politics. It mechanically joins counter-revolutionary and Soviet slogans and in doing so tries to cover up its kulak, pogromist-chauvinist essence with Bolshevik phraseology ('We are Ukrainian Bolsheviks'. 'We are for Soviets but against the Yids and the *katsapy*'; 'We are for an indepdenent Urkraine').[44]

This resolution was by no means a 'backstage' intervention: it was circulated by the Ukrainian Press Bureau (the Ukrainian Sovnarkom's press department) and then subsequently published in both national and local editions of the Party press in mid-April[45] and again on 6 May.[46] Following Rakovskii's 'order' in early February, this was the second public recognition that antisemitism could resonate with sections of the revolution's social base. Moreover, the resolution specifically recognized that antisemitism could find traction through an appropriation of Bolshevik discourse, and that consequently the Bolshevik movement in Ukraine had become a battleground where the politics of antisemitism were playing out.

---

[42] On Rosava, see Heifets, *The Slaughter of the Jews in the Ukraine in 1919*, 85. On Uman', see Miliakova, *Kniga pogromov*, 118–20.

[43] RGVA f.25860 o.1 d.262, 263. I wish to thank Dimitri Tolkatsch for bringing this source to my attention.

[44] RGASPI f.71 o.35 d.512 l.118; f.17 o.6 d.369 l.87-88. *Katsapy* is a pejorative term for ethnic Russians. The Central Committee had been formed at the Third Congress of the Ukrainian Communist Party, held in Kharkiv in early March, and comprised Piatakov, Bubnov, Meshcheriakov, Voroshilov, Rakovskii, Hamarnyk, Khmel'nitskii, Kviring, Farbman (Rafail), Ivanov, Zatonskii, Kharechko, Rovner, Drobnis and Kosior. Of these fifteen Party leaders, only three were Ukrainian. Borys, *The Sovietization of Ukraine, 1917–1923*, 153. The full protocols from the Third Congress of the Ukrainian Communist Party are published in S. I. Gurenko, *Tretii zizd Komunistychnoi Partii (bilshovykiv) Ukrainy. 1–6 Bereznia 1919 g. Protokoly.* (Kiev: Parlamentske vid-vo, 2002).

[45] It was published in *Odesskii Kommunist*, the Party's local Odessa newspaper, on 18 April.

[46] *Bol'shevik*, 6 May 1919. See also RGASPI f.71 o.35 d.512 l.248-252.

In response to more reports of peasant rebellions and outbreaks of Red Army antisemitism came a further announcement from the central authorities in Ukraine, this time in the shape of an appeal from the All-Ukrainian Central Executive Committee (hereafter *VUTsIK*), issued on 8 May. Although the Ukrainian Sovnarkom had legislative rights, these were subject to confirmation by the *VUTsIK*.[47] An appeal from the *VUTsIK*, therefore, arguably carried more political weight than did the decrees already issued by the Sovnarkom in February 1919. The *VUTsIK* appeal was distributed widely by both the government and Party: for example, it took up the entire front page of the 8 May editions of the two main Bolshevik newspapers, *Kommunist*[48] and *Bol'shevik*.[49] In addition, in mid-June it was published as a separate leaflet and distributed in the countryside.[50] Addressed specifically to the peasantry, the appeal covered a range of issues from the food crisis to the *kombedy* (Committees of the Poor). From its opening sentence, however, the question of antisemitism within the Bolsheviks' social base loomed large:

Comrade peasants! Recently a dirty pogromist counter-revolutionary wave has swept across practically the whole of Ukraine. In throwing themselves over to our side, the provocateurs claim that they stand for the workers and the peasants, [but then] turn you against Soviet power, against the power of the workers and the peasants.

This was now the *third* public admission by the Bolshevik leadership in Ukraine that antisemitism could be found in the ranks of the Party's support. The 'provocateurs' were not depicted as an abstract class enemy in the shape of 'the bourgeoisie' or 'the capitalists', as had been the case in the interventions of Lenin and Preobrazhenskii in late March; instead, they were framed as a real social force working under the rubric of 'Bolshevism'. This appeal was a direct attempt to address the growing disjuncture between the Party leadership's vision of 'Soviet power' on the one hand, and the popular conception of that term, which increasingly was taking on an antisemitic inflection. It was also an attempt to deconstruct the explosive, antisemitic 'Judeo-Communist'[51] construction:

The Soviet government is your government ... [but] they try to set you against it by saying it is a Jewish government. The counter-revolutionaries and provocateurs understand very well that the only way out for them is to destroy the unity and

---

[47] Borys, *The Sovietization of Ukraine, 1917-1923*, 218. [48] *Kommunist*, 8 May 1919.
[49] *Bol'shevik*, 8 May 1919. [50] GARF f.9550 o.4. d.10345.
[51] On the myth of Judeo-Bolshevism, see André Gerrits, *The Myth of Jewish Communism: A Historical Interpretation* (New York: P.I.E. Peter Lang, 2009); P. Hanebrink, *A Specter Haunting Europe: The Myth of Judeo-Bolshevism* (Cambridge, MA: Harvard University Press, 2018).

solidarity [*splochennost'*] of the working people of different nationalities ... They say that Jewish Commissars rule over Ukraine. This is the most malicious and pernicious lie. You yourself elect the soviets and the local commissars at your own congresses.

The 8 May appeal by the *VUTsIK* also contained a special section dedicated specifically to antisemitism, titled 'Pogroms Undercut the Unity of the Working People', in which it was announced that the Soviet government would 'mercilessly punish all villains' who take part in pogroms.[52]

Just two days later, on 10 May, an unprecedented outbreak of Red Army antisemitism erupted in the Ukrainian south, in the shape of the Grigor'ev rebellion. In haste, the Central Committee of the Ukrainian Bolsheviks once more intervened, this time issuing an urgent appeal of its own. Again, it tried to take on the explosive articulation between antisemitism and the popular conception of 'Soviet power':

Comrade peasants! ... Do not listen to those villains who shout 'beat up the Yids, down with the Yids and the Commissars'! Remember, if a Jew stands on the side of the workers' and peasants' revolution, they are one of us, like a Ukrainian or a Russian. And you yourself know that the issue is not whether they are a Jew, a Russian or a Ukrainian, but whether they are oppressed or an oppressor, a peasant or a landowner, a worker or a bourgeois.[53]

This statement offers an exemplar of some of the discursive tensions that defined the Soviet confrontation with antisemitism during this period. First, in appealing to a Ukrainian and Russian subjectivity through the first-person personal pronoun '*us*', the Central Committee simultaneously positioned itself in such a way as to undercut the antisemitic conception of Soviet power as a (third person) 'Jewish' power. In so doing, however, the statement appeared also to represent the Soviet government as part of a Russian/Ukrainian formation ('one of us, like a Ukrainian or a Russian'). In taking the important step of rejecting its association with an antisemitic conception of 'Jewishness', the Central Committee therefore appeared to open itself up to an accommodation with a Russian/Ukrainian ethno-national identification, which was evidently at odds with the Bolsheviks' self-avowed internationalist worldview. Perhaps aware of this, the following sentence rejected such a move and instead pushed the narrative into an ethnically non-specific space: 'the issue is not whether he is a Jew, a Russian or a Ukrainian ...'. The

---

[52] RGASPI f.71 o.35 d.486 l.51-57; f.71 o.35 d.512 l.175-184.
[53] TsDAHO f.57 o.2 d.342 l.106-109. The appeal was signed by the Central Committee members: Piatakov, Bubnov, Khorechko, Zatonskii, Khmel'nitskii, Drobino, Tarskii, Rafail, Ivanov, Antonov-Ovseenko, Kviring, Kossior, Meshcheriakov and Rakovskii.

terrain here was *class*, not ethnicity: '... but whether he is oppressed or an oppressor ... a worker or a bourgeois'. Yet far from resolving the tensions inherent in the text, this last passage merely revealed new difficulties. The Central Committee counterposed class ('worker' and 'bourgeoisie') to ethno-national ('Jew' and 'Russian') categories. However, this neat distinction did not hold within a political field in which antisemitic constructions of Jewishness bore *both* class and ethnic overdeterminations. In this context, 'the Jews' and 'the bourgeoisie' were, in the antisemitic imagination, one and the same thing. When terms such as 'the bourgeoisie' gained traction at the level of everyday social relations, they did so in ways which departed significantly from the Bolsheviks' own Marxist conceptualizations. Popular anti-bourgeois sentiment, an important reservoir of revolutionary socialism, could, at the same time, be a resource of antisemitic mobilization. In other words, these were categories and concepts over which the Bolsheviks often had little control. Such were the contradictions and tensions facing the Bolsheviks as they tried to navigate a coherent response to the dramatic escalation of anti-Jewish violence; each discursive step taken in this field opened up the possibility of a new articulation with antisemitism.

Confronting Antisemitism at the Local Level

It has already been demonstrated that the directives and appeals issued from the Party centre often found limited traction on the ground, owing to the nature and extent of antisemitism within the lower echelons of the state apparatuses. The reception of the Party leadership's campaign was not wholly negative, however. Amidst the near breakdown of Soviet power as the Grigor'evshchina took hold, real attempts were made by Bolshevik activists at the local level to confront antisemitism within the Red Army. For example, in late April and early May, a group of communists within the 6th Regiment of the Second Division of the Red Army[54] issued a leaflet addressed to their fellow comrades, warning: 'the enemy is secretive and cunning ... you probably don't know but ... these enemies are all around you in their thousands ... and their main weapon is antisemitism'.[55] The same leaflet went on to say:

---

[54] The 6th Regiment was formed in late 1918 by merging the 9th Oskol'skii regiment, 6th Korochanskii regiment and the Mikhailovskii battalion; Korolivskii, Kolensnik and Rybalka, *Grazhdanskaia voina na Ukraine 1918-1920. Tom pervyi, Kniga pervaia*, 492.

[55] TsDAHO f.57 o.2 d.342 l.79-84.

Everywhere the Red Army gathers you hear them shout the black-hundred slogan 'beat the Yids!' Is this really a slogan of the Red Army? Is this really a slogan of those who are conscious? No! This is the slogan of Nicolas II ... We must say as one that for us there is no difference between Russians, Jews, Germans, and Ukrainians. For us there is only one difference – that between workers [*trudiashchiisia*] and capitalists. We know that it is not the workers but the capitalists who are our enemy, regardless of their nationality.[56]

The challenges this group of communists faced in their confrontation with antisemitism in the 6th Regiment were considerable. The regiment itself was huge, comprising over 3,000 troops by mid-April 1919.[57] Those communists opposed to antisemitism within the regiment, however, were a minority current: in late February they numbered only forty-two activists,[58] and by late April, when the leaflet quoted above was issued, that number had been reduced to a mere twenty.[59] According to internal reports, this small group was operating within a huge regiment which remained deeply antisemitic, 'politically illiterate', 'undisciplined' and prone to 'terrorizing the local population'.[60] Despite their important political work against antisemitism, it was not enough to stem the flow of anti-Jewish violence: in mid-April, the 6th Regiment carried out a pogrom in Vasylkiv.[61] As this case illustrates, even when there was a willingness to confront antisemitism at the local level, such Bolsheviks often found themselves in a minority. In early to mid-1919, they frequently found their efforts blocked by antisemitism embedded in the local state apparatus.

Despite working in such perilous conditions, groups of communists within other sections of the Red Army continued to tackle the question of antisemitism during this period. In the critical weeks between mid-April and late May, meetings and lectures on antisemitism were successfully held for troops of the Third Division of the Red Army. According to one report, they helped 'eradicate' antisemitism within the Division.[62] Similarly positive reports emerged from the Reserve Army in the Podolia

---

[56] TsDAHO f.57 o.2 d.342 l.79-84.   [57] RGASPI f.71 o.35 d.498 l.167ob.
[58] Korolivskii, Kolensnik and Rybalka, *Grazhdanskaia voina na Ukraine 1918-1920. Tom pervyi, Kniga pervaia.*, 645. Incidentally, this was one of the largest groups of communists in the Red Army; Korolivskii, Kolensnik and Rybalka, *Grazhdanskaia voina na Ukraine 1918–1920. Tom pervyi, Kniga pervaia*, 492.
[59] RGVA f.25860 o.1 d.148 l.119ob. I am grateful for Dimitri Tolkatsch's help in finding this source.
[60] RGVA f.25860 o.1 d.148 l.119ob.
[61] Committee of the Jewish Delegations, *The Pogroms in the Ukraine under the Ukrainian Governments (1917-1920)*, 264.
[62] TsDAHO f.1 o.20 d.35 l.122-123.

region in late May.⁶³ Other such initiatives were taken within the 14th Army near the Donbass.⁶⁴

Perhaps the most significant of these attempts came at a conference of Red Army Communists of the Kyiv Garrison, held over four days in early June 1919. On the first day of the conference a standard resolution was passed, declaring antisemitism to be the work of 'counter-revolutionaries and provocateurs who want to destroy soviet power'.⁶⁵ This was a safe, and in the context of ongoing Red pogroms, somewhat empty statement which simply framed the problem of antisemitism as an external issue, as something outside of the Bolshevik and Soviet milieu (in this respect it echoed Lenin's and Preobrazhenskii's interventions in March 1919, discussed earlier). On the third day of the conference, however, a more substantial resolution was passed which put in strikingly clear terms the extent to which antisemitism had found traction within the Bolsheviks' own social base: 'The Red Army, composed mainly as it is by the peasant masses, has become main centre of attention for pogromists.'⁶⁶ This was perhaps the *only* time during the entire Russian Revolution that anyone within the Bolshevik party made the claim that the Red Army had become the *principal* site of antisemitism and pogromist 'agitation'. What is more, this statement was printed in *Bol'shevik*, the main Party newspaper in Ukraine.

In some regions, local Party institutions also addressed the question of Red Army antisemitism. For example, at the Third Party Conference of the Chernihiv Region in June, a resolution was passed expressing a 'categorical protest against those who call for the Jews to be beaten up, against those who carry out their counter-revolutionary work under the flag of 'Bolshevism' ... There is no place for pogromists among the poor [*bednoty*]!'⁶⁷ The significant element of this resolution, like the others quoted above, was its recognition of the presence of antisemitism among those fighting for 'Bolshevism'. Again, this resolution was not kept to a 'backstage' context: it was published in the local Chernihiv Soviet press.⁶⁸ Similar measures were taken elsewhere in June. In Odessa, the Party newspaper *Odesskii Komunist* published a letter from

---

⁶³ TsDAHO f.1 o.20 d.35 l.139-141.
⁶⁴ RGVA f.9 o.4 d.66 l.18 and GARF f.9550 o.14 d.134 l.1. See also RGASPI f.71 o.35 d.497 l.183.
⁶⁵ *Bol'shevik*, 15 June 1919, 3.
⁶⁶ *Bol'shevik*, 18 June 1919, 3. See also RGASPI f.71 o.35 d.497 l.242-243; f.71 o.35 d.500 l.142-143; f.71 o.35 d.519 l.39-40. Emphasis added.
⁶⁷ RGASPI f.71 o.35 d.486 l.373.
⁶⁸ *Izvestiia Gubernskogo Ipolnitel'nogo Komiteta Soveta Rabochikh Selianskikh i Krasnoarmeiskikh Deputatov Chernigovshchiny*, 22 June 1919, 1.

a reader who warned that antisemites were going about 'in Red Army clothes'.[69] As we shall see, however, such public admissions of Red Army antisemitism in the Soviet press were rare, and in fact, the Party leadership regularly went out of its way to ensure that information regarding Red pogroms was kept *out* of the front stage debate on antisemitism.

The Soviet Press Campaign, Early to Mid-1919

Despite the demand from the Ukrainian Sovnarkom in early February 1919 that the Party press carry regular features on antisemitism,[70] such articles appeared only sporadically in the months of February and March. In the two most widely read Red Army newspapers in Ukraine – the Kharkiv-based *Krasnaia Zvezda* (Red Star) and the Commissariat for Military Affairs organ *Krasnaia Armiia* (The Red Army) – not one article on antisemitism was published in the month of April.[71] In Russia, the situation was even starker: when the Grigor'evshchina commenced in early May, the main Bolshevik newspaper *Pravda* had yet to publish a single article devoted specifically to the question of antisemitism. This did not go unnoticed by Jewish Sections of the Party (the Evsektsiia). On 11 May, as the crisis in Ukraine unfolded, Dimanshtein, head of the Evsektsiia, made an urgent appeal at a meeting of the Party Central Committee in Moscow for the Soviet press 'to pay more serious attention to the fight against antisemitism'.[72] This evidently stirred the Party leadership: later that same day the Orgburo met in Moscow to discuss the proposal, and it noted with bitterness the fact that although the Central Committee had apparently informed the provincial Party committees about the 'necessity of republishing leading articles from the central Soviet newspapers', the central newspapers themselves had failed to provide such articles in the first place, and in fact had been 'entirely silent' on the issue of antisemitism.[73] The Orgburo's complaint can be seen to have had at least some impact: on 14 May, the *first* full-length lead article in *Pravda* against antisemitism since the October Revolution

---

[69] See RGASPI f.71 o.35 d.486 l.371-372. For attempts by the local Malyn Committee of the Poor in Kyiv to stop antisemitism, see RGASPI f.71 o.35 d.500 l.159 and *Bol'shevik*, 24 July 1919, 4.
[70] TsDAVO f.2 o.1 d.16 l.17.
[71] RGASPI f.71 o.35 d.499 l.100-160. There were vast numbers of Red Army newspapers. For example, each Red Army division had its own specific publication. See RGASPI f.71 o.35 d.916 l.68-73 for further information. Future studies might attempt to cover these publications more systematically than was possible here.
[72] RGASPI f.17 o.65 d.91 l.14-16.
[73] RGASPI f.17 o.112 d.4 l.25. I have been unable to find any evidence that such directives were issued by the Central Committee in Russia.

was duly published.[74] However, the editors of the main Party newspapers were evidently not doing enough as far as the Party leadership was concerned: the following week, on 22 May, at another meeting of the Orgburo, leading Bolsheviks felt moved to point out *'for the third time'* how 'essential it is' that the main Bolshevik newspapers *Pravda* and *Izvestiia* devote special articles to the question of antisemitism.[75] This directive, however, failed to alter the established pattern. When a second piece appeared in *Pravda* on 12 June,[76] it would be the last time during the entire Civil War period that the Bolsheviks' main newspaper carried a lead article on the topic of antisemitism. In Russia, the confrotation with antisemiitism in the national Party press failed to materialize.[77]

Not so in Ukraine. Despite an uneven and sporadic beginning in February and March 1919, the press campaign in Ukraine fared better than its Russian counterpart. After its establishment in early April 1919, the main newspaper of the Central Committee of the Ukrainian Party – *Bol'shevik* – ran weekly articles on antisemitism until late June.[78] Local Party and government newspapers also published their own articles on the topic of antisemitism.[79] Even more extensive was the propaganda campaign carried out through the medium of leaflets and brochures. In May 1919 alone, the Commissariat for Military Affairs in Ukraine

---

[74] I. Vardin, 'Protiv evreia – za tsaria [To be against the Jews is to be for the Tsar]', *Pravda*, 14 May 1919, 1.

[75] RGASPI f.17 o.112 d.4 l.73 (emphasis in the original).

[76] I. Vardin, 'Pogromnaia 'demokratiia'' [The Pogromist Democracy]', *Pravda*, 12 June 1919, 1.

[77] At the local level, some newspapers did initiate a press campaign against antisemitism. For example, the Petrograd edition of *Pravda* (*Petrogradskaia Pravda*) ran a fairly consistent series of articles on antisemitism in June and July. See, for example, the articles in the following issues: 'Antisemitizm i kontrrevoliutsiia [Antisemitism and Counter-revolution]', 5 June 1919, 2–3; 'Pogromy pod egidoi "sotsializma" i "demokratii"' [Pogroms under the Aeigis of "Socialism" and "Democracy"]', 17 June 1919, 1 (the second half of this article was published twelve days later); 'Pogromy na Ukraine [Pogroms in Ukraine]', 6 July 1919, 2; 'Gosudarstvennaia propaganda i antisemitizm v Kolchakovskom tsarstve [State Propaganda and Antisemitism under Kolchak Rule]', 29 July 1919, 1. A further article was published on 22 August 1919, titled 'Rost antisemitizma [The Growth of Antisemitism]', 1.

[78] See, for example, the following articles: 'Kulatskie bunty' [The Kulak Revolt], 12 April 1919, 1; 'Doloi kulakov' [Down With the Kulaks], 25 April 1919, 2; 'Prichina pogromov' [The Reason for the Pogroms], 28 May 1919, 1; 'Pogromshchikov k stenke!' [Pogromists to the Firing Squad!], 31 May 1919, 1; 'Na bor'by s kulakami' [To War with the Kulaks], 5 June 1919, 1; and 'Smert'' pogromshchikam!' [Death to the Pogromists!], 20 June 1919, 2. Other articles that dealt more tangentially with antisemitism were published on 6 May 1919 (p. 1), 8 May 1919 (pp. 1–2) and 13 June 1919 (p. 3).

[79] For example, *Kommunar*, the Party newspaper in the Kharkiv province, published articles against antisemitism on 3 May 1919 and again on 2 August 1919.

published at least ten individual brochures[80] and seven leaflets[81] dedicated specifically to the question of antisemitism. Further leaflets were issued by other sections of the Party and Ukrainian Soviet government, such as the aforementioned appeal by the Central Committee in mid-May[82] and a further two leaflets by the Kyiv Military District.[83] Some historians, such as Richard Pipes, have suggested that the Bolsheviks were 'conspicuously silent' about antisemitism in 1919.[84] The evidence presented here suggests otherwise: while the campaign in the main Bolshevik newspapers in Russia failed to get off the ground, in Ukraine, despite beginning sporadically in February and March, the campaign was consistent and extensive by April and May.

---

[80] According to a report compiled by Podvoiskii, the head of the Commissariat for Military Affairs, the Commissariat for Military Affairs published the following eight titles in April and May (circulation figures and language are in brackets): 'Pochemu Petliurovtsy ustraivaiut pogromy' [Why The Petliurists Organise Pogroms] (50,000); 'Doloi pogromy' [Down With Pogroms] (50,000); 'Pochemu i kak kulaki vedut travliu protiv evreev' [The Reasons Why the Kulaks Carry out the Persecution of the Jews] (35,000); 'O pogromakh' [On the Pogroms] (75,000); 'Pogromy – vozvrat k proshlomu' [Pogroms - a Return to the Past] (35,000 – this brochure was issued on three separate occasions in April and May alone); 'Get' pogromshchykiv!' (100,000, Ukrainian); 'Dlia chogo i iak kulaki tskuiut protiv evreev' [Why and for What Reason do the Kulaks Persecute the Jews?] (65,000, Ukrainian); and 'Pogromi – povorot do mynulogo' [Pogroms - a Return to the Past] (65,000, Ukrainian). RGASPI f.71 o.35 d.691 l.123ob-124. In addition to these eight, I have been able to track down two further titles published by the Commissariat in mid-1919: see I. Shelit, I. *Doloi pogromy* (Kyiv: Izdatel'stvo narodnogo kommisariata po voennym delam Ukrainy, 1919) and P. Eletskii, *O evreiakh*, Khar'kov: Ukrainskaia sotsialisticheskaia respublika, 1919). These publications formed part of a much wider propaganda campaign waged by the Soviet government: in May 1919, the Commissariat for Military Affairs in Ukraine circulated nearly 2 million leaflets, some 1.6 million newspapers, 929,000 brochures and 32,300 posters. RGASPI f.71 o.35 d.691 l.129.

[81] The aforementioned report by Podvoiskii notes that the following three leaflets were published in May 1919 (circulation in parentheses): 'Pochemu Petliurovtsy ustraivaiut pogromy (50,000 – this item is held in GARF f.9550 o.4 d.10514 l.1); 'Get' pogromshchykiv' (100,000, Ukrainian); and 'Pogromy – vozvrat k proshlomu' (50,000 – this was also published as a leaflet in Ukrainian, under the title 'Pogromy – tse vertannia do starogo'. A copy is held in GARF f.9550 o.4 d.10639 l.1-1ob). In addition to these three, a further four leaflets published by the Commissariat during this period can be located in the archives: 'Oni budut sterty s litsa zemli' (GARF f.9550 o.4 d.10506 l.1); 'Tovarishchi krest'iane i rabochie!' (GARF f.9550 o.4 d.10466 l.1 and TsDAHO f.57 o.2 d.342 l.66-69); 'Doloi pogromy' (GARF f.9550 o.4 d.10625 l.1); and 'Doloi zverstva i grabezhi' (GARF f.9550 o.4 d.10561 l.1).

[82] TsDAHO f.57 o.2 d.342 l.106-109.

[83] These were: 'Doloi predatelei', GARF f.9550 o.5 d.1801 l.1, also available at TsDAHO f.57 o.2 d.273 l.49-50; and 'Get' Pogromshchykiv!', GARF f.9550 o.5 d.1796 l.1.

[84] R. Pipes, *Russia under the Bolshevik Regime* (New York: Alfred A. Knopf, 1993), 111.

Silence and Denial: The Soviet Press on Red Army Antisemitism

Cultivating a discussion about antisemitism in the Party press was one thing; addressing the explosive issue of Red Army antisemitism, quite another. Over the course of the Civil War, the Party press singularly failed to address the specific question of antisemitic violence within the Red Army. Whenever articles documenting individual cases of pogromist violence appeared in Soviet newspapers, they almost exclusively focussed on attacks carried out by Petliura's army or the forces loyal to the Directory.[85] Concrete descriptions and reports on Red Army pogroms were notable by their absence.[86] There was, in other words, a striking reluctance by the Party to publicly acknowledge the *nature and extent* of antisemitism within the Red Army.

Amidst the silence, readers of the Party press would have been far more likely to encounter stories depicting the Red Army in a decidedly positive light. In a front-page article published in the Party newspaper *Kommunar* (formerly *Kommunist*) on 12 April, titled 'Pozornoe nasledie proshlogo' (The Shameful Legacy of the Past), antisemitism was presented in highly reductive terms, as a phenomenon of the 'Russian bourgeoisie'. Soviet institutions like the Red Army, claimed the author, were places where 'everyone works in friendship, both Russian and Jewish workers hand in hand together, and in these places you will never hear any talk about the so called 'Jewish power''.[87] Such depictions were at odds with the messiness of the political field, where antisemitism could and did find traction within the Bolshevik movement. Another case in point is a letter written by the Central Committee member Boris Magidov, published in the Party newspaper *Bol'shevik* on 8 August, in which he gives his impressions of the 'political mood' within the Red Army following an inspection:

> I did not encounter one single instance of antisemitism. This greatly impressed me from my arrival. Each day I spent amidst the Red Army I heard all sorts of colloquial talk, but not once did I hear that term from everyday life – 'Yid'.[88]

---

[85] See, for example, *Petrogradskaia Pravda* on 6 July 1919 and RGASPI f.71 o.35 d.490 l.111-112.

[86] I have come across just one case in which the Soviet press ran a special report on pogroms carried out by the Red Army: *Zhizn' Natsiona'nostei*, 16 March 1919, 3.

[87] *Kommunar. Organ Khar'kovskogo Gubernskogo Komiteta Kommunisticheskoi Partii (bol'shevikov) Ukrainy*, 12 April 1919, 1.

[88] *Bol'shevik*, 8 August 1919, 2. Magidov does not state which regiment or division this was.

Alongside this silence on individual cases of 'Red antisemitism', the Party press carried reports documenting the role the Red Army had played in stopping pogroms.[89] The editors of Party newspapers were evidently selective in the information they shared with their readership regarding the extent of anti-Jewish violence within the Red Army.

At times, the Party press went as far as to knowingly deny that Red Army pogroms had taken place. One such case is an article on pogroms published in the newspaper of the Commissariat for National Affairs, *Zhizn' Natsional'nostei* (The Life of Nationalities), in late August. The article was based on a report carried out by the Russian Red Cross into the pogroms of January–August 1919. In the original, *unpublished* report, specific mention was made of the complicity of the Red Army in the pogroms of March, April and May.[90] It included, for example, a table detailing the total number of recorded instances of pogroms broken down by the military units responsible. In total, 120 pogroms were recorded with an estimated 15,000 fatalities. Included in this table was a column for all known pogroms carried out by 'Soviet units' (13 out of the 120 pogroms, a total of 11 per cent, were attributed to the Red Army). This section of the table further stated that pogroms carried out by the Red Army had been responsible for approximately 500 fatalities.[91] In the *published* version of the report that appeared in *Zhizn' Natsional'-nostei*, however, the section on 'Soviet units' was *deleted* from the table. What is more, even the number of fatalities attributed to Grigor'ev's troops (who, if we recall, were formally attached to the Red Army until their rebellion) were reduced from 6,000 to 4,000 in the published version. In short, readers of the newspaper were presented with a picture of the pogrom wave between January and August 1919 in which the role of the Red Army was denied outright and the extent of the violence downplayed.[92] This was no isolated case: in other reports on the pogroms published in the Soviet press, the role of the Red Army was also omitted.[93]

The practice of rendering Red Army antisemitism invisible actually informed the Party's process of gathering information on pogroms. For example, in a questionnaire drafted by the Jewish Commissariat in early

---

[89] *Izvestiia VtsIK Sovetov, Rabochikh, Krest'ianskikh i Krasnoarmeiskikh Deputatov i Ispolnitel'nogo Komiteta Kievskogo Soveta Rabochikh Deputatov*, 12 April 1919. See also RGASPI f.71 o.35 d.499 l.18-21.
[90] The original is held at HUL f.3050 o.1 d.162 l.3ob-4ob.
[91] HUL f.3050 o.1 d.162 l.6-6ob.   [92] *Zhizn' Natsional'nostei*, 28 August 1919, 3.
[93] See *Izvestiia VtsIK Sovetov, Rabochikh, Krest'ianskikh i Krasnoarmeiskikh Deputatov i Ispolnitel'nogo Komiteta Kievskogo Soveta Rabochikh Deputatov* and RGASPI f.71 o.35 d.486 l 412-413.

July 1919 and issued to Soviet institutions in regions affected by pogroms, respondents were asked the following question: 'Who participated in the pogrom – retreating and advancing white-guard bands or local kulak elements?'[94] Two things can be noted here: first, the question is a closed one, with the categories of pogromist agency prescribed for those filling out the questionnaire. Second, and more important, the Red Army and the various partisan units attached to it are left out of the options on offer. They were not, it seems, legitimate categories of antisemitic agency.[95]

Into the 1920s: The Soviet Press Denial of Civil War–Era 'Red Antisemitism', 1920–1926

These practices continued, and indeed intensified, in the early 1920s. In 1920, the Russian writer and friend of Maksim Gor'kii, Sergei Gusev-Orenburgskii, carried out extensive research into the 1919–20 pogrom wave in Ukraine using testimonies of survivors collected by the Russian Red Cross.[96] When he presented the Soviet government with a finished manuscript, entitled *Bagrovaia Kniga* (The Crimson Book),[97]

---

[94] *Zhizn' Natsional'nostei*, 6 July 1919, 4.

[95] Other questionnaires released in 1920–21 were more open-ended. For example, in a 1921 questionnaire issued by the Jewish Social Committee for the Relief of Victims of Pogroms (*Evobshchestkom*) – a Jewish relief agency which worked in the early 1920s under the auspices of the Soviet government – respondents were simply asked, 'Who led the pogrom? Who participated in the pogrom?' One question even appeared to *invite* the participants to reflect on the role of the local Soviet regime: 'What was the position of the local Soviet organs of power in relation to the pogrom?' Miliakova, *Kniga pogromov*, 502–03. Similarly, in early July 1920, Evobshchestkom activists were instructed to ask participants about the 'attitude of the local Soviet government' to the pogrom; RGASPI f.272 o.1 d.80 l.3. See GARF f.1318 o.1. d.761 l.146; f.R-1339 o.1 d.421 l.20-21 for a further example.

[96] Copies of these testimonies are held in HUL f.3050 o.1. The Red Cross study was led by Il'ia Kheifets. In June 1919, Dimanshtein, head of the Central Jewish Commissariat, sent Heifets to New York to publicize the 'awfulness of the pogroms carried out by the counter-revolutionary agents of the Entente'; GARF f.1318 o.1 d.570 l.245. Kheifets's book on the pogroms was duly published in New York in 1921, but contrary to Dimanshtein's framing of the subject, he included Red pogroms in his narrative; Heifets, *The Slaughter of the Jews in the Ukraine in 1919*. The book was never published in the Soviet Union. Although in the mid-1920s Kheifets went on to publish two monographs in Soviet Russia, their empirical focus was on pogroms in Hungary: I. Ia. Kheifets, *Mirovaia reaktsiia i evreiskie pogromy. Tom vtoroi: Vengriia 1918-1922* (Moscow: Gosizdat Ukrainy, 1925); and Poland: I. Ia. Kheifets, *Mirovaia reaktsiia i evreiskie pogromy. Tom pervyi: Pol'sha 1918–1922* (Moscow: Gosizdat Ukrainy, 1925). In the latter case, Kheifet's book passed over Budennyi's Red Cavalry pogroms in silence.

[97] The original manuscript was republished in full in 1983 by the New York–based Russian-language publishing house Ladoga. See Gusev-Orenburgskii, *Bagrovaia kniga. Pogromy 1919-1920 gg. na Ukraine*.

Into the 1920s: Soviet Press Denial of 'Red Antisemitism' 133

Gusev-Orenburgskii included detailed discussion of the complicity of the Red Army in the Civil War pogrom wave. The following year, in 1921, the book was duly published in Petrograd under the title, *Kniga o evreiskikh pogromakh na Ukraine v 1919 g.* (The Book of Jewish Pogroms in Ukraine in 1919).[98] However, the book was heavily redacted by Soviet censors such that *each and every* reference to Bolshevik and Red Army antisemitism was deleted in the published version, thus shortening the manuscript by some 100 pages. Entire chapters were removed, meaning that Soviet readers would learn nothing of the Red Army pogrom in Rosava in March 1919, to which Gusev-Orenburskii had devoted fifteen pages in the original manuscript.[99]

In other Soviet publications on the Civil War pogroms, the role of the Red Army was similarly elided. For example, in 1926, an illustrated book commemorating the 1918–21 pogrom wave was published by the Bolshevik controlled Jewish Social Committee for the Relief of Victims of Pogroms (*Evobshchestkom*).[100] The book was based on a series of testimonies and photographs presented at an exhibition held by the Evobshchestkom in Moscow in 1923. Purporting to give its Soviet readership a 'short overview' of anti-Jewish violence in the Russian Revolution, the book passed over the role of the Red Army in silence. Responsibility for the pogrom in Uman', for example, was placed with Grigor'ev's 'counter-revolutionary bandits'. The Soviet army, in contrast, was depicted as the 'class conscious liberator'. If we recall, however, after Grigor'ev's pogromist army had been pushed out of Uman' by the Bolsheviks, the Soviet 8th Army *continued* the pogrom for another six weeks.[101] Such refusal to recognize the Red Army as an antisemitic agent was most clearly illustrated in a pictorial representation of pogromist violence, included in the Evobshchestkom volume.

The caption at the top of the image, given in both Russian and Yiddish, reads: 'A breakdown of Jewish pogroms according to their organizers'. The bulk of the pogroms (430) are attributed to 'bandits', who are represented by the tall figure on the right of the image. The following four additional modalities of pogromist agency are then presented: 'Denikin's Army (171 pogroms)'; 'Petliura's Army (129)'; 'The

---

[98] Gusev-Orenburgskii, *Kniga o evreiskikh pogromakh na Ukraine v 1919 g. Sostavlena po ofitsial'nym dokumentam, dokladam s mest i oprosam postradavshikh.*
[99] Gusev-Orenburgskii, *Bagrovaia kniga. Pogromy 1919–1920 gg. na Ukraine*, 69–83.
[100] Ostrovskii, *Evreiskie pogromy 1918–1921.*
[101] Miliakova, *Kniga pogromov*, 126–27; Heifets, *The Slaughter of the Jews in the Ukraine in 1919*, 87–88.

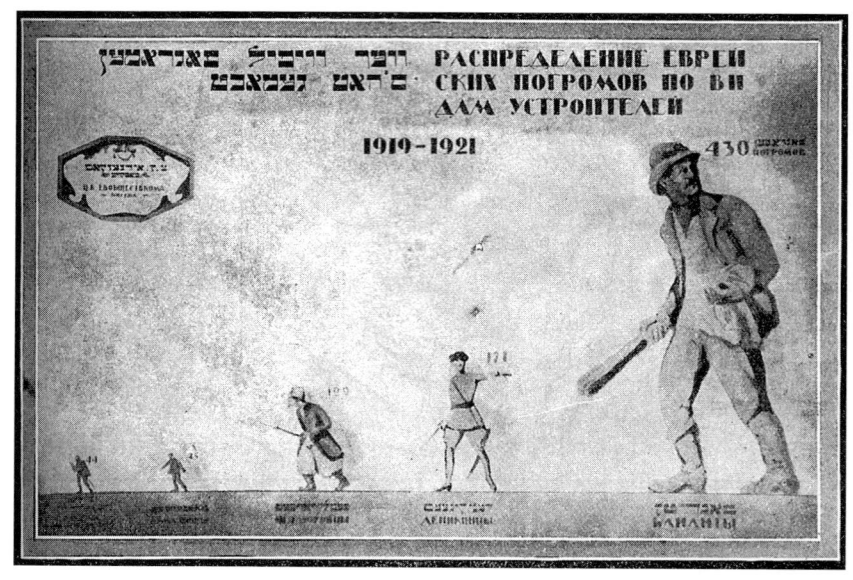

Figure 4 Poster produced by the Jewish Social Committee for the Relief of Victims of Pogroms (*Evobshchestkom*) for an exhibition on pogroms in Moscow in 1923. The caption at the top of the image, given in both Russian and Yiddish, reads: 'A breakdown of Jewish pogroms according to their organizers'. The poster was subsequently published in 1926 in Z. S. Ostrovskii, *Evreiskie pogromy 1918–1921 gg.*, 75.
From the Archives of the YIVO Institute for Jewish Research, New York

Polish Army (45)'; and 'Balakhovich's soldiers¹⁰² (44)'. The complicity of the Red Army is not addressed.¹⁰³

---

¹⁰² General Stanislav Bulak-Balakhovich was a former tsarist officer who served in the White Army under General Yudenich and Petliura, and then formed his own independent army and fought against the Bolsheviks during the Soviet–Polish war of 1919–20. A. Polonsky, *The Jews in Poland and Russia: Volume III: 1914 to 2008* (Oxford: The Littman Library of Jewish Civilization, 2012), 51.

¹⁰³ This was noticed by the Ukrainian anarchist Nester Makhno in 1927, who, having read Ostrovskii's book in Paris, complained that it failed to account for the Red Army pogroms; N. I. Makhno, *Na chuzhbine 1923-1934 gg. Zapiski i stat'i* (Paris: Gromada, 2004), 37. Makhno clearly had his own agenda, since the Bolsheviks repeatedly blamed him and his troops for a number of the Civil War pogroms, an accusation that he vigorously rejected. The question of antisemitism among Makhno's troops is still deeply contested in the literature. Some, such as Shubin, argue that Makhno's army was free of antisemitism, and wherever such cases did exist (and they were few and far between, argues Shubin), Makhno took strong measures against them. See A. Shubin, 'The Makhnovist Movement and the National Question in the Ukraine, 1917-1921', in *Anarchism and Syndicalism in the Colonial and Postcolonial World, 1970-1940. The Praxis of National Liberation, Internationalism and Social Revolution* (London: Brill, 2010). However, in March 1935, the Jewish historian and chronicler of pogroms Elias

The omission of the Red Army as a legitimate category of pogromist agency was far from accidental: internal correspondences reveal that very deliberate steps were taken to ensure that such material was kept out of the public domain. In early 1922, having received notification that the Ukrainian subcommittee of the Evobshchestkom included information about Red Army antisemitism in a draft version of a book on pogroms (possibly an early version of Ostrovskii's 1926 book discussed above), the Moscow-based Central Committee of the Evobshchestkom wrote to the Ukrainian subcommittee, reminding it that 'the publication of such information is, for understandable reasons, *completely out of the question* [*sovershenno nedopustimo*]' (emphasis added). The telegram further instructed the subcommittee to reveal exactly who had been shown the draft copy of the book and to whom copies of it had been sent.[104] This particular intervention was motivated by a concern that the international reputation of Bolshevism would be damaged by revelations of 'Red pogroms', particularly since the Party was about to send representatives to the Genoa Conference[105] to discuss, among other things, relief for Jews suffering from pogroms. These concerns were not merely conjunctural, but were expressive of Bolshevik practice across the Civil War period and beyond. For example, when the former Bundist Rafes wrote to the Party Central Committee and the Ukrainian Sovnarkom to inform them of a Red pogrom in Elisavetgrad in May 1919, he felt moved to add 'I have not forwarded this report or made copies, and nor has it been distributed widely'.[106] In other words, it was a well-established practice within the Bolshevik state apparatus that antisemitism in the Red Army was something to be kept out of the public domain at all costs.

Tcherikower wrote in a private correspondence: 'There cannot be the slightest doubt that he [Makhno] is implicated in a series of pogroms. I have enough substantiated evidence in my archive to show that his men were exactly the same sort of bandits as all the others. Whether they perpetrated the pogroms with his permission or on their own initiative is difficult to say; either way – he is responsible ... In some cases he sternly punished his men for individual pogrom-excesses. In many cases, however, no punishment was meted out for pogroms ... For me it suffices to know that the ordinary Jew in Ukraine consistently held Makhno for a pogromist and that the fear of Makhno was immense.' Tcherikower, *Di Ukrainer Pogromen in Yor 1919*, 348. I thank Lars Fischer for bringing this quote to my attention.

[104] Miliakova, *Kniga pogromov*, 814.
[105] The Genoa Conference in the spring of 1922 was a major international gathering of representatives from thirty-four states to discuss the famine in Russia and the general social and economic crises that had emerged after World War I; R. Pipes, *The Unknown Lenin. From the Secret Archive* (New Haven: Yale University Press, 1996), 139.
[106] TsDAHO f.1 o.20 d.91 l.23-24.

Figure 5 Leningradskii, S. *Kto i za chto ustraival pogromy nad evreiami* [*Who Organised the Pogroms against the Jews and for What Reason?*] (Moscow: Izdatel'stvo Krasnaia Nov', 1924)

Conclusion 137

The historian Oleg Budnitskii has argued that the Bolsheviks 'refused to keep quiet' about the problem of Red antisemitism.[107] On the basis of the evidence presented here, however, it seems that this was far from the case. Although from April 1919 the Party in Ukraine certainly carried out a relatively consistent press campaign against antisemitism *in general*, the Bolsheviks' default position was to downplay – at times even to the point of denial – the particular problem of antisemitism in the Red Army and wider Party.[108]

Conclusion

In contrast to the spring of 1918, when the response to antisemitism emanated specifically from non-Bolsheviks in the regional Moscow Evkom, in early to mid-1919 the Bolshevik leadership in Ukraine *did* take measures of its own to confront antisemitism. Perhaps most importantly, it was the Party leadership itself that first raised the issue of antisemitism in February 1919. In this case, the elaboration of a Soviet campaign did not rely on a group of non-Bolshevik Jewish radicals, as had been the case in the spring of the previous year. How might we account for this seemingly greater readiness on the part of the Ukrainian Bolshevik leadership to confront antisemitism? An answer may be found in the way the question of antisemitism became acutely bound up with the survival of the Soviet state in Ukraine in 1919. This needs explication.

The pogroms of the spring of 1918, as violent as they were, did not pose a significant military threat to the Soviet regime in Russia. Far more pressing for Lenin and his government during this period was the rebellion of the Czech Legion near the Ural Mountains.[109] Neither did the 1918 pogroms present a direct threat to the Ukrainian republic: if we recall, they frequently (though not exclusively) took place on the back of a defeat at the hands of the advancing German army. The pogroms in spring 1918, then, were often carried when the Red Army was in retreat, after the Bolsheviks had already lost power at the local level.[110]

---

[107] Budnitskii, *Russian Jews*, 368.
[108] To give one further illustration of this, in a 1922 report by the Jewish Department of the Commissariat for National Minorities marking the fifth anniversary of the October Revolution, it was claimed that 'in 1919 ... under Petliura and Denikin the whole of Ukraine was awash with the blood of the poor Jews ... but the Red Army saved the Jews from total extermination ... and thus thanks to the heroic efforts of the Red Army the Jewish population was, in the end, able to breathe freely'; GARF f.1318 o.24 d.7 l.30-43.
[109] Mawdsley, *The Russian Civil War*, 62–68; Rabinowitch, *The Bolsheviks in Power*, 242–43.
[110] Tcherikower, *Istoriia pogromnogo dvizheniia na Ukraine 1917-1921*, 147–49.

The conjuncture of 1919, however, was altogether different. By the time of the Grigor'evshchina in mid-May, antisemitism now posed fundamental problems for Soviet power not only in Ukraine itself, but in Russia also. It did so in two ways. First, antisemitism threatened the Soviet regime in Ukraine in terms of its 'counter-revolutionary' manifestation. That is to say, anti-Jewish violence appeared initially in the shape of pogroms carried out by anti-Soviet military forces such as the Petliura Army, whose attacks on Jews were often coterminous with attacks on Bolshevik state power. Second, antisemitism threatened the Bolshevik movement from within. The contradictory nature of popular conceptions of 'Bolshevism' and 'Soviet power' were such that by early 1919, antisemitism had become the current through which many peasants, workers, Red partisan soldiers and local Bolsheviks moved back and forth between 'revolution' and 'counter-revolution'. In 1919, the question of antisemitism was no longer of secondary importance to the leadership in the way it had been in 1918; it was now intimately bound up with the very survival of the Soviet state in Ukraine. As one activist put it, it was a fundamental issue upon which 'the fate of the revolution in Ukraine depended'.[111] In these circumstances, antisemitism demanded a more immediate, and proactive, response.

In these ways the Bolshevik response to antisemitism in Ukraine in 1919 differed from the campaign initiated by the Moscow Evkom the previous year. For most of the Bolshevik leadership, fighting antisemitism did not mean protecting Jews *as Jews*. Bolshevik opposition to antisemitism was certainly a matter of principle, but the overriding principle was to defend the revolution. The activists in the Jewish Commissariat in 1918 approached the confrontation with antisemitism from a different standpoint: for them, the question of antisemitism was directly bound up with the survival of Jewish life. They responded to antisemitism not just as revolutionaries, but *as Jews*. These subtle but no less important differences would come into view during the course of 1919.

In the first instance, the Ukrainian Bolshevik leadership response to antisemitism in 1919 was reactive: the vast majority of Party leaflets, brochures and newspaper articles against antisemitism came in mid- to late May, that is, *after* the Grigor'evshchina had already erupted across the southern regions of the former Pale of Settlement. Indeed, in May 1919, there was no centrally organized or coordinated strategy for dealing with the phenomenon of Red pogroms. During the first five months of 1919, neither the Sovnarkom nor the Central Committee in Moscow

---

[111] RGVA f.25860 o.1 d.263 l.13-14.

Conclusion

(to which its Ukrainian counterpart was more or less subservient) issued anything resembling a set of directives for combating the explosion of antisemitism already underway. In a context in which Red Army antisemitism was a problem in virtually every province in Ukraine and several parts of western Russia, the Soviet state in Moscow failed to elaborate a concrete strategy to prevent it.

Reflecting on the explosive wave of antisemitic violence within the Red Army in mid-1919, a Bolshevik by the name of 'Grinfarb' demanded at a local Party meeting on 30 May in the town of Illintsi (Lypovets, Vinnytsia province) that a more extensive, and above all consistent, political response to antisemitism be developed. In order to put a stop to attacks on the local Jewish community, Grinfarb insisted that 'it is essential to strengthen our agitation ... to organize schools for educationalists, set up meetings, public events, lectures and disseminate our literature'.[112] Evidently, for such a campaign to be launched in Illintsi, let alone in the rest of the country, a co-ordinated and centralized strategy to deal specifically with antisemitism was required. This is precisely what emerged in the *second half* of 1919. However, it emanated *not* from the Party leadership, but rather, just as in the spring of 1918, from a group of non-Bolshevik Jewish socialists who, having broken with their respective parties, joined the Soviet government to deepen and extend the Soviet confrontation with antisemitism. They brought with them a different modality of antiracism – one born not of tactical or strategic concerns, but of an urgency and ethical imperative characteristic of the campaign that had emerged in the spring of 1918.

[112] RGASPI f.71 o.35 d.512 l.427; f.71 o.35 d.486 l.205-206.

6 Jewish Communists and the Soviet Response to Antisemitism, May–December 1919

Introduction

After the full extent of antisemitism within the Red Army came into view in the summer of 1919, a renewed campaign emerged from the peripheral apparatuses of the Soviet state. Just as in the spring of 1918, it emanated *not* from the Party leadership, but from a group of non-Bolshevik Jewish socialists who had recently joined the Soviet government. As before, these activists elevated and singled out the fight against antisemitism as a *separate* sphere of Party work. The Soviet confrontation with antisemitism in late 1919 was the product, therefore, of a distinctly Soviet-Jewish political project, and to understand it, we must first account for the trajectory of the Jewish socialist movement in Ukraine between 1917 and 1919.

During this period, divisions emerged within the Bund, the United Jewish Socialist Workers' Party and the Poalei Zion party, and in each case, pro-Soviet communist factions (and eventually, separate parties) were formed. Although the splintering of the Jewish socialist movement after 1917 has been covered in a now fairly extensive secondary literature,[1] what has gone unnoticed are the significant consequences these developments had for the Soviet confrontation with antisemitism in the second half of 1919, and as such, they deserve a careful re-examination.

---

[1] See, for example, Gitelman, *Jewish Nationality and Soviet Politics*; Shneer, *Yiddish and the Creation of Soviet Jewish Culture*; Shternshis, *Soviet and Kosher*; Moss, *Jewish Renaissance in the Russian Revolution*; Bemporad, *Becoming Soviet Jews*; Sloin, *The Jewish Revolution in Belorussia: Economy, Race, and Bolshevik Power*; M. Kessler, 'The Comintern and the Left Poale Zion, 1919-1922', *The Australian Journal of Jewish Studies* 24 (2010): 116–33; Serhiy Hirik, 'Jewish National Communist Parties and the Comintern: A Non-Mutual Association', *Judaica Ukrainica* 2 (2013): 113–25; Gurevitz, *National Communism in the Soviet Union, 1918–1928*.

The Fragmentation of the Jewish Socialist Movement

The first signs of a fragmentation in Jewish socialist politics along 'left' (pro-Soviet) and 'right' (Menshevik-leaning/anti-Soviet) lines became apparent in the Poalei Zion party in Russia in mid-1917.[2] At the party's Moscow conference in April 1917, a small, broadly pro-Bolshevik current led by Zvi Fridliand emerged.[3] By the time of its August conference, the party had split into three factions: a rightist group close to the Mensheviks; a centrist grouping that campaigned for an end to the war; and a left-wing camp which openly supported the Bolsheviks. Fridliand, who was on the party's Central Committee, led the left faction. At the first party conference following the October Revolution, in early March 1918, Fridliand and the seven left delegates walked out, and shortly after helped to establish the Moscow Jewish Commissariat.[4] It was out of this milieu, and from the Jewish Commissariat specifically, that the first Soviet response to antisemitism emerged (see Chapter 3).

Similar divisions would surface in Ukraine, though they were slower to emerge owing to the fact that until late-1918, Jewish socialist parties generally still supported the Ukrainian Central Rada.[5] However, as early as May 1918, small groupings of 'left-Bundists' in various regions began to openly declare their support for a pro-Soviet Bundism.[6] At the leadership level of the Bund, similar divisions began to emerge in September 1918, with Abram Kheifets forming a left grouping in support of 'Soviet power'.[7] These developments were accelerated by the German Revolution in November 1918 and the renewed attempt by the Bolsheviks to retake Ukraine in December. Faced with what appeared to be a choice between the very real prospect of world revolution on the one hand and nationalist reaction in Ukraine on the other, sections of the Bund's core activists flocked to the left camp which they increasingly saw as the only way to secure and extend the revolution.[8] Just as had been the

---

[2] These party factions were initially pro-Soviet but not pro-Bolshevik.
[3] See *Listok Petrogradskogo Komiteta Evreiskoi Sotsial-Demokraticheskoi Rabochei Partiii (Poalei Tsiona)*, 17 April 1917. See also Fridliand, *Kommunisticheskii Internatsional i Kommunisticheskii Poalei-Tsionizm*, 92.
[4] Fridliand, 96–97.   [5] Abramson, *A Prayer for the Government*, 87.
[6] *Evreiskaia Tribuna*, no. 3–4, 2 June 1918, 13; *Razsvet*, 26 May 1918, 23. See also Agurskii, *Evreiskii rabochii v kommunisticheskom dvizhenii (1917-1921)*, 65, 188–91.
[7] Agurskii, *Evreiskii rabochii v kommunisticheskom dvizhenii (1917-1921)*, 119.
[8] Gitelman, *Jewish Nationality and Soviet Politics*, 169–83. For a broader discussion on the reception of the German Revolution among communists in Russia in 1918 and 1919, see G. J. Albert, '"German October Is Approaching": Internationalism, Activists, and the Soviet State in 1923', *Revolutionary Russia* 24, no. 2 (2011): 111–42.

case in Russia in 1917, the *fact* of Soviet power in Ukraine in late 1918 provoked a reconsideration of the long-standing ideological conflict between Bundism and Bolshevism.

By early 1919, matters had come to a head, and on the eve of the party's third All-Ukrainian Conference on 18 February, a group of left Bundists in Kyiv voted to split the party and form a new, *Communist* Bund. Following the conference, similar divisions emerged at the local level in Poltava, Kharkiv and Ekaterinoslav, leading to the formation of the *Idisher Komunistisher Arbeter-Bund*, or *Kombund* (Communist Bund) as it came to be known.[9] The Kombundists had not yet committed themselves to Bolshevism, and remained sharply critical of the tactics of the Communist Party. Instead, they pledged their support to 'Soviet power', the Red Army and a defence of the revolution. The Kombund's pro-Soviet standpoint was underlined on 12 May, when on the eve of the Grigor'evshchina, it was given representation on one of the main Soviet legislative bodies in Ukraine, the All Ukrainian Central Executive Committee.[10]

The formation of the Kombund represented the emergence of a new united front, or, as a meeting of Communist Bundists in Saratov put it, a new 'united *revolutionary* front' against the counter-revolution.[11] It was an alliance born of a radically changed conjuncture: the actuality of the *socialist* revolution. With this new development, some of the most experienced and most militant revolutionaries within the Jewish socialist movement gravitated towards Bolshevism. This process would have significant consequences for the Soviet confrontation with antisemitism: in mid- to late 1919, the Kombund leadership not only participated in the Soviet government's response to the devastating pogroms of the summer of 1919; in the second half of that year they *led* that response. Among the key activists were Moishe Rafes[12] and Abram Iakovlevich

---

[9] *Zhizn' Natsional'nostei*, 9 March 1919. See also Gitelman, *Jewish Nationality and Soviet Politics*, 171–74; G. D. Hundert, ed., *The YIVO Encyclopedia of Jews in Eastern Europe* (New Haven: Yale University Press, 2008), 919–20. On the Sovietization of the Bund in Belorussia, see Sloin, *The Jewish Revolution in Belorussia*; Gitelman, *Jewish Nationality and Soviet Politics*, 177–83.

[10] Korolivskii, Kolensnik and Rybalka, *Grazhdanskaia voina na Ukraine 1918-1920. Tom vtoroi*, 43.

[11] *Zhizn' Natsional'nostei*, 11 May 1919.

[12] Moishe Rafes (1883–1942) was born in Vilna into a family of wine merchants. As a child, Rafes received a traditional Jewish education (*heder*). By his teenage years, he was an active member in the Bund and by the early 1900s was a significant figure in the party. In 1912, at the Bund's 9th Conference, he was elected onto the party's Central Committee. During this period, he also played an active role in promoting Yiddish language in Jewish schools. By mid-1917, Rafes was the Bund's leader in Ukraine. Following the October Revolution, he initially opposed Bolshevism. In late 1918, however, he was pivotal in

Kheifets,[13] who would be pivotal figures in the Soviet response to the dramatic escalation of antisemitic violence in the summer of 1919. Another key figure was David Lipets, who initially rejected the formation of the Kombund, instead opting to stay with the Bund proper. By April 1919, however, Lipets would join Kheifets and Rafes in aligning himself with a pro-Soviet Jewish politics, and with them he helped shape the Soviet state confrontation with antisemitism in the second half of 1919.[14]

---

bringing about the Bundist turn towards Soviet power, leading the split and subsequent formation of the Kombund. Rafes became a central figure in the Jewish Sections of the Russian Communist Party (Evsektsiia) and was elected onto its Central Bureau in 1920. Thereafter, he worked mostly in the Comintern, spending much of the 1920s engaged in Chinese affairs. Although Rafes largely moved away from Jewish-related work from 1921 onwards, he wrote a number of important studies on the Bund and the Jewish labour movement in the course of the 1920s. He was arrested in 1938, sentenced to 10 years in prison, and died in 1942. See M. G. Rafes, *Dva goda revoliutsii na Ukraine (Evoliutsiia i raskol 'Bunda')* (Moscow: Gosudarstvennoe izdatel'stvo, 1920); Hundert, *The YIVO Encyclopedia of Jews in Eastern Europe*, 1514.

[13] Kheifets was born in Riga on 10 April 1890 to a family of Jewish school teachers. He became a member of the Bund at the age of fourteen, in 1904, and in December 1917 was elected as a member of the party's Central Committee. Though the Bund was highly critical of the October Revolution, Kheifets was part of a small grouping of 'internationalists' who took a more favourable stance towards the Bolsheviks. Indeed, Kheifets soon distinguished himself as one of the most outspoken advocates of a pro-Soviet split in the Bund, and in late 1918 formally joined the Bolshevik party. In September 1919, Kheifets was commandeered to work for the Comintern in Germany, where in 1923 he became a member of the Central Committee of the KPD under the name August Kleine. He was also known as Guralskii, Lepetit, Juan de Dois and Rustico. RGASPI f.495 o.65a d.4573 l.3, 6. Further biographical information about Kheifets is available in A. Pantsov, *The Bolsheviks and the Chinese Revolution 1919-1927* (London: Routledge, 2013), 284; Rafes, *Dva goda revoliutsii na Ukraine (Evoliutsiia i raskol 'Bunda')*, 155; M. Panteleev, *Agenty Kominterna: soldaty mirovoi revoliutsii* (Moscow: EKSMO, 2005), 38–56; H. Weber and A. Herbst, *Deutsche Kommunisten: Biographisches Handbuch 1918 bis 1945* (Berlin: Karl Dietz Verlag, 2004), 453–55.

[14] David Lipets was born in Berdychiv in 1886. His father owned a cloth shop and was a merchant of the second guild. Lipets received a Jewish education (*heder*), and in 1902, aged sixteen, he joined the Bund along with his sister Fanie. He studied in Paris in 1903, but the revolution of 1905 saw him return to Russia. Following arrest, he fled abroad once more, this time to London, where he would take part in the 5th Congress of the RSDRP in 1907. In 1906, he was elected onto the Bund's Central Committee at the party's 7th Conference in Bern, which he chaired at the age of just nineteen. By this point he was known by the name Max Goldfarb, and was widely regarded as a brilliant orator and a key figure in the Bund's leadership and intelligentsia. Lipets remained in Europe in the immediate years following the 1905 Revolution, earning a PhD in economics at the Free University of Belgium. From 1912 onwards, he moved to New York, where he would take up an editorial position specially created for him at the Yiddish socialist newspaper *Forverts*. While in the United States, Lipets became friends with Leon Trotsky, with the two briefly living together in the Bronx in early 1917. Like so many others, the unfolding revolution would bring Lipets back to Russia. Initially, he opposed the October Revolution and remained a leading Bundist. Between the end of 1918 and January 1919, he served as mayor of Berdychiv, doing so as a Bundist. In the spring of 1919, however, he shifted towards a pro-Soviet standpoint, moved to Kyiv, and began

Coterminous with these developments in the Bund were a set of emerging divisions in the *Fareynikte* – the United Jewish Socialist Workers Party, which was formed in May 1917 following a merger of the Socialist Zionist Workers Party (SSRP) and the Jewish Socialist Workers Party (SERP).[15] The SSRP had been founded in December 1904, and despite its avowedly Zionist programme, the party explicitly fought for the political rights of Jews in Russia. The SERP, which was established in 1906, was even more forthright in its campaign for Jewish diasporic nationalism and for Jewish 'national personal autonomy' in a future Russian democratic state. The merger party, the Fareynikte, was thus born of both Zionist and diasporic attempts at political mobilization. Although ardently critical of Bolshevik policy throughout 1918, by the end of that year, just as in the Bund, clear divisions began to emerge within the Fareynikte along 'leftist' and 'rightist' lines. Following the party's Third Conference on 25 February 1919, the Kyiv branch formally split and formed itself into a new entity, the United Jewish Communist Party (*Fareynikte Yidishe Komunistishe Partey*).[16] Among the leaders of this movement were Iu. Novakovskii and Mikhail Levitan. By the summer of 1919, they too would go on to play leading roles in developing the Soviet confrontation with antisemitism.

We should not be surprised to find support for Bolshevism among left Zionists. Recent scholarship has shown that socialist Zionists were often the most ardent supporters of the diasporic claim for Jewish rights in the 'here and now' of revolutionary Russia.[17] In other words, the broader project of establishing a future Zion in Palestine did *not* forestall an active participation in the political struggle in revolutionary Russia. These developments were long in the making: the pogroms of 1905 had forced

working in the Red Army as a lecturing instructor. In April 1919, he joined the Bolsheviks and became known as 'David Petrovskii'. After arriving in Moscow in the early summer of 1919, he took up a senior position in Soviet military education. In March 1920, he was promoted to director of the military academy itself, a position he held until 1924. In the mid- to late 1920s, he worked in the Anglo-American Secretariat of the Comintern under the name David Bennett. He was murdered in Stalin's purges in September 1937. D. Petrovskii, *Voennaia shkola v gody revoliutsii* (Moscow: Vysshii voennyi redaktsionnyi sovet, 1924), 8; G. Estraikh, 'Mnogolikii David Lipets: Evrei v russkoi revoliutsii', in *Arkhiv evreiskoi istorii, Tom 7*, ed. O. V. Budnitskii (Moscow: ROSSPEN, 2012), 225–27; Anderson, Shelokhaev and Amiantov, *Bund*, 1286; Meyers, 'A Portrait of Transition'. See also RGASPI f.495 o.65a d.13497 l.12-15.

[15] B. Gurevitz, *The Bolshevik Revolution and the Foundation of the Jewish Communist Movement in Russia*, Slavic and Soviet Series 4 (Jerusalem: The Russian and East European Research Center, 1976), 13.

[16] Hundert, *The YIVO Encyclopedia of Jews in Eastern Europe*, 501–02; Gitelman, *Jewish Nationality and Soviet Politics*, 197–201.

[17] Moss, *Jewish Renaissance in the Russian Revolution*; Karlip, *The Tragedy of a Generation*, 8–9.

the socialist Zionist movement to reorient its focus to the immediate needs of Jews in Russia.[18] By the February Revolution of 1917, the politics of the 'here and now' arguably dominated over the prospect of settlement in Palestine.[19] The Soviet response to antisemitism was closely connected to these developments within the Jewish political world.

Soon after their emergence, attempts were made to unite the Kombund and the Fareynikte Communists into a single pro-Soviet Jewish communist formation. In March 1919, the Evsektsiia (the Jewish Section of the Russian Bolshevik party) oversaw meetings between the Kombund and the Fareynikte leadership in an attempt to bring about such a merger.[20] It was in the context of the outbreak of the Grigor'evshchina, however, that discussions over the unification began to accelerate. In mid-May, as pogroms raged across southern and central Ukraine, the Evsektsiia leader Semen Dimanshtein made the perilous trip from Moscow to Kyiv. His aim was to consolidate the new Jewish communist movements into a singular political formation. Yet he was driven by another, related ambition: 'to work out', as one Soviet newspaper put it, 'a strategy for combatting antisemitism'.[21] On both counts he was successful.

On 23 May, as the Red Army and Grigor'ev pogroms reached their crescendo, the decision was formally taken to establish the *Komfarband* – the *Yidisher Komunistisher Farband* (the Jewish Communist Alliance), a new, joint party composed of the two communist groupings of former Bund and Fareynikte members.[22] Although the Komfarband was formed as an independent party, it sought formal membership as a Jewish organization within the Ukrainian Bolshevik Party.[23] This proposal was initially rejected by the Ukrainian Bolshevik leadership, who opposed the notion of a semi-autonomous Jewish formation within its ranks. However, Komfarband activists were eventually incorporated into the Party in mid-August 1919 on an individual basis at the insistence of the

---

[18] Trachtenberg, *The Revolutionary Roots of Modern Yiddish, 1903-1917*, 21.
[19] S. Rabinovitch, 'Alternative to Zion: The Jewish Autonomist Movement in Late Imperial and Revolutionary Russia' (PhD dissertation, Brandeis University, 2007), 230–300.
[20] Gitelman, *Jewish Nationality and Soviet Politics*, 200.
[21] 'Dimanshtein is currently en route to Kyiv. The goals of his journey are to unite all Jewish communist parties and work out a strategy to fight antisemitism.' *Kommunar Organ Khar'kovskogo Gubernskogo Komiteta Kommunisticheskoi Partii (Bol'shevikov) Ukrainy*, 20 May 1919, 1.
[22] RGASPI f.17 o.66 d.57 l.2-6; f.445 o.1 d.1 l.78. See also *Zhizn' Natsional'nostei*, 8 June 1919.
[23] On Rafes's attempt to bring about a merger with the Ukrainian Communist Party, see *Bol'shevik*, 18 July 1919, 4; *Zhizn' Natsional'nostei*, 3 August 1919.

Russian Bolshevik leadership in Moscow.[24] Lenin, it seems, was particularly willing to work more closely with the Jewish communists: in a private correspondence with Dimanshtein around this time he stated, 'I am for a compromise with the new Bundists, for bargaining with them and ceding a little ground to them.'[25] In securing the formation of the Komfarband, Dimanshtein introduced a new layer of Jewish activists into the Soviet government, and immediately they began to play a critically important role in deepening the Soviet response to antisemitism.

Similar developments were underway within the Poalei Zion party. As already noted, in March 1918, a leftist, pro-Bolshevik faction of the Poalei Zion led by Zvi Fridliand had actively collaborated with the Soviet government, and the Moscow Evkom specifically (see Chapter 3). In doing so, they had established and led the first Soviet response to antisemitism since the October Revolution. Despite their expulsion from the Soviet government in May and June 1918, many left Poalei Zion activists retained a pro-Soviet politics. This was particularly so in Ukraine, where the bulk of the party's activists remained. For example, on 21 April 1919, the party mobilized all members in Ukraine to serve in the Red Army.[26] On 27 May 1919, a leftist faction broke to form an explicitly pro-communist organization. At the local level in Odessa and Chernihiv similar divisions emerged, and in each case the new communist groupings pledged their support for both communism and the Red Army.[27] Finally, in August 1919 at the party conference in Gomel, the Communist faction formally split and declared itself a separate party, the Jewish Communist Party (Poalei Zion). Among its leaders was Zvi Fridliand, the architect of the first Soviet response to antisemitism in April 1918.[28] Although Poalei Zion communists did not join the Bolshevik Party, they

---

[24] Agurskii, *Evreiskii rabochii v kommunisticheskom dvizhenii (1917-1921)*, 122–24; V. Gusev, *Bund, Komfarband, Evsektsiia KP(b)U: stranitsy politicheskoi biografii. 1917-1921 gg.* (Moscow: Obshchestvo 'Evreiskoe Naselenie', 1994), 17.

[25] V. I. Lenin, *V. I. Lenin neizvestnye dokumenty 1891-1922* (Moscow: ROSSPEN, 2000), 283.

[26] *Zhizn' Natsional'nostei*, 4 May 1919.

[27] *Zhizn' Natsional'nostei*, 8 June 1919. On Poalei Zion in Ukraine in 1919, see Gurevitz, *National Communism in the Soviet Union, 1918-1928*, 42–64. On the party's split in Vitebsk, see Zel'tser, *Evrei sovetskoi provintsii: Vitebsk i mestechki 1917-1941*, 43–44. See also Hirik, 'Jewish National Communist Parties and the Comintern: A Non-Mutual Association'; J. Frankel, *Crisis, Revolution, and Russian Jews* (Cambridge: Cambridge University Press, 2008), 166–80; Z. Galili, 'Zionism in the Early Soviet State: Between Legality and Persecution', in *Revolution, Repression and Revival: The Soviet Jewish Experience*, ed. Z. Gitelman and Y. Ro'i (Lanham: Rowman & Littlefield Publishers, 2007); O. Bertelsen, 'GPU Repressions of Zionists: Ukraine in the 1920s', *Europe-Asia Studies* 65, no. 6 (2013): 1080–1111.

[28] Gurevitz, *National Communism in the Soviet Union, 1918-1928*, 47–52.

nevertheless played a key role in extending, from the margins, a Soviet response to antisemitism in mid- to late 1919, and as we shall see, they did so in a unique way.

The emergence of Jewish communist formations in the shape of the Jewish Communist Party (Poalei Zion), the Kombund, the Fareynikte Communists and, later, the Komfarband, was emblematic of a conjunctural rupture in Jewish politics during the Russian Revolution. The consequences of this for the Bolshevik confrontation with antisemitism were significant: once again, a group of loosely connected Jewish radicals from outside of the Bolshevik milieu played a crucial role in developing the Party and governmental response to the crisis of antisemitism.

Antisemitism: The 'Modality in Which the Revolution Was Lived'

Within the literature on the history of the Jewish socialist movement in revolutionary Russia, the German Revolution of November 1918 is identified as a key factor in bringing about the turn to Bolshevism.[29] Crucial though this was, the Sovietization of Jewish politics was accelerated by another development: the sharp escalation of pogromist violence by the troops of Petliura's Central Ukrainian Rada, beginning first in Berdychiv in January 1919 and then, most dramatically, in Proskuriv in mid-February. Many Jews who enlisted in the Red Army in early 1919 did so, in part, out of an experience of pogromist violence, and in particular the pogroms carried out by *anti*-Bolshevik forces. This is strikingly captured in the memoirs of L. Shapiro:

> In the station at Klinovka I was amazed to see a Red Army company composed entirely of Jews, even some with earlocks. These were *Yeshiva* students from Proskurov who had joined the Red Army in the wake of Petliura's pogroms in order to take revenge ... and I, the Zionist opponent of Communism, I who saw it as a fatal danger to Judaism – I was filled with pride seeing those Jewish fellows.[30]

The route to Bolshevism, for many Jewish Red Army recruits, was paved by the experience of pogromist violence. As another memoir from the period put it,

> A Jewish [Red Army] soldier from Berdichev ran amok. He would wipe his bayonet in the grass to remove the blood and with every head he cut off he

---

[29] Zel'tser, *Evrei sovetskoi provintsii*, 40; Gitelman, *Jewish Nationality and Soviet Politics*, 175–76.
[30] Gitelman, *Jewish Nationality and Soviet Politics*, 166.

screamed, 'This is my payment for my murdered sister, this is my retribution for my murdered mother!'[31]

When the leaders of the Kombund, the Fareynikte Communists and the Communist Poalei Zion agitated among the Yiddish-speaking Jewish masses in April and May 1919, they drew on these narratives of pogromist violence in an attempt to engender support for the Red Army. As a circular of the Fareynikte Communists dated 26 April 1919 declared, 'The Jewish worker in this situation has no choice: either fall, as silent victims, or fight, as heroes, to the last drop of blood.'[32] Another leaflet issued by Fareynikte Communists around the same time struck a similar tone: 'The decisive hour is now upon us ... it is better to die in struggle than live in slavery and shame. The Red Army awaits you!'[33] Indeed, the very title of this leaflet underlines the connection between the Sovietization of Jewish politics and the spectre of antisemitism: *A ruf zikh ranglen mit de pogromshchikes* ('A Call to Fight the Pogromists').[34] The confrontation with pogromist violence acted, then, as a conduit through which non-Bolshevik Jewish communists tried to mobilize the Jewish masses; in turn, it was the current through which Jewish workers themselves made the journey from (Jewish) socialism to communism. At the founding conference of the Komfarband on 22 May, this process was captured in stark terms:

[T]he wave of pogroms against the Jews has not been able to stop the revolutionary process, on the contrary, it has acted to further raise the level of revolutionary energy among the urban [Jewish] poor, before whom stands the *prospect of physical extermination*.[35]

The radicalization of Jewish life and murderous antisemitism were interlocking experiences. In a remarkable account of the revolution in Belorussia, Sloin demonstrates how no series of events did as much to foster the Soviet–Jewish alliance as the pogrom wave during the Polish–Soviet war of 1919–20. For rank-and-file Jewish workers, it was often the direct experience of anti-Jewish violence that drove the process of radicalization. Eighteen-year-old needleworker Roza Yoktelevna Gutman joined the Komsomol in early 1919 in the town of Mozyr, 'still not

---

[31] Gitelman, 165.　[32] Abramson, *A Prayer for the Government*, 150.
[33] *Zhizn' Natsional'nostei*, 15 June 1919, 3.
[34] Gurevitz, *National Communism in the Soviet Union, 1918–1928*, 62.
[35] RGASPI f.71 o.35 d.503 l.42; RGASPI f.17 o.66 d.57 l.3ob-4. Emphasis added. See also Rafes, *Dva goda revoliutsii na Ukraine (Evoliutsiia i raskol 'Bunda')*, 165; Anderson, Shelokhaev and Amiantov, *Bund*, 1140–41. In the latter source the date of the conference is mistakenly noted as 2 May 1919; it took place on 22 May 1919.

Figure 6 Jewish Red Army Unit, 1918. Banner reads: '1st Red Army Unit of the Jewish Social-Democratic Workers' Party Poalei Zion'. From the Archives of the YIVO Institute for Jewish Research, New York

knowing, but feeling, that this was *my* party, the party of the humiliated and the exploited'. When Petliura's army arrived in March that year, it was the 'pillaging and animal acts' of the pogromists that drove her to join the Bolsheviks. Such experiences of pogromist violence, Sloin contends, 'did as much, if not far more, to drive young Jews into the Bolshevik camp than did the writings of Lenin, Trotsky, and all of the party pamphleteers combined'.[36]

None of this was lost on the leadership of Jewish Bolsheviks. A circular published by the Central Bureau of the Evsektsiia in late 1919 noted that 'the defence of Soviet power [for Jewish communists] has merged with the task of defending oneself against physical extermination (*istreblenie*)'.[37] When they joined, these new recruits played a critical role in combatting antisemitism within the Red Army itself. As the Central Bureau of the Evsektsiia noted in late-1919, these Jewish cadres '*were often the only source of local resistance*' to Red Army pogroms and anti-Soviet uprisings in mid-1919.[38] The experience of pogroms drew them

---

[36] Sloin, *The Jewish Revolution in Belorussia*, 34. [37] RGASPI f.445 o.1 d.1 l.78.
[38] RGASPI f.445 o.1 d.1 l.78 (emphasis in the original).

to the Red Army, and having enlisted, they then made extensive efforts to interrupt the surge of antisemitism within sections of the Bolsheviks' social base.

However, the notion that Jews had flocked to the Red Army to combat anti-Jewish violence did not sit easily with the Evsektsiia leadership. In a report in late February 1920, the Evsektsiia Central Bureau admitted that those Jews who had entered the Red Army in 1919 had done so, 'in part, out of a hatred for the White pogromists', before adding that they were therefore largely 'apolitical elements under the influence of a petit-bourgeois mentality'.[39] Trotsky, too, in a newspaper article in October 1919, noted that these Jews had moved to Bolshevism out of 'national', not 'class' experiences, and as a consequence, these cadres 'were not, of course, the best communists'.[40] For the Evsektsiia leadership, this political trajectory was problematic, for to be seen to have reached Bolshevism through racialization risked implying that ethnic and national experiences were at least as important as class determinations. At the Third Congress of the Ukrainian Bolsheviks in March 1919, the Kombund leader Moishe Rafes insisted that it was not antisemitism but the advance of world revolution in Germany that was bringing about a split in the Bund.[41] In his 1920 memoirs, Rafes addressed the issue even more directly:

> I have heard it said on more than one occasion that the swing to the left of the Bund in Ukraine was the result of pogromist politics of Petliura ... We focussed all of our attention on the *general* questions of the revolutionary struggle ... the pogroms of May–August 1919 brought horrors that outstripped all previous pogroms, and this of course provoked our natural indignation, but they did not provoke in us any kind of specifically *national* reaction.[42]

The picture presented here by Rafes, however, requires careful scrutiny. Backstage internal correspondences involving the Bund's leadership during the spring of 1919 offer a different view, one in which antisemitism plays a critical role in bringing about the turn to Bolshevism. In an April 1919 letter sent by the Central Committee of the Bund to the Central Committee of the Communist Party of Lithuania and Belorussia, the experience of pogromist violence is identified as the key force mobilizing Jews into the Red Army:

---

[39] *Zhizn' Natsional'nostei*, 29 February 1920.   [40] *Izvestiia*, 19 October 1919.
[41] Gurenko, *Tretii zizd Komunistychnoi Partii (bilshovykiv) Ukrainy. 1–6 Bereznia 1919 g. Protokoly*, 167–68.
[42] Rafes, *Dva goda revoliutsii na Ukraine (Evoliutsii i raskol 'Bunda')*, 132.

Over and above the Red Army's overall significance as the armed force of the revolutionary proletariat ... the issue of support for the Red Army is of *particular significance* for the Jewish proletariat in our young republic, insofar as the counter-revolutionary forces endangering our country are *at one and the same time also antisemitic forces*, threatening the Jewish proletariat and the Jewish working masses with mass annihilation and death.[43]

Rafes sat on the Central Committee of the Bund at this time and was likely involved in writing this document. What is more, despite Rafes's own protestations in his memoirs that antisemitism had *not* informed the turn to Bolshevism, his own political practice in 1919–20 suggests otherwise: from the moment of the formation of the Komfarband in 1919 he played a critical role in shaping the Soviet response to antisemitism both in Ukraine and Russia. Between June 1919 and March 1920, he served as Chairman of the Central Commission for Providing Help to Victims of the Counter-revolution,[44] an organization within the Ukrainian Soviet government tasked with assisting those Jews suffering from the ruination brought about by the Grigor'evshchina.[45] In July, Rafes wrote directly to the Soviet government and Party leadership in Ukraine to warn of outbreaks of antisemitism in the Red Army,[46] and furthermore, he organized for the Komfarband to disseminate information to Western Europe about the pogroms.[47] Upon formally joining the Bolshevik Party in August 1919, he further consolidated his role as a leader of the Soviet response to antisemitism by helping to steer the Evsektsiia campaign against pogroms, a role he maintained throughout the rest of the year.[48] Above all, though, in September 1919 he helped to establish and develop the work of the *Committee for the Struggle against Antisemitism*, a new Soviet state institution specifically dedicated to confronting antisemitism[49] (discussed later here). Rafes, the former Bundist who claimed that the pogroms did not provoke a 'Jewish' response in him, was appointed to the Committee as a 'specialist' on antisemitism.[50]

In other words, the Soviet confrontation with antisemitism shaped Rafes's *entire* backstage political practice in the immediate period following the formation of the Komfarband and its subsequent

---

[43] Budnitskii, '"Evreiskie batal'ony" v Krasnoi Armii', 240.
[44] TsDAHO f.1. o.20 d.126 l.3. The Central Commission was established within the Commissariat for Social Welfare in the Ukrainian Sovnarkom. It was the precursor to the *Evobshchestkom*, established in 1920. See also RGASPI f.445 o.1. d.1 l.57,71,88-89 and RGASPI f.445 o.1. d.2 l.149
[45] *Dekrety sovetskoi vlasti*, vol. 5 (Moscow: Gosudarstvennoe izdatel'stvo politicheskoi literatury, 1971), 525–26.
[46] TsDAHO f.1 o.20 d.91 l.23-24.   [47] TsDAHO f.1 o.20 d.126 l.8.
[48] RGASPI f.445 o.1 d.1 l.57, 68ob, 71.   [49] GARF f.A2306 o.1 d.3289 l.5-6.
[50] RGASPI f.445 o.1 d.1 l.50.

Figure 7 Moishe Rafes, 1917.
From the Archives of the YIVO Institute for Jewish Research, New York

incorporation into the Bolshevik party. The seeming centrality of antisemitism to Rafes's political radicalization can be traced back further still: when, in March 1917, the Petrograd Soviet established a special commission to stop 'black hundreds' from 'sewing national hatred among the population' in the wake of the February Revolution, it was the Bundist Rafes who took on the role of heading the institution (see Chapter 1). His first task, we should note, was to confront antisemitism.[51] In other words, Rafes's assertion in his memoirs that antisemitism played no role in his and other Bundists' move towards Bolshevism should not be taken at face value.

We can garner further insight into the role of antisemitism in the Sovietization of Jewish politics by exploring David Lipets's journey to Bolshevism. Born in 1886, he was a Bundist by sixteen and a member of the party's Central Committee by his twentieth birthday. When the revolution of 1917 broke out, Lipets was based in New York, serving as editor for the Yiddish socialist newspaper *Forverts*. Though the overthrow of the tsar inevitably pulled him back to Russia, his enthusiasm

---

[51] Gal'perina, *Petrogradskii Sovet*, 84, 132, 176, 190, 342.

Antisemitism: The 'Modality in Which the Revolution Was Lived' 153

Figure 8 David Lipets and David Davidovich (L'vovich) at the Stockholm Peace Conference, June 1917. Lipets is furthest left; Davidovich is third from left.
Image courtesy of Michael Petrovsky

was qualified by a fear that 'Jewish blood' would be used to 'quench the fires of the Russian Revolution'. Shortly before leaving New York, Lipets warned that in Russia, 'freedom and Jewish pogroms [have] a strange connection, a wild insanity'.[52] These predictions would soon come to pass.

Lipets was confronted by the realities of antisemitism soon after his arrival in Russia. In mid- to late 1917, he was sent by the Bund to Volyn, in Ukraine, where he found himself organizing Jewish self-defence units and producing reports on pogroms.[53] It was in his role as elected mayor of his native town Berdychiv, however, that he experienced firsthand the realities of antisemitic violence. On 5 January 1919, Lipets heard pogromists gathering outside his flat, shouting, 'Give us that Yid who runs this city!' Lipets's mother in law, who was also in the house, cried out to

---

[52] Meyers, 'A Portrait of Transition', 113.
[53] On Lipets's account of his role in organizing self-defence units in late 1917 and early 1918, see RGASPI f.495 o.65 d.13497 l.14. For a report by Lipets on pogromist violence in Volyn during this period, see TsDAHO f.41 o.1. d.8 l.10-13. I would like to thank Joshua Meyers for sharing this latter source with me.

Lipets in Yiddish, 'Get [my daughters] and throw them out the window, it is better they die out there than be raped [*oskverneny*] by the pogromists'. Upon hearing this 'non-familiar' language, pogromists entered the apartment and lined Lipets, his mother in law and her daughters up against the wall. They survived only after Lipets was able to pay off the soldiers with money and personal valuables. Others were not so fortunate: over the course of 5 January 1919, at least seventeen Jews were murdered in Berdychiv, around forty were left wounded and beaten, and many hundreds more were robbed and looted.[54] Lipets described the nightmare as 'a wild dance of the dead'.[55]

Four days later, on 9 January, Lipets and other representatives from the local Jewish community made an attempt to bury the victims. Yet again, however, the pogromists struck, prefiguring Walter Benjamin's 1940 warning that 'not even the dead will be safe from the enemy'.[56] In the violent attack on the funeral, two were killed and a further three were left wounded. Lipets yet again survived.[57] Later that day, on 9 January, he led a delegation of Bundists and Jewish socialists – which included Moishe Rafes – to Kyiv, where they appealed to the head of the Directory Vynnychenko to put a stop the violence. When a second pogrom broke out in the city two months later, Lipets left Berdychiv for good, moving first to Kyiv, before eventually settling in Moscow where he changed his surname to David Petrovskii, joined the Red Army and later the Bolshevik party too.[58]

Though Lipets survived these encounters with anti-Jewish violence, he was left profoundly scarred by the experience. A close friend, Shakhne Epshteyn, observed that before the pogrom Lipets had been 'full of life and initiative'. Afterwards, however, he had 'utterly collapsed'.[59] Having joined the Bolsheviks, one of Lipets' first roles was to lead, alongside former Bundists Rafes and Abram Kheifets, the Soviet response to antisemitism.[60] Like Rafes, Lipets's entry into Bolshevism

---

[54] Estraikh, 'Mnogolikii David Lipets', 229–30; E. I. Melamed and G. Estraikh, '"O pogrome v Berdicheve" (Novonaidennaia zapiska D. Lipetsa 1919 G.)', 174. Lipets gives a brief account of his experience of the pogrom in an autobiographical note composed for the Comintern in late 1928. See RGASPI f.495 o.65a d.13497 l.140b.
[55] Meyers, 'A Portrait of Transition', 118.
[56] W. Benjamin, *Illuminations* (London: Pimlico, 1999), 247.
[57] Committee of the Jewish Delegations, *The Pogroms in the Ukraine under the Ukrainian Governments (1917-1920)*, 141.
[58] Estraikh, 'Mnogolikii David Lipets', 229–30; Melamed and Estraikh, '"O pogrome v Berdicheve" (Novonaidennaia zapiska D. Lipetsa 1919 G.)', 170–72.
[59] Meyers, 'A Portrait of Transition', 120. For an account of Lipets's appeal to Vynnychenko, see A. Revutsky, *Wrenching Times in Ukraine: Memoir of a Jewish Minister* (Newfoundland: Yksuver Publishing, 1998), 118–27.
[60] GARF f.A2306 o.1 d.3289 l.2. See discussion later in the chapter.

Figure 9 David Lipets, March 1927.
Russian State Archive of Social-Political History

was shaped, at the level of political practice, by the confrontation with antisemitism. And in Lipets's case, the passage to Bolshevism was paved by firsthand experiences of pogromist violence, something he would later testify to.[61]

Just as in 1918, the Soviet response to antisemitism once again emerged from, and was dependent upon, a wider set of developments within the Jewish socialist world. Like their counterparts in the Moscow Evkom, this new layer of Jewish revolutionaries was born into a world transformed by the pogroms of 1881–83. While their childhood was shaped by a Jewish education, their adolescence was defined by the revolution of 1905 and the politics of self-defence. As Jonathan Frankel once put it, 'to them the revolution meant a struggle not only for social equality and political freedom, but also for national, for Jewish, liberation'.[62] Upon joining the Soviet government in 1919, Bundists such as Rafes, Kheifets and Lipets – now in their late twenties and early thirties –

---

[61] In an autobiographical statement held in his personal files in the Comintern archive, Lipets writes that his turn to Communism was accelerated by three events: the German Revolution, the pogrom in Berdychiv, and the 'turn to counter-revolution on the part of the Directory government in Ukraine'. See RGASPI f.495 o.65a d.13497 l.14ob. The statement is undated but was almost certainly taken in late 1928.
[62] Frankel, *Prophecy and Politics*, 329.

threw themselves into the Soviet confrontation with antisemitism. If the German Revolution was the rationale for doing so offered in front-stage debates, their backstage activism indicated that other reasons were also at play. As the Evsektsiia leader and former Bundist Avrom Merezhin put it in 1921, 'It is no secret that we have members who were won over to the Party *solely because* the Soviet government does not pogromize the Jews. *The Jewish question was the door through which they came to us.*'[63] The cultural theorist Stuart Hall once suggested that race may be the modality in which class is lived. Paraphrasing Hall, we might say that for these Jewish revolutionaries, antisemitism was the modality in which the revolution was lived.[64]

Antisemitism and the Sovietization of Jewish Socialism

The experience of antisemitism led a significant number of radicalized Jewish socialists to move towards the Soviet regime. At precisely the same time, however, the Red pogroms of 1919 demonstrated the fluidity with which scores of peasants, workers, Red partisan soldiers and local Bolsheviks moved back and forth between the seemingly antithetical camps of 'revolution' and 'counter-revolution'. When Ester Frumkina declared at the Bund's 11th Conference in Minsk in late March 1919, 'the Red Army is our Army',[65] Red pogroms were in full flow in Rosava and elsewhere. Even more striking is the fact that the founding conference of the Komfarband took place on 22 May, just as Red antisemitism reached its zenith in the Grigor'evshchina. Two seemingly contradictory developments were concurrently in motion: Jewish revolutionaries in Ukraine moved to Bolshevism in precisely the same moment as 'Bolshevism' in Ukraine turned against Jews in various localities. How can this be explained?

It is essential to remember that despite the severity of antisemitism within the Red Army, the vast bulk of the pogroms in early to mid-1919 were carried out by *anti-Soviet* forces. According to Gergel's calculations, forces loyal to the Directory government were responsible for some 40 per cent of all fatalities in the 1918–21 pogrom wave.[66] The revolution thus presented itself to many Jews as a stark choice between life and death, and in this context, an increasing number of Jewish socialists came

---

[63] Gitelman, *Jewish Nationality and Soviet Politics*, 222–23 (emphasis added).
[64] S. Hall, 'Race, Articulation, and Societies Structured in Dominance', in *Sociological Theories: Race and Colonialism* (Paris: United Nations Educational Scientific and Cultural, 1980), 341.
[65] Budnitskii, '"Evreiskie Batal'ony" v Krasnoi Armii', 239.
[66] Gergel, 'The Pogroms in the Ukraine in 1918–1921', 248.

to the view that Soviet power represented 'the best chance of survival'.[67] As the writer Vladimir Mikhailovskii put it in 1922, even 'Rabbis realised that it was better for Jews to lose their faith than their lives'.[68] This sentiment is perhaps captured most sharply by an unknown Bundist in mid-February 1919:

> To whom can we turn? ... To civilised Europe which signs treaties with the antisemitic Directory? [The Bolsheviks] ... the armed carriers of socialism, are now the only force which can oppose the pogroms ... for us there is no other way ... This is the best and perhaps the only way to combat the horrible Jewish pogroms.[69]

In these ways, the Bolshevik leadership's opposition to antisemitism – despite its uneven realization on the ground – played a vital role in cementing what Elissa Bemporad has referred to as the 'Soviet-Jewish alliance'.[70] The decision to join the Red Army, however, was often made in the knowledge that the Red Army itself was a source of antisemitism. As one eyewitness account observed,

> The Jewish youth leave the *shtetls* and run to Kyiv for one purpose – to enter into the Red Army. They are not Bolsheviks ... but they go to the Red Army because there one can die 'gun in hand'. And yet when they pass by a Soviet military post the Red Army men call out after them, 'you bloody Yids, you're going to speculate aren't you?'[71]

One Bundist complained of the 'strongly developed antisemitism of the Red Army soldiers ... who constantly swear at the "Yids"',[72] but this apparently did not deter him from committing himself to the fight for Soviet power. The leaders of the newly formed pro-Soviet Jewish communist parties who actively campaigned for Jews to enlist in the Red Army were equally aware of the dangers of doing so. For example, in the very moment that Poalei Zion communists issued leaflets encouraging Jews to mobilize to defend Soviet power,[73] the Moscow Bureau of the

---

[67] Kenez, 'Pogroms and White Ideology in the Russian Civil War', 301; Heifets, *The Slaughter of the Jews in the Ukraine in 1919*, 98; Budnitskii, *Rossiiskie evrei mezhdu krasnymi i belymi*, 498. Of course, it need not be stated that not all Jews chose Bolshevism in 1919. On the participation of Jews in the White movement, see Budnitskii, 158–218.
[68] Shternshis, *Soviet and Kosher*, 154.
[69] Gitelman, *Jewish Nationality and Soviet Politics*, 175–76.
[70] E. Bemporad, 'From Berdichev to Minsk and Onward to Moscow: Jewish Voices of the Russian Revolution' (27 November 2017), www.pearsinstitute.bbk.ac.uk/events/past-events/2017-events/from-berdichev-to-minsk-and-onward-to-moscow-jewish-voices-of-the-1917-russian-revolution/.
[71] Gitelman, *Jewish Nationality and Soviet Politics*, 166–67.
[72] Budnitskii, '"Evreiskie batal'ony" v Krasnoi Armii', 244.
[73] GARF f.9550 o.9 d.531 l.1.

party wrote to Lenin directly on 25 April 1919 to complain that the pogroms had 'washed over an entire series of towns and *shtetls* like a mighty wave, leaving its influence in the ranks of the Red Army'.[74] Similarly, on 22 May, when Kombund and Fareynikte Communists merged to form the Komfarband, the leadership felt moved to 'put on record' how 'utterly essential' it was to remove the 'enemy elements' who had 'taken up key positions in the Red Army and the Soviet state apparatus to carry out their counter-revolutionary activities'.[75]

Amidst the drama and the tragedy of the Russian Revolution in the former Pale of Settlement, left-wing currents of the Jewish socialist movement moved towards Bolshevism in the full knowledge that the Red Army was pervaded by antisemitism. That many *shtetl* Jews followed them speaks volumes about the starkness of the choice facing Russian and Ukrainian Jews in 1919. The Bolshevik 'promise', despite the unevenness of its delivery, presented the best chance of survival in the face of ferocious antisemitism of the White Army and various Ukrainian nationalist insurgence movements. In the latter half of 1919, those Jewish socialists who moved over to a Soviet standpoint now began to address the imbalance between the promise and the actuality of the Bolshevik project.

From the Margins to the Centre: Poalei Zion

From the very moment of their formation in May–June 1919, the new Jewish communist groupings worked in close contact with the Bolshevik leadership to extend, deepen and renew the Soviet confrontation with antisemitism.[76] Poalei Zion, in particular, played a key role in this process. The beginnings of this initiative emanated from the Poalei Zion's 'Pogrom Department', an institution within the party structure tasked with carrying out reports into anti-Jewish violence during the spring and summer of 1919.[77] On 2 June, when the full extent of the Grigor'evshchina came into view, the head of the department, Moishe Rekis, wrote to the Poalei Zion leadership to suggest that it issue a proclamation to the 'Russian proletariat' and the 'whole of the civilized world' about the 'brutal extermination [*istreblenie*]' of the Jews in

---

[74] RGASPI f.17 o.66 d.57 l.22-22ob; RGASPI f.272 o.1 d.79 l.3-4.
[75] RGASPI f.17 o.66 d.57 l.4ob.
[76] The first such communication is an appeal from the Bolshevik N. Podvoiskii on 16 April to the leaders of the Kombund, Fareynikte and Poalei Zion to mobilize Jews to fight the pogroms. RGASPI f.71 o.35 d.498 l.165.
[77] RGASPI f.272 o.1 d.81 l.98-102; f.272 o.1 d.141 l.78.

Ukraine.[78] Eight days later, on 10 June, such an appeal was published. Contrary to Rekis's request, however, it was addressed not to the 'Russian proletariat' or the 'civilized world', but instead to the Bolshevik leadership.[79] It was perhaps the most important intervention in the debate on antisemitism by the Poalei Zion during the Russian Revolution:

> The counter-revolutionary gangs of Grigor'ev and Zelenyi[80] ... try to use the darkness of the people ... to drown the social revolution in Jewish blood. These nightmarish horrors ... clearly illustrate the ominous danger of *complete extermination* [*pogolovnnogo istrebleniia*] which stands before the *entire Jewish population of Ukraine.*[81]

In this opening passage, the Poalei Zion Main Bureau began by strategically positioning themselves in accordance with the dominant Bolshevik conceptualization of antisemitism as something both 'counter-revolutionary' and external to the regime itself: the pogroms were, in essence, framed as the work of the *non-Bolshevik* 'gangs' of Zelenyi and Grigor'ev. It was important that the Poalei Zion positioned themselves in this way, since what was to follow was a dramatic depiction of antisemitism within the Red Army:

> This danger has become all the more threatening, owing to the sad fact that several Red Army units which are sent to fight the counter-revolution ... are themselves perpetrating identical criminal pogroms against the Jewish population ... It is particularly bitter for us to have to point out the tragic situation of Jewish workers in the Red Army who, having volunteered out of a deep feeling of brotherhood and solidarity with the international proletariat...are met with hatred from their fellow Red Army soldiers, which in many cases results in brutal violence.[82]

This was the most open and frank discussion of Red Army antisemitism in the presence of the Bolshevik leadership since the October Revolution. The most stinging criticism, however, was reserved for the Soviet government itself:

> To our deep regret we must state that the measures taken by the Soviet government in Ukraine in the fight against pogroms have been insufficiently

---

[78] RGASPI f.272 o.1 d.78 l.15.   [79] RGASPI f.272 o.1 d.141 l.14-19.
[80] Otaman Zelenyi (Danil Terpilo) was a military leader from Kyiv. In January 1919, he deserted Petliura's army and temporarily sided with the Bolsheviks. By March he again changed sides and fought against the Red Army until his death in November 1919. B. Gurevitz, 'An Attempt to Establish Separate Jewish Units in the Red Army during the Civil War', *Michael* 6 (1980): 90.
[81] RGASPI f.272 o.1 d.141 l.14 (emphasis in the original).
[82] RGASPI f.272 o.1 d.141 l.15.

successful. For example, those Red Army units that have taken part in pogroms or have exhibited an openly pogromist character have still not been disbanded or punished. Similarly, several openly counter-revolutionary bandits remain in local *ispolkomy* and *revkomy*. And even in the press of the Soviet leadership these pogromist events have been reported rather poorly, and with a few exceptions all of these nightmarish facts have been passed over in silence.[83]

If we recall, there had indeed been a 'silence' in the Soviet press regarding the Red Army pogroms. The message from the Poalei Zion leadership here bore a striking resemblance to the discourse articulated in the spring of 1918, when non-Bolshevik Jewish radicals in the Evkom took it upon themselves to *remind* the Soviet government that the fight against antisemitism was its responsibility. A year on, in 1919, the Poalei Zion now emphasized to the Bolshevik leadership that a principled and consistent confrontation with antisemitism would 'correspond to the interests, honour and conscience of the great revolution'.[84] Once again, the agency of anti-antisemitism flowed from the margins to the centre.

Such sentiment was not confined to the Poalei Zion communists, but was in fact shared across the Jewish communist left. Perhaps out of concern that the Bolshevik leadership might not take seriously an appeal from the Poalei Zion party, a group of communists aligned to the Evsektsiia[85] wrote to the Ukrainian Commissariat for Military Affairs to state their *full agreement* with the Poalei Zion letter, adding that it

accurately reflects the prevalence of the antisemitic climate within the Red Army ... [and that we] too encounter innumerable complaints from Jewish Red Army soldiers about threats to kill them at the front ... This situation demands serious attention from military authorities, especially in the provinces, where Jewish workers are frequently subjected to a great deal of insult and humiliation by units that claim to be [pro]'Soviet'.[86]

As is clear, the constellation of a group of Jewish communist activists around a pro-Soviet standpoint was generating a deeper, more extensive critique of the Soviet government's strategy on antisemitism. Never before had such pointed criticisms been levelled at the Bolsheviks for their record on the question of antisemitism. What is most striking, particularly in the appeal issued by the Poalei Zion, is the urgency of the intervention, an urgency born not of instrumentalism but an ethical

---

[83] RGASPI f.272 o.1 d.141 l.18-19.   [84] RGASPI f.272 o.1 d.141 l.18-19.
[85] The group in question was the Jewish Section of the Department for International Propaganda of the Political Directorate of the Ukrainian Commissariat for Military Affairs (*Evvoensek*). It was responsible for recruiting Jews into the Red Army; Gurevitz, 'An Attempt to Establish Separate Jewish Units in the Red Army during the Civil War', 87.
[86] Budnitskii, '"Evreiskie batal'ony" v Krasnoi Armii', 252.

imperative. The response of these Jewish socialists to antisemitism differed from that of the Soviet government in that they spoke from a *subject position* of 'racialized outsiders', to borrow a concept from the sociologist Satnam Virdee.[87] This was illustrated in another appeal issued by Poalei Zion to the Soviet government at the very end of the Civil War, in 1922, which complained bitterly that, 'at the local level, [Soviet] power is taking no measures whatsoever against [pogromists] ... *we are standing before great danger*'.[88] It was from this revolutionary *Jewish* subjectivity ('we') that a particular and urgent form of political action was made possible.

Yet this response to antisemitism flowed not as much from the 'Jewishness' of the activists per se, but rather from the fact that they had embraced an explicitly *Jewish socialist* politics. This needs careful explication. Each of the political formations that coalesced around a pro-Soviet politics in 1919 – the Poalei Zion, the Fareynikte and the Kombund – were located within a Jewish national politics that ranged from Marxist Zionism to territorialism to national-cultural autonomy.[89] Their profound disagreements notwithstanding, each of these parties moved towards Bolshevism through the prism of *Jewish* socialism. In his exploration of the sociological moorings underlying ideological divergences among Russian-Jewish intellectuals in the late nineteenth century, Robert Brym argued that the 'degree of affinity to Jewish nationalism varied proportionately with the degree of embeddedness in the Jewish community'.[90] The analysis here suggests that the degree of embeddedness in Jewish life identified by Brym also shaped the socialist confrontation with antisemitism. That is to say, *affinity to Jewish national politics bore implications for the ways in which Jewish communists developed their response to antisemitism*. The closer one stood politically to a Jewish socialist-national project in the Russian Revolutionary context, the more likely one would be to elevate the question of antisemitism in one's own political practice. The case of the Poalei Zion is instructive.

The party's founder and leading theoretician of Marxist Zionism, Ber Borochov, had long insisted on a non-reductive Marxist conceptualization of antisemitism. In 1905, he argued emphatically that it was a mistake to explain antisemitism in strictly economic terms. In a passage remarkably similar in spirit to Walter Benjamin, he rejected the fatalistic

---

[87] Virdee, *Racism, Class and the Racialized Outsider*.
[88] GARF f.6990 o.1 d.6 l.22; RGASPI f.17 o.84 d.165 l. 39-40 (emphasis in the original).
[89] Frankel, *Prophecy and Politics*.
[90] R. J. Brym, *The Jewish Intelligentsia and Russian Marxism: A Sociological Study of Intellectual Radicalism and Ideological Divergence* (London: Palgrave Macmillan, 1978), 45.

conception of the relationship between Marxism and oppression, so dominant in Marxist circles at the time: 'We do not put our trust in progress ... Progress is a double-edged sword. If the good angel in man advances, the Satan within him advances also.'[91] Similarly, while some Bolsheviks such as Lenin had been reluctant to address the participation of workers in the 1903–05 pogrom wave,[92] Borochov addressed the matter directly. In a 1906 essay, he argued:

> If anti-Semitism were the hobby of only a few psychopathic and feeble-minded individuals, it would not be dangerous. But anti-Semitism is very popular among the masses, and very frequently its propaganda is tied up closely with the social unrest of the lowest elements of the working class.[93]

After the October Revolution of 1917, Poalei Zion communists continued to 'stretch' Russian Marxism[94] by advancing non-reductive conceptions of antisemitism. For example, at the Poalei Zion 4th Party Congress in Moscow in early September 1919, a resolution was passed exhibiting a startling reformulation of the then dominant currents in Marxism:

> The oppression of capitalism concretises in a national form, and only in these concrete forms do the contents of that oppression and the experience of the working people of all nations develop. This is the result of the interaction of capitalism with the historical conditions of national life, and it follows that the working class therefore experience national-class oppression.[95]

This striking passage predates Stuart Hall's classic conception of racism as the 'modality in which class is lived' by some sixty years.[96] In short, Poalei Zion premised its politics in such a way as to elevate the status of ethnicity and nationality to a level at least equal to that of 'class'. In contrast, the Bolsheviks at times marginalized the specificity of the experience of racialization and oppression in their attempt to bolster a universalist conception of the 'working class'. Of all the Jewish communist formations in the Russian Civil War, the Poalei Zionists were the most likely to insist on the signification of the particular, and this facilitated a

---

[91] B. Borochov, *Class Struggle and the Jewish Nation: Selected Essays in Marxist Zionism* (Pistcataway: Transaction Publishers, 1983), 36–37. Compare this with Benjamin's famous *Theses on the Philosophy of History*, where 'progress' is akin to a 'storm', a 'catastrophe which keeps piling wreckage upon wreckage', producing a 'pile of debris' that 'grows skyward'; Benjamin, *Illuminations*, 249.
[92] See Introduction to this chapter.
[93] Borochov, *Class Struggle and the Jewish Nation*, 78.
[94] Fanon, *The Wretched of the Earth*. [95] RGASPI f.17 o.60 d.974 l.51.
[96] Hall, 'Race, Articulation, and Societies Structured in Dominance'.

clear-sighted critique of the Bolshevik attempt to get to grips with antisemitism.

There were significant divisions, of course, between these Jewish communists. Given their background in the politics of national-cultural autonomy, the Kombundists were sharply critical of the Poalei Zion insistence on a territorial nation-building project in Palestine. Even more critical of the theoretical and political foundations of Marxist Zionism was the Bolshevik, and head of the Evsektsiia, Semen Dimanshtein, who in a 1919 newspaper article publicly accused the Poalei Zionists of 'crying about antisemitism'.[97] Nevertheless, their disagreements notwithstanding, these Jewish communists provided the most consistent reservoir of opposition to antisemitism within the Soviet state apparatuses, and taken together, their politics acted as a buffer to the pitfalls of a race-blind class reductionism. The hub of such activism in mid- to late 1919 was, unquestionably, the Central Bureau of the Evsektsiia.

From the Margins to the Centre: The Evsektsiia

The first major gathering of these new Jewish communists came at the Second Conference of the Evsektsiia, held in Moscow on 1 June 1919. Such was the precariousness of the military situation in Ukraine following the Grigor'evshchina, only thirty-four delegates were able to attend: twenty-five representing Evsektsiia organizations in Russia and nine delegates from the newly formed Komfarband. The question of how to revitalize the Soviet campaign against antisemitism was a key theme at the conference. These discussions, however, were marked by sharp disagreement. Frustrated by the 'abstract' nature of the debate about whether or not the Evsektsiia should orientate itself to the Jewish 'middle class', the Komfarbandist Mandel'sberg interjected that 'the main enemy of the Jewish working class is *antisemitism*, and to fight it we need to urgently outline a set of concrete measures'. This provoked a stinging critique from Dimanshtein, who was eager to frame antisemitism as a threat to the revolution, not the Jews per se: 'Antisemitism is *not* a special Jewish question, as Mandel'sberg thinks ... it is a plague on the revolution; it is the slogan of the counter-revolution'.[98] This disagreement underlined the existence of competing conceptions of antisemitism

---

[97] *Zhizn' Natsional'nostei*, 6 July 1919; L. S. Gatagova, L. P. Kosheleva and Rogovaia, eds., *TsK RKP(b)-VKP(b) i natsional'nii vopros. Kniga 1. 1918-1933 gg.* (Moscow: ROSSPEN, 2005), 24. Despite such criticisms, Bolsheviks continued to work with Poalei Zionists at the local level. See TsDAHO f.1 o.20 d.35 1.125 and Miliakova, *Kniga pogromov*, 148.

[98] *Zhizn' Natsional'nostei*, 21 June 1919.

among the now enlarged group of Jewish communists within the Evsektsiia. For the Komfarbandist Mandel'sberg, antisemitism had a relative autonomy from the 'revolution', it was a phenomenon affecting Jews *as Jews*; in contrast, in Dimanshtein's formulation, antisemitism did not have 'the Jews' as its object, but instead 'the 'revolution'. These tensions were played out in quite dramatic fashion when Mikhail Kalinin, President of the All-Russian Executive Committee (*VTsIK*) and titular president of the Soviet state, entered into the debate. Aware of the feeling among the delegates that the Party leadership had not done enough to tackle antisemitism, Kalinin began by insisting:

> The Central Committee of our Party *does* pay special attention to the political struggle against antisemitism. *Your struggle* against antisemitism is part of our general work because it is pure counter-revolution ... *Your work* is of paramount importance to us because we are faced with a fight against an antisemitism that permeates soviet government institutions.[99]

Three observations can be made on these striking comments. First, in identifying the fight against antisemitism as '*your struggle*' and '*your work*', Kalinin implied that the Evsektsiia activists bore an intimate connection to this campaign *as Jews*; it was a campaign that they seemingly possessed by virtue of their Jewishness, whereas for the Party leadership it was part of its general political work. Second, the 'paramount importance' of the Evsektsiia, for Kalinin, lay in its contribution to the campaign against antisemitism. They were the activists who were best placed to confront antisemitism within the Soviet state apparatus. Third, and relatedly, we should also note Kalinin's remarkably frank admission that Soviet institutions had been 'permeated' by antisemitism.

Kalinin continued:

> There are no other people who have shed as much blood as the Jewish people have ... no honest person can remain indifferent to the current mass murder of the Jews. The spectre of literal destruction hangs over the Jewish people, and for you, Jewish Communists, there looms a very difficult task.[100]

This provoked a strong response from the floor, particularly from those who shared Dimanshtein's conception of antisemitism. M. Al'skii[101]

---

[99] *Zhizn' Natsional'nostei*, 21 June 1919 (emphasis added).
[100] Agurskii, *Di yidishe komisariatn un di yidishe komunistishe sektsies*, 218.
[101] Arkadii Al'skii (born Mal'skii, pseudonym: M. Al'skii) had been a member of the Jewish Commissariat since mid- or late 1918, during which time he headed the local *Evkom* in Voronezh; GARF f.1318 o.21 d.13 l.38. In August, Al'skii was elected to the Central Bureau of the Evsektsiia; Agurskii, *Evreiskii rabochii v kommunisticheskom dvizhenii (1917-1921)*, 133. In later years, he was a member of Trotsky's Left Opposition. He was executed in Stalin's purges in 1936.

Figure 10 Second Conference of Jewish Sections of the Communist Party, June 1919. Abram Kheifets is on the far right, second row.
From the Archives of the YIVO Institute for Jewish Research, New York

immediately rose to his feet to refute Kalinin's appeal to the Jewishness of the Evsektsiia, insisting that 'Jewish communists fight under the banner of the Russian Communist Party against all enemies of the revolution, no matter who they are'.[102] For Al'skii, members of the Evsektsiia approached the question of antisemitism as 'communists', not as 'Jews'. As if to underline this point, Al'skii felt moved to inform Kalinin that the conference was composed not of 'Jewish national-Communists, but Communist Jews who have no connection with the Jewish bourgeoisie'. Following this fraught exchange, Kalinin walked out of the conference, to the astonishment of the Evsektsiia delegates.[103] The row was settled by the passing of a delicately framed resolution which stated the centrality of the Evsektsiia's contribution to the fight against antisemitism, but in such a way as to make it clear that Jewish Communists did not posses any special ownership over this campaign: 'We, the Jewish communists ... must support Soviet power in its fight [*v ee bor'be*] against antisemitism.'

[102] *Zhizn' Natsional'nostei*, 21 June 1919.
[103] Gitelman, *Jewish Nationality and Soviet Politics*, 248.

Figure 11 Presidium of the Second Conference of Jewish Sections of the Communist Party. From left to right: Samuel Agurskii, Ia. Mandelsburg, Semon Dimanshtein, Abram Kheifets, Shafir, Arkadii Al'skii.
From the Archives of the YIVO Institute for Jewish Research, New York

The state confrontation with antisemitism, then, belonged not to the Evsektsiia, but to the Soviet government. It was *its* campaign, not the Evsektsiia's. Immediately following this statement, however, was an accompanying commitment on the part of the Evsektsiia activists to shape and indeed *lead* the campaign:

The conference instructs the Central Bureau of the Evsektsiia to work out a set of concrete measures for the struggle against antisemitism and to enter into dialogue with the Central Committee of the [Russian] Party about this.[104]

This is precisely what the Central Bureau of the Evsektsiia did over the course of the next six months during its weekly meetings. With its membership now enlarged by the presence of Kombundists such as Rafes, Kheifets and Novakovskii,[105] the Moscow-based Central Bureau

[104] RGASPI f.17 o.65 d.91 l.5. *Zhizn' Natsional'nostei*, 15 June 1919, 2. The resolutions for the congress have been republished in full in Gatagova, Kosheleva and Rogovaia, *TsK RKP(b)-VKP(b) i natsional'nii vopros. Kniga 1. 1918–1933 gg.*, 22–25, and more recently in V. P. Sapon, *Evrei v obshchestvenno-politisheskoi zhizni nizhegorodskoi gubernii (1914–1920 gg.)* (Nizhii-Novgorod: Evreiskii tsentr 'Khesed Sara', Istoricheskii fakul'tet Nizhegorodskogo Gosudarstvennogo Pedagogicheskogo Universiteta im. Koz'my Minina, 2012), 149–54. See also Agurskii, *Di yidishe komisariatn un di yidishe komunistishe sektsies*, 230.

[105] Orshanskii (Komfarband), Dimanshtein, Mandel'sberg, Epshtein, Sverdlov, Segal', Al'skii, Tominskii and Charnii were also elected to the Central Bureau. See Agurskii, *Evreiskii rabochii v kommunisticheskom dvizhenii (1917–1921)*, 133–34.

immediately positioned itself as the focal point of the Soviet response to antisemitism in both Russia *and* Ukraine.[106] It had some immediate successes. Just twenty-four hours after the Evsektsiia passed its motion on antisemitism at its Second Conference, the question was taken up at a joint meeting of the Orgburo and Politburo (essentially a gathering of the Party leadership). The meeting resolved to develop a fully 'worked-out plan' for confronting antisemitism at both Party and governmental levels. Lev Kamenev, specifically, was instructed to present such a plan at the next session of the Orgburo.[107] However, the issue was not taken up by Kamenev; no plan was ever presented to the Orgburo over the course of its regular meeting in the summer of 1919.

In the face of such difficulties, one of the key strategies of the Evsektsiia was to maintain pressure on the Bolshevik leadership to ensure that it followed through on its own anti-racist promise. For example, following a two-day meeting of the Central Bureau in late July 1919, the Komfarbandist Mandel'sberg wrote to the Central Committees of both the Russian and Ukrainian Communist Parties to demand that those accused of pogroms be brought to justice before Revolutionary Tribunals.[108] Far from viewing antisemitism as a *general* political question, the Central Bureau in fact approached it as a *particular* problem requiring a dedicated state response. However much Dimanshtein and others insisted that antisemitism was not specific to Jews as Jews, for the rest of 1919, the Soviet confrontation with antisemitism was led and directed by the Jewish Sections of the Communist Party – the Evsektsiia.

The Evsektsiia and the Reconstitution of the Soviet Confrontation with Antisemitism

From its very inception in June 1919, the Central Bureau of the Evsektsiia dedicated itself to the re-establishment of an intensive Soviet state response to antisemitism. Whereas in the first half of 1919 the Soviet government's approach to antisemitism had been reactive and sporadic in Ukraine and almost non-existent in Russia, the Evsektsiia now sought

---

[106] For example, at the second meeting of the newly elected Central Bureau on 8 June 1919, the Evsektsiia established a commission to determine the scale and scope of the recent pogrom wave and provide aid to its victims. The overall 'control' and 'political leadership' of the commission was to lie with the Central Bureau. See RGASPI f.445 o.1 d.1 l.7-8.
[107] RGASPI f.17 o.3 d.11 l.4. Present at the meeting were: Lenin, Rakovskii, Krestinskii, Dzerzhinskii, Kamenev, Smigla, Kalinin, Serebriakov, Mitskevich, Tomskii, Muranov, Sklianskii and Tsiurupa.
[108] RGASPI f.445 o.1 d.1 l.20ob.

to re-establish a campaign of a different type, one that had not been seen since the spring of 1918. On 26 June 1919, at one of its very first meetings, the head of the Central Bureau Semen Dimanshtein appealed directly to the VTsIK to set up a dedicated state institution for tackling antisemitism,[109] something that had been lacking since the dissolution of the Moscow Evkom back in May 1918. The following week, on 6 July, Dimanshtein publicly admitted that 'the Bolsheviks had not done much up to now in the fight against antisemitism'. He added, however, the party was 'now taking it more seriously, and the Soviet government is taking concrete steps and has set up institutions for the fight against antisemitism in all its manifestations'.[110]

In reality, no such institutions had been established. What was in fact taking place was a struggle on the part of the Central Bureau to create such an institution; and it was a struggle that had been ongoing since the dismantling of the Moscow Evkom the previous year. If we recall, in both May and October 1918, the Central Evkom (headed by Dimanshtein) appealed to the Presidium of the Cheka for a specific institution to be established within the Cheka structure to combat antisemitism. Neither of these attempts was successful.[111] After the outbreak of the Grigor'evshchina in May 1919, Dimanshtein tried again, this time appealing in person at a meeting of the Bolshevik Central Committee in Moscow on 11 May 1919 to demand a more coherent and consistent opposition to antisemitism. In his speech before the Central Committee, Dimanshtein noted 'with horror' the fact that 'antisemitism, particularly in the provinces, is growing more and more and is becoming a threat to the social revolution'. To address the crisis, Dimanshtein demanded that the Party leadership permit the formation of a dedicated department to tackle antisemitism.[112] Despite gaining a favourable response,[113] no progress was made. In June 1919, Dimanshtien tried yet again by appealing to the VTsIK, but it fell on deaf ears. On July 17, the Central Bureau of the Evsektsiia decided to write instead to the Cheka once more to ask that it establish a special department to fight against antisemitism. Again, however, no such apparatus was formed.[114]

---

[109] RGASPI f.445 o.1 d.1 l.13.   [110] *Zhizn' Natsional'nostei*, 6 July 1919, 1.
[111] GARF f.1318 o.1 d.563 l.465-456ob.   [112] RGASPI f.17 o.65 d.91 l.16.
[113] Dimanshtein's suggestions were discussed at a session of the Orgburo of the Central Committee on 11 May. Although the meeting noted its 'approval' of Dimanshtein's proposal, no state apparatus for confronting antisemitism was actually formed. RGASPI f.17 o.112 d.4 l.25.
[114] RGASPI f.445 o.1. d.1 l.16. A 'Jewish Section' headed by the Evsektsiia activist Ainshtein *was* in fact established within the Cheka on July 28, but it existed to arrest Zionists rather than combat antisemitism; RGASPI f.445 o.1 d.1 l.46; f.445 o.1 d.2 l.215-216. For more on Evsektsiia campaigns against Zionism in mid-1919, see V. Iu.

The Committee for the Struggle against Antisemitism

On 6 August, the Central Bureau changed tack and appealed instead to the Extramural Department of the Commissariat of Enlightenment in Moscow.[115] This time, their efforts were met with success: three weeks later, on 26 August, the Committee for the Struggle against Antisemitism was formed within the Extramural Department.[116] After more than a year of campaigning and petitioning by the Jewish Commissariat and the now enlarged Central Bureau of the Evsektsiia, a new, dedicated state institution for combatting antisemitism had finally been established within the Soviet government – the first such institution since the dissolution of the Moscow Evkom in the spring of 1918.

The committee had been formed, however, at a time of abject crisis for the Party: no sooner had the Bolsheviks defeated Grigor'ev in May than the White Army, with substantial support from Western governments, moved into Ukraine from the south in June, and in July Petliura's Army returned from the west. By late August, the Red Army was entirely overrun and the Bolsheviks lost power completely in Ukraine.[117] Amidst the chaos, many former Komfarband activists fled Ukraine to the western borderlands of Gomel and Vitebsk where they helped to establish local Evsektsiias in the towns and cities not occupied by the Whites.[118] Leaders of the Jewish communist movement such as Rafes, Kheifets and Lipets, however, fled to Moscow where they joined up with other members of the Central Bureau such as Dimanshtein and Mandel's-berg.[119] It was here, in Moscow, that the work of the Committee for the Struggle against Antisemitism was carried out. Just as in 1918, the Soviet confrontation with antisemitism was once again located not in the former Pale of Settlement, where the vast bulk of pogroms continued, but in the heartland of Soviet power: Moscow.

Vasil'ev, ed., *Evreiskii vopros. Poiski otveta. Dokumenty 1919–1921 gg. Vypusk pervyi* (Vinnitsa: Globus-Press, 2003), 63; Gatagova, Kosheleva and Rogovaia, *TsK RKP(b)-VKP(b) i natsional'nii vopros. Kniga 1. 1918–1933 gg.*, 27–28.

[115] RGASPI f.445 o.1 d.2 l.213. The Extramural Department's sphere of work included adult education, the news agency ROSTA and, most significantly, Prolekul't, the artistic institution that promoted an avant-garde proletarian culture; S. Fitzpatrick, *The Commissariat of Enlightenment. Soviet Organization Education and Arts under Lunacharsky, October 1917–1921* (Cambridge: Cambridge University Press, 1970), 25.

[116] GARF f.A2306 o.1 d.291 l.46-47; f.A2306 o.1 d.3289 l.1, 7; TsGAMO f.66 o.12 d.694 l.12-12ob.

[117] Yekelchyk, *Ukraine*, 81.

[118] Rafes, *Dva goda revoliutsii na Ukraine (Evoliutsiia i raskol 'Bunda')*, 166.

[119] RGASPI f.445 o.1 d.1 l.51.

The work of the committee was formally overseen by two of the Party's most senior members: Anatolii Lunacharskii, head of the Commissariat for Enlightenment; and Nadezhda Krupskaia, leader of the Extramural Department and wife of Lenin. In practice, however, the committee was sustained by a core of individuals: the Bolshevik Semen Dimanshtein (the head of the Evsektsiia), Abram Kheifets and David Lipets (formerly of the Bund), and, most curiously, the anarchist Apollon Karelin,[120] a non-Jew, who since June 1919 had been actively publishing articles in the Bolshevik press against antisemitism.[121] On 9 September, two weeks after its formation, the former Kombund leader Moishe Rafes and former Fareynikte Communist Ia. Novakovskii were also appointed to the committee as 'specialists' on antisemitism.[122] We might note that this decision was taken not by the committee itself, but by the Central Bureau of the Evsektsiia. This underlines the fact that behind the scenes, the Central Bureau played a key role in overseeing the direction of the committee's work.[123] Owing to a long-standing track record in publishing articles on antisemitism stretching back to the pre-revolutionary years, Maksim Gor'kii was also elected as a member of the committee's Literary-Publishing Section.[124] Gor'kii's involvement also led to the inclusion of the well-known writer and publisher Ivan Gorbunov-Posadov, who, like Gor'kii, had written literary texts denouncing the Kishinev pogrom of 1903.[125] In total, by the end of August 1919, the committee boasted nine staff members,[126] and it is unlikely that this number increased significantly over the rest of the year. However, the importance of the committee's work extended beyond its small activist base.

---

[120] Karelin (1863–1926) was a veteran theorist of Russian anarchism. Following the October Revolution, Karelin became a leader of the 'All-Russian Federation of Anarcho-Communists', a group that offered critical support to the Soviet regime. For more on Karelin, see V. P. Sapon, *Apollon Andreyevich Karelin: Ocherk zhizni* (Niznii Novgorod: Yu. A. Nikolaev, 2009).

[121] See, for example, Karelin's article on antisemitism in *Krasnaia Zvezda*, 17 June 1919, 3

[122] RGASPI f.445 o.1 d.1 l.50.   [123] RGASPI f.445 o.1 d.1 l.38-39; 49-50; 60-60ob.

[124] GARF f.A2306 o.1 d.3289 l.1, 3, 5-6, 12-12ob, 14. For an anthology of Gor'kii's writings on the so-called Jewish question, see M. Gor'kii, *Iz literaturnogo naslediia. Gor'kii i evreiskii vopros* (Jerusalem: Evreiskii Universitet v Ierusalime, 1986).

[125] GARF f.A2306 o.1 d.3289 l.3. Between 1897 and 1940, Gorbunov-Posadov was head of the publishing house Posrednik (The Intermediary), which had been originally founded by Tolstoy in 1884. In 1903, after the Kishinev pogrom, Gorbunov-Posadov published a highly emotive poem simply titled *Pogrom*. Racism more broadly was something he took an interest in: the previous year he had also been responsible for the publication of a Russian-language edition of *Uncle Tom's Cabin*. For a critical discussion, see J. MacKay, *True Songs of Freedom: Uncle Tom's Cabin in Russian Culture and Society* (Madison: University of Wisconsin Press, 2013), 48–53.

[126] GARF f.A2306 o.1 d.291 l.47, 49.

In its founding document drafted at its inaugural meeting on 26 August 1919, the committee declared itself 'the central organ for leading the ideological struggle against antisemitism in all its manifestations and in all areas of Soviet life'.[127] Its scope was exceptionally broad and covered the writing and publication of brochures, leaflets and posters; the organization of public lectures and special courses of antisemitism in higher education; the provision of materials on antisemitism for both local and central newspapers; and, perhaps most important of all, directives for political agitators in the Red Army.[128] The founders of the committee clearly saw their work as much more than just stopping pogroms: instead, the task was a deeply cultural struggle against antisemitism 'in all its manifestations'. An anecdotal incident at the inaugural meeting on 26 August underscores this crucial point: when taking down the minutes, the stenographer incorrectly noted down the name of the newly formed institution as 'The Committee for the Struggle against Pogroms'. When the first draft of the minutes was circulated, the word 'pogroms' was scored out in red pen (perhaps by Dimanshtein or Lipets) and replaced with 'Antisemitism'.[129]

Following this first meeting, an Executive Bureau composed of the former Kombundists Kheifets and Lipets was tasked with mapping out the committee's strategy for confronting antisemitism.[130] The document produced by these two Jewish communists gives a strikingly clear insight into the ethical standpoint of those who led the Soviet campaign against antisemitism during this period:

We are unable to remain passive viewers ... the most decisive and urgent measures are required ... The struggle against antisemitism, having been part of the *general* educational work of Soviet propaganda, must now be *singled out as a special branch* and be taken up by an *independent active organization*. The Committee for the Struggle against Antisemitism represents such an organization.[131]

There is an urgency with which Kheifets and Lipets write: their inability to 'remain passive' speaks of a perspective born not of strategic or tactical considerations, but rather of an ethical imperative characteristic of the Moscow Evkom's campaign against antisemitism in the spring of 1918. For Lipets and Kheifets, it was insufficient to merely designate antisemitism a place in the 'general educational work' of the Soviet state. Instead, Lipets and Kheifets were now insisting – as Dimanshtein and others in the Evkom/Evsektsiia milieu had been since 1918 – that antisemitism be

---

[127] GARF f.A2306 o.1 d.291 l.46-47.   [128] GARF f.A2306 o.1 d.291 l.46-47.
[129] GARF f.A2306 o.1 d.3289 l.1.   [130] GARF f.A2306 o.1 d.3289 l.2.
[131] GARF f.A2306 o.15 d.749 l.13 (emphasis added).

Figure 12 Abram Kheifets, around 1917.
Russian State Archive of Social-Political History

'singled out' as a 'special' area of political work. In refusing to reduce antisemitism to the 'general' fight against 'counter-revolution', the activists of the committee elevated the question of antisemitism and gave it the degree of relative autonomy that had previously been lacking in the Soviet government campaigns in the first half of 1919.

The committee's approach to antisemitism was above all underpinned by an educative praxis. At the meeting on 26 August, it was noted that '[t]he success of antisemitic persecution is rooted in … hatred towards the Jews which is a result of the centuries-old politics of the autocracy'. Rather than being explained (away) as mere 'counter-revolution', antisemitism was instead framed as a specifically '*cultural*' phenomenon to be tackled by an educative and interventionist politics.[132] The committee therefore identified schools, theatres, cinema, drama, art and music as important fora for tackling antisemitic attitudes.[133] This is further underlined by the fact that the committee had very little in the way of dealings with repressive state apparatuses such as Revolutionary Tribunals; instead, it dedicated its attention to collaborating with activists in the ideological state apparatuses of the Soviet government, in particular its

[132] GARF f.A2306 o.15 d.749 l.13.   [133] GARF f.A2306 o.15 d.749 l.13-14, 22.

press departments and publishing houses.[134] The aim was to confront antisemitism through the politics of *consent* rather than coercion.

The committee's work was targeted at the Bolsheviks' social base. As a resolution passed on 8 September stated, 'in bypassing the intellectual stratum of society [the committee] direct itself mainly at the working masses'.[135] In particular, the committee identified the Red Army as the primary audience for its work.[136] Unlike other bodies within the Soviet government, then, the committee refused to ignore the specificity of Red Army antisemitism. Previously, when the Soviet government issued information-gathering questionnaires about pogroms, respondents were prescribed categories to explain the pogromists (i.e. 'white guards' or 'kulak elements') (see Chapter 5).[137] The Red Army was noticeable by its absence. In contrast, when the committee issued a questionnaire to Bolshevik agitators in the provinces, it included a specific and pointed question about the nature and extent of antisemitism within the Red Army.[138]

The committee's strategy was clarified on 1 September, when the former Kombundist Kheifets contacted the Bolshevik Central Committee in Moscow to request that a permanent group of educators be recruited to support the campaign against antisemitism.[139] The committee further organized a series of lectures for students in higher education institutions, with the anarchist and committee member Karelin making a guest appearance at one of these in Moscow on 18 September.[140] Lectures were delivered in Moscow throughout September on the themes: 'Jews and the Army'; 'The Church and the Army'; 'The Church and the Synagogue'; 'The Attitude of the State to Churches and Synagogues'; and the somewhat provocatively titled 'The Privileged Position of the Jews'. Further lectures were also planned for a whole series of local Party meetings, and plans were put in place to issue instructions for agitators and educationalists on the subject of antisemitism.[141]

The publication of agitational materials was overseen by Karelin and Kheifets. One of their first tasks was to delegate the former Bundist David Lipets to write two brochures on the pogroms in Ukraine.[142] These were published in early 1920 under Lipets's newly adopted name,

---

[134] See GARF f.A2306 o.1 d.3289 l.5-6, 12-13; GARF f.A2306 o.15 d.749 l.1-3ob, 39-40, 46-49.
[135] GARF f.A2306 o.1 d.3289 l.5-6. [136] GARF f.A2306 o.15 d.749 l.14.
[137] *Zhizn' Natsional'nostei*, 6 July 1919, 4. [138] GARF f.A2306 o.15 d.749 l.5.
[139] GARF f.A2306 o.1 d.3289 l.24. [140] GARF f.A2306 o.1 d.3289 l.5-6.
[141] GARF f.A2306 o.1 d.3289 l.12-12ob. [142] GARF f.A2306 o.1 d.3289 l.3.

'David Petrovskii'.[143] Karelin also wrote two pamphlets of his own: one, a twenty-five-page guide for Bolshevik agitators engaged in the campaign against antisemitism[144]; the other, a short eight-page piece written in colloquial Russian for peasants.[145] According to the minutes of a committee meeting on 31 August, Karelin also wrote a third brochure on antisemitism.[146] A collaborative piece on antisemitism was also written by the three committee members Moishe Rafes, Maksim Gor'kii and Semen Dimanshtein in the late summer of 1919.[147] Dimanshtein also enlisted Lenin's former secretary Vladimir Bonch-Bruevich to publish a collection of articles on antisemitism.[148] Lastly, in his role as a 'specialist' on antisemitism, Rafes put plans in motion for a major publication on the Civil War pogroms based on archival materials. The finished monograph was to total some 1,300 pages, but it apparently never saw the light of day.[149]

In addition to these political texts, the committee oversaw the re-publication of popular pre-revolutionary fiction dealing with the subject of antisemitism. These included Maria Konopnicka's *Mendel' Gdansk*, published in a new translation in 1920 under the title *Staryi Perepletchik i Ego Vnuk* ('The Old Bookbinder and His Grandson').[150] Further planned publications included Vladimir Korolenko's classic 1903 account of the Kishinev pogrom *Dom 13* ('House No. 13') and G. Machtet's 1888 short story *Zhid* ('Yid'). However, owing to the committee's inability to find an author willing to do the required editorial work, the latter two remained unpublished.[151] The committee also oversaw the publication of a collection of poems by the popular Soviet poet Dem'ian Bednyi which sought to challenge, again in colloquial Russian, a whole range of antisemitic stereotypes.[152]

---

[143] D. Petrovskii, *Revoliutsiia i kontr-revoliutsiia na Ukraine* (Moscow: Gosudarstvennoe izdatel'stvo, 1920); D. Petrovskii, *Kontr-revoliutsiia i evreiskie pogromy* (Moscow: Gosudarstvennoe izdatel'stvo, 1920).
[144] A. A. Karelin, *Zlye spletni na ugnetennykh* (Moscow: Gosudarstvennoe izdatel'stvo, 1919).
[145] A. A. Karelin, *Zlye rosskazni pro evreev* (Moskva: Izdatel'stvo Vserossiiskogo Tsentral'nogo Ispolnitel, nogo Komiteta Sovetov R., S., K. i K Deputatov, 1919).
[146] GARF f.A2306 o.1 d.3289 l.3
[147] Gor'kii, *Iz literaturnogo naslediia. Gor'kii i evreiskii vopros.*, 280.
[148] Agurskii, *Di yidishe komisariatn un di yidishe komunistishe sektsies*, 15; Bonch-Bruevich, *Krovavyi navet na khristian*.
[149] GARF f.A2306 o.1 d.3289 l.5-6
[150] M. Iu. Konopnitskaia, *Staryi perepletchik i ego vnuk* (Moscow: Gosudarstvennoe izdatel'stvo, 1920).
[151] GARF f.A2306 o.1 d.3289 l.3, 14. *Dom 13* had in fact been published by the Bund during the 1905 revolution; M. G. Rafes, *Ocherki po istorii Bunda* (Moskva: Moskovskii rabochii, 1923), 439–40.
[152] D. Bednyi, *Kainovo nasledstvo* (Moscow: Gosudarstvennoe izdatel'stvo, 1919).

Amidst all this activity, the committee's work did not go unnoticed. In mid-September, the committee began to receive letters from the public offering advice on how best to confront antisemitism.[153] Soviet government institutions also looked to the committee to supply it with much needed materials on antisemitism. On 30 September, the Political Enlightenment Department of the Commissariat for Military Affairs made a special appeal to the committee, asking it to address '*the complete absence*' of educational materials on antisemitism. The appeal also noted that because of the shortage of propaganda materials, 'very little work was being carried out' among the troops of the Red Army.[154] Other institutions also wrote to the committee to inform it about outbreaks of antisemitism at the local level.[155]

The Committee Dismantled

At a meeting on 23 September, it was agreed that the committee should look to increase staff levels to consolidate itself as the main government body responsible for leading the Soviet response to antisemitism.[156] This was partly a response to one of its key members, Abram Kheifets, being commandeered to work for the Comintern just a few weeks into his post in the committee. On 14 October, the Sovnarkom headed by Lenin in Moscow agreed to issue one million roubles to the committee to facilitate this enlargement.[157] However, later that *same day* a meeting of the Presidium of the Extramural Department decided to close down the committee:

> The Extramural Department considers it unwise to have a special committee for the struggle against antisemitism owing to the fact that the fight against antisemitism ought to be interspersed with all the work of the Extramural Department as an ordinary [*ocherednykh*] question of agitation and propaganda.[158]

The Presidium's sudden closure of the committee seemed driven by a rejection of its elevation of antisemitism as a 'special' area of political struggle. Against the wishes of the committee, the Presidium reframed the campaign against antisemitism, and in so doing insisted that it be 'interspersed' as an 'ordinary' sphere of work.[159] Following this announcement, a meeting of the Central Bureau of the Evsektsiia was

---

[153] GARF f.A2306 o.15 d.407 l.2-7.   [154] GARF f.A2306 o.15 d.749 l.1-4.
[155] For example, a group of trade unionists in Gomel appealed to the committee for assistance after an antisemitic attack at a local commune. See GARF f.A2306 o.15 d.749 l.43.
[156] GARF f.A2306 o.1 d.3289 l.12-12ob.   [157] GARF f.A2306 o.15 d.407 l.1.
[158] GARF f.A2306 o.15 d.407 l.12.   [159] GARF f.A2306 o.15 d.407 l.12.

immediately called on 17 October to salvage the work of the committee. With Dimanshtein, Mandel'sberg and Orshanskii present, it was agreed that an appeal be made to the Presidium of the VTsIK for the work of the committee to continue.[160] Just as in late June, however, no progress was made on this front.

On 21 January 1920, the Presidium of the Extramural Department announced the formal dissolution of the committee on the disingenuous grounds that it had been a 'stillborn' project 'as evidenced by its own productivity'.[161] In truth, its closure had been forced through by the Extramural Department a mere *six weeks* after its formation, at the peak of its activity. On 5 February, Krupskaia presented the case for the committee's closure to the Commissariat of Enlightenment,[162] and with that, just as in May 1918, a dedicated Soviet state institution for combatting antisemitism had been dismantled almost as soon as its work had begun.

How can this be explained? A brief announcement by the Commissariat for Enlightenment, tucked away on the back page of *Zhizn' Natsional'nostei* on 21 March 1920, revealed the reasons for the *Committee's* dissolution:

[T]he critical moment of antisemitic propaganda *has passed* and therefore the continued existence of a special committee is no longer necessary.[163]

This was, by all accounts, an astonishing statement. Just as the Commissariat for Enlightenment declared the 'critical moment' to have 'passed', reports of antisemitism from across Ukraine continued to flood in throughout the first weeks and months of 1920.[164] Some reports pointed to an exponential growth of antisemitism in the Red Army specifically.[165] Indeed, the continued problem of Red Army antisemitism was revealed when one of the Soviet government's most trusted and decorated army units, the First Red Cavalry, carried out a series of brutal pogroms during the 1920 Soviet–Polish War.[166] Moreover, reports from Jewish

---

[160] RGASPI f.445 o.1 d.1 l.60-60ob.   [161] GARF f.A2306 o.1 d.394 l.37.
[162] GARF f.A2306 o.1 d.394 l.36.
[163] *Zhizn' Natsional'nostei*, 21 March 1920 (emphasis added).
[164] For reports on pogroms between January and May 1920, see Miliakova, *Kniga pogromov*, 344–82. See also TsDAVO f.3204 o.1 d.75 l.21; RGVA f.4 o.1 d.17 l.8-11; YIVO RG80 folder 43, 3606; and GARF f.6990 o.1. d.1. Scores of reports were also sent to the Jewish Commissariat and Evsektsiia warning of the continued problem of antisemitism in early 1920. See, for example, GARF f.1318 o.24 d.9 l.51; f.1318 o.1 d.655 l.1-2; and RGASPI f.445 o.1 d.14 l.125.
[165] Miliakova, *Kniga pogromov*, 358–62.
[166] RGASPI f.17 o.109 d.73 l.60-60ob; GARF f.R-1339 o.1 d.424 l.119-119ob. See also Babel, *Red Cavalry*; Budnitskii, 'The Reds and the Jews, or the Comrades in the Arms of the Military Reporter Liutov'; Figes, 'The Red Army and Mass Mobilization during

communists in early July 1920 indicated that an 'oppressive' anti-Jewish atmosphere had prevailed in the Kyiv Party apparatuses since the re-establishment of Bolshevik power in late 1919, and that scores of Jewish workers had decided not to re-register for Party membership as a consequence.[167] One letter to the Central Committee even claimed that 'the provincial Kyiv committee [*gubkom*] of the Party is *entirely* antisemitic'.[168] Whilst it is true that the White Army was all but defeated by early 1920, the 'critical moment' had far from 'passed', and antisemitism remained a problem in the Red Army and state apparatus. What is more, pogroms continued right throughout the first few years of the 1920s.[169]

The closure of the Committee reflected an underestimation of antisemitism on the part of the Soviet government. What is more, it was emblematic of the sporadic and reactive way in which the Bolshevik leadership approached the issue: whenever cases of antisemitism arose in 1919, the Party would respond; when the 'critical moment' appeared to have passed, the campaign fell away. For the Jewish communists in the Evsektsiia and the Committee for the Struggle against Antisemitism, however, the campaign against antisemitism was born not of strategic considerations, but of a commitment to what Raymond Williams once called the 'long revolution'.[170] It was a strategy which had, as its end goal, the supplanting of antisemitism with a new worldview; at the same time it recognized the deeply entrenched nature of antisemitism and, in turn, the long-term cultural confrontation required to overcome it.

Into the 1920s: The Evsektsiia Continues Its Work

The Committee for the Struggle against Antisemitism was to be the last dedicated state institution for combating antisemitism during the revolutionary period. Its dismantling, however, did not stop the Evsektsiia and other Jewish communists from trying to revive a Soviet response to antisemitism. In early December 1919, with the committee all but disbanded, a series of debates were conducted within both the Central Bureau and the Ukrainian Bureau of the Evsektsiia over how best to

---

the Russian Civil War 1918–1920', 195–96; Brown, 'Communists and the Red Cavalry', 86–89. On the Soviet–Polish War more generally, see Fiddick, *Russia's Retreat from Poland*.

[167] RGASPI f.445 o.1 d.14 l.125.   [168] RGASPI f.17 o.65 d.92 l.39.

[169] On pogroms in 1922, see GARF f.1318 o.1 d.761 l.4, 12, 25-26, 40-41, 99, 113; f.6990 o.1 d.6 l.16, 26-28; f.6990 o.1 d.19 l.26; RGASPI f.17 o.84 d.165 l.19, 33. For an overview of the pogrom wave in Ukraine between mid 1920 and late 1922, see Miliakova, *Kniga pogromov*, 379–750.

[170] R. Williams, *The Long Revolution*, Revised edition (Harmondsworth: Penguin Books, 1965).

confront antisemitism.[171] These discussions culminated on 10 December in one of the single most significant interventions undertaken by the Evsektsiia, when its Central Bureau issued the Russian and Ukrainian Bolshevik leadership with a set of directives on antisemitism. It insisted, not for the first time, that 'the Party and Soviet government must give more consideration to the fight against antisemitism ... which has started to poison the minds of the workers and has even penetrated the ranks of local Party organizations'.[172] These directives and the extensive debates that preceded them are discussed in greater detail in Chapter 7. It is important to note here that after its demise, the activists who had worked in and around the committee – Dimanshtein, Rafes, Lipets, Mandel'berg and Orshanskii – continued to take it upon themselves to attempt to direct the Party leadership on the question of antisemitism, and they continued to do so well in to the early 1920s.

For example, on 28 July 1920, the former Kombundist and newly elected member of the Evsektsiia Central Bureau, Avrom Merezhin,[173] spoke before the Second Congress of the Comintern to propose a special resolution devoted to the question of the pogroms.[174] Later that same

[171] RGASPI f.445 o.1 d.1 l. 67-68ob; f.445 o.1 d.5 l.91; f.17 o.65 d.92 l.26-28; TsDAHO f.1 o.20 d.89 l.61.
[172] Copies of these directives are held in various archives, including: RGASPI f.272 o.1 d.141 l.87-90; f.272 o.2 d.9 l.23; f.17 o.65 d.92 l.120-125; f.445 o.1 d.1 l.74-79ob; f.445 o.1 d.5 l.80-85; GARF f.9550 o.9 d.648 and IJ f.19 o.1 d.4 l.25. See also *Zhizn' Natsional'nostei*, 1 February 1920. According to Dimanshtein, these directives were written largely by the Ukrainian Evsektsiia leadership, that is, the former members of the Komfarband; Lenin, *O evreiskom voprose v Rossii*, 18. See also RGASPI f.17 o.65 d.92 l.26-28; TSAGOV f.1 o.20 d.89 l.61.
[173] Avrom Merezhin (Avrom-Moishe Grubshtein) was born in Odessa in 1880, where he attended a Jewish school. By the beginning of the century he was an active supporter of Zionism. His transition to Bolshevism was, like so many others, made through the Bund and the experience of the Civil War. Having joined the Bund in 1917, he went on to become a founding member of the Kombund in mid-1919. He was elected to the Central Bureau of the Evsektsiia at its third congress in July 1920. In the 1920s, he helped establish The Society for Agricultural Settlement of Jewish Toilers (OZET), an organization formed by the Soviet government to promote the agricultural settlement of Jews on Soviet territory. Merezhin was also active in promoting Jewish agricultural settlement in Birobidzhan in the late 1920s and early 1930s. On 27 February 1937 he was murdered in the Stalinist purges (material taken from http://newswe.com/index.php?go=Pages&in=view&id=1020. Accessed 6 July 2019). See also Gitelman, *Jewish Nationality and Soviet Politics*, 259–62.
[174] Merezhin's proposed resolution read: 'The Second Congress of the Communist International, which expresses the will of the revolutionary proletariat of the world, therefore raises the most decisive protest against the pogroms against the Jews, which are the work of the international counter-revolution. It calls on the workers of every country to fight against them actively in word and deed ... to tear down all the barriers that divide nations and to bring about the true fraternity of nations all over the globe" *Vestnik Evotdela Narkomnatsa* No. 1–2, August–September 1920, available in GARF f.1318 o.24 d.8 l.9ob-10. For an English translation, see J. Riddell, *Workers of the World*

year, as news filtered through to Moscow in early to mid-October 1920 of the brutal pogroms carried out by the Soviet Red Cavalry in the war with Poland, again the Evsektsiia were among the first to inform Lenin and the Bolshevik leadership and demand that something be done.[175] The Evsektsiia also held rallies in late October 1920 to discuss the continued growth of antisemitism in the Red Army and the seeming lack of any stringent response from the Party leadership. Following these meetings, appeals were made to the Ukrainian Bolshevik Central Committee, demanding that a series of lectures on antisemitism be delivered in all regions where the Red Army was stationed.[176]

Similarly, in early July 1921, Merezhin, now head of the Evsektsiia Central Bureau, wrote to Lenin to inform him and the Politburo that in parts of the former Pale 'the Jewish population is gaining the impression that the Soviet government is not capable of defending the civilian population from bandits' and, even worse, that 'the pogroms against the Jews are made with the knowledge of the Soviet government'.[177] The following month, at the Forth Congress of the Evsektsiia in August 1921, Merezhin also drafted a set of recommendations for combating the ongoing pogroms.[178] Such praxis was sustained throughout 1922 as the fallout from the Red pogroms in the Soviet–Polish war continued.

It was noted previously that the Soviet press invariably kept silent about the phenomenon of antisemitism in the Red Army. In both 1921 and 1922, however, the Evsektsiia and Jewish Commissariat leadership consistently appealed to the Soviet government for details of the Red Army pogroms to be made public.[179] Relatedly, on 5 July 1922, the

---

and *Oppressed Peoples, Unite! Proceedings and Documents of the Second Congress, 1920. Volume 1.* (Pathfinder, 1991), 266–69, 296–98.

[175] Lenin, *V. I. Lenin neizvestnye dokumenty 1891-1922*, 401–02; Pipes, *The Unknown Lenin*, 116–17.

[176] RGASPI f.445 o.1 d.14 l.116. In late 1919, for example, Rafes took additional measures to pressure the Soviet government to do more to tackle antisemitism. RGASPI f.445 o.1 d.1 l.68ob, 71.

[177] Pipes, *The Unknown Lenin*, 128.

[178] Copies of the recommendations are preserved in RGASPI f.445 o.1 d.91 l.105, 107, 149, 239-241. An edited version was published in the journal of the Jewish Commissariat, *Vestnik Evotdela Narkomnatsa*, no. 5, October 1921. See GARF f.1318 o.24 d.8; f.1318 o.24 d.13a l.37-37ob; f.1318 o.1 d.726 l.57; and RGASPI f.445 o.1 d.91 l.240ob.

[179] On 13 April 1921, Merezhin wrote to the Politburo to complain that a request by the Evsektsiia leadership in December the previous year to publicize pogroms carried out by Budennyi's Red Army cavalry had been ignored. RGASPI f.17 o.84 d.165 l.1, 3-3ob. For further examples, see Miliakova, *Kniga pogromov*, 814–15, and GARF f.1318 o.1 d.761 l.31-32, 126.

former Bundist (turned Evsektsiia leader) Orshanskii wrote to the Party leadership to complain that antisemites in the Red Army responsible for the pogroms in the Soviet–Polish war had either escaped arrest altogether or were sent to Revolutionary Tribunals, only to be released without punishment.[180] Orshanskii was not entirely correct in his accusations: scores of Red Army soldiers from the 6th Division of the First Red Cavalry (perhaps even as many as 400) had indeed been executed for their involvement in the pogroms of 1920.[181] Nevertheless, Orshanskii's letter underscored the fact that the flow of anti-racist agency continued to move from the margins to the centre – from the Evsektsiia to the Party leadership. Other such interventions from activists in the Evsektsiia, the Jewish Commissariat and Poalei Zion in the early 1920s give further evidence of this pattern.[182]

Conclusion

In late November 1921, the Bolshevik A. Morozov wrote to Trotsky to warn him of the depth of antisemitic sentiment among sailors and Red Army soldiers in Odessa, Ekaterinoslav and Petrograd. In his letter he suggested that a broad Party-led 'project' be initiated to counter the ongoing problem of antisemitism. Morozov even went as far as to map out what such a strategy might look like: it should, he argued, above all entail a cultural struggle involving a series of lectures and rallies in the central cities of Soviet Russia and Ukraine. What is more, Morozov recommended that antisemitism be marked out as a *specific* area of struggle, suggesting, for example, that the Party establish a dedicated newspaper on combating antisemitism.[183] This was *precisely* the kind of 'project' that had been actualized, however fleetingly, by the Committee for the Struggle against Antisemitism in the late summer of 1919. More

---

[180] GARF f.1318 o.1 d.761 l.39.

[181] Budnitskii, 'The Reds and the Jews, or the Comrades in the Arms of the Military Reporter Liutov', 79.

[182] For examples from the Jewish Commissariat, see GARF f.1318 o.1 d.761 l.12-13, 40-41ob, 45, 88, 92. In July 1920, the Poalei Zion leadership wrote directly to Zinov'ev, then Chairman of the Executive Committee of the Comintern, to complain that 'for over two years the persecution of the Jewish population has continued ... and the Soviet government has been unable to put a stop to it ... in the spring of this year in Cherkasy and Chernihiv "Red partisans" carried out yet more pogroms'; RGASPI f.272. o.1 d.87 l.83. See also RGASPI f.272. o.1 d.82 l.71-72, 84, 91-93; f.272 o.1 d.141 l.44-45; f.17 o.84 d.165 l.39-40; and GARF f.6990 o.1 d.6 l.22 for similar examples of Poalei Zion opposition to antisemitism in the early 1920s.

[183] RGASPI f.17 o.60 d.49 l.211-213. My thanks to Gleb Albert for bringing this source to my attention.

Conclusion

than two years on from its dissolution, the strategy developed by the committee remained as vital as ever.

Who were the agents of Soviet anti-antisemitism in mid- to late 1919 and the early 1920s? Writing in his diary on 21 March 1919 from Poltava, the Russian writer Vladimir Korolenko noted: 'There are many people here who want to start bloody pogroms against the Jews. To their credit the Bolsheviks are decisively against the pogroms, but unfortunately, this is only so because there are many Jewish men and women among them'.[184] Given the material presented in this chapter, such accounts are not surprising. The Soviet state response to antisemitism was not solely dependent on the agency of Jewish Bolsheviks. The previous chapter showed emphatically that non-Jewish Party leaders *were* committed to putting a stop to pogromist violence. However, when we begin to disaggregate the *nature* of the different currents of Soviet state responses to antisemitism, three important conclusions can be drawn.

First, it is clear that the most consistent and urgent form of opposition to antisemitism emerged specifically from the broad grouping of non-Bolshevik Jews who moved over to a pro-Soviet standpoint in mid-1919. These activists coalesced primarily around the apparatuses of the Evsektsiia and Jewish Commissariat, and their political trajectory is striking: of the 144 delegates who attended the 4th Congress of the Evsektsiia in 1921, 116 had previously belonged to either the Bund or the United Jewish Socialist Workers' Party.[185] In mid- to late 1919, just as had been the case in the spring of 1918, the Soviet confrontation with antisemitism flowed from the margins to the centre.

Second, this campaign was born not of strategic considerations, but of a distinctly ethical imperative. In the numerous documents detailing the Evsektsiia's sphere of work, antisemitism is rarely, if ever, listed. For instance, in a set of instructions written in December 1919 for Evsektsiia activists at the national and regional levels, twenty-seven tasks are identified: antisemitism is notable by its absence.[186] The question of antisemitism was similarly absent from the founding documents of the Jewish Commissariat when it was established in early 1918.[187] In other words, the campaigns discussed at length here emerged *organically* from this social formation of Jewish communists. More specifically, they emerged out of a continued disappointment with the record of those institutions of

---

[184] Korolenko, *Dnevnik. Pis'ma 1917–1921*, 146–47.
[185] Gitelman, *Jewish Nationality and Soviet Politics*, 223–24.
[186] TsDAHO f1 o.20 d.90 l.5-7.
[187] RGASPI f.272 o.1 d.71 l.5; GARF f.1318 o.1 d.22 l.12; Agurskii, *Evreiskii rabochii v kommunisticheskom dvizhenii (1917–1921)*, 40.

the Soviet leadership that *were* expected to deal with antisemitism. It was out of this frustration that Jewish communists took matters into their own hands, went beyond their identified sphere of work, and set about establishing dedicated Soviet state institutions to combat antisemitism. The sporadic approach taken by the Party leadership, however, combined with the tendency towards centralization, ensured that these institutions were dissolved, and with them went the most promising strand of opposition to antisemitism to emerge in the Russian Revolution.

Third, and perhaps most contentiously, we can say that the closer one stood politically to a Jewish socialist-national project in the Russian Revolution, the more likely one was to elevate the status of (and hence take more seriously) the campaign against antisemitism in one's political practice. In short: proximity to a Jewish socialist-national project facilitated a more urgent form of political practice on the question of antisemitism.

7 Reinscribing Antisemitism?
The Bolshevik Approach to the 'Jewish Question'

In revolutionary Russia, antisemitism resurfaced even within those campaigns designed to combat it. Whenever Bolsheviks responded to antisemitism, they did so on a terrain fraught with great difficulty. Antisemitism at times overdetermined the revolutionary process, its entry points being multiple and often unpredictable. In their actions against antisemitism, Bolsheviks often found themselves reinscribing what they had set out to confront.

Antisemitism and Revolutionary Class Discourse

The mobilization of class injuries was pivotal to the growth of the workers' movement and the stunning success of the Bolshevik party in 1917. Long-standing popular conceptions of 'us', the disadvantaged, and 'them', the rich and powerful, had been forged among the subaltern classes out of tangible social and political inequalities, and Bolshevik agitators knew how to channel these grievances better than anyone.[1] Yet the politics of class conflict did not always provide a buffer to racialization and nationalist resentments. The Russian Revolution was a crucible in which the discursive architectures of 'revolution' and 'counter-revolution' could overlap, particularly in the former Pale, where class concepts such as 'bourgeoisie' frequently bore ethnic (and sometimes specifically antisemitic) overdeterminations. In the popular imaginary, 'the Jew' was often positioned in an antagonistic class relation to the 'working people' (the *trudiashchiesia* or *trudovoi narod*).

This presented the Bolshevik leadership with an acute problem: the categories of class struggle were vulnerable to antisemitic appropriations and interpretations, especially in the former Pale. On the ground, the reception of the Bolshevik message was something the Party leadership

---

[1] M. D. Steinberg, *Voices of Revolution, 1917* (London: Yale University Press, 2001), 17–21; O. Figes and B. I Kolonitskii, *Interpreting the Russian Revolution. The Language and Symbols of 1917* (New Haven: Yale University Press, 1999), 167–70.

could not always control. For example, when partisan Red Army units in Ukraine received directives from above in mid-1919 to 'sweep away the speculators who have stolen from you',[2] how could the Bolshevik leadership be certain that a category so porous and malleable as 'speculator' would be understood in its Marxist, and not antisemitic, sense? Similarly, when Red Army posters were put up around central Kyiv in 1919 with the words 'beat the bourgeoisie!' (*'burzhuev bit'!'*),[3] could the Bolsheviks be sure that the message would not evoke the most long-standing and notorious of all antisemitic slogans in Russia: 'beat the Yids!'? In so far as 'bourgeois' and 'Jew' were interchangeable in the popular imaginary, the Bolshevik strategy of confronting antisemitism with the categories of class ran into difficulties. The Bolsheviks were sometimes reminded of this by their political opponents. An article in the Odessa-based Menshevik newspaper *Iuzhnyi Rabochi* (Southern Worker) in late January 1919 argued: 'If the Bolsheviks are honest, then they must admit that these 'communists' [who have joined the Red Army] have gathered not to fight the bourgeoisie, but, above all, to fight the Yids.'[4] While such claims were evidently motivated by a desire to discredit the Bolsheviks, they correctly identified that the 'Jew'/'bourgeois' construction could, and did, find traction within sections of the Bolsheviks' social base.

The Bolsheviks made several attempts to undercut the scope for such antisemitic interpretations of their revolutionary class discourse. The primary means for doing so was to clarify and re-emphasise the anti-bourgeois basis of their political project. As one pamphlet on antisemitism put it, 'Understand, comrade workers and peasants, that our real enemies are the landlords, the bourgeoisie and the capitalists of all hues and all nationalities. 'Class against class' – that is our slogan.'[5] The Bolsheviks also tried to clarify the *intention* of their anti-bourgeois message by insisting, emphatically, that the bourgeoisie of *all* nationalities were the target, not simply the 'Jewish bourgeoisie'. Another pamphlet against antisemitism, issued in late summer 1919, informed its readers:

Every nation has its own bourgeoisie, which exploits ... the peasants, workers and all working people. There are, of course, bourgeois among the Jews, and they are also the enemies of the working people, just like the Russian bourgeoisie are for our working people. But among the Jews there are also many worker-people,

---

[2] RGVA f.9 o.4 d.66 l.17.   [3] RGVA f.9 o.13 d.699 l.31.
[4] *Iuzhnyi Rabochii*, 31 January 1919; RGASPI f.71 o.35 d.527 l.140-142. For more on *Iuzhnyi Rabochii*, see V. Faitel'berg-Bland and V. Savchenko, *Odessa v epokhu voin i revoliutsii (1914-1920)* (Odessa: Optimum, 2008), 21, 82, 221.
[5] Shelit, *Doloi pogromov*, 7.

prepared to work just as diligently as we Russians ... and these Jew-workers are the friends of the Russian working people, and we must relate to them just like we relate to our own fellow villagers and workers.[6]

The Bolshevik strategy, then, was to counterpose class to ethnicity. As the same pamphlet argued,

> The world is split into two camps ... and every worker and each peasant must look to see which camp one stands in – that of the working people or that of the parasites and exploiters, and not which people or which nation one was born into.[7]

Such interventions attempted to uncouple the articulation between antisemitism and class struggle, and instead push the narrative into an ethnically non-specific space: class. However, the categories of class were *not* guaranteed to cut through racialized conceptions of Jewishness. Racialization and class formation were interlocking, not separate processes. Popular anti-bourgeois sentiment – a vital resource of Bolshevik mobilization – was vulnerable to antisemitism in certain regions of the Pale. The attempt to navigate an anti-racist Marxism was therefore laden with great difficulty; each discursive step taken seemingly opened up yet another entry point for antisemitism.

On occasion, the Bolsheviks recognized this dynamic. In mid-February 1919, the head of the Ukrainian Sovnarkom Rakovskii issued an 'order' (*prikaz*) threatening all those participating in 'antisemitic propaganda' with arrest (see Chapter 5 for a discussion). In this document, published widely in the Soviet press,[8] Rakovskii addressed the antisemitic potential of the category 'speculation', noting that whilst the Soviet government 'takes a firm hand to eliminate [the speculators], we do not need pogroms to do so'.[9] This was a seeming recognition that Bolshevik policy on speculation often translated, on the ground, as a call for pogromist violence. Similarly, on 31 March 1919, a Party member by the name 'Kagorovskaia' wrote directly to Podvoiskii, the Commissar for Military Affairs, to warn that if the Soviet state was seen to be attacking the 'petit-bourgeoisie' *in general*, then a green light would be given for the masses to *specifically* attack Jews, owing to the fact that they are so associated with trade.[10] Even more striking was the lead article in the 12 April 1919 edition of the main Party newspaper in Ukraine, *Bol'shevik*, which implored its readers not to fall prey to the antisemitic slogan 'beat the Yids'. 'The Soviet government', it

---

[6] Karelin, *Zlye spletni na ugnetennykh*, 16. [7] Ibid.
[8] See *Kommunist*, 12 February 1919, 1, and *Zhizn' Natsional'nostei*, 23 March 1919, 3.
[9] IJ, f.19 o.1 d.4 l.50.
[10] RGVA f.25860 o.1 d.263 l.15. I wish to thank Dimitri Tolkatsch for bringing this source to my attention.

warned, 'will not permit pogroms ... we need only empty the pockets of the peaceful bourgeois, and not by force.'[11] There was an awareness within the Bolshevik camp, then, that the mobilization of class resentment could, and sometimes did, translate into antisemitic violence.

'Jews' in the Red Army

Yet in countering antisemitism, Bolsheviks sometimes reinscribed certain antisemitic representations of Jewishness. A cornerstone of antisemitism in 1919 was the racialized notion of the Jewish body and its unsuitability for military combat. Another, related canard was that those Jews who did serve in the Red Army managed to secure lucrative administrative positions far from the front. The prevalence of these stereotypes among Red Army units is documented in a series of internal Bolshevik reports from 1919,[12] and they survived well into the late 1920s.[13] In front-stage contexts the Party tried to convince non-Jewish Red Army soldiers that Jews really were like 'them'.[14] For example, pamphlets were published pointing to the baseless nature of these and other related antisemitic depictions of Jewishness.[15] However, in backstage contexts, a more common strategy adopted by the Bolsheviks was to try to get the Jews to be less like the antisemites said they were. Consider, for example, the following telegram sent to the Central Committee of the Russian Bolshevik Party on 19 November 1919 by the Bolshevik Kozlovskii[16]:

> Jewish Red Army soldiers, including mobilized Party members, are leaving the rear in great numbers not only for political work but for ordinary clerical and administrative work as well. As a result, Jewish Commissars are reproached by Red Army soldiers, and this sometimes takes on an antisemitic inflection. We must review the lists of all Jewish Red Army soldiers in the rear and in the front and redistribute them so as to eliminate this abnormal situation.[17]

For Kozlovskii, the problem was not just that people within the Bolshevik social base subscribed to an antisemitic worldview, but that Jews seemingly confirmed those antisemitic projections. This revealed a certain acquiescence with the logic of antisemitism itself: Jews, in other words, were part of

---

[11] *Bol'shevik*, 12 April 1919.   [12] See, for example, TsDAHO f.1 o.20 d.39 l.7.
[13] See Larin, *Evrei i antisemitizm v SSSR*, 241; G. Ledat, *Antisemitizm i antisemity: Voprosy i otvety* (Leningrad: Priboi, 1929), 55.
[14] Y. Slezkine, *The Jewish Century* (Princeton: Princeton University Press, 2006).
[15] See, for example, Karelin, *Zlye rosskazni pro evreev*. For a discussion of Karelin's pamphlet, see Shternshis, *Soviet and Kosher*, 153–54.
[16] This was most likely Mechislav Kozlovskii, who worked in the Sovnarkom in Moscow and the Commissariat for Justice.
[17] RGASPI f.17 o.65 d.92 l.36.

the problem. Such an outlook was widespread in backstage Bolshevik interventions against antisemitism. In a report into the activities of the 1st Ukrainian Soviet Army in May 1919, several references are made to the extent of antisemitism within the unit. However, when it came to providing the Party leadership with a set of recommendations for overcoming such antisemitism, the report suggested that Jews be mobilized to fight on the front line 'side by side with the peasants, so as to reduce this counter-revolutionary sentiment in the Red Army'.[18] Similarly, when another report the following month stated that antisemitism among the same Red Army soldiers had become so 'strongly developed' that pogroms had become an 'ordinary occurrence', the proposed solution was the same: 'one of the best means of fighting this antisemitism is to enlist mobilized and volunteer Jews into the regiment'.[19] When, in August 1919, yet another report detailed antisemitism in the 1st Ukrainian Soviet Army, the solution was by now a familiar one: 'To weaken antisemitism in the Red Army, it would be advisable to mobilize Jewish volunteers.' Only this, the author argued, 'would have the effect of reducing counter-revolutionary sentiments among the Red Army milieu'.[20] Although motivated by a desire to confront antisemitism, such strategies appeared to place the emphasis on changing Jews, not than those who subscribed to antisemitic ideas.

These were not isolated cases: over the course of the Civil War, Bolshevik responses to antisemitism regularly betrayed a preoccupation with Jews rather than antisemites.[21] Take, for example, an internal security report covering the 'political composition' of the First Cavalry during the period of 15 July–15 August 1920. Despite growing Party concern that the First Cavalry was deeply interpolated with antisemitism in July and August[22], the author of the report, Il'ia Vardin (Illarion Mgeladze),[23] head of the Political Division, insisted:

It is absolutely necessary to emphasize that there is no active antisemitism in the Army. There are anti-Jewish prejudices, and there is a purely peasant,

---

[18] RGASPI f.71 o.35 d.692 l.23-34; 42ob.   [19] TsDAHO f.1 o.20 d.35 l.95.
[20] RGVA f.4 o.1 d.10 l.47.
[21] See, for example, Budnitskii, *Rossiiskie evrei mezhdu krasnymi i belymi*, 470–71.
[22] A report on the First Cavalry dated 30 June noted that in the Fourth Division, 'antisemitic agitation is displayed almost openly'. Meanwhile, in the Sixth, Eleventh and Fourteenth Divisions, antisemitism was similarly widespread. Budnitskii, 'The Reds and the Jews, or the Comrades in the Arms of the Military Reporter Liutov', 70–71. On antisemitism in the First Cavalry in the summer of 1920, see Babel, *Red Cavalry*, 209, 225, 279.
[23] Vardin, we should note, authored the only *Pravda* article on antisemitism during the *whole* Civil War period. Unlike his internal report into the First Cavalry, his *Pravda* article did not broach the question of 'Jewish behaviour', but instead depicted antisemitism as a 'counter-revolutionary phenomenon'; *Pravda*, 14 May 1919.

unconscious (*bezotchetnaia*), passive dislike for the Jew, but nothing more. There are practically no malicious, pogromist-hooligan attitudes towards the Jew. The best way to fight antisemitism is to have good Jewish communists. Jewish communists (and unfortunately there are few of them) work rather idly.[24]

Not only does Vardin downplay the seriousness of what he terms 'passive dislike for the Jew' (the First Cavalry was about to embark on a series of devastating pogroms), but the responsibility for antisemitism is clearly outlined: if only Jews worked harder and were not so 'idle', then antisemitism would necessarily subside. Moreoever, Vardin's report actually served to confirm, rather than subject to criticism, existing antisemitic stereotypes about Jews' alleged lack of 'productivity'. What this and other such examples illustrate is that some Bolsheviks saw a 'kernel of truth' to the representations of Jewishness articulated by their antisemitic opponents.[25]

'Jews' in the Soviet State Apparatus

Bolshevik responses to antisemitism were further complicated by the pernicious 'Jewish-Bolshevik' construct, so widely perpetuated by

---

[24] RGASPI f.71 o.35 d.778 l.37-39.
[25] Budnitskii, 'The Reds and the Jews, or the Comrades in the Arms of the Military Reporter Liutov', 70–71. On the 'kernel of truth' approach to antisemitism of socialists in Weimar Germany, see Fischer, *The Socialist Response to Antisemitism in Imperial Germany*. The preoccupation with the role of Jews in the Red Army sometimes resonated at the highest levels of Party leadership. When Trotsky received a warning from Akradii Rozengol'ts on 2 June 1920 about the 'serious danger of increased antisemitism in the Red Army', he responded the next day by dispatching the following memorandum to the Orgburo: 'The same story is repeating itself on the Western and Southwestern fronts. There are only a very insignificant number of Jews serving in active units. *From this antisemitism inevitably grows.* We must immediately command the Jewish communist organizations to mobilize the maximum number of Jewish workers ... this measure must be carried out with particular energy in Ukraine'; Budnitskii, '"Evreiskie batal'ony" v Krasnoi Armii', 258 (emphasis added). This was not the first time Trotsky had intervened in such a manner. At a Politburo meeting on 18 April 1919, at which Lenin, Stalin and Krestinskii were also present, he complained that a 'huge percentage of workers in the Cheka ... and central Soviet institutions consist of Latvians and Jews', and that the number serving in the ranks of the Red Army on the front is 'comparatively small'. For Trotsky, it was '*for this reason* [that] chauvinistic agitation finds a response among Red Army soldiers'; RGASPI f.17 o.3 d. 2 l.1 (emphasis added). For a discussion of this document, see Kostyrchenko, *Tainaia politika Stalina*, 59. The belief that mobilizing Jews into the Red Army was the best means of undercutting antisemitism was shared by the Party leadership in Ukraine as well. Antonov-Ovseenko, Commander of the Red Army in Ukraine, argued in April 1919 that the most effective way to reduce Bolshevik antisemitism was to have Jews fight side by side with non-Jews in the Red Army; RGASPI f.71 o.35 d.498 l.164-165. Antonov-Ovseekno's suggestion was seconded by the Bolshevik leader Podvoiskii; RGASPI f.272 o.2 d.25 l.52.

the White Army during the Civil War.²⁶ The antisemitic claim that Bolshevism was 'Jewish', or that Jews 'controlled' the Soviet state apparatus, was something Party leaders could ill-afford to ignore: the Bolshevik project was entangled in the antisemitic projection. On a terrain such as this, each step taken risked perpetuating the politics of antisemitism and unleashing the ferocity of anti-Jewish violence, so often coterminous with anti-Communism. How, then, did the Bolsheviks proceed?

Internal reports show that throughout 1919, local Party activists were intensely preoccupied by the role Jews played in the regime. Equally, they saw the management of that 'role' as one of the most effective means of countering antisemitism. A report sent to the Central Committee from Elisavetgrad in early April noted that factory and railway workers were 'strongly against the Jews' and saw Soviet power as a 'government of Yids'. Local institutions of Soviet government, it argued were unable to function owing to the fact that key positions had been given to Jews. The solution, according to the author, was to immediately send 'Orthodox Christians [*pravoslavnye*]' to replace the Jews currently staffing these positions.²⁷ Such reports implied that local state apparatuses were collapsing not because of endemic levels of antisemitism, but because too many Jews were staffing these departments. Similar conclusions were reached in Mogilev in mid-May, when Party officials stressed the 'urgent need' for 'Russian [*russkie*]' communists after a peasant uprising against Soviet power had been conducted under the slogan 'beat the Yids'.²⁸ A few weeks prior to this, Grigorii Moroz, a member of the central Cheka Collegium and himself Jewish, wrote to the Central Committee in Moscow to express his dismay at the depth of antisemitism in Ukraine. His solution? Remove Jews from office and replace them with Russians.²⁹ Elsewhere, Party leaders received a letter from local Bolsheviks in Kremenchuk in late May requesting that 'the number of Jewish Commissars be kept to a

---

[26] In 1919, the White Army distributed leaflets to workers, peasants and soldiers that repeatedly identified Bolshevism as a 'Yid' project. See, for example, RGASPI f.17 o.66 d.75 l.1-2, 18-18ob. See also Budnitskii, *Russian Jews*, 180. As is well known, the Jewish-Bolshevik construct reached its apex in Nazi Germany. See J. Herf, *Jewish Enemy: Nazi Propaganda during World War II and the Holocaust* (Cambridge, MA: Harvard University Press, 2006).

[27] TsDAHO f.1 o.20 d.35 l.1-3. See also RGASPI f.17 o.6 d.369 l.109-111

[28] TsDAHO f.1 o.20 d.35 l.45-46, 55, 57-59.

[29] S. A. Pavliuchenkov, *Voennyi kommunizm v Rossii: Vlast' i massy* (Moscow: RKT-Istoriia, 1997), 256–59; S. Velychenko, *State Building in Revolutionary Ukraine: A Comparative Study of Governments and Bureaucrats, 1917–1922* (Toronto: University of Toronto Press, 2011), 189.

minimum ... in order to save the revolution'.³⁰ By mid-June, similar reports were sent to the Party leadership from a host of towns and cities – including Vasylkiv, Bila Tserkva, Fastiv, Pereiaslav, Vorozhba, Valki, Vapniarka, Mogilev, Ivankiv, Radomyshl, Cherkasy, Lypovets, Skvyra and Ruzhyn – all demanding that Russian (*russkie*) Party workers be sent to replace Jews.³¹

These developments added two new dimensions to the Bolshevik approach to antisemitism in 1919. First, the blowback of antisemitism in local party and government institutions in Ukraine had put the Bolshevik leadership under immense strain: antisemitism now threatened to undo Soviet power from within. Second, when mid-level Bolsheviks responded to the emerging crisis, they did so by reinscribing certain antisemitic representations of Jewishness. In their attempts to combat antisemitism, these Bolshevik actors indicated that they believed those representations to hold truth, and in doing so they focussed their attentions not on antisemites, but on Jews. Such practices, which initially emerged at the local level, were eventually adopted by the Party leadership as well.

Recent scholarship has shown that in the second half of 1919, Bolshevik leaders were engaged in a contentious set of discussions about restricting the number of Jews in the Soviet government in Ukraine.³² This was an explosive policy move that Lenin and other Party leaders sought to keep out of public view. The debate was initiated at leadership level in mid-1919. At a meeting of the regional Kyiv Party Committee (Kyiv *gubkom*) on 31 May, Central Committee Secretary Stanislav Kosior revealed that Party leaders in Ukraine had, just the previous day, debated 'for a long time' the question of removing Jews from the government in an attempt to reduce antisemitism. The Central Committee, Kosior suggested, had agreed on the following approach:

We must attract the *muzhik* [Russian peasant³³] ... the whole situation [regarding antisemitism] has come to pass because the peasantry has become convinced that

---

[30] YIVO RG80 folder 39, 3535. This letter was apparently printed in *Izvestiia Kremenchugskogo gorodskogo i uezdnogo Ispolnitel'nogo Komiteta Sovetov Rabochikh, Krest'ianskikh i Krasnoarmeiskikh Deputatov i Kremenchugskogo Komiteta Kommunisticheskoi Partii (Bol.) Ukrainy* on 31 May 1919.
[31] TsDAHO f.57 o.2 d.283 l.1-9; 15-16. For a discussion of this theme, see Velychenko, *State Building in Revolutionary Ukraine*, 189.
[32] Velychenko, *State Building in Revolutionary Ukraine*; S. Velychenko, *Painting Imperialism and Nationalism Red: The Ukrainian Marxist Critique of Russian Communist Rule in Ukraine, 1918-1925* (Toronto: University of Toronto Press, 2015); Kostyrchenko, *Tainaia politika Stalina*, 63; Pipes, *The Unknown Lenin*, 76–77.
[33] The term *muzhik* formally translates as 'peasant', but the meaning is far more diffuse than this. Often, it can take on an almost derogatory meaning; R. May, *The Translator in*

the 'Yids' take up the places in the Party committees, and that all they do is speculate there. It is essential that we persuade the peasantry *in practice* that this is not the case.[34]

What, exactly, did it mean to 'persuade in practice'? Kosior was clear: 'We need to have a sufficiently cautious policy, such that *we do not put in key posts those comrades who might irritate the population*.'[35]

Some Party leaders in Ukraine were evidently concerned about this change in policy: the Ukrainian Orgburo, for example, intervened to request that it be kept firmly out of the public view, and certainly until it had been approved by the Central Committee in Moscow.[36] According to Velychenko, no such approval was granted, and the policy was dropped at the insistence of Piatakov.[37] However, from this point onwards, the Bolshevik debate about antisemitism in 1919 proceeded from a basic premise: the presence of Jews in the state apparatus was understood as a cause of antisemitism, and for some Party leaders this meant the Soviet government should reduce the number of Jews in office. By the end of 1919, this controversial policy would eventually come to be the official Party position. Its chief architect was Lenin.

Jews and Soviet Power: Lenin Intervenes

When the Bolshevik leadership fled Ukraine in August 1919 following Denikin's advance, there began in Moscow a three-month period of reflection on the reasons for the Party's defeat. A fierce debate ensued about how Bolshevik power in Ukraine might be restored, not just militarily, but politically as well. Two main proposals were put forth: the first insisted on a genuinely autonomous and independent Ukrainian Soviet state with its own government and Communist Party; the second, viewing Ukraine merely as an extension of 'southern Russia', advocated the full subordination of any future Ukrainian Soviet government to Moscow. Arguing against both positions, Lenin outlined a policy of greater sensitivity to Ukrainian national sentiment.

Lenin's thinking was shaped in part by advice he received from the Bolshevik Ordzhonikidze. Writing on 19 November 1919,

the Text: On Reading Russian Literature in English (Evanston: Northwestern University Press, 1994), 76, and this seems to be the way in which Kosior deployed it here (consider, for example, the fact that in the next sentence he refers to the region as being a 'nasty kulak town'). These were 'simple' people in Kosior's meaning, and they were often interpolated with reactionary worldviews (such as antisemitism).

[34] RGASPI f.71 o.35 d.512 l.430-431.   [35] RGASPI f.71 o.35 d.512 l.431.
[36] The full account by Kosior is available in RGASPI f.71 o.35 d.512 l.429-431.
[37] Velychenko, *Painting Imperialism and Nationalism Red*, 50.

Ordzhonikidze stressed to Lenin that the Party must 'find, at all costs, a common language [*obshchii iazyk*] with the Ukrainian peasant'. Ordzhonikidze further suggested that those Bolsheviks who had previously staffed the state apparatuses be prevented from returning to Ukraine. The Party, advised Ordzhonikidze, should rely largely on 'local forces' should the Bolsheviks come to power in Ukraine again.[38] On the face of it, this exchange bore no relation to the question of antisemitism. However, Ordzhonikidze's careful choice of words, '*local* forces', was in fact a coded reference to the *ethnicity* of Bolshevik cadres in Ukraine. This would be confirmed two days later at a meeting of the Politburo on 21 November, when debate turned to the specific question of the Jewish presence in the Soviet government in Ukraine.

In preparation for the Politburo meeting on 21 November, Lenin drafted a set of guidelines on behalf of the Party Central Committee outlining a new Bolshevik strategy in Ukraine. In a strong critique of the 'Great Russian chauvinists' in the Party who had refused to give any concession to the national question in Ukraine, Lenin now insisted that all Bolsheviks exercise the 'greatest caution in relation to nationalist traditions and the strictest observance of equality of the Ukrainian language and culture'.[39] According to the annotated notes in the fifth (and most comprehensive) edition of Lenin's *Complete Works*, the draft theses were agreed 'in principle' by the meeting of the Politburo on 21 November and then submitted to a 'commission' for final editing before being officially ratified at a meeting of the Party Central Committee the following week, on 29 November. The theses then became the basis of the Party's resolution 'On Soviet Power in Ukraine', which was passed at the Eighth Party Conference four days later, on 3 December, and published widely in the Soviet press.[40]

Since the opening of the archives, however, we now know that Lenin's *original* draft theses, written for the Politburo meeting on 21 November, in fact contained an additional, unpublished recommendation. Drafted by hand, Lenin advised the Party

---

[38] G. K. Ordzhonikidze, *Stat'i i rechi. Tom 1* (Moscow: Gosudarstvennoe izdatel'stvo politicheskoi literatury, 1956), 106–07.

[39] Lenin, *V. I. Lenin neizvestnye dokumenty 1891–1922*, 306; Pipes, *The Unknown Lenin*, 76. These directives can be seen to have had some impact: shortly after this, a set of instructions from the Party centre were issued to all Red Army agitators and local Party workers in Ukraine insisting that they relate 'very carefully to national and religious and other such remnants of the cultural way of life'; RGASPI f.71 o.35 d.503 l.179–180.

[40] V. I. Lenin, *Polnoe sobranie sochinenii*, 5th edition, Vol. 39 (Moscow: Izdatel'stvo politicheskoi literatury, 1970), 334–37.

to keep a tight rein[41] on Jews and urban inhabitants in Ukraine [*Evreev i gorozhan na Ukraine vziat' v ezhovye rukavitsy*], transferring them to the front, not letting them into government agencies (except in an insignificant percentage and in particularly exceptional circumstances, under class control).[42]

This remarkable passage was consistently omitted from all published versions of Lenin's works, and only became available after the opening of the archives following the collapse of the Soviet regime.[43] It reflected two significant insecurities harboured by the Party leadership in 1919: that Jews were *underrepresented* in the Red Army and *overrepresented* in the state apparatuses. Lenin's solution, as is clear, was to increase the number of Jews in the Red Army by transferring them to the front, and second – and here he was quite explicit – to reduce their presence in Party and government institutions by preventing them from working there.

In the official resolution passed by the Eighth Party Conference on December 3 (and subsequently published widely in the Soviet press), all reference to Lenin's controversial resolution on 'the Jews' was omitted.[44] Instead, the dramatic passages quoted above were reformulated with the demand that 'measures be taken immediately to prevent Soviet institutions from being flooded with the Ukrainian urban petty-bourgeoisie [*gorodskogo meshchanstva*], who have no conception of the living conditions of the peasant masses'.[45] As is clear, the jarring terminology in

---

[41] Pipes translates this as 'Treat the Jews and urban inhabitants in the Ukraine with an iron rod'; Pipes, *The Unknown Lenin*, 77. However the phrase 'keep a tight rein' seems to me to be a better translation of Lenin's original: '*vziat' v ezhovye rukavitsy*' ; Lenin, *V. I. Lenin Neizvestnye dokumenty 1891-1922*, 307. The document is widely discussed in the existing literature: Kostyrchenko, *Tainaia politika Stalina*, 63; Velychenko, *State Building in Revolutionary Ukraine*; Velychenko, *Painting Imperialism and Nationalism Red*; Y. Petrovsky-Shtern, *Lenin's Jewish Question* (New Haven: Yale University Press, 2010), 91.

[42] Lenin, *V. I. Lenin neizvestnye dokumenty 1891–1922*, 307. In the original handwritten version, 'under class control' is written in the margins in place of 'under special supervision'.

[43] The passage was omitted from both the fourth and fifth editions of Lenin's complete works, as well as the officially issued protocols of the Eighth Party Conference at which the theses were discussed; N. N. Popov, ed., *Vos'maia konferentsiia RKP(b), dekabr' 1919 g.* (Moscow: Partiinoe izdatel'stvo, 1934). Excerpts of the draft theses were published in *Pravda* on 11 July 1956, but all references to the controversial passages on 'the Jews' were removed. The full draft theses were first published in English in Pipes, *The Unknown Lenin*. A more comprehensive and fully annotated documentation was subsequently included in the Russian-language collection: Lenin, *V. I. Lenin neizvestnye dokumenty 1891–1922*.

[44] The discussion on Ukraine took place during the fourth session of the conference on the evening of 3 December, with Rakovskii, Bubnov, Zatonskii, Manuil'skii, Drobnis and Lenin all taking part. Popov, *Vos'maia konferentsiia RKP(b), dekabr' 1919 g.*, 93–115.

[45] Popov, *Vos'maia konferentsiia RKP(b), dekabr' 1919 g.*, 186.

Lenin's original draft theses was reframed such that the new resolution now appeared to be grounded in a more readily recognizable Marxist schema; the language of ethnicity ('Jews') had been replaced by the language of class analysis ('petty bourgeoisie').

However, the resolution was carefully worded such that its original target ('the Jews') was in fact still signposted, if now in a coded form. The category 'Jew' bore *both* ethnic and class overdeterminations in revolutionary Russia. In the Ukrainian context, the seemingly non-racialized class concept 'urban petty-bourgeoisie' in fact captured and retained the very thrust of Lenin's original thesis: the groups to be kept out of office were those that were *non-Ukrainian*, and in this context that meant, above all, Jews.[46] The change in language was in fact suggested by Lenin himself: in his original draft theses, next to the controversial line 'keep a tight rein on Jews', Lenin added in the margins the following note: 'express it politely: the Jewish petty-bourgeoisie'. In other words, Lenin tried to push the narrative away from ethnicity towards class.

Lenin's interventions in late 1919 were not without consequence: according to Velychenko, Lenin's *original* draft theses were passed down through the Party apparatuses and issued as a secret directive to Party functionaries instructing them to exclude Jews from office.[47] When a thousand experienced Party workers were sent to Ukraine between December 1919 and April 1920 to re-establish Soviet power, the Central Committee in Moscow apparently issued a special memorandum insisting that checks be carried out on the nationality of all those who took up key positions in the state apparatus.[48] Other documents suggest that in late 1919 and early 1920, the Central Committee had *specifically* instructed Party cadres in Ukraine to replace Jews with Russians. For example, during a debate about the Red Army's defeat in Poland at the Ninth Party Conference in September 1920, Lenin was handed a note from a conference delegate Grigorii Zaitsev which made reference to a decision by the Central Committee in late 1919 to address 'the question of "Jewish domination" [*evreiskom zasil'e*] in Party and Soviet institutions' by replacing Jews with Russians.[49] That a lower-mid-level Bolshevik in Ukraine was aware of these directives perhaps indicates that Lenin's *original* version of the draft theses was passed down through the Party and government apparatuses, not the coded version that replaced 'Jews'

---

[46] Velychenko, *State Building in Revolutionary Ukraine*, 190.   [47] Ibid., 192.
[48] Pavliuchenkov, *Voiennyi kommunizm v Rossii*, 261; Borys, *The Sovietization of Ukraine, 1917–1923*, 255.
[49] Pavliuchenkov, *Voennyi kommunizm v Rossii*, 254.

with 'urban petty-bourgeoisie'.[50] Some years later, in 1922, Zinoviev spoke openly of Lenin's policy of removing Jews from office.[51]

How can we interpret these dramatic passages bearing Lenin's name? The revelation of the original draft theses was first made in Richard Pipes's controversial 1996 collection, *The Unknown Lenin: From the Secret Archive*.[52] According to Pipes, Lenin was entirely indifferent to antisemitism, and throughout 1919 steadfastly refused to take action against Red Army pogroms. This, however, is a baseless claim. Writing shortly after Lenin's death in 1924, the head of the Evsektsiia Dimanshtein recalled:

Whenever I informed Lenin about the information we had gathered in the Jewish Commissariat about the scope and form of antisemitism, he was full of rage, and, it seemed to me, even shame at the disgracing of the revolution with such a shameful relic of the past. He said that antisemitism is a dangerous weapon of the counter-revolution and that we must fight it with decisive measures.[53]

In depicting Lenin as indifferent to the issue, Pipes misses the key issue: in his intervention *against* antisemitism in November 1919, Lenin reinscribed a set of antisemitic representations of Jewishness. Lenin and other Bolshevik leaders no doubt believed that the less Jews appeared to confirm antisemitic representations of Jewishness, the easier it would be to fight antisemitism – hence the decision to reduce the number of Jews in office. But in doing so, their actions betrayed a certain acquiescence with the antisemitic projection: they implied that there really were 'too many Jews' in government. These contradictions were illustrative of a much deeper, conjunctural problem: every step taken by the Bolsheviks in the campaign against antisemitism risked perpetuating the racializing logic they sought to critique.

The Evsektsiia Responds to Lenin

A core argument of this book is that Jewish socialists who staffed the Jewish Commissariats (Evkom) and Jewish Sections (Evsektsiia) offered

---

[50] For a further discussion, see Velychenko, *Painting Imperialism and Nationalism Red*, 50.
[51] When Zinoviev met a group of Communists from the United States at a session of the 4th Congress of the Comintern on 1 December 1922, he apparently informed them: 'When we finally got a grip of Ukraine, Lenin announced: we have too many Jews in Ukraine. Real Ukrainian workers and peasants must be called upon to take power'; G. Estraikh, 'Letters to the Editor', *East European Jewish Affairs* 23, no. 1 (1993): 123–24.
[52] For an excellent critique, see A. Rabinowitch, 'Richard Pipes's Lenin', *Russian Review* 57, no. 1 (1998): 110–13.
[53] Lenin, *O evreiskom voprose v Rossii*, 15.

the most consistent strand of opposition to antisemitism in early Soviet Russia. How, then, did they respond to Lenin's explosive suggestion that Jews be prevented from entering the Soviet government?

Once news filtered through about the passing of Lenin's resolution at the Eight Party Conference, the Central Bureau of the Evsektsiia called a meeting for 6 December to formulate an immediate response. Five of the ten Evsektsiia Central Bureau members present at the meeting were leading activists in the state campaign against antisemitism: Mandel'sberg, Dimanshtein, Novakovskii, Lipets and Rafes.[54] The latter four had all been instrumental in establishing and coordinating the activities of the Committee for the Struggle against Antisemitism, recently disbanded by the Party leadership (see Chapter 6).

Rafes opened the meeting on 6 December by insisting that the Central Bureau draft a special memorandum addressed to the Party Central Committees both in Russia and in Ukraine, outlining an alternative approach to antisemitism and the 'Jewish question' more generally. More substantively, Rafes argued that the 'Jewish working masses' had to be drawn *into* Party work in Ukraine, and in this sense he signalled his disagreement with the suggestion that Jews, in general, had to be kept *out* of office. On the other hand, however, he added that the 'Jewish petty bourgeoisie' had to be 'proletarianized' and 'encouraged to take up productive labour'. Although rejecting the controversial view that Jews had to be removed from the Soviet state apparatuses, Rafes clearly signalled his agreement that the Jewish 'petty-bourgeoisie' represented some sort of problem.[55]

More forthright was the former Farband activist Mikhail Levitan, who insisted that the Evsektsiia response to Lenin's theses 'must point out that the exclusion of Jewish workers from Soviet work as a means of fighting antisemitism is the wrong path to take [*lozhnyi put'*]'.[56] This was then seconded by the Evsektsiia activist Cheskis, who added that it was simply 'out of the question' for the Party to even discuss the notion of 'excluding Jews from work in Ukraine'.[57] Clearly, within the Evsektsiia

---

[54] Also in attendance at the meeting on 6 December were Mikhail Levitan (a former United Jewish Socialist Workers' Party/Farband activist), Ainshtein, Cheskis (who in 1921 was placed in charge of the Jewish Bureau of the Comintern Executive Committee), Shakhno Epshtein (a former Bundist who in 1921 would go on to become editor of the official Soviet Yiddish newspaper *Emes*) and Yankel Kantor, a former Poalei Zionist and expert on Jewish demography and statistics. For more on these individuals, see Gitelman, *Jewish Nationality and Soviet Politics*, 197, 245, 259, 261–62.
[55] RGASPI f.445 o.1 d.1 l.67.   [56] RGASPI f.445 o.1 d.1 l.67.
[57] RGASPI f.445 o.1 d.1 l.68.

Central Bureau there was strong opposition to Lenin's and the Party leadership's strategy on the question of antisemitism.

The former Bundist and recently turned Communist David Lipets was next to take the floor. Just three months earlier, Lipets had been instrumental in mapping out a strategy for confronting antisemitism in his capacity as Executive Bureau member of the Committee for the Struggle against Antisemitism. Back then, he had insisted that the fight against antisemitism had to be 'singled out' as a 'special area' of Party work.[58] With the committee now disbanded and a new, controversial strategy on antisemitism now in place following the Eighth Party Conference, the stage was set for Lipets to make a key intervention. Like Levitan, he directly challenged the premise of Lenin's resolution. Lipets went further, though, and drafted a set of new theses for inclusion in the new memorandum proposed by Rafes. The first thesis stated, emphatically, that it is not 'the participation of Jews that was the main reason for the failures in Ukraine, but chiefly the errors of the Russian Communist Party and the Ukrainian Communist Party themselves'. In his second thesis, Lipets contended that antisemitism was caused not by the number of Jews in the Soviet state apparatus, but by the presence in the Party of the 'chauvinistic and nationalist bourgeoisie'. Lipets went so far as to argue that such elements had been brought into the Party at the expense of Jewish workers. Accordingly, for Lipets, the resolution passed at the Eighth Party Conference three days previously was an 'error' that 'had to be corrected'. The reasons for antisemitism, argued Lipets, were to be found in the fact that there were antisemites in the Party.[59]

However, towards the end of his speech Lipets added a caveat: 'In welcoming the idea of removing [*ustraneniia*] the Jewish petty-bourgeoisie, it follows that we must attract Jewish workers [to Party work].'[60] Despite declaring Lenin's theses to be an 'error', Lipets nevertheless agreed that the 'Jewish petty-bourgeoisie' needed removing. Like Rafes, Lipets rejected, then, the suggestion that Jews *in general* be prevented from taking up positions in the Soviet government. In opposition to Lenin, Lipets suggested that 'Jewish workers' be *attracted* to work in the state apparatuses. The terrain of Lenin's argument was ethnicity; Lipets sought to shift it to that of class.

There was evidently great concern among the Evsektsiia leadership about the direction the Party was taking on antisemitism. Lipets con-

---

[58] GARF f.A2306 o.15 d.749 l.13.   [59] RGASPI f.445 o.1 d.1 l.68.
[60] RGASPI f.445 o.1 d.1 l.68.

cluded by warning that 'we must hurry with our memorandum in order to prevent the misinterpretation of the resolution from the conference concerning the participation of Jews in the government in Ukraine'.[61] This concern was echoed by Mandel'sberg, who added that the need for a memorandum from the Evsektsiia was urgent, since 'the whole question has become confused and this threatens all of our Party work in Ukraine'.[62] Mandel'sberg did not elaborate on the nature of this 'threat', but it seems plausible that he and other Evsektsiia activists were concerned that Lenin's resolution was open to an antisemitic interpretation.

At the conclusion of the meeting, it was resolved that a commission formed of Dimanshtein, Rafes and Novakovskii would draft the memorandum. Perhaps most interestingly of all, though, it was further agreed that Dimanshtein and Rafes would consult Lenin directly during the drafting process. Such was the urgency to respond to the resolution passed by the Eighth Party Conference, the commission was given twenty-four hours to complete its task, and all members of the Evsektsiia Central Bureau were instructed to remain in Moscow until further notice.[63] At the next meeting of the Central Bureau on 8 December (two days later), a version of the draft memorandum was presented by Rafes and accepted on the grounds that it helped to clarify the 'correct treatment of the Jewish question and the place of Jewish work in the Party'.[64] On 10 December, the finished version, entitled 'On the Tasks and Organisation of Jewish Work within the Party', was duly presented to the Russian and Ukrainian Central Committees.[65] What did the memorandum say, and did it differ from the position outlined by Lenin in his controversial draft theses?

---

[61] RGASPI f.445 o.1 d.1 l.68.   [62] RGASPI f.445 o.1 d.1 l.68.

[63] RGASPI f.445 o.1 d.1 l.68-68ob. Writing in 1924, Dimanshtein recalled that the memorandum had been drafted mainly by Ukrainian-Jewish members of the Evsektsiia Lenin, *O evreiskom voprose v Rossii*, 18. Given that we know from the meeting on 8 December that the commission tasked with drafting the memorandum was composed of Dimanshtein himself plus Mandel'sberg and Rafes, we may deduce that Rafes, as the only 'Ukrainian' of the three, was its chief author.

[64] RGASPI f.445 o.1 d.1 l.91; f.17 o.65 d.92 l.28; TsDAHO f.1 o.20 d.89 l.61. The Central Bureau met again on 9 December and 11 December, but the memorandum was seemingly not discussed. TsDAHO f.1 o.20 d.89 l.74-77.

[65] M. G. Rafes, *Natsional'nye voprosy (Sbornik statei i materialov)* (Moscow: Gosudarstvennoe izdatel'stvo, 1921), 62. Here Rafes mistakenly noted down the date as 20 December. It was, in fact, 10 December.

The Evsektsiia's Memorandum of December 1919

Over the course of the memorandum's six pages,[66] the question of the origins of antisemitism occupied centre stage, and it is clear that the document's chief interlocutor was Lenin. In one of its opening paragraphs, the memorandum stated:

> War, revolution, the intensification of the Civil War, the economic policies of the Soviet government and, finally, the devastating pogrom wave have all destroyed the lives of the Jewish petty traders and artisans ... This counter-revolutionary pogrom wave has devastated all towns and cities. Arising as a product of the contradictions between the peasantry and the Jews, it has poisoned the whole social life of the region with antisemitism.[67]

This was a non-committal statement that sidestepped Lenin's contentious recommendation that Jews be prevented from taking up key positions in the Soviet government. However, the statement implicitly raised a crucial question: how, exactly, did the 'poison of antisemitism' gain traction and embed itself in the 'social life of the region'? In the following paragraph, the Central Bureau began to hint at an explanation: antisemitism, the memorandum stated, is rooted in the 'contradictions between the peasantry and Jews' (note here the counterposing of class and ethnicity), contradictions which only took the form of antisemitism in 1919 in light of the 'general crisis and the dissatisfaction of the peasantry with Soviet politics'.[68] Here, the argument appeared to identify the *policies* of the Soviet government, not the presence of Jews, as the reason for the sharp growth of antisemitism. If we recall, this was precisely the argument put forward by the former Bundist Lipets during the debate at the meeting of the Central Bureau of the Evsektsiia two days previously, on 8 December, where he had insisted that 'it is not the participation of Jews which was the main reason for the failures in Ukraine, but chiefly the errors of the Russian Communist Party and the Ukrainian Communist Party themselves'.[69] So far, then, the

---

[66] Copies of the memorandum are held in various archives. It can be found in the files of the Party Central Committee in Moscow: RGASPI f.17 o.65 d.92 l.120-125; and the Ukrainian Central Committee in Kyiv: TsDAHO f.1 o.20 d.89. Copies are also held in the archives of the Poalei Zion party, which indicates that they too were kept abreast of these discussions; RGASPI f.272 o.1 d.141 l.87-90; f.272 o.2 d.9 l.23. The memorandum was also issued as a double-sided leaflet, presumably for distribution among Party activists. See GARF f.9550 o.9 d.648 and IJ f.19 o.1 d.4 l.25. The versions consulted for this discussion are those held in the archives of the Central Bureau of the Evsektsiia, in Moscow: RGASPI f.445 o.1 d.1 l.74-76ob; f.445 o.1 d.1 l.77-79ob; f.445 o.1 d.5 l.80-85.

[67] RGASPI f.445 o.1 d.1 l.77ob.   [68] RGASPI f.445 o.1 d.1 l.77ob.

[69] RGASPI f.445 o.1 d.1 l.68.

memorandum was shaping up to be a *critique* of the position outlined in Lenin's draft theses. However, the argument soon took a sharp and dramatic turn.

Towards the end of the document, in a special section devoted to the question of antisemitism, a quite different perspective emerges – one much closer to Lenin's draft theses.

> The contradictions between the city and the countryside *inevitably* had to lead to the strengthening of nationalist ideology within the peasantry in Ukraine, where the city is *overly painted in Jewish colours* (*gorod slishkom okrashen v evreiskie tsveta*).[70]

Suddenly, antisemitism was no longer framed as a problem deriving from the policies of the Soviet government. Instead, the role played by Jews themselves was now centre stage: it was the *presence* of the Jews in the city – denoted by the provocative phraseology 'overly painted in Jewish colours' – which had strengthened antisemitism. This signalled what was to follow in the next paragraph:

> Concerning the question of Jews filling up the organs of Soviet power ... far too many specialists have been employed ... and in this capacity many elements from the Jewish petty and even big bourgeoisie have poured in, thus demoralizing the state from within.[71]

The key issue raised in Lenin's draft theses had now been broached. However, far from subjecting it to criticism, as Lipets, Levitan and Cheskis had at the meeting of the Central Bureau just two days previously, the memorandum now seemed to *concur* with the logic of Lenin's argument. The implication here was that one of the main reasons for the dramatic rise in antisemitism in 1919 was the specific problem of the 'Jewish bourgeoisie' 'pouring in' to the state apparatuses. The locus of antisemitism now shifted to Jews, not antisemites; the city, 'overly painted in Jewish colours', and the Jewish bourgeoisie 'pouring' into the state apparatuses – these familiar, and troubling, representations now formed the crux of the antisemitism question.

Indeed, the very title of this section of the memorandum revealed as much: 'The Development of Antisemitism. Jews – Soviet State Employees' (*Razvitie antisemitizma. Evrei – sovetskie sluzhashchie*). Clearly, the focus was not on the antisemitism of the peasantry or the prevalence of deeply entrenched antisemitic conceptions of Jewishness both inside and

---

[70] RGASPI f.445 o.1 d.1 l.78 ob (emphasis added). Note how ethnic and class concepts ('Jews' versus 'peasant') are replaced by a set of spatial categories ('city' versus 'countryside').

[71] RGASPI f.445 o.1 d.1 l.78ob.

outside of the Party. Rather, the 'development' of antisemitism was framed as a problem deriving from the *presence* of 'Jewish-Soviet state employees'. Like Lenin's draft theses discussed earlier, the memorandum was predicated on the 'kernel of truth'[72] approach to antisemitism: that the antisemites really were correct in what they said about the Jews.

As if aware of the contentious terrain onto which they had stepped, the authors of the memorandum immediately appeared to backtrack:

> It is necessary to point out, however, that a similar and perhaps even worse situation has transpired in Ukraine with the allocation of key positions [in the government] to petty-bourgeois Ukrainian and Russian [members of the] intelligentsia, who are almost completely imbued with reactionary Great Russian and Ukrainian ideas ... and even if there had not been a single Jewish commissar, this would not have changed the root of the situation: the struggle against the hegemony of the city, the struggle against communism, had to take an antisemitic form because of the special structure [*original'nogo uklada*] of national-social and revolutionary relations. However, the essence of this struggle does not lie in its antisemitic form. *The reason for the antisemitic sentiments of the peasantry must be found in the social-political basis – in the undisciplined nature of the peasantry, in the general agrarian politics of Soviet power etc.*[73]

This, quite evidently, was a contradictory argument. The explanatory emphasis had shifted once again, away from Jews and back to the Soviet state, its economic policies and the fact that it harboured non-Jews with 'reactionary Great Russian and Ukrainian ideas'. Further, the peasantry's lack of 'discipline' was invoked *without* recourse to the alleged role played by Jews in provoking it. In other words, antisemitism was now framed as something *independent* of Jews. If this was the Bureau's position all along, why, in earlier passages, had it invoked notions of Jews 'filling up' Soviet institutions and the 'Jewish colours' of the city? The memorandum concluded by insisting that 'the Party and Soviet government must give more consideration to the fight against antisemitism ... which has started to poison the minds of the workers and has even penetrated the ranks of local Party organisations'.[74] Yet which side of the argument was to be emphasized? Were the Central Committees in Moscow and Kyiv to challenge the lack of 'discipline' within the peasantry, re-think the Soviet state's agrarian policies and expel the antisemites in the Party who harboured 'reactionary Great Russian and Ukrainian ideas'? Or, conversely, were they instead to address the 'problem' of Jews 'filling up' Soviet institutions? The memorandum did not give any indication as to

---

[72] Fischer, *The Socialist Response to Antisemitism in Imperial Germany*.
[73] RGASPI f.445 o.1 d.1 l.78ob (emphasis in the original).
[74] RGASPI f.445 o.1 d.1 l.79.

which side of this contradictory argument did, in fact, point towards the real solution to the problem of antisemitism.

At the meeting on 8 December, members of the Evsektsiia Bureau had flatly rejected the notion that removing Jews from office could act as a block on antisemitism. Yet two days later, the Evsektsiia memorandum presented to the Central Committee seemed to argue just this very point. How can this contradiction be explained? And how can we account for the fact that those key individuals who actualized the Soviet response to antisemitism in the summer of 1919 were now, just weeks later, reproducing antisemitic representations of Jewishness themselves?

Jewish Self-Reconstruction and the Politics of Antisemitism

The highly contentious statements contained in the Evsektsiia's memorandum flowed from a deep internal critique of Jewish economic and social life that Jewish radicals had been engaged in for a number of years. It is a critique that is traceable in the theory and practice of the Evsektsiia throughout the Civil War years.

One of the key points of ideological convergence between antisemitism and revolutionary discourse centred on the concept of 'speculation'. This tension flowed from the fact that the Soviet state's designation of 'speculation' as a criminal (not to mention 'counter-revolutionary') act coincided and at times overlapped with the widespread antisemitic identification of 'speculation' as a defining feature of Jewishness. At stake here was the capacity for racialized conceptions of Jewishness to be reinscribed through Bolshevik economic policy. As Andrew Sloin has perceptively observed, there was a 'tendency inherent in the Soviet project to conflate Jewish economic practices with the workings of "merchant capital" and problematically impute to Jewish actors a certain agency over basic economic functions'.[75] Although this was a *general* feature of the revolutionary conjuncture, these dynamics took a particular hold on Soviet-Jewish politics, and the Evsektsiia in particular.

The most fervent advocates of the campaign to transform Jewish social and economic life were the activists within the Evsektsiia.[76] A central component of this drive was the fight to eradicate speculation, and 'Jewish speculation' specifically. A whole range of sources attest to this. For example, at the Second Congress of the Evsektsiia in June 1919,

---

[75] Andrew Sloin, 'Speculators, Swindlers and Other Jews: Regulating Trade in Revolutionary White Russia', *East European Jewish Affairs* 40, no. 2 (2010): 112.
[76] Gitelman, *Jewish Nationality and Soviet Politics*.

Dimanshtein outlined his plan to transform Jewish economic life, a task he identified as placing 'idle hands in the service of the country in a *productive* way; we want to cut down the number of small speculators'.[77] In the debate following Dimanshtein's speech, the Evsektsiia activist Samuil Agurskii drew a link between Jewish economic transformation and the Party campaign against antisemitism:

> If I thought speculation could be wiped out by repression, by driving the *shtetl* to the wall, I should be the first to advocate establishing Jewish detachments of the Cheka, but since repression won't work, we must put the Jewish petty bourgeois on the way to becoming useful to society, instead of a parasite and a burden. As soon as possible we must use exceptional measures to rescue the Jewish masses from hunger and want – and from engaging in speculation – *which will surely weaken antisemitism also*.[78]

In combatting antisemitism, Agurskii mobilizes a set of concepts frequently associated with *antisemitic* conceptions of Jewishness – Jews as 'unproductive' 'speculators' and 'parasites' – and in so doing makes a causal link between the overcoming of 'Jewish speculation' and the eradication of antisemitism: the latter depends on the former. Agurskii was hardly alone in reaching for these kinds of arguments.[79]

Similar formulations were expressed by Dimanshtein in a speech before a meeting of the Central Committee on 11 May 1919.[80] The primary reason for Dimanshtein's appearance was to demand of the Party leadership that it outline a more coherent campaign against antisemitism. He began his case by stressing that 'economic ruination has created favourable conditions for the development of antisemitism'. Furthermore, he noted the role played by the 'enemies of Soviet power ... who try to spread among the masses the alleged idea that there are no Jews in the Red Army, or that you only see them in commander positions'.[81] By emphasizing the '*alleged*' nature of these claims, Dimanshtein appeared to be mapping out a materialist analysis, one that pointed towards a deconstruction of antisemitic representations of Jewishness. However, when it came to suggesting concrete measures to tackle

---

[77] Schwarz, *The Jews in the Soviet Union*, 161.   [78] Ibid., 162 (emphasis added).
[79] In an article written immediately after the conference, and published on 15 June, Dimanshtein echoed this logic when he argued that settling Jews on the land would help to weaken antisemitism. See *Zhizn' Natsional'nostei*, 15 June 1919, 1.
[80] A copy of Dimanshtein's speech is held in RGASPI f.17 o.65 d.91 l.14-16. It has been reprinted in full in Gatagova, Kosheleva and Rogovaia, *TsK RKP(b)-VKP(b) i natsional'nii vopros. Kniga 1. 1918-1933 gg.*, 18–21. The meeting was attended by Dimanshtein, Krestinskii, Sverdlov and Stasova.
[81] Gatagova, Kosheleva and Rogovaia, *TsK RKP(b)-VKP(b) i natsional'nii vopros. Kniga 1. 1918-1933 gg.*, 20.

antisemitism, his position instead revealed, once more, a signification of 'Jewish agency' as the basis of antisemitism:

> One of the best means of struggling against antisemitism in these circumstances is to attract the Jewish masses towards agriculture ... this will put an end to, or in the worst-case scenario, significantly weaken their current *harmful activities* and *speculation*, which is *so damaging* for the Soviet Republic and *so irritating* for the surrounding non-Jewish population. Joint agricultural work between Jews and non-Jews is the best means of fighting antisemitism in the peasant environment'.[82]

Here, Jews are identified as the social agents who must overcome antisemitism. In contrast, other collectivities, such as the non-Jewish peasantry, do not appear to be social actors in this process. Dimanshtein left unanswered the question as to how their attachment to antisemitism was to be weakened. What is more, when Dimanshtein invoked the notion of 'speculation ... so irritating for the non-Jewish population', he drew a causal conection between 'Jewish behaviour' and antisemitism. This contrasts markedly with the deconstructivist position hinted at earlier in his speech. The basis of antisemitism had now shifted from a combination of 'economic ruination' and counter-revolutionary propaganda about the 'alleged' number of Jews on the front, to a perspective that holds Jewish speculation accountable. For Dimanshtien, Jews needed to become less irritating to the peasantry, and the best means for doing so was for their labour power to become 'normalized' through agricultural work.[83] The appearance of such highly charged representations of Jewishness was not coincidental; rather, it flowed from the broader Evsektsiia project of Jewish self-reconstruction. This requires further explication.

Campaigns to 'productivize' the Jews and render them 'useful' through agriculaturalization programmes and other such initiatives were a fundamental feature of Jewish social reform in Europe throughout the Emancipation age.[84] In late-Imperial Russia, proponents of the Jewish Enlightenment movement were particularly strong advocates of such practices through organizations such as the ORT, the Society for Handicraft and Agricultural Work among the Jews of Russia (*Obshchestvo*

---

[82] Ibid., 20–21.
[83] We should note that these comments by Dimanshtein provoked no criticism from the members of the Orgburo and Politburo, who later accepted his recommendations; RGASPI f.17 o.112 d.4 l.25.
[84] Sloin, 'Speculators, Swindlers and Other Jews', 106.

remeslennogo i zemledel'cheskogo truda sredi Evreev v Rossii).[85] Evsektsiia campaigns against the 'undesirable' elements of Jewish life in the early Soviet period were part of this long tradition of internal Jewish critique and the transformative politics of the Jewish Enlightenment. Discourse about 'the city being painted in Jewish colours', as found in the memorandum of the Evsektsiia in December 1919, cannot be explained only with reference to Lenin or Bolshevism; their historical moorings were as much 'Jewish' and as they were 'Bolshevik'.[86]

In 1919, Evsektsiia campaigns for Jewish economic reform took place against a backdrop of the outright criminalization of 'speculation' by the Bolshevik regime.[87] In such a highly contentious political field, antisemitic depictions of 'speculators' risked conjoining with the politics of revolutionary Bolshevism. Put differently, the 'internal' Jewish critique expressed by the Evsektsiia was vulnerable to an antisemitic interpretation. Paradoxically, then, those Bolsheviks most prone to perpetuating racialized conceptions of Jewishness were, in fact, the architects of the Bolshevik confrontation with antisemitism.

The critique of the 'Jewish bourgeoisie' was foundational to the Evsektsiia and Evkom political habitus, and can be traced throughout the Soviet Yiddish press of the period. Conversely, Russian Soviet journalists, no doubt sensitive to the dynamics of antisemitism, generally refrained from broaching this explosive issue during the Civil War. Not so with the Evsektsiia.[88] When pogroms broke out in February 1919, Evsektsiia activist Zalman Khaikin identified Jewish speculators as the cause.[89] This perspective endured throughout the revolutionary period. When the Evsektsiia press reported on a small pogrom in Smolensk towards the end of the Civil War, in March 1922, it suggested that locals had turned against the Jews because large numbers of the 'Jewish bourgeoisie' were engaged in speculation.[90] Such criticisms of 'Jewish

---

[85] For more on the history of the ORT, see R. Bracha, A. Drori-Avraham and G. Yantian, eds., *Educating for Life: New Chapters in the History of the ORT* (London: World ORT, 2010); Shapiro, *The History of the ORT*.

[86] For more on Jewish agricultural colonization programmes in the early Soviet period, see Dekel-Chen, *Farming the Red Land*.

[87] Sloin, 'Speculators, Swindlers and Other Jews', 106.

[88] Sloin, 'Speculators, Swindlers and Other Jews'.

[89] Sloin, *The Jewish Revolution in Belorussia*, 65.

[90] G. Estraikh, 'Simulating Justice: The Blood Libel Case in Moscow, April 1922', in *Ritual Murder in Russia, Eastern Europe, and Beyond. New Histories of an Old Accusation*, ed. E. Avrutin, J. Dekel-Chen and R. Weinberg (Bloomington: Indiana University Press, 2017), 208.

speculation' were almost entirely absent from the non-Jewish Soviet press. These differences were emblematic of the fact that while Russian was the language of the campaign against antisemitism, these Yiddish-language materials were part of the Evsektsiia project of Jewish self-reconstruction.[91] These two projects overlapped and informed each other, but in complicated and often contradictory ways.

This discussion allows us to view the Evsektsiia memorandum of 10 December 1919 in a different light. The Evsektsiia's concern about Lenin's draft theses stemmed not so much from the content of the theses – which as we now know was largely shared by many in the Evsektsiia. Rather, it was the *context* and *audience* to which these views were aired that was most problematic. For the Evsektsiia, this was a profoundly 'internal' 'Jewish' question. It was one thing to raise these criticisms in a 'Jewish' context (either in a Yiddish-speaking or specifically Evsektsiia setting), but quite another to do so at a Party conference where the decisions taken would have consequences extending far beyond the Jewish communist milieu, and where the scope for a whole range of differing 'interpretations' of the criticisms was significantly enlarged. If we recall, among the main concerns raised by Lipets and Mandel'sberg at the 8 December meeting of the Esvekstiia Central Bureau was the need to prevent the *'misinterpretation'* of Lenin's theses, and the need to address the *'confusion'* it had brought among the Party at large and to limit the damage it would cause.[92]

That the Evsektsiia leaders harboured concerns regarding the *reception* of this whole debate can be further illustrated by noting how they altered the memorandum depending on the audience at which it was addressed. The full version of the memorandum was presented to the Russian and Ukrainian Central Committees, and in this way it was a decidedly backstage document.[93] However, the memorandum was also published by the Evsektsiia in the Russian-language Soviet press, presumably to inform its non-Jewish readership about the direction the Party was taking in Jewish affairs. Significantly, in this *front-stage* context, the contentious

---

[91] Shternshis, *Soviet and Kosher*, 150–61. At times, activists within the Evsektsiia criticized Russian-language pamphlets against antisemitism on the grounds that they had not broached (and subjected to sufficient critique) the issue of 'Jewish behaviour'. For example, speaking at the Second Conference of the Evsektsiia on 5 June, M. V. Brener observed that while the Soviet government had 'from time to time' issued Russian-language pamphlets against antisemitism, they were too often written by Party members 'unfamiliar with those facts of Jewish life that especially outrage the backwards Russian society', and as such, the texts failed to achieve their 'intended aims'. *Zhizn' Natsional'nostei*, 26 June 1919, 2.
[92] RGASPI f.445 o.1 d.1 l.68.   [93] RGASPI f.445 o.1 d.1 l.77–79ob.

section on 'antisemitism' was studiously deleted. One of the most provocative elements of the memorandum was the title of the section – 'The Development of Antisemitism. Jewish-Soviet State Employees'; provocative because it explicitly linked the presence of Jews in the state apparatus to the question of antisemitism. In the version published in the Soviet press, however, this title was abridged to 'The Development of Antisemitism'; the second, contentious half was deleted, thereby reducing the scope for an antisemitic interpretation by the non-Jewish readership.[94] Similarly, when Dimanshtein published the memorandum in his 1924 collection of Lenin's writings on the Jewish question (which he edited), he claimed to have made 'no changes whatsoever to the document'. In truth, however, Dimanshtein had edited out the provocative title of the section on antisemitism, and he had also removed those sections containing the passages on the city being 'painted in Jewish colours' and Jews 'filling up' the state apparatuses.[95]

What this demonstrates is that the leadership of the Evsektsiia held complicated and contradictory views on antisemitism. On the one hand, their commitment to the project of Jewish self-reconstruction left them wedded to racialized conceptions of Jewishness that invoked a 'causal connection' between 'Jewish behaviour' and antisemitism. At times, these assumptions informed their policies and political decision-making in backstage contexts. Yet, on the other hand, the Evsektsiia's opposition to antisemitism led them to confront these same representations of Jewishness when they appeared in non-Jewish contexts. The contradictory response to Lenin's draft theses in December 1919 provides an illustration of the Evsektsiia's difficulties in navigating the politics of antisemitism across Jewish and non-Jewish situations.

Conclusion

In the Russian Revolution, Bolsheviks found themselves caught in an inescapable articulation with the politics of antisemitism. Anti-bourgeois sentiment overlapped with, and at times found expression through, antisemitic constructions of Jewishness. In these ways, class politics and the 'Jewish question' were brought together; the Bolshevik message, independently of its intent, was susceptible to an antisemitic reception. Similarly, the 'Jewish-Bolshevik' construct posed significant obstacles for Bolshevik strategy on antisemitism. When Bolsheviks sought to refute the

---

[94] See *Zhizn' Natsional'nostei*, 1 February 1920, 2–3.
[95] See Lenin, *O evreiskom voprose v Rossii*, 84–92.

charge that Jews avoided fighting in the Red Army or that Bolshevism was a 'Jewish project', their responses often revealed a level of acquiescence with those very stereotypes. These tensions were revealed, most dramatically, in Lenin's policy of restricting the number of Jews in the Ukrainian Soviet government in late 1919.

Jewish communists in the Evsektsiia were also caught in this entanglement between antisemitism and revolutionary politics, though in different ways and for different reasons. On the one hand, they offered the most sustained Soviet response to antisemitism by establishing institutions such as the Committee for the Struggle against Antisemitism (see Chapter 6). Yet in their attempts to politically marginalize antisemitism, they at times recirculated antisemitic representations of Jewishness. The appearance of contentious discourses on Jewish identity within the politics of the Evsektsiia was not coincidental, but instead flowed from the Evsektsiia project of Jewish self-reconstruction. In its quest to remake Soviet Jewry, Evsektsiia activists reinscribed certain racialized conceptions of Jewish life identified as socially harmful. In this way, antisemitism could be reproduced by the very same individuals responsible for leading the state campaign against it.[96]

Yet these contentious discourses on Jewishness were generally kept to backstage, Yiddish-speaking contexts, and Evsektsiia activists took measures to minimize their exposure in Russian-speaking forums. To borrow a phrase from W. E. B. Du Bois, this revealed a degree of 'double consciousness' on the part of the Evsektsiia, a 'sense of always looking at one's self through the eyes of others'.[97] This was powerfully captured in 1922 by the former Bundist, now turned Evsektsiia leader, Ester Frumkina,[98] when she remarked: 'You [non-Jewish communists] do not understand the danger Jews face. If the Russian people begin to feel

---

[96] Sloin, *The Jewish Revolution in Belorussia*, 16.
[97] W. E. B. Du Bois, *The Souls of Black Folk* (New York: Dover Publications, 2000), 2.
[98] Frumkina (Khaye Malke Lifshits) was a Bundist and Evsektsiia leader. Born in Minsk in 1880, she was the most prominent woman in the Bund, and a leading proponent of Yiddish secular schools during the late imperial period. Like the vast majority of Bundists, she initially denounced the Bolshevik 'coup' of 1917. Later, in 1919–21, she became a leading figure in the Communist Bund (Kombund), and after joining the Bolsheviks she held various prominent positions in the Evsektsiia throughout the 1920s. See N. Shepherd, *A Price Below Rubies: Jewish Women as Rebels and Radicals* (London: Weidenfeld & Nicolson, 1993), 137–71; R. Gechtman, 'Lifshits, Il'ia Mikhailovich', in *The Yivo Encyclopedia of Jews in Eastern Europe*, ed. D. H. Gershon, vol. 1, 2 vols (New Haven: Yale University Press, 2008), 1038–39. For a detailed overview of Frumkina's published writings, see S. S. Faigain 2018 'An Annotated Bibliography of Maria Yakovlena Frumkina (Esther)', PhD Dissertation, The Australian National University.

Conclusion

that we are partial to the Jews, it will be harmful to Jews.'[99] Dimanshtein spoke from the same place in late 1919, when he pleaded with Lenin to halt the publication of a pamphlet by Maksim Gor'kii which praised the role of Jews in the Russian Revolution. Though ostensibly written to counter antisemitsim, Dimanshtein feared the pamphlet gave credence to the explosive myth of 'Judeo-Bolshevism'.[100] Jewish Communists were acutely aware of the inextricable ways in which they were bound up in the antisemitic projection.

Trotsky was similarly unable to escape the racializing process, no matter how much he stated his internationalism and his aloofness from all things 'Jewish'. Both in 1917 and in 1922, Trotsky refused invitations from Lenin to take up a senior position in the Soviet government. During the struggle for power with Stalin in 1923, he found himself having to explain these refusals at a joint plenum of the Central Committee and the Central Control Committee on 26 October 1923. His explanation is worth quoting at length, since it captures the contradictions and dilemmas that Jewish Communists faced in the Russian Revolution.

> The thing is, comrades, that there is a personal element in my work, which, being of no importance in my private life, so to speak, is of great political importance in my everyday life. This is my Jewish origin. I remember quite well that on October 25, 1917, lying on the floor in the Smolny, Vladimir Ilyich said: 'Comrade Trotsky! We will make you People's Commissar for Internal Affairs. You will crush the bourgeoisie and nobility'. I opposed. I said that, in my opinion, one should not place such a trump card in our enemies; I thought that it would be much better if there were no Jews in the first revolutionary Soviet government. Vladimir Ilyich said: 'Nonsense. Never mind!' ... When [in 1918] it was necessary to organize our military forces, they chose me; I should say that I opposed the office of People's Commissar of War still more resolutely. Well, comrades, after all my work done in this sphere, I can tell you with certainty that I was right ... Remember what a hindrance it was in some acute moments ... when our enemies in their agitation used the fact that the Red Army was headed by a Jew. It interfered greatly. Comrades, I should repeat once again that [although] in my private life this fact meant nothing; it is very serious as a political moment. I have never forgotten this. Vladimir Ilyich considered it to

---

[99] N. Levin, *The Jews in the Soviet Union since 1917: Paradox of Survival. Volume 1* (New York: I. B. Tauris & Co. Ltd, 1990), 72–73. Frumkina made these comments in the context of the Soviet government's anti-religious campaigns of 1922. For background on the 1922 anti-religion campaigns, see J. W. Daly, "Storming the Last Citadel': The Bolshevik Assault on the Chruch, 1922', in *The Bolsheviks in Russian Society. The Revolution and the Civil War Years*, ed. V. Brovkin (New Haven: Yale University Press, n.d.), 235–68.
[100] Lenin, *O evreiskom voprose v Rossii*, 16.

be my 'eccentricity', and he often said in conversations with me and with other comrades that it was my 'eccentricity'.[101]

Despite his assimilatory internationalism, Trotsky could not fail to be cognisant of the force of the antisemitic projection: acutely aware that he was its object, he refused senior roles in the government to avoid confirming those projections. When Evsektsiia activists argued that Jews should stop 'flooding' the state apparatuses, or that they should stop 'speculating', or stop 'shirking' from taking up positions at the front, they too were trying to take the sting out of antisemitism. Such Evsektsiia attempts to 'disprove' antisemitism were born, in part, out of the experience of 'looking at one's self through the eyes of others'.[102] It was a strategy that betrayed a certain acquiescence with the same antisemitism they had devoted their revolutionary lives to confronting.

At times, there was no way out of this bind: every step taken risked reinscribing antisemitism within the revolutionary process. In his recollections of Petrograd in 1919, Victor Serge was similarly aware of the grip antisemitism had on the political moment: '[It] was the enemy, the counter-revolution … We could feel it all around us, on the watch, looking for our weakness, our mistakes, our follies, skilfully making us stumble, ready at the slightest lapse to pounce on us and tear us to pieces.'[103] Like Serge, Lenin no doubt felt the presence of the counter-revolution when he sat down to compose his contentious draft theses. Though Trotsky and the activists in the Evsektsiia led markedly different Jewish lives, they too felt it keenly. This was a revolution that promised liberation from antisemitism; its actuality, however, overdetermined them *as Jews*. No one, it seems, escaped the racializing logic of the 'Jewish question' in the Russian revolution.

---

[101] V. P. Vilkova, *The Struggle for Power: Russia in 1923* (New York: Prometheus Books, 1996), 183–84. These comments are from a rough draft of Trotsky's speech made by B. V. Bazhanov. According to Vilkova, it is almost certain that Trotsky did not check the draft for corrections; Vilkova, *The Struggle for Power*, 188. The draft is held in RGASPI f.17 o.2 d.685 l.39-49 and was first published in Russian in Vilkova, *RKP(b) vnutripartiinaia bor'ba v dvadtsatye gody*, 258–59. The version quoted above is the English translation in Vilkova, *The Struggle for Power*, 183–84. Writing in his autobiography in 1929, Trotsky offered a now frequently cited, though significantly revised, version of this dynamic. Contrary to the picture he offered in 1923, he now claimed that during the Civil War, the question of his 'Jewish origin' interfered only marginally in his ability to act as War Commissar, and that antisemitism only became an issue in the mid-1920s alongside 'anti-Trotskyism'; L. Trotsky, *My Life: An Attempt at an Autobiography* (Middlesex: Penguin Books, 1975), 376.

[102] Du Bois, *The Souls of Black Folk*, 2.

[103] V. Serge, *Revolution in Danger: Writings from Russia, 1919–1921* (Chicago: Haymarket Books, 2011), 21–22.

Epilogue: In the Shadow of Pogroms

By the early 1920s, the architects of the Soviet confrontation with antisemitism had left the scene. After his expulsion from the Jewish Commissariat in 1918, Zvi Fridliand continued to lead the Poalei Zion party, before eventually joining the Bolsheviks in 1921. Shortly after, he became a professor of French history, and later, the first dean of Moscow University. In the course of the 1920s, he mostly left the question of antisemitism to one side. Seconded to work for the Comintern in China, Moishe Rafes also moved away from Soviet Jewish politics after the Civil War. Abram Kheifets followed a similar path, and moved to Germany under the auspices of the Comintern, where he later joined the German Communist Party under the name 'August Kleine'. In the 1920s, David Lipets found a new life too: now known as 'Petrovskii', he became a decorated general in the Red Army. The territorialist David Davidovich (L'vovich) had been the first to raise the question of antisemitism to the Soviet government in April 1918. Unlike the others, he deepened his immersion in the fate of Soviet Jewry, but did so from a distance, as Director of the ORT in Berlin and Paris. Of the core activists who initiated and then led the Soviet response to antisemitism, only Dimanshtein remained within the Evsektsiia orbit by the end of the Civil War.

Antisemitism gradually faded from view in the work of the Evsektsiia from 1922 onwards, with attention increasingly shifting towards consolidating the revolution on the 'Jewish street'.[1] But when the spectre of antisemitism returned with explosive force in 1926, the Evsektsiia sought to position itself once again at the heart of the Soviet response. In the social and economic crisis of the mid- to late 1920s, anti-Jewish sentiment rose sharply in Soviet society. From accusations of ritual murder to small-scale pogroms and shop-floor discrimination in the factory, a surge in antisemitism became apparent across all spheres of social life in Russia, Ukraine and

---

[1] Gitelman, *Jewish Nationality and Soviet Politics, 1917–1930*.

Belorussia.² When the warnings emerged in 1926, the Evsektsiia was in line to direct and lead the Party campaign.

On 26 August 1926, the Party held a meeting to address the growing crisis. Though formally called by the Department of Agitation and Propaganda (Agitprop) of the Central Committee of the Communist Party, the drive for the initiative came not from the Party leadership, but from Dimanshtein and the Evsektsiia, which was now located within the Agitprop as a subdepartment.³ The Evsektsiia prepared and gave direction to the meeting. Its leading members – Vainshtein, Merezhin and Chermerisskii – all spoke from the podium, as did a number of other Party officials, including the prominent Soviet economist, Iurii Larin. But it was Dimanshtein who led the proceedings. His opening address struck a familiar tone: antisemitism had become common occurrence within Soviet institutions, in part because no campaign against it was being waged amongst workers and Party members. And the problem would continue to grow while no state response was in place. He insisted that a new set of concrete measures be developed: 'We had a decree against antisemitism signed by Lenin and Bonch-Bruevich [in 1918]', noted Dimanshtein, but 'what we need to develop here is *a whole system of measures against antisemitism*' (emphasis added).

Just as in 1918 and 1919, he called for the formation of a special commission to direct the Party response. At the close of the meeting, Dimanshtein and Chemerisskii of the Evsektsiia were elected to lead the initiative alongside Petr Smidovich, a member of the VTsIK, and Meer Trilisser, Vice-Chairman of the OGPU (the secret police). The latter two individuals, however, played no role in the Commission's work; it was Evsektsiia-led. The following week, on 2 September, the Commission held its first meeting and sketched a detailed plan for a renewed confrontation with antisemitism in Party and Soviet institutions.⁴

---

² Schwarz, *The Jews in the Soviet Union*, 241–73; Sloin, *The Jewish Revolution in Belorussia*, 218–19; L. S. Gatagova, '"Antisemit est' kontrrevoliutsioner…" Soveshchanie o vyrabotke mer po bor'be s antisemitizmom pri Agitpope TkK VKP(b)', in *Arkhiv evreiskoi istorii, Tom 4*, ed. O. V. Budnitskii (Moscow: ROSSPEN, 2007), 147–49. On the emergence of antisemitism within Soviet society in 1926, see GARF f.374 o.27 d.1096.

³ Gatagova notes that there is no evidence in the files of the Politburo that the initiative came from the Party leadership. Gatagova, 'Antisemit est' kontrrevoliutsioner…', 158.

⁴ Gatagova, 'Antisemit est' kontrrevoliutsioner…', 147–62; O. V. Budnitskii, ed., 'Soveshchanie o vyrabotke mer po bor'be s antisemitizmom pri Agitprope TsK VKP (B)', 163–65, 178–79. Dimanshtein's speech at the 26 August meeting is also republished in Gatagova, Kosheleva and Rogovaia, *TsK RKP(b)-VKP(b) i natsional'nii vopros. Kniga 1. 1918-1933 gg.*, 425–27. On the 26 August Party meeting, see also D. Dumitru, *The State, Antisemitism, and Collaboration in the Holocaust: The Borderlands of Romania and the Soviet Union* (Cambridge: Cambridge University Press, 2016), 109–13; Kostyrchenko, *Tainaia politika Stalina*, 106.

The proposals were met with stunning success. At the next (and 15th) Party Congress, in December 1927, it was announced from the rostrum that the Party would directly confront antisemitism.[5] What followed was an unprecedented campaign exceeding in scale and scope anything seen during the Civil War years. From mass meetings to official investigations and scores of newspaper articles and published materials, the issue of antisemitism was brought before Soviet audiences like never before.[6] The impact, at least for Soviet Jews, was profound. Work by Anna Shternshis has shown how the campaign of the late 1920s left a lasting imprint on a generation of Soviet Jewry and helped foster a sense of belonging and identification with the Bolshevik project, despite the continuation of antisemitism in everyday social life.[7] Similarly, in her comparative study of the Holocaust in Bessarabia and Transnistria, Diana Dumitru suggests that Soviet educational campaigns against antisemitism of the Civil War and the 1920s had a determinate effect on the non-Jewish population as well, and helped to instil a certain acceptance of Jewish integration.[8]

While Dimanshtein and the Evsektsiia had drawn attention to the growing crisis and given it crucial urgency in August and September 1926,[9] the campaign was sustained 'from above' from 1927 onwards by the Party leadership, and not by the Evsektsiia. How can this be explained? What had changed since the Civil War period? The Soviet state was a qualitatively different entity under Stalin. By 1929 – the peak

---

[5] Kostyrchenko, *Tainaia politika Stalina*, 105.
[6] In addition to a wide-ranging press campaign, the Soviet state also released a number of films on the subject of antisemitism. For a discussion, see V. Pozner, 'Le cinéma contre l'antisémitisme: La campagne de la fin des années 1920', in *Kinojudaica. Les représentations des juifs dans le cinéma de Russie et d'Union Soviétique*, ed. V. Pozner and N. Laurent (Paris: Nouveau Monde Editions, 2012). For a dated but nevertheless useful overview of print publications on the topic of antisemitism in the 1920s, see B. Pinkus and A. A. Greenbaum, *Russian Publications on Jews and Judaism in the Soviet Union 1917-1967* (Jerusalem: Society for Research on Jewish Communities, 1970), 51–66.
[7] Shternshis, *Soviet and Kosher*, 161–62.
[8] According to Dumitru, after the Romanian and German attack on the Soviet Union in 1941, civilians in Ukrainian Transnistria were considerably more tolerant of Jews than their counterparts in Romanian Bessarabia. The decisive factor, argues Dumitru, was state-sponsored opposition to antisemitism in the Soviet territories during the preceding two decades. Whether these findings are specific to Transnistria or generalizable to other parts of the Soviet Union remains an open question. Dumitru, *The State, Antisemitism, and Collaboration*. For a counter-view, which suggests civilians and local collaborators were often the major, even sole forces in the extermination of Jews in the German-occupied territories of the Soviet Union, see Y. Arad, *The Holocaust in the Soviet Union* (Lincoln: University of Nebraska Press, 2009).
[9] Dimanshtein's commission met for a second time on 9 September 1926, but no records of the meeting have survived. It is not clear if it met again. Gatagova, 'Antisemit est' kontrrevoliutsioner...', 153.

of the antisemitism campaign – it eclipsed in resources and sheer human labour anything enjoyed by the regime in 1918 or 1919. But politically, it had been transformed too. As Andrew Sloin has compellingly argued, the state response to antisemitism in the late 1920s was unleashed within the context of the Stalin Revolution, whose defining practice was to identify and mark out for exclusion a range of rhetorically constructed enemies. These campaigns mobilized the extraordinary might of the Stalinist state: 'antisemites' joined an ever-growing list of harmful enemies alongside kulaks, priests, wreckers, speculators and hooligans.[10] The campaign of the late 1920s, then, was not so much motivated by a desire to protect Jewish life, but by the larger state project of targeting those sections of society deemed to pose a threat to *the regime*. Its aim, Sloin argues, was to consolidate Stalinism's hold on domestic power and its control over the language of politics in a period of deep instability. The new campaign against antisemitism flowed first and foremost from the Stalin Revolution's model of total control, not from a straightforward commitment to liberating Jews from enduring oppression. In this way, the state could, without much contradiction, mobilize opposition to antisemitism while unleashing it as the same time. It is no paradox, for example, that the campaign of the late 1920s occurred alongside the emergence of state-sponsored antisemitism in the shape of 'anti-Trotskyism' and the campaign against the United Opposition.[11]

There is a crucial difference to draw out here between the Civil War years and the late 1920s. In the earlier period, the Soviet response to antisemitism was actualized by a layer of Jewish radicals within the Evsektsiia and Evkom; a decade later, it was sustained not through the agency of a small grouping of individuals, but by an authoritarian state with unprecedented resources at its disposal to realize its often-conflicting agendas. But the Evsektsiia leadership did continue to play a role. As late as 1929, on the eve of the Evsektsiia's demise, its leader, Chemeriskii, regularly informed the Soviet government of the extent of antisemitism on the shop floor and in the wider Party, especially the Komsomol. In Smolensk, the local Evsektsiia took the lead in exposing such incidents. Tellingly, Jewish victims of antisemitism continued to look to the Evsektsiia as a source of authority in this area and

---

[10] Sloin, *The Jewish Revolution in Belorussia*, 209–10.
[11] Sloin, *The Jewish Revolution in Belorussia*; I. Deutscher, *The Prophet Unarmed. Trotsky: 1921–1929* (Oxford: Oxford University Press, 1970), 258; Kevin Murphy, *Revolution and Counter-revolution: Class Struggle in a Moscow Metal Factory* (Chicago: Haymarket Books, 2007), 167–69.

wrote scores of letters to its leaders detailing their experiences throughout the late 1920s.[12]

Yet the Evsektsiia's response to antisemitism during this period was tempered by its need to demonstrate a preoccupation with 'Jewish nationalism'. By the late 1920s, as Stalinist hostility to 'particularism' began to take hold, Evsektsiia activists devoted more energy and resources to the confrontation with 'Jewish chauvinism', increasingly identified as a right 'deviation'.[13] There was a cruel irony to this. When Bundists and Left Zionists joined the Soviet government during the Civil War, their 'Jewish nationalism' had provided a resource that helped bring the Soviet confrontation with antisemitism to fruition. As Stalinism was consolidated a decade later, these routes were closed down. The Stalin Revolution entailed total organization of power from above, and ultimately brought about the abolition of relatively autonomous political formations such as the Evsektsiia, the Women's Department (the Zhenotdel), the Polish Section and other 'particularist' state institutions.[14] The closure of the Evsektsiia in 1930 signalled the end of the state's cultivation of a Jewish cultural politics. Concurrently, the state campaign against antisemitism ground to a halt, and by 1932, publications on the topic more or lease ceased. Worse was to follow. As the nightmare of High Stalinism descended in the middle of the decade, an entire layer of Soviet Jewish activists, including many of the key figures encountered in this study, were murdered in the Great Terror that scarred Soviet society for the rest of the century and beyond. Soviet antisemitism survived Stalinism; the campaign against it did not.

---

[12] M. Fainsod, *Smolensk Under Soviet Rule* (Boston: Unwin Hyman, 1989), 445.
[13] Gitelman, *Jewish Nationality and Soviet Politics*, 455; Sloin, *The Jewish Revolution in Belorussia*, 244.
[14] Bemporad, *Becoming Soviet Jews*, 80.

Conclusions: Anti-Racist Praxis in the Russian Revolution

The Soviet response to antisemitism during the Russian Revolution was actualized, and often sustained, by group of non-Bolshevik Jewish socialists. Bolshevism unquestionably had an inbuilt opposition to antisemitism stretching back to the late-imperial period, but in the Civil War years, the move from 'standpoint' to 'actuality' relied, to a significant extent, on the agency of this grouping of Jewish radicals. It was a remarkably small assemblage, consisting, at times, of a mere handful of individuals. The Moscow Jewish Commissariat led by Zvi Fridliand and other Poalei Zion activists boasted, at its peak in early 1918, ten staff. Its department for combatting antisemitism was even smaller, its work resting on the shoulders of just six individuals.[1] When a layer of Bundists and Fareynikte activists entered the Evsektsiia in 1919 and established the Committee for the Struggle Against Antisemitism, they too relied on a similarly sized pool of resources.[2] Yet the importance of these institutions extended well beyond their small activist base: they helped to instil, in practice, a Soviet response to antisemitism where often there was none.

Though drawn from rival parties, these individuals held much in common. It was a network formed of personal connections. The Zionist turned Territorialist, David Davidovich (L'vovich) – the first to raise the issue of antisemitism to the Soviet government in 1918 – knew the Bundist David Lipets, who would go on to lead the Soviet campaign in the summer of 1919. In June 1917, they travelled together from New York to Russia to take part in the unfolding revolution. En route, they stopped off in Stockholm to participate in the third Zimmerwald international socialist conference.[3] The association between Lipets and Moishe Rafes – the two key figures in the Soviet response to antisemitism in 1919 – ran deeper still. As fellow Bundists, they had been connected through revolutionary politics for nearly fifteen years. Before joining the

---

[1] GARF f.1318 o.1 d.561 l.258ob. [2] GARF f.A2306 o.1 d.291 l.47, 49.
[3] Estraikh, 'Mnogolikii David Lipets', 228–29.

Bolsheviks, they undertook joint initiatives to confront antisemitism, such as in January 1919, when they made a direct appeal (in person) to the head of the Directory, Vinnychenko, to request that pogroms be brought to a halt in Berdychiv and elsewhere.[4] Having joined the Bolsheviks later that summer, they together established the Committee for the Struggle Against Antisemitism within the Soviet government. When Abram Kheifets entered the fray shortly after, he was joined by fellow Bundist Lidiia Rabinovich (his wife[5]), who directed the Committee's work among working-class women. Soon after this, Lidiia Abramovich's brother, the poet and playwright Nikolai Aduev, was appointed Secretary of the Committee's press department and tasked with overseeing publications on antisemitism.[6] In other words, a third of the Committee's staff were members of a single family.

Their biographies overlapped in crucial ways, too. As children, Dimanshtein, Rafes, Kheifets and Lipets each received a Jewish education (*kheder*), and by their teens they were immersed in revolutionary organizations. Born amidst the tumult of the 1881–82 pogrom wave, this was a generation that entered adolescence in the slipstream of one of the most decisive turning points in East European modern Jewish history.[7] Unlike their predecessors, they studied not in the *yeshiva* but in universities aboard.[8] Dimanshtein, a fully ordained rabbi, was the exception to this rule. By the time they were young adults in 1905, they found themselves in the throes of revolution and antisemitic violence. Frankel captures it vividly:

They were extremely young in 1905, utterly committed both the cause of revolution and to that of armed Jewish self-defence against pogroms ... By 1906, the revolution had absorbed their every waking moment, every ounce of strength and every hope. However, to them the revolution meant a struggle not only for social equality and political freedom, but also for national, for Jewish, liberation.[9]

---

[4] Melamed and Estraikh, '"O pogrome v Berdicheve" (Novonaidennaia zapiska D. Lipetsa 1919 G.)', 172.

[5] RGASPI f.445 o.1 d.1 l.39, 49; GARF f.A2306 o.15 d.761 l.48. Born in Saint Petersburg in 1891, Lidiia Abramovich was a Bundist from her teenage years. In 1919, together with Abram Kheifets, she joined the Kombund. Her main sphere of work was in the Zhenotdel during this period. In 1920, she left Russia with Kheifets, having been commandeered by the Comintern to work in Germany. After divorcing Kheifets in 1922, Abramovich changed her name to Kathe Pohl and became a leading member of the German Communist Party. RGASPI f.495 o 205 d.5805 l.50-52. See also Weber and Herbst, *Deutsche Kommunisten*, 484–85.

[6] GARF f.A2306 o.1 d.3289 l.1, 5-6, 24. Unfortunately, there are no records detailing the extent of Lidia Abramovich's work among women in the archives of the Committee.

[7] Frankel, 'The Crisis of 1881–1882 as a Turning Point in Modern Jewish History'.

[8] Trachtenberg, *The Revolutionary Roots of Modern Yiddish, 1903–1917*, 40.

[9] Frankel, *Prophecy and Politics*, 329.

This was a socialism that was at once revolutionary, proletarian and Yiddish. And it was profoundly inflected by the actuality of antisemitism. The Soviet response to antisemitism that emerged in 1918 and 1919 had its moorings in these biographies and in the Jewish politics through which they were lived out. Marxist Zionism and Bundism may have been peripheral in Bolshevik power in Russia and Ukraine, but they were central to the Soviet confrontation with antisemitism.

Jewish socialism provided a resource of Soviet anti-racism in the Russian Revolution, and often a crucial one. Its marginality generated a 'radical openness', to paraphrase bell hooks, from which flowed a consistent and clear-sighted politics.[10] This route from national liberation through to Communism was well trodden. In 1920, the Jamaican American poet Claude McKay wrote: 'Although an international socialist ... I believe that, for subject peoples, at least, Nationalism is the open door to Communism'.[11] Just a few months later, Evsektsiia leader Avrom Merezhin adopted a strikingly similar metaphor to describe those Bundists who had moved over to Bolshevism amidst pogromist violence: 'The Jewish question was the door through which they came to us.'[12] For both McKay and Merezhin, Black and Jewish, the door that opened the way to communism and to the politics of the 'universal' was something profoundly *particular*: the experience of racialized violence.

In opening itself up to these cadres, Bolshevism inherited a generation of radicals who would play a critically important role in elevating the politics of liberation within class struggle. Again, these dynamics were not peculiar to Jewish politics. In the formative late imperial period (1897 to 1914), an effective anti-colonial struggle was articulated not by the Bolshevik leadership, but by 'borderland Marxists' of Ukrainian, Georgian and Finnish origin.[13] Similarly, wihtin the Comintern the development of an anti-racist and anti-colonial communism often came from the margins, from the colonized themselves, not the Russian centre.[14] It was

---

[10] b. hooks, *Yearning: Race, Gender and Cultural Politics* (Boston: South End Press, 1990), 145–54. The discussion here draws on Satnam Virdee's work on clear-sightedness and anti-racist politics. See Virdee, 'The Second Sight of Racialised Outsiders in the Imperialist Core'.

[11] A. Dawahare, *Nationalism, Marxism, and African American Literature Between the Wars: A New Pandora's Box* (Jackson: University Press of Mississippi, 2003), 65.

[12] Gitelman, *Jewish Nationality and Soviet Politics*, 222–23.

[13] E. Blanc, *Revolutionary Social Democracy: Marxist Politics Across the Tsarist Empire (1882-1917)* (Leiden: Brill, 2019). See also E. Blanc, 'National Liberation and Bolshevism Reexamined', 2014, https://johnriddell.wordpress.com/2014/05/20/national-liberation-and-bolshevism-reexamined-a-view-from-the-borderlands/.

[14] J. Riddell, 'The Comintern in 1922: The Periphery Pushes Back', *Historical Materialism* 22, no. 3–4 (2014): 52–103.

Conclusions: Anti-Racist Praxis in the Russian Revolution

M. N. Roy, Mirsaid Sultan-Galiev and others who pushed Bolshevism into a theoretical and political space that was more attentive to questions of race and coloniality.[15]

Though principally a history of antisemitism in the Russian Revolution, this book contains a broader offering to the political left. The Bolshevik encounter with antisemitism in 1917 presents a vivid illustration that anti-racism does not flow automatically from socialist politics. Within the Soviet government of the Civil War period, opposition to antisemitism had to be cultivated and renewed, continually – and often by those at the margins of the Party. The Bolshevik response to antisemitism was most effective when the voices of those racialized internal 'others' were amplified and listened to. A century on, as we grapple with the global damage done by racism to class politics, the Russian Revolution may yet have something to tell us about how reactionary ideas can take hold, but also how they can be challenged and confronted.

---

[15] For a pioneering theorization of the role of racialized minorities in the making of the working class and socialist movements, see Virdee, *Racism, Class and the Racialized Outsider*.

Bibliography

Archival Collections

Moscow, Russia

Gosudarstvennyi arkhiv Rosiiskoi Federatsii (GARF), State Archive of the Russian Federation

f. 130	*Sovet narodnykh komissarov RSFSR*. Soviet of People's Commissars of the RSFSR
f. 374.	*Tsentral'naia kontrol'naia komissiia VKP(b) - Narodnyi komissariat raboche-krest'ianskoi inspektsii SSSR (TsKK VKP(b) - NK RKI SSSR)*. The Central Control Commission VKP(b) - The People's Commissariat of the Worker-Peasants' Inspectorate SSSR (TsKK VKP(b) - NK RKI SSSR).
f. 504	*Komissiia po obespecheniiu novogo stroia pri ispolnitel'nom komitete moskovskikh obshchestvennykh organizatsii*. The Commission for Ensuring New Order under the Executive Committee of Moscow Public Organisations
f. 1235	*Vserossiiskii tsentral'nyi ispolnitel'nyi komitet sovetov rabochikh, krest'ianskikh i krasnoarmeiskikh deputatov (VTsIK)*. The All-Russian Central Executive Committee of Workers, Peasants, and Red Army Deputies
f. 1318	*Narodnyi komissariat po delam natsional'nostei RSFSR (Narkomnats RSFSR), predstavitel'stva Narkomnatsa RSFSR v dogovornykh i avtonomykh respublikakh i ikh prestavitel'stva pri Narkomnatse RSFSR*. The People's Commissariat of Nationalities of the RSFRS (Narkomnats RSFSR), Representatives of the Narkomnats RSFSR in the Autonomous Republics, and Representatives of the Republics at the Narkomnats RSFSR
f. 1339	*Tsentral'nyi komitet Vserossiiskogo evreiskogo obshchestvennogo komiteta po okazaniiu pomoshchi postradavshim ot pogromov i stikhiinykh bedstvii (Evobshchestkom)*. The Central Committee of the All-Russian Jewish Social Committee to Aid Victims of Pogroms and Natural Disasters
f. 2306	*Ministerstvo prosveshcheniia RSFSR*. The Ministry of Education of the RSFSR
f. 6990	*Polnomochnaia komissiia vserossiiskogo tsentral'nogo ispolnitel'nogo komiteta po bor'be s banditizmom na zapadnom fronte*. The Plenipotentiary Commission of the All-Russian Central Executive Committee of the Committee for the Struggle against Banditry on the Western Front

f. 9550 Kollektsiia listovok sovetskogo perioda. Collection of Leaflets from the Soviet Period

Rossiiskii gosudarstvennyi arkhiv sotsial'no-politicheskoi istorii (RGASPI), Russian State Archive of Social-Political History

f. 17 Tsentral'nyi komitet Kommunisticheskoi Partii Sovetskogo Soiuza. The Central Committee of the Communist Party of the Soviet Union

f. 19 Protokoly Sovnarkoma i Malogo Sovnarkoma RSFSR. The Minutes of the Council of People's Commissars and the Small Council of People's Commissars of the RSFRS

f. 71 Institut Marksizma-Leninizma pri TsK KPSS. The Institute of Marxism-Leninism under the Central Committee of the Communist Party of the Soviet Union

f. 272 Organizatsii Poalei-Tsion v SSSR. The Organisations of the Poalei-Zion Party in the Soviet Union

f. 445 Tsentral'noe biuro evreiskikh kommunisticheskikh sektsii pri TsK VKP(b). The Central Bureau of the Jewish Communist Sections under the Central Committee of the All-Russian Communist Party (Bolsheviks)

f. 495 Ispolnitel'nyi Komitet Kommunisticheskogo Internatsionala. The Executive Committee of the Communist International

Rossiiskii gosudarstvennyi voennyi arkhiv (RGVA), Russian State Military Archive

f. 4 Upravleniia delami pri narodnom komissare oborony SSSR. The Administrative Department of the People's Commissariat of Defence of the USSR.

f. 9 Politicheskoe upravlenie Revoliutsionnogo Voennogo Soveta Respubliki. The Political Department of the Revolutionary Military Council of the Republic.

f. 103 Politotdel ukrainskogo fronta. The Political Department of the Ukrainian Front.

f. 25860 Narodnyi komissariat po voennym delam Ukrainskoi SSR. The People's Commissariat for Military Affairs of the Ukrainian SSR.

Rossisskii gosudarstvennyi arkhiv literatury i iskusstva (RGALI), Russian State Archives of Literature and Art

f. 631 Souiz sovetskikh pisatelei SSSR. The Union of Soviet Writers of the USSR.

Tsentral'nyi gosudarstvennyi arkhiv moskovskoi oblasti (TsGAMO), Central State Archive of Moscow Oblast

f. 66 Moskovskii Sovet. The Moscow Soviet

f. 4619 Sovet narodnykh komissarov g. Moskvy i Moskovskoi oblasti. The Council of People's Commissars for the city of Moscow and the Moscow Region

Kyiv, Ukraine

Tsentral'nyi derzhavnyi arkhiv hromads'kykh ob'iednan' Ukrainy (TsDAHO), Central State Archive of Public Organisations of Ukraine

f. 1 Tsentral'nyi komitet kompartii Ukrainy. The Central Committee of the Communist Party of Ukraine

222   Bibliography

f. 57   *Kollektsiia dokumentov po istorii Kommunisticheskoi Partii Ukrainy.* Collection of Documents on the History of the Communist Party of Ukraine

Tsentral'nyi derzhavnyi arkhiv vyshchykh orhaniv vlady ta upravlinnia Ukrainy (TsDAVO), Central State Archive of the Supreme Organs of Government and Administration of Ukraine
f. 2   *Sovet ministrov ukrainskoi SSR.* The Council of Ministers of the Ukrainian SSR
f. 5   *Narodnyi komissariat vnutrennikh del Ukrainskoi SSR, g. Kiev.* The People's Commissariat for Internal Affairs of the Ukrainian SSR, Kyiv
f. 3204   *Postoiannoe soveshchanie po bor'be s banditizmom pri SNK USSR, g. Khar'kov.* The Permanent Forum of the Struggle against Banditry under the Sovnarkom of the Ukrainian SSR, Kharkiv
f. 4572   *Revoliutsionnyi voennyi tribunal vooruzhennykh sil Ukrainy i Kryma, g. Khar'kov.* The Revolutionary Military Tribunal of the Armed Forces of Ukraine and Crimea, Kharkiv.

Institut Iudaiki (IJ), The Judaica Institute
f. 19   *Kollektsiia evreiskikh predvybornykh plakatov i agitatsionnykh listovok nachala XX veka.* Collection of Jewish Campaign Posters and Agitational Leaflets from the Beginning of the Twentieth Century

Zhytomyr, Ukraine

Derzhavnyi arkhiv zhytomyrs'koi oblasty (DAZhO), State Archive of Zhytomyr Oblast'
f. R-1820   *Volyns'kyi huberns'kyi revoliutsiinyi tribunal m. Zhytomyr* (Volhynia Guberniia Revolutionary Tribunal, Zhytomyr)

Boston, United States

Harvard University Library (HUL), Archives and Special Collections
f. 3050   *Evreiskie Pogromy na Ukraine, 1918-1924. g.g. Dokumenty kievskoi komissii pomoshchi postradavshim ot pogromov.* Jewish Pogroms in Ukraine, 1918–1924. Documents of the Kyiv District Commission for Relief to Victims of Pogroms. [Originals held at the State Archive of Kyiv Oblast, Kyiv]

New York, United States

YIVO Institute for Jewish Research
RG 80   Mizrakh Yidisher Historisher Arkhiv

Munich, Germany

Bayerische Staatsbibliothek (the Bavarian State Library)
f. 272   *Organizatsii Poalei-Tsion v SSSR.* The Organisations of the Poalei-Zion Party in the Soviet Union [Originals held at Russian State Archive of Social-Political History, Moscow]

Glasgow, Scotland
University of Glasgow, Russian and East European Collection
Reel   Russian Revolutionary Literature Collection [Originals held at
47   Houghton Library, Harvard University]

London, England
World ORT Archive (WORTA)
d07a008   David L'vovich files
d07f144   David L'vovich files
d17a001   David L'vovich files

Periodicals

Bol'shevik
Bor'ba
Evreiskaia Nedelia
Evreiskaia Rabochaia Khronika
Evreiskaia Tribuna – Organ Otdela kul'tury i prosviashcheniia Kommissariata po evreiskim natsional'nym delam
Evreiskaia Zhizn'
Evreiskii Rabochii
Iuzhnyi Rabochii
Izvestiia Gubernskogo Ispolnitel'nogo Komiteta Soveta Rabochikh, Selianskikh i Krasnoarmeiskikh Deputatov Chernigovshchiny
Izvestiia Moskovskogo Soveta Rabochikh Deputatov
Izvestiia Sovetov Rabochikh, Soldatskikh i Krest'ianskikh Deputatov gor. Moskvy i Moskovskoi Oblasti
Izvestiia VTsIK
Kommunar. Organ Khar'kovskogo Gubernskogo Komiteta Kommunisticheskoi Partii (bol'shevikov) Ukrainy
Kommunist
Krasnaia Niva
Krasnaia Zvezda
Listok Petrogradskogo Komiteta Evreiskoi Sotsial-Demokraticheskoi Rabochei Partiii (Poalei Tsiona)
Odesskii Kommunist
Ogonek
Petrogradskaia Pravda
Pravda
Rabochaia Gazeta
Rassvet
Russkiie Vedemosti
Soldatskaia Pravda
Vestnik Evotdela Narkomnatsa
Zhizn' Natsional'nostei
Zvezda

Primary and Secondary Published Materials

Abramson, H. *A Prayer for the Government: Ukrainians and Jews in Revolutionary Times, 1917-1920*. Boston: Harvard University Press, 1999.

Abrosimova, T. A., ed. *Peterburgskii komitet RKP(b) v 1918 godu: protokoly i materialy zasedanii*. Sankt-Peterburg: Peterburgskii gosudarstvennyi universitet. Filologicheskii fakul'tet, 2013.

Adams, A. E. *Bolsheviks in the Ukraine: Second Campaign, 1918-1919*. New Haven: Yale University Press, 1963.

Adorno, T. *The Stars Down to Earth*. London: Routledge, 2002.

Agurskii, S. *Di yidishe komisariatn un di yidishe komunistishe sektsies*. Minsk: Gosudarstvennoe Izdatel'stvo Belorussii, 1928.

——— *Evreiskii rabochii v kommunisticheskom dvizhenii (1917-1921)*. Minsk: Gosudarstvennoe Izdatel'stvo Belorussii, 1926.

Akhapkin, Iu. A., M. P. Iroshnikov, and A. V. Gogolevskii. *Dekrety sovetskoi vlasti o Petrograde: 25 oktiabria (7 noiabria) 1917 g - 29 dekabria 1918 g*. Leningrad: Lenizdat, 1986.

Albert, G. J. '"German October Is Approaching": Internationalism, Activists, and the Soviet State in 1923'. *Revolutionary Russia* 24, no. 2 (2011): 111–42.

Althusser, L. *On the Reproduction of Capitalism: Ideology and Ideological State Apparatuses*. London: Verso, 2014.

Amiantov, Iu. N., V. M. Lavrov, A. S. Pokrovskii, and E. Iu. Tikhonova, eds. *Protokoly zasedanii soveta narodnykh komissarov RSFSR. noiabr' 1917 - mart 1918 gg*. Moscow: ROSSPEN, 2006.

Anderson, K. M., V. V. Shelokhaev, and IU. N. Amiantov. *Bund: dokumenty i materialy, 1894-1921*. Moscow: ROSSPEN, 2010.

Antonov-Ovseenko, V. A. *Zapiski o grazhdanskoii voine. Tom 1*. Moscow: Vysshii voennyi redaktsionnyi sovet, 1924.

——— *Zapiski o grazhdanskoii voine. Tom 3*. Moscow: Gosudarstvennoe voennoe izdatel'stvo, 1932.

——— *Zapiski o grazhdanskoii voine. Tom 4*. Moscow: Gosudarstvennoe voennoe izdatel'stvo, 1933.

Arad, Y. *The Holocaust in the Soviet Union*. Lincoln: University of Nebraska Press, 2009.

Aronson, G. Ia. 'Evreiskaia obshchestvennost'' v Rossii v 1917-1918 g.g.' In *Kniga o russkom evreistve 1917-1967*, edited by Ia. G. Frumkin, G. Ia. Aronson, and A. A. Gol'denveizer, 1–21. New York: Soiuz russkikh evreev, 1968.

——— 'Evreiskii vopros v epokhu stalina'. In *Kniga o russkom evreistve 1917-1967*, edited by Ia. G. Frumkin, G. Ia. Aronson, and A. A. Gol'denveizer, 132–59. New York: Soiuz russkikh evreev, 1968.

Aronson, M. *Troubled Waters: Origins of the 1881 Anti-Jewish Pogroms in Russia*. Chicago: University of Pittsburgh Press, 1990.

Artizov, A. N. 'Sud'by istorikov shkoly M. N. Pokrovskogo (seredina 1930-kh godov)'. *Voprosi Istorii* 7 (1994): 34–38.

Babel, I. *Red Cavalry*. New York: W. W. Norton & Company, 2003.

Bednyi, D. *Kainovo nasledstvo*. Moscow: Gosudarstvennoe izdatel'stvo, 1919.

Beizer, M. 'Antisemitism in Petrograd/Leningrad, 1917–1930'. *East European Jewish Affairs* 29, no. 1–2 (1999): 5–28.

Bemporad, E. *Becoming Soviet Jews: The Bolshevik Experiment in Minsk*. Bloomington: Indiana University Press, 2013.

'From Berdichev to Minsk and Onward to Moscow: Jewish Voices of the Russian Revolution'. Pears Institute for the study of Antisemitism, Birkbeck, University of London, 27 November 2017. www.pearsinstitute.bbk.ac.uk/events/past-events/2017-events/from-berdichev-to-minsk-and-onward-to-moscow-jewish-voices-of-the-1917-russian-revolution/.

Benjamin, W. *Illuminations*. London: Pimlico, 1999.

Bergin, C., ed. *African American Anti-Colonial Thought, 1917-1937*. Edinburgh: Edinburgh University Press, 2016.

———, ed. *'Bitter with the Past but Sweet with the Dream': Communism in the African American Imaginary*. Chicago: Haymarket Books, 2016.

Bertelsen, O. 'GPU Repressions of Zionists: Ukraine in the 1920s'. *Europe-Asia Studies* 65, no. 6 (2013): 1080–111.

Bilinsky, Y. 'The Communist Takeover of the Ukraine'. In *The Ukraine, 1917-1921: A Study in Revolution*, edited by T. Hunczak, 104–127. Cambridge, MA: Harvard University Press, 1977.

Blanc, E. 'National Liberation and Bolshevism Reexamined: A View from the Borderlands', 2014. https://johnriddell.wordpress.com/2014/05/20/national-liberation-and-bolshevism-reexamined-a-view-from-the-borderlands/.

——— *Revolutionary Social Democracy: Marxist Politics Across the Tsarist Empire (1882-1917)*. Leiden: Brill, 2019.

Bobrov, I. V. 'Evreiskii vopros v ideologii i politicheskoi deiatel'nosti rossiiskikh marksistov (konets XIX v.-fevral' 1917 g.)'. PhD Dissertation, Tiumenskii gosudarstvenyi universitet, 2003.

Bonch-Bruevich, V. *Krovavyi navet na khristian*. Moscow: Gosudarstvennaia tipografiia, 1919.

Borochov, B. *Class Struggle and the Jewish Nation: Selected Essays in Marxist Zionism*. Piscataway: Transaction Publishers, 1983.

Borys, J. *The Sovietization of Ukraine, 1917-1923: The Communist Doctrine and Practice of National Self-Determination*. Edmonton: Canadian Institute of Ukrainian Studies, 1980.

Bosh, E. B. *God Bor'by: bor'ba za vlast' na Ukraine s aprelia 1917 g. do nemnetskoi okkupatsii*. Moscow: Gosudarstvennoe izdatel'stvo, 1925.

Bracha, R., A. Drori-Avraham, and G. Yantian, eds. *Educating for Life: New Chapters in the History of the ORT*. London: World ORT, 2010.

Brovkin, V. *Dear Comrades: Menshevik Reports on the Bolshevik Revolution and the Civil War*. Stanford: Hoover Press, 1991.

Browder, R. P., and A. F. Kerensky, eds. *The Russian Provisional Government 1917. Documents (in 3 Volumes)*. Stanford: Stanford University Press, 1961.

Brown, S. 'Communists and the Red Cavalry: The Political Education of the Konarmiia in the Russian Civil War, 1918-1920'. *Slavonic and East European Review* 73, no. 1 (1995): 61–81.

Brym, R. J. *The Jewish Intelligentsia and Russian Marxism: A Sociological Study of Intellectual Radicalism and Ideological Divergence*. London: Palgrave Macmillan, 1978.

Budnitskii, O. V. '"Evreiskie batal'ony" v krasnoi armii'. In *Mirovoi krizis 1914-1920 godov i sud'ba vostohnoevropeiskogo evreistva*, edited by O. V.

Budnitskii, O. Belova, V. Kelner, and V. Mochalova, 239–61. Moscow: ROSSPEN, 2005.

'Jews, Pogroms, and the White Movement: A Historiographical Critique'. *Kritika: Explorations in Russian and Eurasian History* 2, no. 4 (2001): 1–23.

Rossiiskie evrei mezhdu Krasnymi i Belymi, 1917-1920. Moscow: ROSSPEN, 2005.

Russian Jews between the Reds and the Whites, 1917-1920. Philadelphia: University of Pennsylvania Press, 2012.

'Soveshchanie o vyrabotke mer po bor'be s antisemitizmom pri Agitprope TsK VKP(B)'. In *Arkhiv Evreiskoi istorii tom 4*, 163–179. Moscow: ROSSPEN, 2007.

'The Reds and the Jews, or the Comrades in the Arms of the Military Reporter Liutov'. In *The Enigma of Isaac Babel. Biography, History, Context.*, edited by G. Freidin, 65–81. Stanford: Stanford University Press, 2009.

Bukharin, N., and E. Preobrazhenskii. *The ABC of Communism*. Wiltshire: The Merlin Press, 2006.

Buldakov, V. P. 'Freedom, Shortages, Violence: The Origins of the "Revolutionary Anti-Jewish Pogrom" in Russia, 1917-1918'. In *Anti-Jewish Violence: Rethinking the Pogrom in East European History*, edited by J. Dekel-Chen, D. Gaunt, N. M. Meir, and I. Bartal, pp. 74–94. Bloomington: Indiana University Press, 2011.

Khaos i Etnos: Etnicheskie Konflikty v Rossii, 1917-1918 gg. Usloviia Vozniknoveniia, Khronika, Kommentarii, Analiz. Moscow: Novyi khronograf, 2010.

'Rossiiskoe evreistvo i bol'shevistskii perevorot v Petrograde, Oktriabr' 1917 - Ianvar' 1918 goda'. In *Arkhiv Evreiskoi istorii, tom 4*, edited by O. V. Budnitskii, pp. 92–124. Moscow: ROSSPEN, 2007.

Butt, V. P., A. B. Murphy, N. A. Myshov, and G. Swain, eds. *The Russian Civil War: Documents from the Soviet Archives*. New York: Palgrave Macmillan, 1996.

Carr, E. H. *The Bolshevik Revolution, 1917-1923, Volume 1*. London: Penguin Books, 1950.

The Bolshevik Revolution, 1917-1923, Volume 3. London: Penguin Books, 1973.

Colton, T. J. *Moscow: Governing the Socialist Metropolis*. Boston: Harvard University Press, 1995.

Committee of the Jewish Delegations. *The Pogroms in the Ukraine under the Ukrainian Governments (1917-1920). Historical Survey with Documents and Photographs*. London: John Bale, Sons and Danielsson, ltd., 1927.

Daly, J. W. '"Storming the Last Citadel": The Bolshevik Assault on the Chruch, 1922'. In *The Bolsheviks in Russian Society. The Revolution and the Civil War Years*, edited by V. Brovkin, 235–68. New Haven: Yale University Press, n.d.

Daniels, R. V. *The Conscience of the Revolution. Communist Opposition in Soviet Russia*. London: Harvard University Press, 1960.

Davies, S. *Popular Opinion in Stalin's Russia: Terror, Propaganda and Dissent, 1934-1941*. Cambridge: Cambridge University Press, 1997.

Dawahare, A. *Nationalism, Marxism, and African American Literature between the Wars: A New Pandora's Box*. Jackson: University Press of Mississippi, 2003.

Dekel-Chen, J. *Farming the Red Land: Jewish Agricultural Colonization and Local Soviet Power, 1924-1941*. New Haven: Yale University Press, 2005.

Dekel-Chen, J., D. Gaunt, N. M. Meir, and I. Bartal, eds. *Anti-Jewish Violence: Rethinking the Pogrom in East European History*. Bloomington: Indiana University Press, 2011.
Dekrety sovetskoi vlasti. Vol. 5. Moscow: Gosudarstvennoe izdatel'stvo politicheskoi literatury, 1971.
Denisenko, P. I. *Listovki bol'shevikov Ukrainy perioda pervoi russkoi revoliutsii (1905-1907 gg)*. Kiev: Gosudarstvennoe izdatel'stvo politicheskoi literatury USSR, 1955.
Deutscher, I. *The Prophet Armed: Trotsky, 1879-1921*. London: Oxford University Press, 1970.
The Prophet Unarmed. Trotsky: 1921-1929. Oxford: Oxford University Press, 1970.
Du Bois, W. E. B. *Darkwater: Voices from Within the Veil*. London: Verso, 2016.
The Souls of Black Folk. New York: Dover Publications, 2000.
Dubnov, S. *Kniga zhizni. Materialy dlia istorii moego vremeni: vospominaniia i razmyshleniia*. Moscow: Mosty kul'tury, 2004.
Dumitru, D. *The State, Antisemitism, and Collaboration in the Holocaust: The Borderlands of Romania and the Soviet Union*. Cambridge: Cambridge University Press, 2016.
Eletskii, P. *O evreiakh*. Khar'kov: Ukrainskaia Sotsialisticheskaia Sovetskaia Respublika, 1919.
Engel, David. *The Assassination of Symon Petliura and the Trial of Sholem Schwarzbard 1926-1927: A Selection of Documents*. Göttingen: Vandenhoeck and Ruprecht, 2016.
Engelstein, L. *The Keys to Happiness. Sex and the Search for Modernity in Fin-de-Siècle Russia*. London: Cornell University Press, 1992.
Russia In Flames: War, Revolution, Civil War, 1914-1921. Oxford: Oxford University Press, 2017.
Estraikh, G. 'Evreiskaia literaturnaia zhizn' v poslerevoliutsionnoi Moskve: Moskovskii kruzhok evreiskikh pisatelei i khudozhnikov'. In *Arkhiv Evreiskoi istorii, tom 2*, edited by O. V. Budnitskii, 187–212. Moscow: ROSSPEN, 2005.
'From Berlin to Paris and Beyond: The 1930s and 1940s'. In *Educating for Life: New Chapters in the History of the ORT*, edited by R. Bracha, A. Drori-Avraham, and G. Yantian. London: World ORT, 2010.
'From Foreign Delegation to World ORT Union'. In *Educating for Life: New Chapters in the History of the ORT*, edited by R. Bracha, A. Drori-Avraham, and G. Yantian. London: World ORT, 2010.
In Harness: Yiddish Writers' Romance With Communism. Syracuse: Syracuse University Press, 2005.
'Letters to the Editor'. *East European Jewish Affairs* 23, no. 1 (1993): 123–24.
'Mnogolikii David Lipets: Evrei v russkoi revoliutsii'. In *Arkhiv Evreiskoi istorii, tom 7*, edited by O. V. Budnitskii, 225–41. Moscow: ROSSPEN, 2012.
'Simulating Justice: The Blood Libel Case in Moscow, April 1922'. In *Ritual Murder in Russia, Eastern Europe, and Beyond. New Histories of an Old Accusation*, edited by E. Avrutin, J. Dekel-Chen, and R. Weinberg, 204–18. Bloomington: Indiana University Press, 2017.

'Zalman Wendroff. The Forverts Man in Moscow'. In *Leket: yidishe shtudyes haynt*, edited by M. Aptroot, E. Gal-Ed, R. Gruschka, and S. Neuberg, pp. 509–28. Dusseldorf: Dusseldorf University Press, 2012.

'Zalmen Vendrof'. In *The YIVO Encyclopedia of Jews in Eastern Europe*, edited by D. H. Gershon, 1964–65. New York: YIVO Institute for Jewish Research, 2008.

'EVENTS IN 5679: June 1, 1918, to May 31, 1919'. *The American Jewish Year Book* 21 (1919): 169–302.

Evrei, klassovaia bor'ba i pogromi. Petrograd: Izdatel'stvo Petrogradskogo Soveta, 1918.

Fainsod, M. *Smolensk Under Soviet Rule*. Boston: Unwin Hyman, 1989.

Faitel'berg-Bland, V., and V. Savchenko. *Odessa v epokhu voin i revoliutsii (1914-1920)*. Odessa: Optimum, 2008.

Faigain, S. S. 'An Annotated Bibliography of Maria Yakovlena Frumkina (Esther)', PhD Dissertation, The Australian National University, 2018.

Fanon, F. *The Wretched of the Earth*. London: Penguin Classics, 2001.

Ferro, M. *The Bolshevik Revolution: A Social History of the Russian Revolution*. London: Routledge & Kegan Paul, 1985.

Fiddick, T. C. *Russia's Retreat from Poland. From Permanent Revolution to Peaceful Coexistence*. Basingstoke: Palgrave Macmillan, 1990.

Figes, O. 'The Red Army and Mass Mobilization during the Russian Civil War 1918-1920'. *Past & Present*, no. 129 (1990): 168–211.

Figes, O., and B. I Kolonitskii. *Interpreting the Russian Revolution. The Language and Symbols of 1917*. New Haven: Yale University Press, 1999.

Fine, R., and P. Spencer. *Antisemitism and the Left: On the Return of the Jewish Question*. Manchester: Manchester University Press, 2017.

Fischer, L. 'The Pogromshchina and the Directory: A New Historiographical Synthesis?' *Revolutionary Russia* 16, no. 2 (2003): 47–93.

The Socialist Response to Antisemitism in Imperial Germany. Cambridge: Cambridge University Press, 2010.

Fitzpatrick, S. *The Commissariat of Enlightenment. Soviet Organization Education and Arts under Lunacharsky, October 1917-1921*. Cambridge: Cambridge University Press, 1970.

Ford, C. 'The Crossroads of the European Revolution: Ukrainian Social-Democrats and Communists (Independentists), the Ukrainian Revolution and Soviet Hungary 1917–1920'. *Critique* 38, no. 4 (2010): 565–605.

Frankel, J. *Prophecy and Politics: Socialism, Nationalism, and the Russian Jews, 1862-1917*. Cambridge: Cambridge University Press, 1981.

'The Crisis of 1881-1882 as a Turning Point in Modern Jewish History'. In *The Legacy of Jewish Migration, 1881 and Its Impact*, edited by David Berger, 9–22. New York: Brooklyn College Press, 1983.

Crisis, Revolution, and Russian Jews. Cambridge: Cambridge University Press, 2008.

Fridliand, Ts. 'Antisemitizm'. In *Bol'shaia sovetskaia entsiklopediia*, Vol. 4. Moscow: Gosudarstvennoe slovarno-entsiklopedicheskoe izdatel'stvo 'Sovetskaia Entsiklopediia', 1926.

'Ester: Lenin i ego trudy'. *Pechat' i revoliutsiia*, no. 4 (1925): 176–77.

Kommunisticheskii Internatsional i kommunisticheskii Poalei-Tsionizm. Minsk: Gosudarstvennoe izdatel'stvo Belorussii, 1921.

Galili, Z. 'Zionism in the Early Soviet State: Between Legality and Persecution'. In *Revolution, Repression and Revival: The Soviet Jewish Experience*, edited by Z. Gitelman and Y. Ro'i, 37–68. Lanham: Rowman & Littlefield Publishers, 2007.

Gal'perina, B. D., and V. I. Startsev, eds. *Petrogradskii Sovet Rabochikh i Soldatskikh Deputatov v 1917 godu. Dokumenty i materialy*. Vol. 3. Moscow: ROSSPEN, 2002.

——— eds. *Petrogradskii Sovet Rabochikh i Soldatskikh Deputatov v 1917 godu. Dokumenty i materialy*. Vol. 4. Moscow: ROSSPEN, 2003.

Gal'perina, B. D., O. N. Znamenskii, and V. I. Startsev, eds. *Petrogradskii Sovet Rabochikh i Soldatskikh Deputatov v 1917 godu. Dokumenty i materialy*. Vol. 1. Leningrad: Nauka Leningradskoe otdelenie, 1991.

Gatagova, L. S. '"Antisemit est' kontrrevoliutsioner…" Soveshchanie o vyrabotke mer po bor'be s antisemitizmom pri Agitpope TkK VKP(b)'". In *Arkhiv evreiskok istorii tom 4*, edited by O. V. Budnitskii, 147–162. Moscow: ROSSPEN, 2007.

Gatagova, L. S., L. P. Kosheleva, and Rogovaia, eds. *TsK RKP(b)-VKP(b) i natsional'nii vopros. Kniga 1. 1918-1933 gg*. Moscow: ROSSPEN, 2005.

Gechtman, R. 'Lifshits, Il'ia Mikhailovich'. In *The Yivo Encyclopedia of Jews in Eastern Europe*, Vol. 1, edited by D. H. Gershon, pp. 1038–39. New Haven: Yale University Press, 2008.

Genis, V. L. 'Pervaia Konnaia armiia: Za kulisami slavy'. *Voprosy istorii*, no. 12 (1994): 64–77.

Gergel, N. 'The Pogroms in the Ukraine in 1918-1921'. *YIVO Annual of Jewish Social Science* 6 (1951): 237–51.

Gerrits, André. *The Myth of Jewish Communism: A Historical Interpretation*. New York: P.I.E. Peter Lang, 2009.

Gilley, C. 'Beyond Petliura: The Ukrainian National Movement and the 1919 Pogroms'. *East European Jewish Affairs* 47, no. 1 (2017): 45–61.

——— 'Fighters for Ukrainian Independence? Imposture and Identity among Ukrainian Warlords, 1917–22'. *Historical Research* 90, no. 247 (2017): 172–90.

——— 'Otamanshchyna?: The Self-Formation of Ukrainian and Russian Warlords at the Beginning of the Twentieth and Twenty-First Centuries'. *Ab Imperio* 2015, no. 3 (2015): 73–95.

——— 'The Ukrainian Anti-Bolshevik Risings of Spring and Summer 1919: Intellectual History in a Space of Violence'. *Revolutionary Russia* 27, no. 2 (2014): 109–31.

Gitelman, Z. *A Century of Ambivalence: The Jews of Russia and the Soviet Union, 1881 to the Present*. Bloomington: Indiana University Press, 2001.

——— *Jewish Nationality and Soviet Politics: The Jewish Sections of the CPSU, 1917-1930*. Princeton: Princeton University Press, 1972.

Goldhagen, E. 'The Ethnic Consciousness of Early Russian Socialists'. *Judaism* 23 (1973): 479–96.

Gor'kii, M. *Iz literaturnogo naslediia. Gor'kii i evreiskii vopros*. Jerusalem: Evreiskii Universitet v Ierusalime, 1986.

Gorky, M. *Untimely Thoughts. Essays on Revolution, Culture and the Bolsheviks, 1917-1918*. 1st Edition. London: Garnstone Press, 1968.

Gorlov, N. *Temnye sily, voina i pogromy*. Petrograd: Izdatel'stvo Petrogradskogo Soveta, 1918.

Gosizpolit. *Sed'moi ekstrennyi s'ezd RKP(b) mart 1918 goda. Stenograficheskii otchet*. Moscow: Gosudarstvennoe izdatel'stvo politicheskoi literatury, 1962.

Gurenko, S. I. *Tretii zizd Komunistychnoi Partii (bilshovykiv) Ukrainy. 1-6 Bereznia 1919 g. Protokoly*. Kiev: Parlamentske vid-vo, 2002.

Gurevitz, B. 'An Attempt to Establish Separate Jewish Units in the Red Army during the Civil War'. *Michael* 6 (1980): 86–101.

―― *National Communism in the Soviet Union, 1918-1928*. Pittsburgh: University of Pittsburgh Press, 1980.

―― *The Bolshevik Revolution and the Foundation of the Jewish Communist Movement in Russia*. Slavic and Soviet Series 4. Jerusalem: The Russian and East European Research Center, 1976.

Gusev, V. *Bund, Komfarband, Evsektsiia KP(b)U: Stranitsy politicheskoi biografii. 1917-1921 gg*. Moscow: Obshchestvo 'Evreiskoe Naselenie', 1994.

Gusev-Orenburgskii, S. I. *Bagrovaia kniga. Pogromy 1919-1920 gg. na Ukraine*. New York: Ladoga, 1983.

―― *Kniga o evreiskikh pogromakh na Ukraine v 1919 g. Sostavlena po ofitsial'nym dokumentam, dokladam s mest i oprosam postradavshikh*. St. Peterburg and Berlin: Izdatel'stvo Z. I. Grzhebina, 1921.

Haberer, E. 'Cosmopolitanism, Antisemitism, and Populism: A Reappraisal of the Russian and Jewish Socialist Responses to the Pogroms of 1881-1882'. In *Pogroms: Anti-Jewish Violence in Modern Russian History*, edited by J. D. Klier and S. Lambroza, 98–134. Cambridge: Cambridge University Press, 1992.

―― *Jews and Revolution in Nineteenth-Century Russia*. Cambridge: Cambridge University Press, 2000.

Hall, S. 'Race, Articulation, and Societies Structured in Dominance'. In *Sociological Theories: Race and Colonialism*, UNESCO, 305–45. Paris: United Nations Educational Scientific and Cultural, 1980.

Hanebrink, P. *A Specter Haunting Europe: The Myth of Judeo-Bolshevism*. New Haven: Harvard University Press, 2018.

Heideman, P., ed. *Class Struggle and the Color Line: American Socialism and the Race Question, 1900-1930*. Chicago: Haymarket Books, 2018.

Heifets, E. *The Slaughter of the Jews in the Ukraine in 1919*. New York: Thomas Seltzer, 1921.

Herbeck, U. *Das Feindbild vom 'jüdischen Bolschewiken'. Zur Geschichte des russischen Antisemitismus vor und während der Russischen Revolution*. Berlin: Metropol, 2009.

Herf, J. *Jewish Enemy: Nazi Propaganda during World War II and the Holocaust*. Cambridge, MA: Harvard University Press, 2006.

Hirik, Serhiy. 'Jewish National Communist Parties and the Comintern: A Non-Mutual Association'. *Judaica Ukrainica* 2 (2013): 113–25.

―― 'Neviadomaia pratsa Ryhora (Tsvi) Frydlianda ab levym Paalei-Tsyianiz'me u Belarusi'. *Zapisy BINIM* 39 (2017): 491–99.

Hirsch, F. *Empire of Nations: Ethnographic Knowledge and the Making of the Soviet Union*. Ithaca: Cornell University Press, 2005.

Hirsh, D. *Contemporary Left Antisemitism*. London: Routledge, 2017.

Holquist, P. 'Letter', *Slavic Review* 55, no. 3 (1996): 719.

Bibliography

hooks, b. *Yearning: Race, Gender and Cultural Politics.* Boston: South End Press, 1990.
Hundert, G. D., ed. *The YIVO Encyclopedia of Jews in Eastern Europe.* New Haven: Yale University Press, 2008.
I. I. P. *Listovki moskovskikh bol'shevikov v period pervoi russkoi revoloitsii.* Moscow: Gosudarstvennoe izdatel'stvo politicheskoi literatury, 1955.
Jacobs, J., ed. *Jews and Leftist Politics: Judaism, Israel, Antisemitism, and Gender.* New York: Cambridge University Press, 2017.
 ed. *On Socialists and 'The Jewish Question' After Marx.* New York: New York University Press, 1992.
James, C. L. R. *World Revolution, 1917-1936: The Rise and Fall of the Communist International – The C. L. R. James Archives.* Edited by Christian Høgsbjerg. Durham: Duke University Press, 2017.
James, W. *Holding Aloft the Banner of Ethiopia: Caribbean Radicalism in America 1900-32.* London: Verso, 1999.
Johnson, Kelly. 'Sholem Schwarzbard: Biography of a Jewish Assassin'. PhD Dissertation, Harvard University, 2012.
Johnston, T. *Being Soviet: Identity, Rumour, and Everyday Life Under Stalin 1939-1953.* Oxford: Oxford University Press, 2011.
Kalmina, L. 'The Possibility of the Impossible: Pogroms in Eastern Siberia'. In *Anti-Jewish Violence: Rethinking the Pogrom in East European History,* edited by J. Dekel-Chen, D. Gaunt, N. M. Meir, and I. Bartal, 131–43. Bloomington: Indiana University Press, 2011.
Karelin, A. A. *Zlye rosskazni pro evreev.* Moscow: Izdatel'stvo Vserossiiskogo Tsentral'nogo Ispolnitel'nogo Komiteta Sovetov R., S., K. i K Deputatov, 1919.
 Zlye spletni na ugnetennykh. Moscow: Gosudarstvennoe izdatel'stvo, 1919.
Kariaeva, T. F., and N. N. Azovtsev, eds. *Direktivy komandovaniia frontov Krasnoi Armii, 1917-1922. Sbornik dokumentov.* Vol. 1. 4 vols. Moscow: Voennoe izdatel'stvo Ministerstvo Oborony SSSR, 1971.
 eds. *Direktivy komandovaniia frontov Krasnoi Armii, 1917-1922. Sbornik dokumentov.* Vol. 2. 4 vols. Moscow: Voennoe izdatel'stvo Ministerstvo Oborony SSSR, 1971.
Karlip, J. M. 'Between Martyrology and Historiography: Elias Tcherikower and the Making of a Pogrom Historian'. *East European Jewish Affairs* 38, no. 3 (2008): 257–80.
 The Tragedy of a Generation: The Rise and Fall of Jewish Nationalism in Eastern Europe. Cambridge, MA: Harvard University Press, 2013.
Kenez, P. 'Pogroms and White Ideology in the Russian Civil War'. In *Pogroms: Anti-Jewish Violence in Modern Russian History,* edited by J. D. Klier and S. Lambroza, pp. 293–313. New York: Cambridge University Press, 1992.
Kessler, M. *On Anti-Semitism and Socialism: Selected Essays.* Berlin: Trafo, 2005.
 'The Comintern and the Left Poale Zion, 1919-1922'. *The Australian Journal of Jewish Studies* 24 (2010): 116–33.
Kheifets, I. Ia. *Mirovaia reaktsiia i evreiskie pogromy. Tom pervyi: Pol'sha 1918-1922.* Moscow: Gosizdat Ukrainy, 1925.
 Mirovaia reaktsiia i evreiskie pogromy. Tom vtoroi: Vengriia 1918-1922. Moscow: Gosizdat Ukrainy, 1925.

Khromov, S., ed. *Grazhdanskaia voina i voennaia interventsiia v SSSR*. Moscow: Sovetskaia Entsiklopediia, 1983.
Kirillov, I. N., and A. M. Tarasenko. *Listovki Ivanovo-Voznesenskoi bol'shevistkoi organizatsii 1900-1917 g.g*. Ivanovo: Ivanovskoe khnizhnoe izdatel'stvo, 1957.
Klier, J. D. *Russians, Jews, and the Pogroms of 1881-1882*. Cambridge: Cambridge University Press, 2011.
  'The Pogrom Paradigm in Russian History'. In *Pogroms: Anti-Jewish Violence in Modern Russian History*, edited by J. Klier and S. Lambroza, pp. 13–38. Cambridge: Cambridge University Press, 1992.
Koenker, D. 'The Evolution of Party Consciousness in 1917: The Case of the Moscow Workers'. *Soviet Studies* 30, no. 1 (1978): 38–62.
Kolonitskii, B. I. '"democracy" as Identification. Towards the Study of Political Consciousness during the February Revolution'. In *Social Identities in Revolutionary Russia*, edited by K. P. Madhavan, 161–73. Basingstoke: Palgrave, 2001.
  '"Democracy" in the Political Consciousness of the February Revolution'. *Slavic Review* 57, no. 1 (1998): 95–106.
Konopnitskaia, M. Iu. *Staryi perepletchik i ego vnuk*. Moscow: Gosudarstvennoe izdatel'stvo, 1920.
Koprzhiva-Lur'e, B. Ia. *Istoriia odnoi zhizni*. Paris: Athenuem, 1987.
Korolenko, V. G. *Dnevnik. Pis'ma 1917-1921*. Moscow: Sovetskii pisatel', 1997.
Korolivskii, S. M., N. K. Kolensnik, and I. K. Rybalka,. *Grazhdanskaia voina na Ukraine 1918-1920. Tom pervyi, Kniga pervaia*. Kiev: Izdatel'stvo naukova duma, 1967.
  Grazhdanskaia voina na Ukraine 1918-1920. Tom pervyi, Kniga vtoraia. Kiev: Izdatel'stvo naukova duma, 1967.
  Grazhdanskaia voina na Ukraine 1918-1920. Tom vtoroi. Kiev: Izdatel'stvo naukova duma, 1967.
Kostyrchenko, G. V. *Tainaia politika Stalina: Vlast' i antisemitizm*. Moscow: Mezhdunarodnye otnosheniia, 2003.
Kowalski, R. I. *The Bolshevik Party in Conflict: The Left Communist Opposition of 1918*. Pittsburgh: University of Pittsburgh Press, 1991.
Kozlov, V. P. *Arkhiv noveishei istorii Rossii. Seriia 'Katalogi' tom VII: Protokoly rukovodiashchikh organov narodnogo komissariata po delam natsional'nostei RSFSR 1918-1934 gg. Katalog dokumentov*. Moscow: ROSSPEN, 2001.
Krasnikova, A. V. 'Studencheskaia organizatsiia pri Peterburgskom komitete RSDRP(b) i ee vklad v sovetskoe gosudarstvennoe stroitel'stvo v pervye posleoktiabr'skie mesiatsy 1917 G.' In *Problemy gosudarstvennogo stroitel'stva v pervye gody sovetskoi vlasti*, edited by Iu. S. Tokarev, 67–82. Leningrad: Trudy LOIN, 1973.
Kucherov, S. *The Organs of Soviet Administration of Justice: Their History and Operation*. Leiden: Brill, 1970.
Kurinnyi, P. F. *Uman' ta umanchany ochyma P. F. Kurinnoho (z osobystykh shchodennikiv za 1918-1929 hh.)* Uman: uman'skyi kraieznavchyi muzei, 2014.
Lambroza, S. 'The Pogroms of 1903-1906'. In *Pogroms: Anti-Jewish Violence in Modern Russian History*, edited by J. D. Klier and S. Lambroza, 195–247. Cambridge: Cambridge University Press, 1992.
Larin, Iu. *Evrei i antisemitizm v SSSR*. Moscow: Gosizdat, 1929.

Bibliography

Ledat, G. *Antisemitizm i antisemity: Voprosy i otvety*. Leningrad: Priboi, 1929.
Lenin, V. I. *Collected Works*. Vol. 30. 40 vols. Moscow: Lawrence and Wishart, 1965.
— *Lenin on the Jewish Question*. New York: International Publishers, 1974.
— *O Evreiskom voprose v Rossii*. Moscow: Kooperativnoe izdatel'stvo 'Proletarii', 1924.
— *Polnoe sobranie sochinenii*. Vol. 5. 55 vols. Moscow: Izdatel'stvo politicheskoi literatury, 1967.
— *Polnoe sobranie sochinenii*. Vol. 35. 55 vols. Moscow: Izdatel'stvo politicheskoi literatury, 1974.
— *Polnoe sobranie sochinenii*. Vol. 39. 55 vols. Moscow: Izdatel'stvo politicheskoi literatury, 1970.
— *Neizvestnye dokumenty 1891-1922*. Moscow: ROSSPEN, 2000.
Levin, N. *The Jews in the Soviet Union Since 1917: Paradox of Survival*. Vol. 1. New York: I. B. Tauris & Co. Ltd, 1990.
Lih, L. T. 'The Mystery of the ABC'. *Slavic Review* 56, no. 1 (1997): 50–72.
Lohr, E. 'The Russian Army and the Jews: Mass Deportation, Hostages, and Violence during World War I'. *Russian Review* 60, no. 3 (2001): 404–19.
Lunacharskii, A. *Ob antisemitizme*. Moscow: Gosudarstvennoe izdatel'stvo, 1929.
Luxemburg, R. *Selected Political Writings*. London: Jonathon Cape, 1972.
L'vov-Rogachevskii, V. *Goniteli evreiskogo naroda v Rossii. Istoricheskii ocherk*. Moscow: Moskovskii Sovet Rabochikh Deputatov. Otdel izdatel'stva i knizhnogo sklada, 1917.
MacKay, J. *True Songs of Freedom: Uncle Tom's Cabin in Russian Culture and Society*. Madison: University of Wisconsin Press, 2013.
Makhno, N. I. *Na chuzhbine, 1923-1934 gg. Zapiski i stat'i*. Paris: Gromada, 2004.
Makukhin, I. Ia., ed. *Istoriia gorodov i sel Ukrainskoi SSR. Tom 19. Sumskaia oblast'*. 26 vols. Kiev: Institut istorii Akademii Nauk USSR, Ukrainskoi sovetskoi entsiklopedii Akademii Nauk USSR, 1974.
Martin, T. D. *The Affirmative Action Empire: Nations and Nationalism in the Soviet Union, 1923-1939*. New York: Cornell University Press, 2001.
— 'Obzory OGPU i sovetskie istoriki,' in *"Sovershenno sekretno": Lubianka – Stalinu o polozhenii v strane (1922-1934 gg.)*. Vol. 1, Part 1, pp. 21–26. Moscow: Institut Rossiiskoi Istorii Rossiiskoi Akademii Nauk, 2001.
Marx, K. *Early Writings*. London: Penguin Books Limited, 1992.
Mawdsley, E. *The Russian Civil War*. Edinburgh: Birlinn, 2008.
May, R. *The Translator in the Text: On Reading Russian Literature in English*. Evanston: Northwestern University Press, 1994.
McDonald, T. *Face to the Village: The Riazan Countryside under Soviet Rule, 1921-1930*. Toronto: University of Toronto Press, 2011.
McGeever, B. 'Bolshevik Responses to Antisemitism during the Civil War: Spatiality, Temporality, and Agency'. In *Volume 3: Russia's Home Front in War and Revolution, 1914-22. Book 4*, edited by C. Read and A. Lindenmeyr, Vol. 1, 467–91. Bloomington: Slavica Publishers, 2018.
— 'The Bolshevik Confrontation with Antisemitism in the Russian Revolution, 1917-1919'. Unpublished Ph.D. thesis. University of Glasgow, 2015.

McGeever, B., and S. Virdee. 'Antisemitism and Socialist Strategy in Europe, 1880–1917: An Introduction'. *Patterns of Prejudice* 51, no. 3–4 (2017): 221–34.

Medem, V. *The Life and Soul of a Legendary Jewish Socialist. The Memoirs of Vladimir Medem.* New York: KTAV Publishing House, 1979.

Melamed, E. I., ed. *Dokumenty po istorii i kul'ture evreev v regional'nykh arkhivakh Ukrainy. Putevoditel'. Volynskaia, Zhitomirskaia, Rovenskaia, Cherkasskaia oblasti.* Kiev: Rossiiskii Gosudarstvennyi Gumanitarnyi Universitet, Tsentr Bibleistiki i Iudaiki, 2009.

Melamed, E. I., and G. Estraikh. '"O pogrome v Berdicheve" (novonaidennaia zapiska D. Lipetsa 1919 g.)'. In *Arkhiv evreiskoi istorii tom 8*, edited by O. V. Budnitskii, pp. 156–176. Moscow: ROSSPEN, 2016.

Melamed, E. I., and M. S. Kupovetskii, eds. *Dokumenty po istorii i kul'ture evreev v arkhivakh Kieva.* Kiev: DUKh i LITERA, 2006.

Meyers, J. 'A Portrait of Transition: From the Bund to Bolshevism in the Russian Revolution'. *Jewish Social Studies* 24, no. 2 (2019): 107–34.

'To Dance at Two Weddings: Jews, Nationalism, and the Left in Revolutionary Russia'. Unpublished Ph.D. thesis. Stanford University, 2018.

Miliakova, L. B. *Kniga pogromov: Pogromy na Ukraine, v Belorussii i evropeiskoi chasti Rossii v period grazhdanskoi voiny 1918–1922 gg. Sbornik dokumentov.* Moscow: ROSSPEN, 2008.

Moss, K. *Jewish Renaissance in the Russian Revolution.* Cambridge, MA: Harvard University Press, 2009.

Murphy, Kevin. *Revolution and Counterrevolution: Class Struggle in a Moscow Metal Factory.* Chicago: Haymarket Books, 2007.

Nathans, B. *Beyond the Pale: The Jewish Encounter with Late Imperial Russia.* Berkeley: University of California Press, 2002.

Nedava, J. *Trotsky and the Jews.* Philadelphia: The Jewish Publication Society of America, 1971.

O.K.K. *Gody bor'by. Sbornik materialov po istorii revoliutsionnogo dvizheniia na Zinov'evshchine.* Zinov'evsk: Okruzhnaia Oktiabr'skaia Komissiia, 1927.

Ordzhonikidze, G. K. *Stat'i i rechi. Tom 1.* Moscow: Gosudarstvennoe izdatel'stvo politicheskoi literatury, 1956.

ORT. *The Hope and the Illusion. The Search for a Russian Jewish Homeland: A Remarkable Period in the History of the ORT, 1921 to 1938.* London: World ORT, 2006.

Ostrovskii, E. S. *Evreiskie pogromy 1918-1921.* Moscow: Emes, 1926.

Panteleev, M. *Agenty Kominterna: Soldaty mirovoi revoliutsii.* Moscow: EKSMO, 2005.

Pantsov, A. *The Bolsheviks and the Chinese Revolution 1919-1927.* London: Routledge, 2013.

Pavliuchenkov, S. A. *Voennyi kommunizm v Rossii: Vlast' i massy.* Moscow: RKT-Istoriia, 1997.

Pavloff, V. I. 'Revolutionary Populism in Imperial Russia and the National Question in the 1870s and 1880s'. In *Socialism and Nationalism*, edited by E. Cahm and V. I. Fisera, pp. 69–95. Nottingham: Spokesman, 1978.

Pearce, B. *1903 Second Ordinary Congress of the RSDLP.* New York: New Park Publications, 1978.

Petrovskii, D. *Kontr-revoliutsiia i evreiskie pogromy*. Moscow: Gosudarstvennoe Izdatel'stvo, 1920.
Revoliutsiia i kontr-revoliutsiia na Ukraine. Moscow: Gosudarstvennoe Izdatel'stvo, 1920.
Voennaia shkola v gody revoliutsii. Moscow: Vysshii voennyi redaktsionnyi sovet, 1924.
Petrovsky-Shtern, Y. *Lenin's Jewish Question*. New Haven: Yale University Press, 2010.
Pinkus, B., and A. A. Greenbaum. *Russian Publications on Jews and Judaism in the Soviet Union 1917-1967*. Jerusalem: Society for Research on Jewish Communities, 1970.
Pipes, R. *Russia under the Bolshevik Regime*. New York: Alfred A. Knopf, 1993.
The Unknown Lenin. From the Secret Archive. New Haven: Yale University Press, 1996.
Polonsky, A. *The Jews in Poland and Russia: Volume III: 1914 to 2008*. Oxford: The Littman Library of Jewish Civilization, 2012.
Popov, N. N, ed. *Vos'maia konferentsiia RKP(b), dekabr' 1919 g*. Moscow: Partiinoe izdatel'stvo, 1934.
Postone, M. 'Anti-Semitism and National Socialism: Notes on the German Reaction to "Holocaust"'. *New German Critique*, no. 19 (1980): 97–115.
'History and Helplessness: Mass Mobilization and Contemporary Forms of Anticapitalism'. *Public Culture* 18, no. 1 (2006): 93–110.
Pozner, V. 'Le cinéma contre l'antisémitisme : La campagne de la fin des années 1920'. In *Kinojudaica. Les représentations des Juifs dans le cinéma de Russie et d'Union Soviétique*, edited by V. Pozner and N. Laurent, pp. 131–174. Paris: Nouveau Monde Editions, 2012.
Rabinovitch, S. 'Alternative to Zion: The Jewish Autonomist Movement in Late Imperial and Revolutionary Russia'. PhD Dissertation, Brandeis University, 2007.
Rabinowitch, A. 'Richard Pipes's Lenin'. *Russian Review* 57, no. 1 (1998): 110–13.
The Bolsheviks Come to Power. The Revolution of 1917 in Petrograd. New York: W.W. Norton, 1978.
The Bolsheviks in Power: The First Year of Soviet Rule in Petrograd. Bloomington: Indiana University Press, 2007.
Radar, J. *By the Skill of Their Hands: The Story of the ORT*. Geneva: World ORT, 1965.
Rafes, M. G. *Dva goda revoliutsii na Ukraine (Evoliutsiia i raskol 'Bunda')*. Moscow: Gosudarstvennoe izdatel'stvo, 1920.
Natsional'nye voprosy (Sbornik statei i materialov). Moscow: Gosudarstvennoe izdatel'stvo, 1921.
Ocherki po istorii Bunda. Moscow: Moskovskii rabochii, 1923.
Raleigh, D. J. 'Political Power in the Russian Revolution: A Case Study of Saratov'. In *Revolution in Russia: Reassessments of 1917*, edited by E. R. Frankel, J. Frankel, and B. Knei-Paz, pp. 34–53. Cambridge: Cambridge University Press, 1992.
Reed, J. *Ten Days That Shook the World*. Harmondsworth and New York: Penguin, 1977.

Reese, R. R. *Red Commanders: A Social History of the Soviet Army Officer Corps, 1918-1991*. Lawrence: University Press of Kansas, 2005.

Rendle, M. 'Defining the "Political" Crime: Revolutionary Tribunals in Early Soviet Russia'. *Europe-Asia Studies* 65, no. 9 (2013): 1771–88.

'Revolutionary Tribunals and the Origins of Terror in Early Soviet Russia'. *Historical Research* 84, no. 226 (2011): 693–721.

Retish, A. 'Power, Control, and Criminal Activity: The Peasantry and the Soviet Revolutionary Tribunal in Viatka Province, 1918–1921', 2011. Online at www.cas.miamioh.edu/havighurstcenter/papers/retish.pdf

Revutsky, A. *Wrenching Times in Ukraine: Memoir of a Jewish Minister*. Newfoundland: Yksuver Publishing, 1998.

Riddell, J. 'The Comintern in 1922: The Periphery Pushes Back'. *Historical Materialism* 22, no. 3–4 (2014): 52–103.

Workers of the World and Oppressed Peoples, Unite! Proceedings and Documents of the Second Congress, 1920. Vol. 1. New York: Pathfinder, 1991.

Riga, L. *The Bolsheviks and the Russian Empire*. Cambridge: Cambridge University Press, 2012.

Rimmel, L. A. 'Svodki and Popular Opinion in Stalinist Leningrad,' *Cahiers du Monde Russe: Russie, Empire Russe, Union Soviétique, États Indépendants* 40, no. 1 (1999): 217–34.

Roediger, D. *Class, Race and Marxism*. London: Verso, 2017.

Rogatyns'kyi, I. 'Hlukhivs'ka tragediia. Iz zapysok Ilii Rogatyns'kogo'. *Zhyttia i Znannia* 8, no. 32 (1930): 229–33.

Rogger, H. 'Conclusions and Overview'. In *Pogroms: Anti-Jewish Violence in Modern Russian History*, edited by J. D. Klier, pp. 314–72. New York: Cambridge University Press, 1992.

Sapon, V. P. *Apollon Andreyevich Karelin: Ocherk zhizni*. Nizhnii Novgorod: Yu. A. Nikolaev, 2009.

Evrei v obshchestvenno-politisheskoi zhizni Nizhegorodskoi Gubernii (1914-1920 gg.). Nizhii-Novgorod: Evreiskii tsentr 'Khesed Sara', Istoricheskii fakul'tet Nizhegorodskogo gusodarstvennogo pedagogicheskogo universiteta im. Koz'my Minina, 2012.

Schapiro, L. *The Origin of the Communist Autocracy. Political Opposition in the Soviet State. First Phase: 1917-1922*. 2nd Edition. London: Macmillan, 1977.

Schwarz, S. M. *The Jews in the Soviet Union*. New York: Syracuse University Press, 1951.

Serge, V. *Revolution in Danger: Writings from Russia, 1919-1921*. Chicago: Haymarket Books, 2011.

Shapiro, L. *The History of the ORT: A Jewish Movement for Social Change*. New York: Schocken Books, 1980.

Shechtman, I. B. *Pogromy dobrovol'cheskoi armii na Ukraine (K istorii antisemitizma na Ukraine v 1919-1920 gg.)*. Berlin: Ostjudisches Historisches Archiv, 1932.

Shelit, I. *Doloi pogromy*. Kiev: Izdatel'stvo narodnogo kommisariata po voennym delam Ukrainy, 1919.

Shepherd, N. *A Price Below Rubies: Jewish Women as Rebels and Radicals*. London: Weidenfeld & Nicolson, 1993.

Shneer, D. *Yiddish and the Creation of Soviet Jewish Culture: 1918-1930*. Cambridge: Cambridge University Press, 2004.
Shtakser, I. *The Making of Jewish Revolutionaries in the Pale of Settlement: Community and Identity during the Russian Revolution and its Immediate Aftermath, 1905-1907*. Basingstoke: Palgrave, 2014.
Shternshis, A. *Soviet and Kosher: Jewish Popular Culture in the Soviet Union, 1923-1939*. Bloomington: Indiana University Press, 2006.
Shtif, N. I. *Pogromy na Ukraine (Period Dobrovol'cheskoi armii)*. Berlin: Wostok, 1922.
Shubin, A. 'The Makhnovist Movement and the National Question in the Ukraine, 1917-1921'. In *Anarchism and Syndicalism in the Colonial and Postcolonial World, 1870-1940. The Praxis of National Liberation, Internationalism and Social Revolution*, edited by S. Hirsch and L. van der Walt, 147–92. London: Brill, 2010.
Sicher, E. *Jews in Russian Literature after the October Revolution: Writers and Artists between Hope and Apostasy*. Cambridge: Cambridge University Press, 2006.
Slavin, I. *Evreiskii pogrom na zavode 'Novki'*. Vitebsk: Izdanie Vitebskogo Gubvoenrevkoma, 1920.
Slezkine, Y. *The Jewish Century*. Princeton: Princeton University Press, 2006.
Sloin, Andrew. 'Speculators, Swindlers and Other Jews: Regulating Trade in Revolutionary White Russia'. *East European Jewish Affairs* 40, no. 2 (2010): 103–25.
The Jewish Revolution in Belorussia: Economy, Race, and Bolshevik Power. Bloomington: Indiana University Press, 2017.
Slutskii, A. G. 'Doktor istoricheskikh nauk, professor Grigorii Samoilovich Fridliand (K semidesiatiletiiu so dnia rozhdeniia)'. In *Istoriia i istoriki. Istoriografiia vseobshchei istorii. Sbornik statei.*, edited by M. A. Alpatov, 387–89. Moscow: Izdatel'stvo 'Nauka', 1966.
Smirnov, N. N. 'The Soviets'. In *Critical Companion to the Russian Revolution, 1914-1921*, edited by E. Acton, V. Iu Cherniaev, and W. G. Rosenberg, pp. 429–37. Bloomington: Indiana University Press, 1997.
Smith, J. 'Stalin as Commissar for Nationality Affairs, 1918-1922'. In *Stalin: A New History*, edited by S. Davies and J. Harris, 45–62. Cambridge: Cambridge University Press, 2005.
Smith, S. A. *The Russian Revolution: A Very Short Introduction*. Oxford: Oxford University Press, 2002.
Sol'skii, V. *1917 god v Zapadnoi Oblasti i na zapadnom fronte*. Minsk: Tesei, 2004.
Spargo, J. *The Jew and American Ideals*. New York and London: Harper & Brothers, 1921.
Steinberg, M. D. *Voices of Revolution, 1917*. London: Yale University Press, 2001.
Stevens, M. *Red International and Black Caribbean: Communists in New York City, Mexico and the West Indies, 1919-1939*. New York: Pluto Press, 2017.
Stogov, M. *Komu nuzhny pogromy?* Petrograd: Izdatel'stvo Petrogradskogo Soveta, 1918.
Sukhanov, N. N. *The Russian Revolution, 1917: A Personal Record*. Edited by Joel Carmichael. Princeton: Princeton University Press, 1984.
Suny, R. G. 'Toward a Social History of the October Revolution'. *The American Historical Review* 88, no. 1 (1983): 31–52.

Suny, R. G., and T. D. Martin, eds. *A State of Nations: Empire and Nation-Making in the Age of Lenin and Stalin*. Oxford: Oxford University Press, 2001.
Surh, G. 'Ekaterinoslav City in 1905: Workers, Jews, and Violence'. *International Labor and Working-Class History* 64 (2003): 139–66.
Surh, G. D. 'Russian Jewish Socialists and Antisemitism: The Case of Grigorii Aronson'. *Patterns of Prejudice* 51, no. 3–4 (2017): 253–68.
Sutton, K. A. 'Class and Revolution in Russia: The Soviet Movement of 1905'. Ph.D. Dissertation, University of Birmingham, 1987.
Swain, G. 'Russia's Garibaldi: The Revolutionary Life of Mikhail Artemevich Muraviev'. *Revolutionary Russia* 11, no. 2 (1998): 54–81.
Tcherikower, E. *Di Ukrainer Pogromen in Yor 1919*. New York: YIVO Institute for Jewish Research, 1965.
   Istoriia pogromnogo dvizheniia na Ukraine 1917-1921. Berlin: Osjudisches Historisches Archiv, 1923.
Trachtenberg, Barry. *The Revolutionary Roots of Modern Yiddish, 1903-1917*. New York: Syracuse University Press, 2008.
Traverso, E. *The Marxists and the Jewish Question. The History of a Debate 1843-1943*. New York: Humanity Books, 1994.
Trotsky, L. *My Life: An Attempt at an Autobiography*. Middlesex: Penguin Books, 1975.
   On Lenin: Notes Towards a Biography. London: Harrap, 1971.
   The Permanent Revolution and Results and Prospects. London: New Park Publications Ltd., 1971.
   Trotsky's History of the Russian Revolution, Volume 3. London: Sphere Books, 1967.
Vasil'ev, V. Iu., ed. *Evreiskii vopros. Poiski otveta. Dokumenty 1919-1921 gg. Vypusk pervyi*. Vinnitsa: Globus-Press, 2003.
Veidlinger, J. *The Moscow State Yiddish Theater: Jewish Culture on the Soviet Stage*. Bloomington: Indiana University Press, 2006.
   In the Shadow of the Shtetl: Small-Town Jewish Life in Soviet Ukraine. Bloomington: Indiana University Press, 2013.
   Pogrom: The Origins of the European Genocide of the Jews. New York: Metropolitan Books University.
Velychenko, S. *State Building in Revolutionary Ukraine: A Comparative Study of Governments and Bureaucrats, 1917-1922*. Toronto: University of Toronto Press, 2011.
   Painting Imperialism and Nationalism Red: The Ukrainian Marxist Critique of Russian Communist Rule in Ukraine, 1918-1925. Toronto: University of Toronto Press, 2015.
Vilkova, V. P. *RKP(b) Vnutripartiinaia bor'ba v dvadtsatye gody. Dokumenty i materialy 1923 g.* Moscow: ROSSPEN, 2004.
   The Struggle for Power: Russia in 1923. New York: Prometheus Books, 1996.
Virdee, S. *Racism, Class and the Racialized Outsider*. London: Palgrave Macmillan, 2014.
   'The Second Sight of Racialised Outsiders in the Imperialist Core'. *Third World Quarterly* 38, no. 11 (2017): 2396–410.

Vladimirskii, M. F., A. S. Enukidze, M. N. Pokrovskii, and Iakovleva, eds. *Pervyi Vserossiiskii S'ezd Sovetov Rabochikh i Soldatskikh Deputatov, Tom 2.* Moscow: Gosizdat, 1931.

Vragi li evrei rabochim i krest'ianam? Petrograd: Izdatel'stvo Petrogradskogo Soveta, 1918.

Wade, R., ed. *Documents of Soviet History. Volume 1. The Triumph of Bolshevism, 1917-1921.* New York: Academic International Press, 1991.

Weber, H., and A. Herbst. *Deutsche Kommunisten: Biographisches Handbuch 1918 bis 1945.* Berlin: Karl Dietz Verlag, 2004.

Weinberg, R. 'Demonizing Judaism in the Soviet Union during the 1920s'. *Slavic Review* 67, no. 1 (2008): 120–53.

Stalin's Forgotten Zion: Birobidzhan and the Making of a Soviet Jewish Homeland. An Illustrated History, 1928-1996. Berkeley: University of California Press, 1998.

Williams, R. *Marxism and Literature.* Oxford: Oxford University Press, 1977.

The Long Revolution. Revised Edition. Harmondsworth: Penguin Books, 1965.

Wynn, C. *Worker, Strikes, and Pogroms: The Donbass-Dnepr Bend in Late Imperial Russia, 1870-1905.* Princeton: Princeton University Press, 1992.

Yekelchyk, S. *Ukraine: Birth of a Modern Nation.* Oxford: Oxford University Press, 2007.

Zatonskii, V. P. 'Vodovorot (iz proshlogo)'. In *Etapy bol'shogo puti. Vospominaniia s grazhdanskoi voiny*, edited by V. D. Polikarpov, pp. 154–81. Moscow: Voennoe izdatel'stvo Ministerstvo Oborony SSSR, 1963.

Zel'tser, A. 'Dimanshtein, Semen Markovich'. In *The YIVO Encyclopedia of Jews in Eastern Europe*, edited by G. D. Hundert, Vol. 1, 407–08. New York: Yale University Press, 2008.

Evrei sovetskoi provintsii: Vitebsk i mestechki 1917-1941. Moscow: ROSSPEN, 2006.

Index

Page numbers in *italics* refer to figures; 'n' after a page number indicates the footnote number.

1905 Revolution, 11, 21, 35, 65, 155

Abramson, H., 118
Aduev, Nikolai, 217
Agitprop (Department of Agitation and Propaganda), 212
Agurskii, Samuil, 50, *166*, 203
Al'skii, M., 164, *166*
Alexander II, Emperor of Russia, 10
antisemitism. *See also* Bolshevism and antisemitism; counter-revolution and antisemitism; pogroms; Red Army antisemitism; revolutionary politics and antisemitism
   Jewish agency and, 204
   political practice and, 164, 175, 182
   state antisemitism, 10, 214
   threat to the survival of the Soviet state, 138, 163, 168
   tsarism and, 20–21, 25
Antonov-Ovseenko, Vladimir, 45, 51, 93–94, 96
Aronson, Grigorii, 35
Arosev, Alexandr Iakovlevich, 70
Asarkan, Naum Markovich, 57
Astrov, Isaak, 34
Averin, Vasilii, 113
Axelrod, Pavel, 12

Babel, Isaac, 4
   Red Cavalry, 32, 44
beat the Yids! (slogan), 105, 125, 184–85, 189
Bednyi, Dem'ian, 174
Bemporad, Elissa, 157
Black Hundreds, 22, 32, 34, 152
Bol'shevik (newspaper), 122, 126, 128, 130, 185

Bolshevik revolution. *See* October Revolution
Bolshevism, 12
   racism and, 1, 5, 33
   threat to (1918), 85
Bolshevism and antisemitism, 16–17, 33, 36, 73, 150–51, 183, 207, 219
   centralisation and, 51
   historical setting, 10–17
   Jewish radicals, 8–9
   opposition to antisemitism, 1, 3, 6–8, 13, 29, 37, 87, 216
   overlapping, 29–33, 36, 47, 90, 97, 111
   pogroms, 80
   silence and denial, 129–37
Bonch-Bruevich, Vladimir, 24, 34, 68, 174
Bor'ba (newspaper), 68
Borochov, Ber, 161–62
Brym, Robert, 161
Budennyi, Semen, 109, 179n179
Budnitskii, Oleg, 4, 6, 53n3, 137
Bukharin, N.: *ABC of Communism*, 120
Bulak-Balakhovich, Stanislav, 134n102
Buldakov, Vladimir, 4
Bund, the, 13, 30, 35–36, 70, *See also* Kombund
   Central Committee of the Bund, 37, 150
   conflict with Lenin, 15–16
   Cross-Party Socialist Committee for the Struggle against Antisemitism, 80
   Foreign Committee of the Bund, 15
   ideological conflict between Bundism and Bolshevism, 142
   Jewish Commissariats and, 55, 55n9
   response to 1918 pogroms, 80–81
   split, 37, 141–42, 150

Central Commission for Providing Help to Victims of the Counter-Revolution, 151

Index

Central Evkom (Commissariat for Jewish Affairs), 60, 64, 73–74
  Bolshevism and Jewish revolution, 82
  Department for the Struggle against Antisemitism, 76
  Department for the Struggle against Antisemitism and Pogroms, 83–84
  Moscow Evkom and, 72
  Soviet response to antisemitism, 74, 81–84
Charney, Daniel, 81–82
Cheka (Extraordinary Commission for Combating Counter-Revolution and Sabotage), 69, 75, 83, 168
Chemeriskii, A., 212, 214
Chernihiv, 26, 91
  1918 pogroms, 40–42, 53
Cheskis, A., 196, 200
Chicherin, Georgii, 68
Civil War, 44, 214, 216
  Jewish question, the, 36
Civil War pogroms, 1–2, 19, 49, *See also* Denikin's Army; Petliura's Army; Red Army pogroms; Ukraine
class
  anti-bourgeois resentment and antisemitism, 41, 89, 98, 124, 183, 205, 207
  bourgeois revolution and antisemitism, 20
  bourgeoisie and antisemitism, 15, 76, 120, 130
  class discourse and antisemitism, 17, 183–86, 194
  ethnicity and, 183–84, 194, 199
  racism and class politics, 219
  Ukraine, class and ethnic polarisation, 91, 111
Comintern (Communist International), 218
Commissariat for Jewish Affairs. *See* Central Evkom; Jewish Commissariats; Moscow Evkom
Committee for the Struggle against Antisemitism, 8, 151, 169–75, 217
  antisemitism as cultural phenomenon, 172
  dissolution, 8, 175–77
  members and activists, 170
  Moscow and, 169
  publications and lectures, 173–74
  Red Army antisemitism and, 173
  remit, 170
  strategy against antisemitism, 171–74, 180

Communist Bund. *See Kombund*
Cossacks, 94n35, 97, 101
counter-revolution, 14, 40, 121, 195
  punishment against, 114n12, 118
  Revolutionary Tribunals, 115
counter-revolution and antisemitism, 5–6, 20–21, 25, 32, 44, 79, 138, 159, 210
Czech Legion rebellion, 85, 137

Dan, Fedor, 34–35
dark masses, 14, 33, 35
Davidovich, David (L'vovich), 62–65, 66, 85, 153, 211, 216
demokratiia, 21, 25
Denikin, Anton Ivanovich, 105–6
Denikin's Army, 105
  Civil War pogroms, 4, 89, 133
Dimanshtein, Semen, 54, 60, 62, 75, 82–84, 127, 163, 166, 195–96, 211
  antisemitism and, 164, 203–4, 212
  collection of Lenin's writings on the Jewish question, 207
  Evsektsiia, 168
  Evsektsiia's 1919 Memorandum, 198
  Jewish economic life, 203
  Komfarband, 145–46
  Sovnarkom decree on antisemitism (July 1918), 78
  telegram to Trotsky, on antisemitism (July 1918), 74–77, 79
Dobkovskii, Il'ia, 57, 59, 67–69, 71
  on Red Army pogroms (1918), 67–68, 70
Donbass-Dnepr Bend region, 14
Du Bois, W. E. B., 9, 208
Dubchak, Sergei, 118
Dubnov, Simon, 13n38, 48–49
Dumitru, D., 213
Dzerzhinskii, Feliks, 69

Edinstvo (newspaper), 30
education and Soviet state response to antisemitism, 8, 14, 25–26, 213
  cancellation of workshops and courses, 74
  Commission for the Struggle against Antisemitism and Pogroms, 72
  cross-party alliances, 81
  Moscow Sovnarkom, 69, 71
  Ukrainian Sovnarkom, 113
Ehrenburg, Ilia, 31
Ekaterinoslav, 15, 41–42, 91, 105, 113, 180
Elisavetgrad, 23
  1919 pogrom, 99–101, 135
ethnicity, 8, 91, 192
  class and, 183, 185, 194, 199

European socialism, 9, 15n46
Evkom (Jewish Commissariat of the People's Commissariat of Nationalities). *See* Central Evkom; Jewish Commissariats; Moscow Evkom
Evobshchestkom (Jewish Social Committee for the Relief of Victims of Pogroms), 133–35
   poster for exhibition on pogroms, *134*
Evreiskaia Nedelia (newspaper), 20, 28, 35
Evreiskii Rabochii (newspaper), 43, 80
Evsektsiia (Jewish Sections of the Communist Party), 8, 10, 82, 108, 127, 181, *See also Committee for the Struggle against Antisemitism*
   Agitprop, 212
   confrontation with Jewish chauvinism, 215
   demise, 215
   double consciousness, 208, 210
   formation of Jewish Red Army units, 149–50
   Jewish self-reconstruction and politics of antisemitism, 202–9
   response to Lenin on antisemitism, 196–98
   Second Conference, 163–66, *166*
   Soviet response to antisemitism, 165–67, 195, 216
   Soviet response to antisemitism (1920s), 177–80, 211–15
Evsektsiia's 1919 Memorandum, 198–202
   problematic issues and contradictions, 200–2, 206–7
Extramural Department of the Commissariat of Enlightenment, 169, 175–76

Fanon, Frantz, 16
Fareynikte (United Jewish Socialist Workers Party), 7, 56, 62, 65, 80, 87, 144
   split, 144
Fareynikte Communists, 144, 147–48
February Revolution (1917), 9n19, 19, 145, 152
   antisemitism, 20, 24
First All-Russian Congress of Soviets (1917), 24–26
   On the Struggle against Antisemitism (resolution), 26–27
Frankel, Jonathan, 155, 217
Fridliand, Zvi, 23, 57–58, *59*, 62, *75*, 81, 84, 141, 211, 216
   campaign against antisemitism, 66–68

Central Evkom, 75
Jewish Communist Party (Poalei Zion), 146
Moscow Evkom, 58, 141
Frumkina, Ester, 156, 208

Genoa Conference, 135
Gergel, Nahum, 4, 89, 156
German Revolution (1918), 141, 147, 156
Germany, 38–40, 42, 50, 85, 137
   Brest-Litovsk peace treaty, 39
   Eleven Days War, 38–39, 114n12
   German-Jewish conspiracy, 43
Gor'kii, Maxim, 170, 174
   Novaia Zhizn, 34
Gorbunov-Posadov, Ivan, 170
Gorokhov, A., 113
Gribenko, Fedor, 103
Grigor'ev, Nikifor, 159
   antisemitism, 98–99
   Universal, 98, 100, 104
Grigor'evshchina, 95–97, 104–6, 111–12, 123, 138, 145, 156
   Elisavetgrad pogrom, 100–1
   fatalities, 131
   Uman', 101
Groza (newspaper), 32
Gusev-Orenburgskii, Sergei, 132–33

Hall, Stuart, 156, 162
Herbeck, Ulrich, 7n18, 53n3
Hlukhiv pogrom, 46–48, 73
   agency and responsibility, 49–51
   Bolshevik newspapers and, 48–50
   Jewish press and, 47n46, 49, 68n48
   power consolidation and, 5, 36, 48, 51
   Roslavl'skii regiment, 46, 48–51

Illintsi, 139
Ilyich, Vladimir, 209
imperialism, 39
intelligentsia, 35, 47, 66, 82, 143n14
internationalism, 5, 10, 209–10
Iuzhnyi Rabochi (newspaper), 184
Izvestiia (newspaper), 24, 71–72, 128
   re-launched as pro-Bolshevik organ, 73

Jewish Commissariats, 8, 10, *75*, 82, *See also* Central Evkom; Moscow Evkom
   Bund, the, and, 55, 55n9
Jewish Communist Party (Poalei Zion), 58n20, 146–47, 157
   Pogrom Department', 158
   response to Red Army antisemitism, 146, 158–60, 162

Index

Jewish Enlightenment movement, 204
Jewish national-cultural project, 8–9, 56, 86, 161, 182
  anti-racist praxis, 10
Jewish nationalism, 161, 215
Jewish question, the, 9, 11, 36, 156, 207, 210, 218
  Evsektsiia's 1919 Memorandum, 198, 206
  Jewish radicals on. 56
Jewish radicals. *See also* Jewish socialists
  Bolshevism and antisemitism, 8–9
  radicalisation, 10, 148
  Soviet response to antisemitism, 84, 86–87, 112, 214
Jewish self-defence units, 41–43, 93, 103, 153
Jewish socialism, 218
  antisemitism and the Sovietisation of Jewish socialism, 147–48, 150, 156–58, 161–63, 218
  fragmentation of, 141–47
  Soviet anti-racism, 218
  Ukraine, 140–42
Jewish socialists, 216–17, *See also* Jewish radicals
  1918 pogroms and, 85
  antisemitism and, 7, 17, 23, 84–85, 163, 195, 211, 216–17
Jewish socialists, Soviet response to antisemitism (1919), 139–40, 155, 163, 181–82, *See also Committee for the Struggle against Antisemitism*; Evsektsiia; Jewish Communist Party (Poalei Zion); *Kombund*; *Komfarband*
Jewishness, 123, 164
  antisemitic/racialized conceptions of, 185–86, 188, 190, 194, 203, 205, 207–8
  revolutionary politics/antisemitism overlapping, 24, 97, 124
  speculation and, 202
Jews
  bourgeoisie and, 184–85
  Jewish-Bolshevik construct, 188, 207
  Jews in the Soviet government, 188–90, 195, 200–1, 209–10
  Jews in the Soviet government, restriction of numbers, 190–97, 208
  numerus clausus quota system, 98
  Soviet-Jewish alliance, 148, 157
Jews in the Red Army, *149*, 157, 186–88
  pogroms and, 147, 149–50

Kalinin, Mikhail, 164–65
Kamenev, Lev, 167
Karelin, Apollon, 170, 173–74
Kerensky, Alexander, 31
Khaikin, Zalman, 205
Kharkiv, 43, 91
Kheifets, Abram, 141, 143, *165–66, 171,* 172, *173, 211, 217*
  response to antisemitism, 154–55
Kheifets, Il'ia, 132n96
Kishinev pogrom, 13
Kombund (Communist Bund), 7, 37, 87, 147
  Bolshevism and, 142
  formation of, 142, 143n12
  Soviet response to 1919 antisemitism, 142
Komfarband (Jewish Communist Alliance), 147, 158
  formation of, 145–46, 156
  Soviet response to 1919 antisemitism, 146
Kommunar (newspaper), 130
Kommunist (newspaper), 113–14, 122
Konopnicka, Maria, 174
Kornilov Affair, 20, 22
Korolenko, Vladimir, 174, 181
Kosior, Stanislav, 190
Kozlovskii, Mechislav, 186
Krupskaia, Nadezhda, 170, 176
Kyiv, 16, 39
Kyiv Soviet, 27

L'vov-Rogachevskii, Vasili, 26–27, 33, 35
Lavrov, Petr, 12
left politics. *See* Jewish radicals; Jewish socialism; Jewish socialists; revolutionary politics and antisemitism
Lenin, 7, 33, 38–39, 105
  antisemitism, 16, 35, 54, 120, 195
  draft theses, 191–95, 210
  On the Pogromist Persecution of the Jews (speech), 119–20
  Red Guards/popular militia, 40
  Sovnarkom, 60–61
  Sovnarkom decree on antisemitism (July 1918), 78
Leningradskii, S., *136*
Levitan, Mikhail, 144, 196–97, 200
Liber, Mark, 24, 30
Lipets, David
  role in the Soviet response to antisemitism, 173
Lipets, David (Petrovskii), 35, 143, 152–55, *153,* 154, *155,* 174, 196, 206, 211, 216
  experience of pogromist violence, 153–54
  response to Lenin's theses, 197–98
  role in the Soviet response to antisemitism, 154–55, 171–72

Lunacharskii, Anatolii, 170
Lur'e, Solomon, 31
Luxemburg, Rosa, 40

Machtet, G., 174
Magidov, Boris, 130
Makhno, Nester, 134n103
Mandel'sberg, Ia., 163, *166*, 167, 196, 198, 206
Marxism, 3
  anti-racism and, 10, 185
  antisemitism, 15n46, 161–62
  Marxist Zionism, 9, 87, 161, 218
McKay, Claude, 1, 218
Medem, Vladimir, 15
Menshevik Party, 22, 27, 30, 70, 80
  Petrograd Electoral Committee, 34
Merezhin, Avrom, 9, 156, 178–79, 218
Mezhlauk, V., 113
Mikhailovskii, Vladimir, 157
Morozov, A., 180
Moscow Commissariat for Military Affairs, 69
Moscow Evkom (Moscow Jewish Commissariat), 7, 54–57
  campaign against antisemitism, 56, 66–68, 71, 79
  Commission for the Fight against Pogroms, 56
  Commission for the Struggle against Antisemitism and Pogroms, 72
  Department for the Struggle against Antisemitism, 57
  dissolution, 7, 73–74, 182
  establishment of, 56, 58, 181
  Soviet response to antisemitism, 62–63, 69, 85, 138, 216
  staff, 59–85, 216
  structural weaknesses, 60–61
Moscow Sovnarkom (Council of Peoples' Commissars), 60–61
  dissolution, 73
  education and antisemitism, 69, 71
  key positions in, 60n25
  Soviet response to antisemitism, 69–73
Moscow, capital city relocation to, 39, 60
Moss, Kenneth, 8, 57, 86

Narkomnats (Commissariat for National Affairs), 61
  Collegium of Narkomnats, 62
Nasha Zhizn' (newspaper), 100
Nicholas II, Emperor of Russia, 19
Niger, Shmuel, 82

Nikitin, A. M., 27
Novakovskii, Iu., 144, 170, 196, 198

October Revolution (1917), 37
  antisemitism, 20, 31, 33–36, 38
  far-right and, 32
Odessa, 43, 96, 180
Odessa Soviet, 31
Odesskii Komunist (newspaper), 126
Ordzhonikidze, G. K., 191
Orgburo, 127–28, 167
  Ukrainian Orgburo, 191
Orshanskii, B., 180
ORT (Society for Handicraft and Agricultural Work among the Jews of Russia), 204

Pale of Settlement, 17, 26, 45
  pogroms, 1, 13, 23, 33, 36, 38, 43, 158
Petliura, Simon, 88
Petliura's Army, 169
  Berdychev pogrom, 88, 112, 147, 154
  Civil War pogroms, 4, 88–89, 112, 130, 133, 138, 149
  Proskuriv pogrom, 88, 112, 147
  Zhytomyr pogrom, 88, 112
Petrograd, 39, 76, 180
  pogroms, 23–24
Petrograd Jewish Communal Council, 64
Petrograd Soviet, 19, 21
  antisemitism and, 23
  pamphlets on pogroms, 76
Pipes, Richard, 129
  The Unknown Lenin: From the Secret Archive, 195
Plekhanov, Georgii, 13, 30
Poalei Zion Party, 23, 41, 56, 80, *See also* Jewish Communist Party (Poalei Zion)
  split, 57, 141, 146
Podvoiskii, Nikolai, 91, 93–94, 115n15
pogroms, 10, *See also* Civil War pogroms; Kishinev pogrom; Red Army pogroms; Ukraine
  1871 pogrom, 11n28
  1881–1883 pogroms, 11–12
  1903–1906 pogroms, 12–14
  1920 pogroms, 176
  Bolshevik approach to gathering information on, 131
  causes of, 36
  pogrom, meaning of, 33n74
  populism and, 13
  state organised, 13
  threat to the survival of the Soviet state, 118, 214

Index

tsarist state and, 14
working class and, 15–17, 34
Politburo, 167, 192
Poltava, 91–92, 105, 118
populism
  1881–1883 pogroms, 11–12
  antisemitism and, 6, 202
  pogroms and, 13
  Ukraine, 95, 98, 102, 111
Postone, Moishe, 6
Pravda (newspaper), 30, 48–49, 74, 127–28
Preobrazhenskii, Evgenii, 26–27, 120
  ABC of Communism, 119
Provisional Government, 21, 31
  opposition to antisemitism, 27–28

Rabinovich, D., 70–71
Rabinovich, Lidiia, 29, 217
racialisation, 9, 150, 162, 183, 209
  class formation and, 185
racism, 162
  anti-racism, 10, 71, 139, 218–19
  antisemitism and, 3
  Bolshevism and, 1, 5, 33
  class politics and, 219
  Jewish socialism and anti-racism, 218
Rafes, Moishe, 22–23, 91n16, 142, 150, 152, 196, 211, 216
  Committee for the Struggle against Antisemitism, 151, 170, 174
  Evsektsiia's 1919 Memorandum, 198
  role in the Soviet response to antisemitism, 135, 151–52, 155
Rakovskii, Khristian, 94, 112–14, 119–20, 185
Red Army antisemitism, 4–5, 43, 45, 70–71, 77, 87, 126, 157
  1920s, 180
  centralisation and, 51
  criticism by Jewish communists, 159–61
  mobilising Jewish volunteers, 187, 188n25
  silence and denial, 130–37
  Soviet press on, 130–31
  Ukraine, 92–95, 106, 122–23
  Ukrainian Sovnarkom, 114
Red Army pogroms, 4, 49, *See also* Red Army pogroms of 1918; Soviet-Polish War; Ukraine; Ukraine, Soviet response to antisemitism in
  1920s pogroms, 177
  downplay of Red Army's role in, 50
Red Army pogroms of 1918, 5, 36, 38, 41–46, 51, 137, *See also* Hlukhiv pogrom
  agency and responsibility, 49–51, 67, 80
  Bolshevik power and, 38, 44
  Jewish self defence units and, 43
  Red Army units, composition of, 44–46
Red Army pogroms of 1919. *See* Ukraine; Ukraine, Soviet response to antisemitism in
Red Guards, 29, 40, *See also* Red Army; Red Army pogroms of 1918
  role in stopping pogroms, 44
Red Star (newspaper), 127
Revkom (Revolutionary Committee), 41
revolutionary politics and antisemitism, 4, 6, 25
  1881–1883 pogroms, 11
  overlapping, 2, 24, 26, 97, 124, 202
  Russian Revolution, 4–5
Revolutionary Tribunals, 115–18, 167
  Ukraine, 115–18
Roy, M.N., 219
RSDRP (Russian Social Democratic Labour Party), 12–13, 15
Russian Far East, 28
Russian Red Cross, 102–3, 131–32
Russian Revolution (1917), 1, *See also* February Revolution; October Revolution
  antisemitism, 20, 86, 88
  Jewish Renaissance, 8, 57, 86
  Jews and, 10, 19
  revolutionary politics and antisemitism, 4–5
Russian Social Democracy, 17
  1903–1906 pogroms, 12–14
  antisemitism, conceptualisations of, 14–16
Russian Social Democratic Labour Party. *See* Menshevik Party
Russkie Vedomosti (newspaper), 28

Serge, Victor, 210
SERP (Jewish Socialist Workers Party), 144
Shapiro, L., 147
Shimeliovich, Iu. A., 77
Shneer, David, 87
Shternshis, Anna, 213
Skoropadsky, Pavlo, 88
Sloin, Andrew, 148, 202, 214
Slutsk, 27
Smidovich, Petr, 212
Smolensk, 42, 50, 117, 205, 214
Socialist Revolutionary Party, 13, 16, 22, 70, 80
  Left SR uprising, 76, 81
  Left SRs, 55–56, 60, 99

246   Index

Soviet response to antisemitism (1917), 22–29
Soviet response to antisemitism (1918), 53, 61–68, 84–87, *See also* Central Evkom; Central Sovnarkom; Moscow Evkom
   centralisation, 74, 76
   dismantling of the campaign against antisemitism (1918), 73
   failure to respond, 85
   Jewish politics and, 64
Soviet response to antisemitism (1919). *See* Jewish socialists, Soviet response to antisemitism (1919); Revolutionary Tribunals; Ukraine, Soviet response to antisemitism in
Soviet response to antisemitism (1920s), 211–15
   Evsektsiia, 177–80, 211–15
Soviet-Polish War (1920), 148
   Red Army/First Cavalry Army pogroms, 44, 109, 176, 179–80
Soviets, 21–22
   alliances, 22, 27, 37
   antisemitism, 40, 64, 199
   centralisation, 74, 76, 182
Sovnarkom (Soviet of People's Commissars), 60–62, 73, *See also* Moscow Sovnarkom; Ukrainian Sovnarkom
Sovnarkom decree on antisemitism (July 1918), 6, 78–79
speculation, 202–4
   antisemitism and, 185, 203–5
   criminalisation of, 202, 205
   Jewish speculation, 202–4, 206
SSRP (Socialist Zionist Workers Party), 144
Stalin, Joseph, 61–62, 209
   Great Terror, 55n6, 58n20, 215
   response to antisemitism, 214
   Stalin Revolution, 214–15
   Stalinism, 214–15
Steklov, Iurii, 119
Struk, Il'ia Timofeevich, 117
Sukhanov, Nikolai, 35
Sultan-Galiev, Mirsaid, 219
Surazh, 43
Sverdlov, Yakov, 63, 65–66

Tambov, 29, 72
Tcherikower, Elias, 4, 40, 45, 49, 135n103
Temporary Jewish National Soviet, 64
The Red Army (newspaper), 127
Trilisser, Meer, 212
Trotsky, Leon, 15–16, 39, 105, 150, 209–10

Red Army antisemitism, 188n25
tsarism and antisemitism, 20–21, 25
Tsvibak, S. M., 69, 71, 77–78

Ukraine, 40, 42, 88, 110, *See also* Denikin's Army; Grigor'evshchina; Petliura's Army
   8th Ukrainian Soviet Regiment, 101–3
   antisemitism, 89, 98, 106–8, 110–11
   antisemitism and Red Army composition, 92–95
   antisemitism as threat to Soviet regime in, 138
   Bolshevik revolution in, 89, 92
   Cherkasy pogrom, 104
   class and ethnic polarisation, 90–91, 111
   Elisavetgrad—May 1919, 101–5
   International 4th Soviet Regiment, 103
   Lenin's draft theses, 191–95
   Mykolaiv pogrom, 14
   On Soviet Power in Ukraine (resolution), 192
   pogroms of 1920, 176
   populism, 95, 98, 102, 111
   Red Army 1918 pogroms, 5
   Red Army 1919 pogroms, 5, 7, 89, 101–3, 105, 108–9, 120, 131
   Red Army antisemitism, 106, 122–23
   Rosava pogrom, 121, 133, 156
   Skvyra pogrom, 110
   soviet power and antisemitism, 91–92, 96, 101
   Uman' pogrom, 101–4, 121
   Zolotonosha pogrom, 105
Ukraine, Soviet response to antisemitism in, 112, 138–39, *See also* Jewish socialists, Soviet response to antisemitism (1919); Ukrainian Sovnarkom
   6th Regiment, Red Army, 124–25
   anti-antisemitism measures at local level, 115–19, 124–27
   Civil War and, 117
   contradictions, 118–19, 123–24
   Kyiv Garrison, conference of Red Army Communists, 126
   Lenin, On the Pogromist Persecution of the Jews (speech), 119
   Preobrazhenskii's *ABC of Communism*, 120
   Red Army antisemitism, 112
   Revolutionary Tribunals, 115–18
   silence and denial, 133–37
   Soviet press and, 127–29, 138
   Soviet State, failure to respond, 120

Index

Third Party Conference, Chernyhiv Region, 126
Ukrainian Central Committee, 121, 123–27
VUTsIK appeal, 122–23
Ukrainian Sovnarkom, 112
   campaign against antisemitism (1919), 112–14, 137
   Decree against National Hatred, 114–16
   punishment for antisemitism, 113–14, 116–18
Union of Jewish Soldiers, 41
Union of Socialist Revolutionary Maximalists, 59
United Committee of Social Democrats, 14
Unzer Togblat (newspaper), 47

Vardin, Il'ia, 187
Velychenko, S., 191, 194
Vendrovskii, Zalman, 81–84
Virdee, Satnam, 9, 161
Vitebsk Soviet, 43–44
Vlast' Naroda (newspaper), 34
Vpered (newspaper), 30
VTsIK (All-Russian Central Executive Committee), 62
   antisemitism, 64, 164
   opposition to antisemitism, 29

VUTsIK (All-Ukrainian Central Executive Committee), 122
Vynnychenko, Volodymyr, 88

White Army, 44, 105, 169, 177, 189
   antisemitism, 158
white supremacy, 3
Williams, Raymond, 111, 177
Winter Palace, 29, 31–32, 58
Wynn, Charters, 14

Yiddish and Bolshevism, 10, 55, 82–83
Yiddishists, 82, 85

Zaitsev, Grigorii, 194
Zatonskii, V. P., 110
Zelenyi (Danil Terpilo), 159
Zhenotdel (Women's Department), 215
Zhizn' Natsional'nostei (newspaper), 131, 176
Zinoviev, Grigory, 76, 195
Zionism, 82, 144
   left Zionists and the Bolshevik revolution, 144
   liberal press, 35n84
   Marxist Zionism, 9, 87, 161, 218
Zionist Socialist Workers' Party, 65
Zvezda (newspaper), 48